I0709771

OREGON

MY OREGON

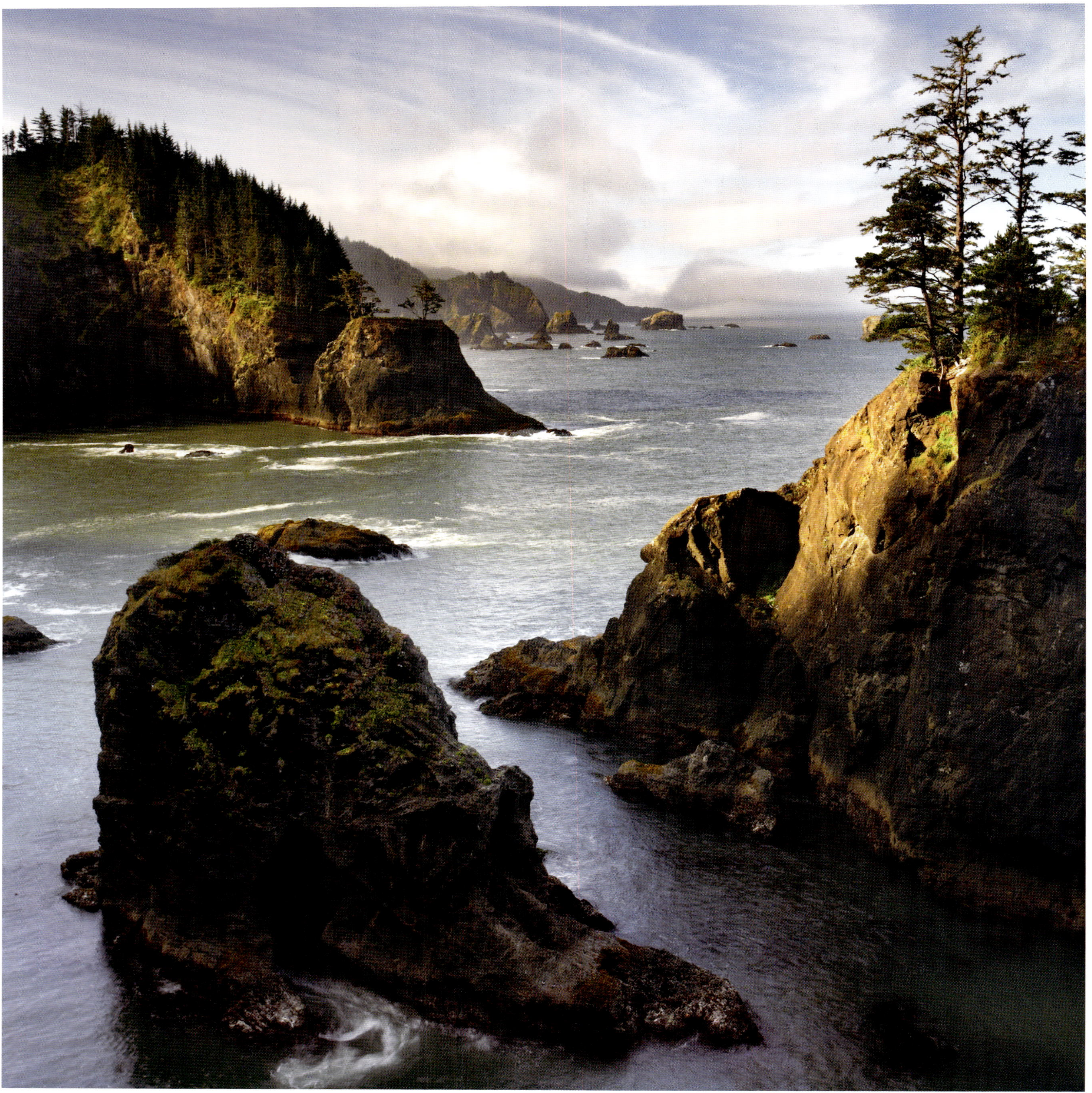

OREGON

LAND *of* NATURAL WONDERS

PHOTO CASCADIA

foreword by NICHOLAS D. KRISTOF

TIMBER PRESS · PORTLAND, OREGON

FOREWORD

NICHOLAS D. KRISTOF

A *real* Oregonian, as everybody knows, is a hardy outdoors type who licks banana slugs to relish the way they make your tongue go numb. Nope. A *real* Oregonian is a sophisticate with a delicate tongue refined by a thousand tastings of pinot noir.

No, not at all. A *real* Oregonian is a cowboy from Wallowa, limping from a hard-earned broken leg after a bull ride. Or a grizzled fishing boat operator heading out on a foggy dawn from Depoe Bay. Or a loving craftsman of the Best Bicycle in the World at a small shop in Portland. Or a distance runner in Eugene dreaming of becoming another Prefontaine. Or a baker of marionberry pies so delectable that after you eat one slice, you feel your life has peaked and you may as well die—oh, but how about another slice first? Or a volunteer at Adelante Mujeres, the Forest Grove nonprofit working with the Latina immigrants who constitute the new Oregonians pivotal to the economy. Or an ophthalmology researcher at Oregon Health & Science University trying to beat glaucoma. Or a costume designer at the Oregon Shakespeare Festival in Ashland, trying to plant Hamlet in the 1920s. Or maybe a fourteen-year-old girl careering along remote Eastern

Oregon roads each Sunday evening, using a special driver license allowing her to drive the 120 miles from her Steens Mountain ranch to Crane Union High School, one of the few public schools in America with a dormitory, serving ranch kids who live too far from school to commute daily.

The point is that Oregon contains multitudes, for this is a state that spans a tremendous range of people, cultures, and terrains. It's a range that this book seeks to illuminate, along with Oregon's spectacularly beautiful and varied landscape.

Ever since I was a kid growing up on a farm between Yamhill and Gaston in the northern end of Yamhill County, I've seen how we Oregonians feel a profound and sometimes ostentatious pride in our state. Perhaps our chauvinism isn't unique, but there is something special—occasionally over the top—about our affection for our state. Newly elected Secretary of State Norma Paulus proposed in 1976 that Oregonians line up at the southern border and throw rocks at cars arriving with California license plates. (During the next recession, she swallowed her words in the search for investors and tourists. "Those were the days when we were so arrogant," Paulus told me ruefully. "There's nothing like poverty to change your attitude.")

If we're proud of our state, well, we do have plenty to be proud of. The Oregon Trail brought pioneers in their Conestoga wagons through unimaginable perils to settle in the Willamette Valley. For more than a century, Oregon has also been known for practical and progressive innovations, often involving the environment: the first state to provide for ballot initiatives and referendums, hence known as the "Oregon system" (1902), the first to impose a gasoline tax to pay for roads (1919), the first to preserve public access to all beaches (1967), the first to require deposits on bottles (1971), the first to decriminalize marijuana (1973), the first to legalize physician-assisted suicide (1994), the first to vote by mail in a federal election (1995), the first to provide over-the-counter access to birth control pills (2016), and the first to elect an openly LGBT governor (2016)—and it's a particular tribute to Oregon that this last one wasn't even much of an issue, nor was her gender. Then there are other ways in which Oregon has led the way for America that aren't political but certainly improve wellbeing: think of the bike path system in Portland and many other towns.

We have been a pioneering state in protecting the environment, partly because we have such a lovely environment to protect. I've had the chance to backpack across the entire state on the Pacific Crest Trail and, friends, we are blessed. Can there be any more beautiful sight than the snow-clad Three Sisters looming over an alpine meadow? Maybe a herd of pronghorn antelope at the Hart Mountain National Antelope Refuge? A dazzling tide pool abounding with starfish and sea urchins at Strawberry Hill Wayside between Yachats and Florence?

It's because of this pride in our state that I firmly count myself an Oregonian, even though I've lived much of my adult life abroad and in New York. My wife, Sheryl, a New Yorker, and I raised our three kids partly on our family farm in Yamhill, where they built a tree house and learned the hard way how to recognize poison oak. Every year we still try to backpack as a family around Mount Hood on the Timberline Trail, and we have an annual family expedition to Ashland for a few days of intensive theater. One of the kids' favorite restaurants is Mo's in Lincoln City, and their first kiss was a sloppy one from a seal at the aquarium in Newport. This is a state that earns the sense of wonder we feel for it.

And yet.

If we are to be honest, we must acknowledge that there is more, a side that we have often whitewashed. In school, I studied Oregon history—so how was it that the books and teachers never uttered a peep about our state's malignant history on race? One of Oregon's first legal actions, in 1844, well before it was a state, was to ban blacks and declare that any black person attempting to settle would be subjected to a public whipping. When Oregon became a state in 1859, the new state constitution explicitly barred blacks. After the Civil War, Oregon refused to ratify the Fifteenth Amendment, giving the vote to black men, and the Ku Klux Klan became very active in Oregon, helping elect Walter Pierce as governor in 1922. These days, East Main Street in Ashland seems a bastion of culture and liberalism; in the 1920s, it was a scene of KKK parades. Oregon law explicitly banned whites from marrying not only blacks but also Native Americans or Chinese; it even provided for the imprisonment of anyone who performed such a wedding ceremony, and that law remained on the books until the 1950s.

Likewise, I learned nothing of the destruction of native tribes. We children vaguely knew that Yamhill was named for the Yamhill Indians who preceded us, but we never discussed how they had disappeared. We knew nothing of the systematic thievery of native lands. Nor did we know of the massacre of some thirty-four Chinese miners in 1887 near Wallowa, a crime for which no one was ever punished. We were ignorant of the racist laws passed to bar ethnic Japanese from buying or leasing land in Oregon, and of the efforts to bar them from returning to Oregon after they were shamefully interned during World War II. We as a state have never come to terms with the reasons Oregon is so white.

As long as we are excavating painful truths, we also have to acknowledge that much of our beloved state is struggling. The Willamette Valley has thrived with Intel, technology, trade, and wine. But farm towns and logging towns have been left behind, along with the people in them. "I have seen such a change in forty-five years, it is pitiful," one of my childhood friends, Bobby Stepp, once wrote me, describing in particular how meth roared through rural Oregon. "It has hurt my family very bad … If meth was a nuke, at least one-third of the people in Oregon would be dead from it." Bobby was exaggerating, but it doesn't feel like it when you're in a blue-collar family in a small town. Bobby, my closest neighbor growing up, wrote me from the prison where he is serving a life sentence, and his younger brother Mike is homeless and living in a park in McMinnville. As I wrote in our last book, *Tightrope*, a quarter of the kids on my old No. 6 school bus in Yamhill are now dead from drugs, alcohol, suicide, reckless accidents, and other pathologies. That too is a side of Oregon, and it's one we must do more to acknowledge and address.

Maybe it seems tonally dissonant to discuss this grim side of a state in a book dedicated to its wonders? I mention these failures partly because our state has shown remarkable resilience—where it squarely faces its challenges. Beginning with the terrible recession of the early 1980s, economic planners saw that traditional agriculture, forestry, and fisheries could no longer drive Oregon's future, so they lured in tech companies and nurtured ties with Asia. The little town of Carlton was a poor community of farmers and foresters when I was growing up, but it reinvented itself (partly through the heroic work of winemaker Ken Wright) into a pinot noir tourist hub, and it now boasts several superb restaurants, excellent wine tasting rooms, and a shop for fine chocolates. No phoenix ever had more remarkable a rebirth, reminding us that reinvention and renaissance are also part of our Oregon heritage.

I risk becoming sentimental here, but I also think that one of the threads in our state's social fabric is a decency, a desire to do the right thing, a willingness to acknowledge mistakes. As an eighteen-year-old, I spent a year traveling every county in Oregon as a state officer in the Future Farmers of America, and I felt that decency. A conservative Republican in The Dalles won't agree with a liberal Democrat in Eugene about the policy implications of that decency—indeed, they will torment each other—but both want to do the right thing for the state and its people.

Few people realize it, but Oregon is the only part of the American mainland ever to have been bombed from an enemy plane. It was 1942, and a Japanese submarine with a crew of one hundred surfaced off the southern Oregon coast. A small, foldable seaplane in the submarine was assembled and then catapulted into the air, flown by a pilot named Nobuo Fujita. Fujita headed inland and dropped two incendiary bombs in the forests of the coastal range near the town of Brookings, hoping to set off large forest fires. The Japanese military hoped that forest fires would force the United States to bring back troops from Asia to protect the homeland. Fujita then returned to the submarine, landed on floats and helped stow the plane back in the submarine

In fact, the fires didn't amount to much. But after the war, in 1962, the town of Brookings was looking for someone to highlight its annual parade, so it invited Fujita. Not entirely understanding that he was to be honored rather than pilloried, and feeling deeply guilty for the bombings, he somberly agreed. He took with him a four-hundred-year-old samurai sword that had been handed down in his family from generation to generation. "He thought that perhaps people would still be angry and would throw eggs at him," his daughter, Yoriko Asakura, explained to me. "He wanted to take responsibility for what he had done." She meant by committing seppuku, or ritual suicide by disemboweling himself.

Fortunately, that proved unnecessary. To Fujita's astonishment, he found that the people of Brookings forgave him and warmly welcomed him, showering him with affection and respect. So he gave the sword to the Brookings library, where it now hangs. In later years, Fujita paid two more visits to Brookings, and donated money to its library so that it could buy books about Japan. When he was dying of lung cancer in 1997, the Brookings city council named him an honorary citizen, which moved him deeply. So, yes, we Oregonians rarely have demonstrated a capacity for racism and bigotry, but we've also shown that we can muster the magnanimity to forgive and embrace.

In trying to explain why some areas do better than others, scholars offer the concept of social capital, a sense of community that binds people together. Well, we Oregonians may no longer manufacture much steel or furniture, but we're a social capital factory. It was the social capital of Brookings that led it to invite Fujita back and later to name him an honorary citizen. It is the social capital of Oregon that led our people to protect the beaches, pass the bottle bill, and preserve so much of our wilderness. This social capital ties us in a shared fabric of pride in our state, even as we acknowledge that the fabric has had its tears. It is this sense of community and shared purpose—we are all so damn lucky to claim this state as our own!—that inspired this book, and it's what binds you and me together forever as Oregonians.

OREGON'S
SEVEN REGIONS

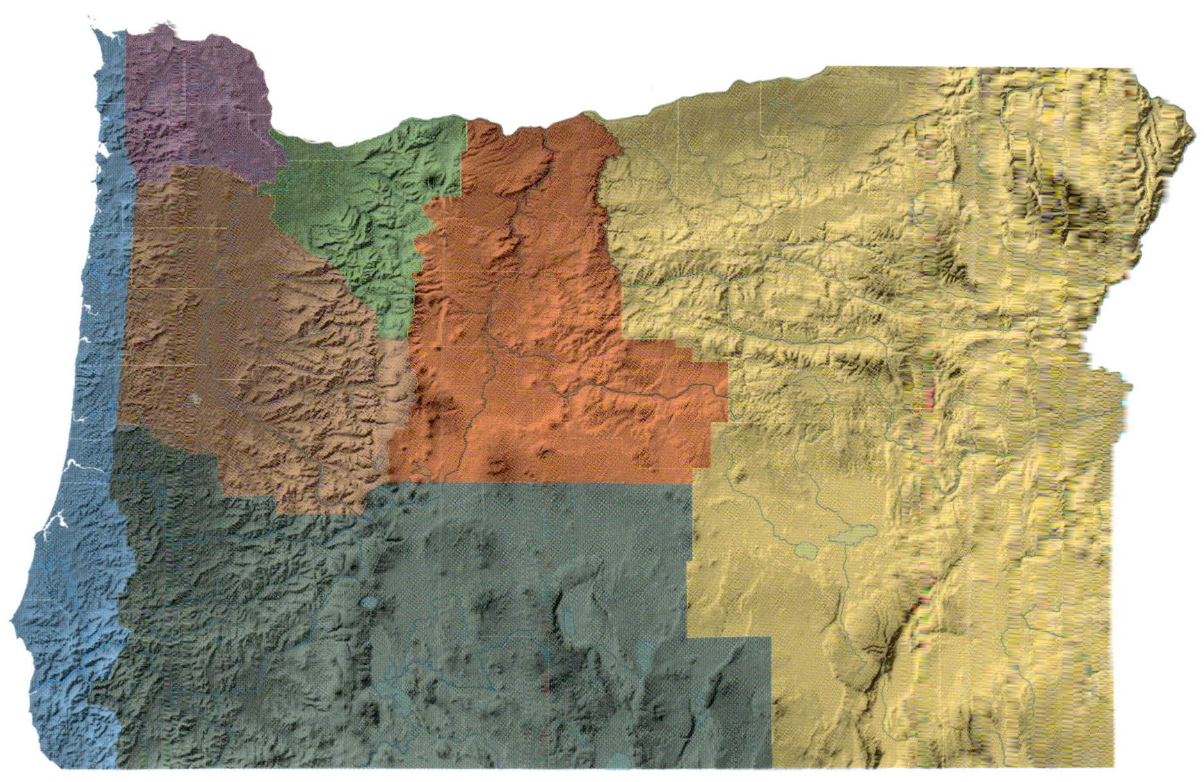

The colored dots next to the captions that
follow coordinate with the region of the featured image.

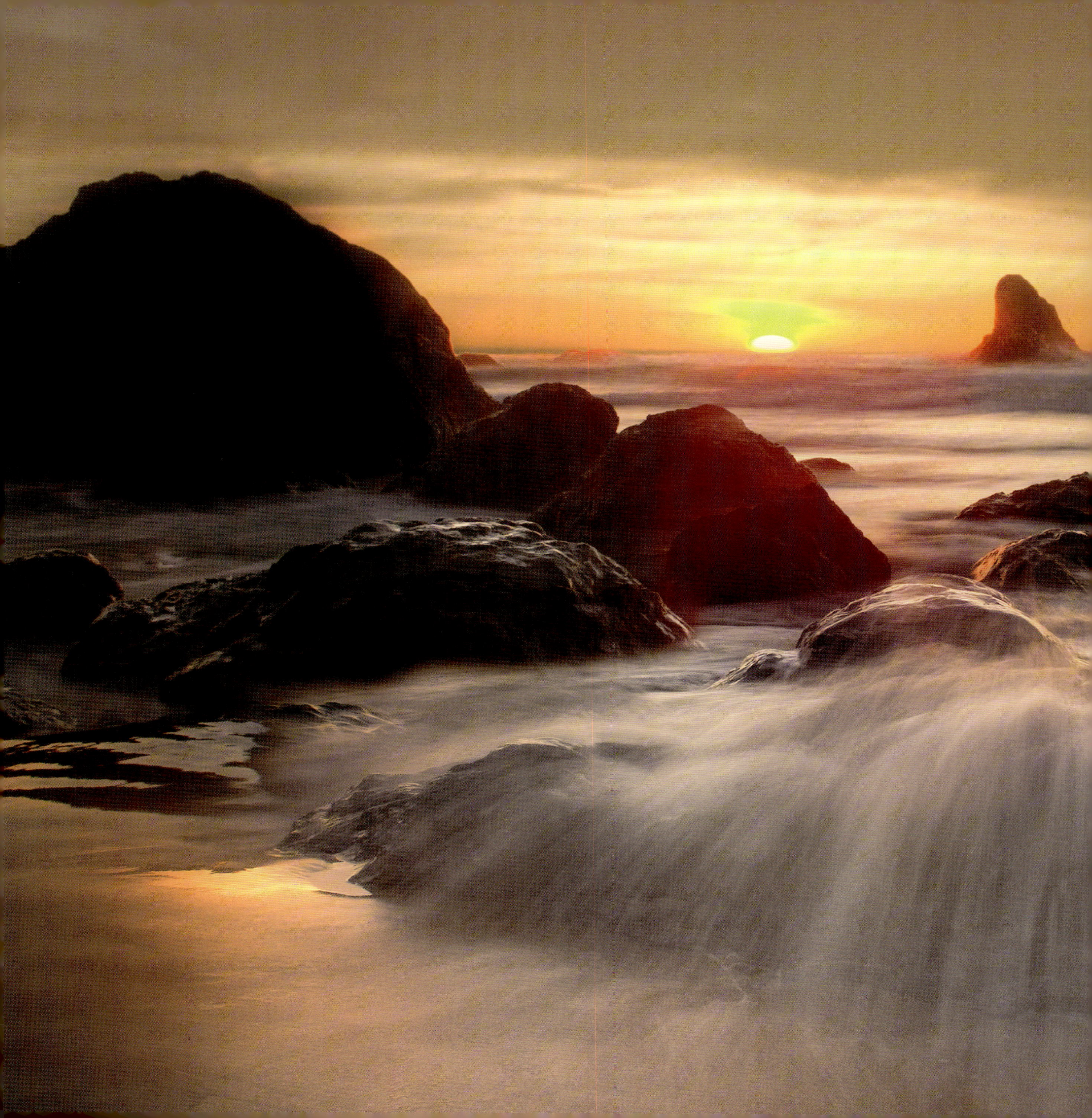

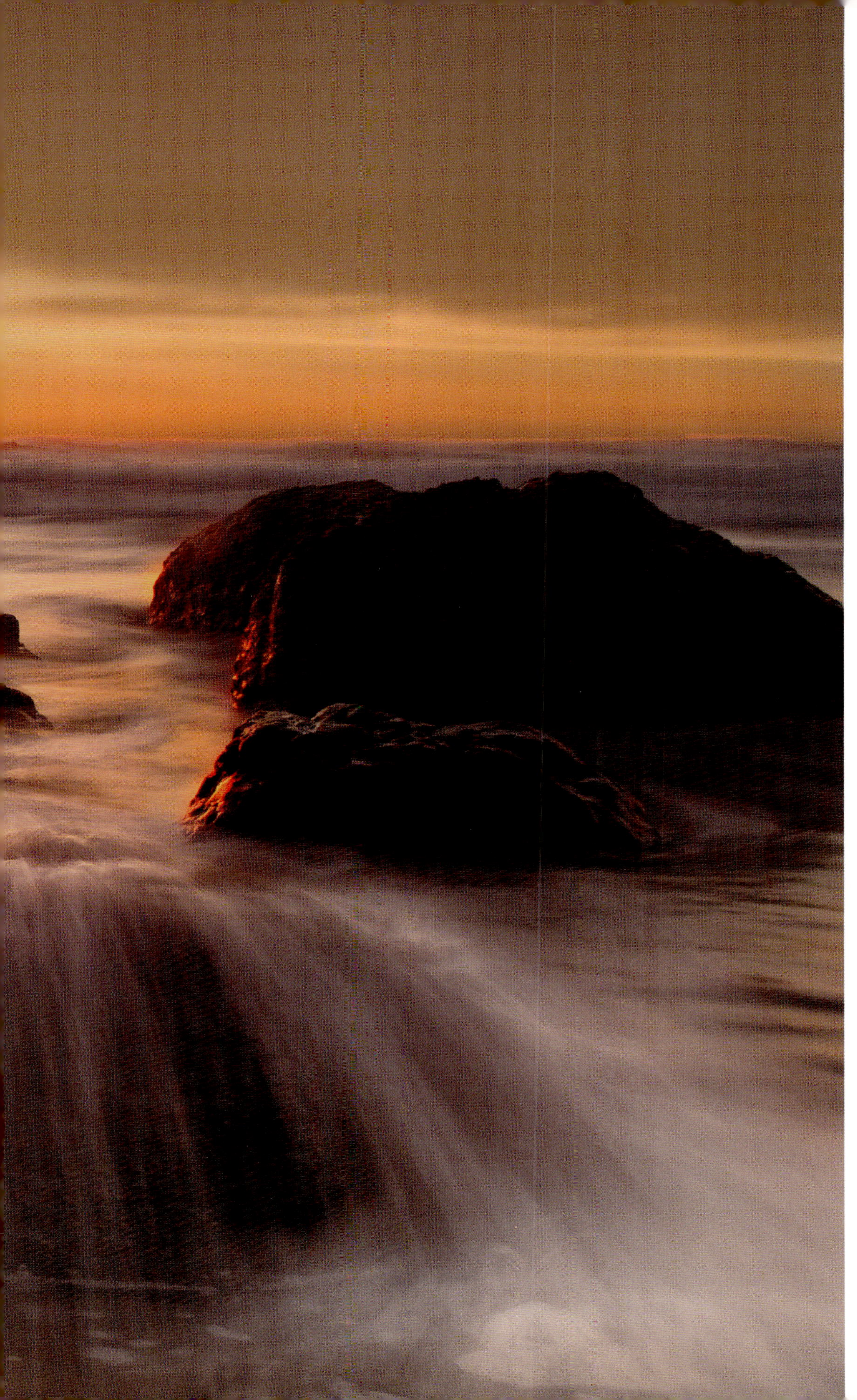

Sunset on Indian Beach, near Ecola
State Park on the northern coast. ◆

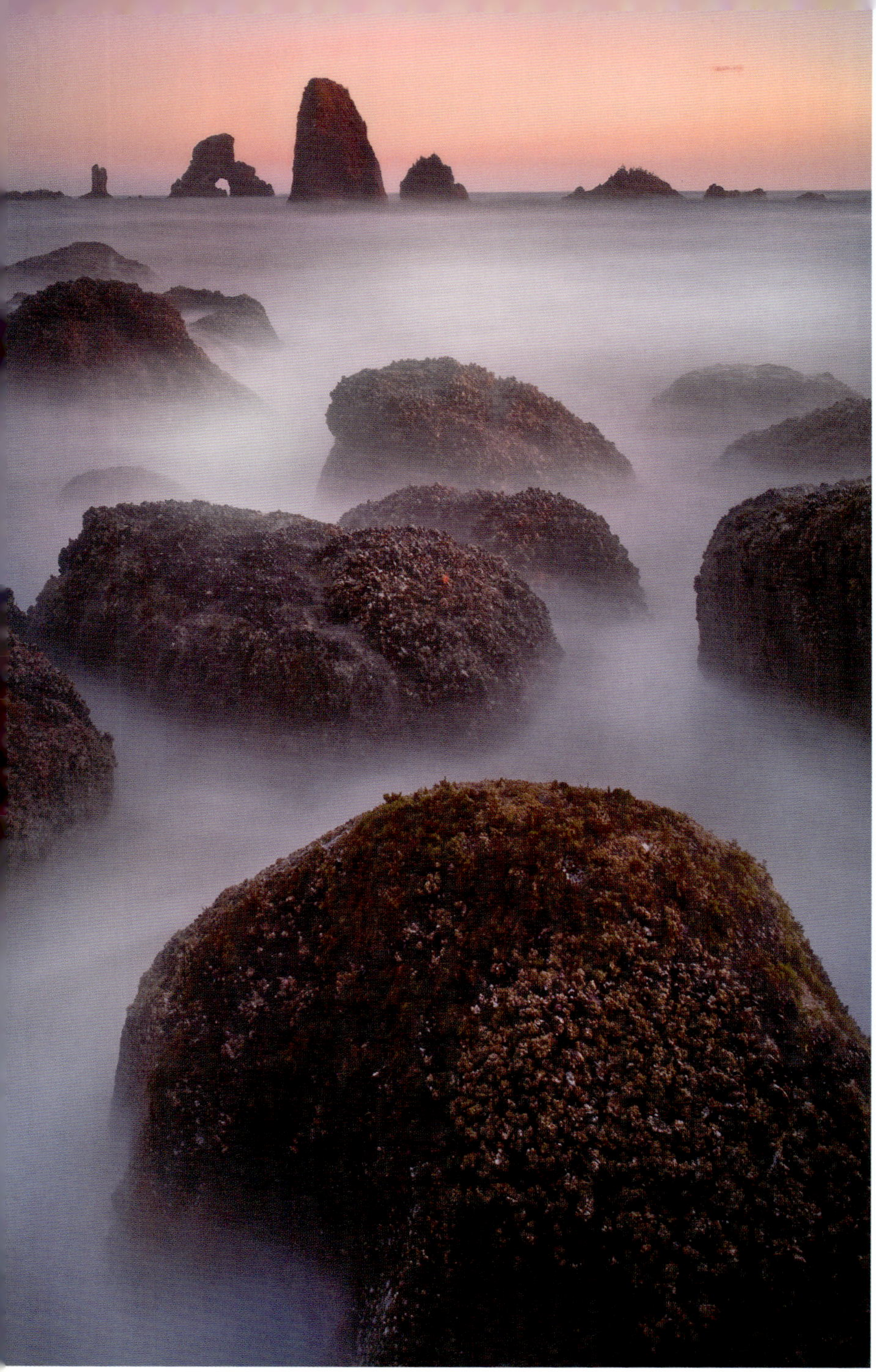

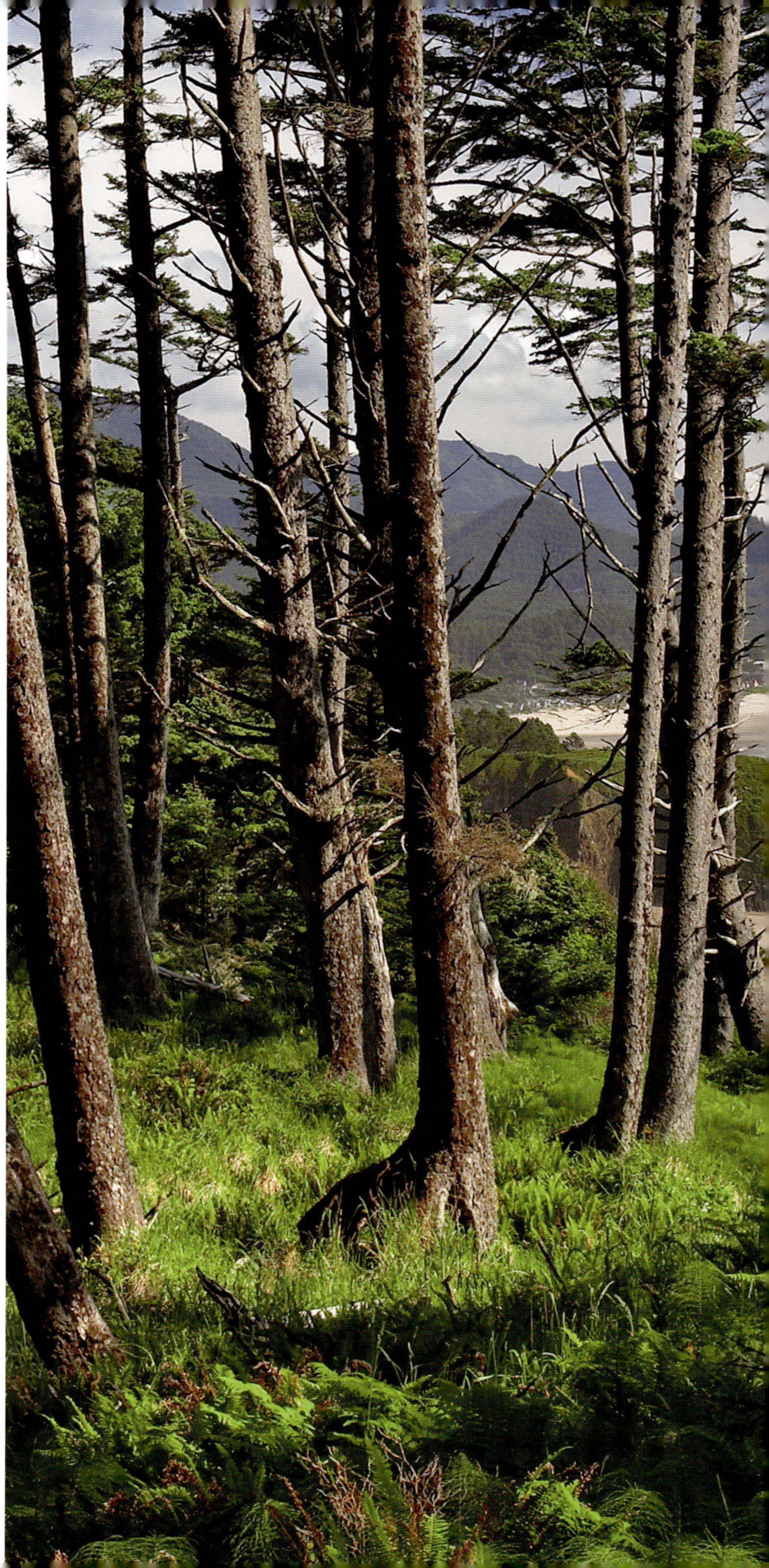

ABOVE Ocean spray seems to float
around Indian Beach's rock formations
at twilight. •

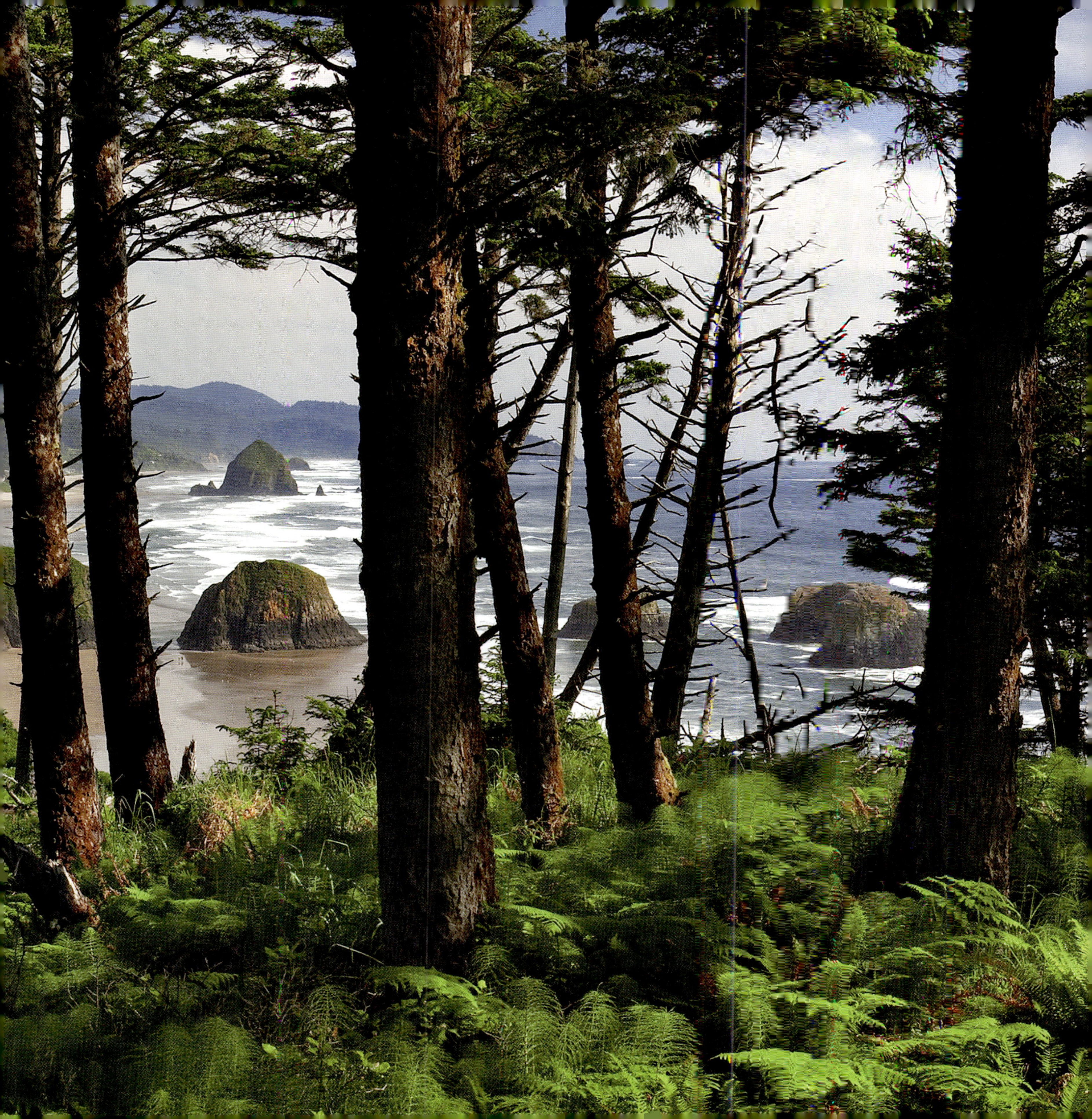

PREVIOUS PAGES Cannon Beach
as seen through the trees of Ecola
State Park. •

RIGHT A marine layer wraps
Haystack Rock in mist during
sunset on Cannon Beach. •

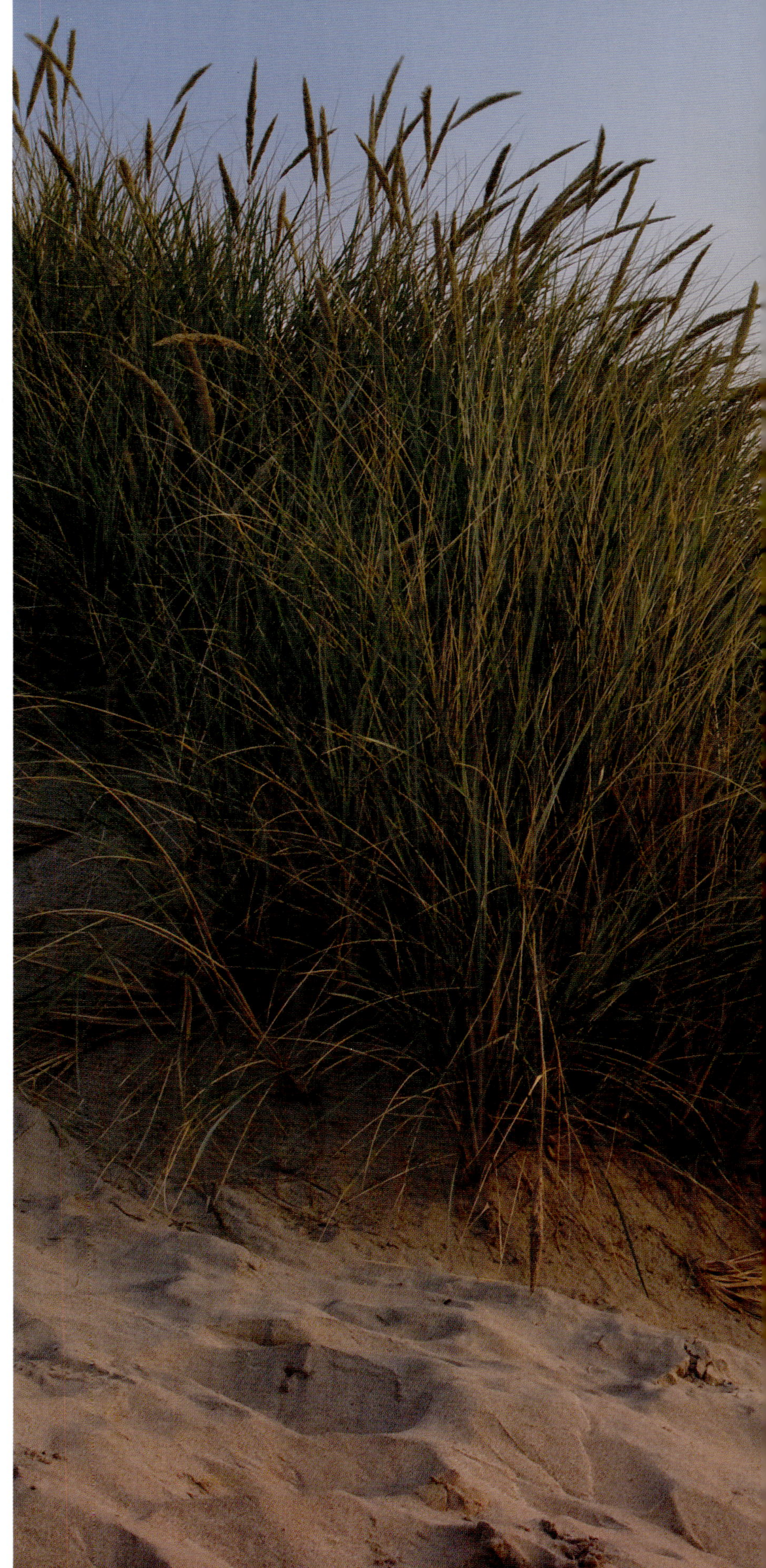

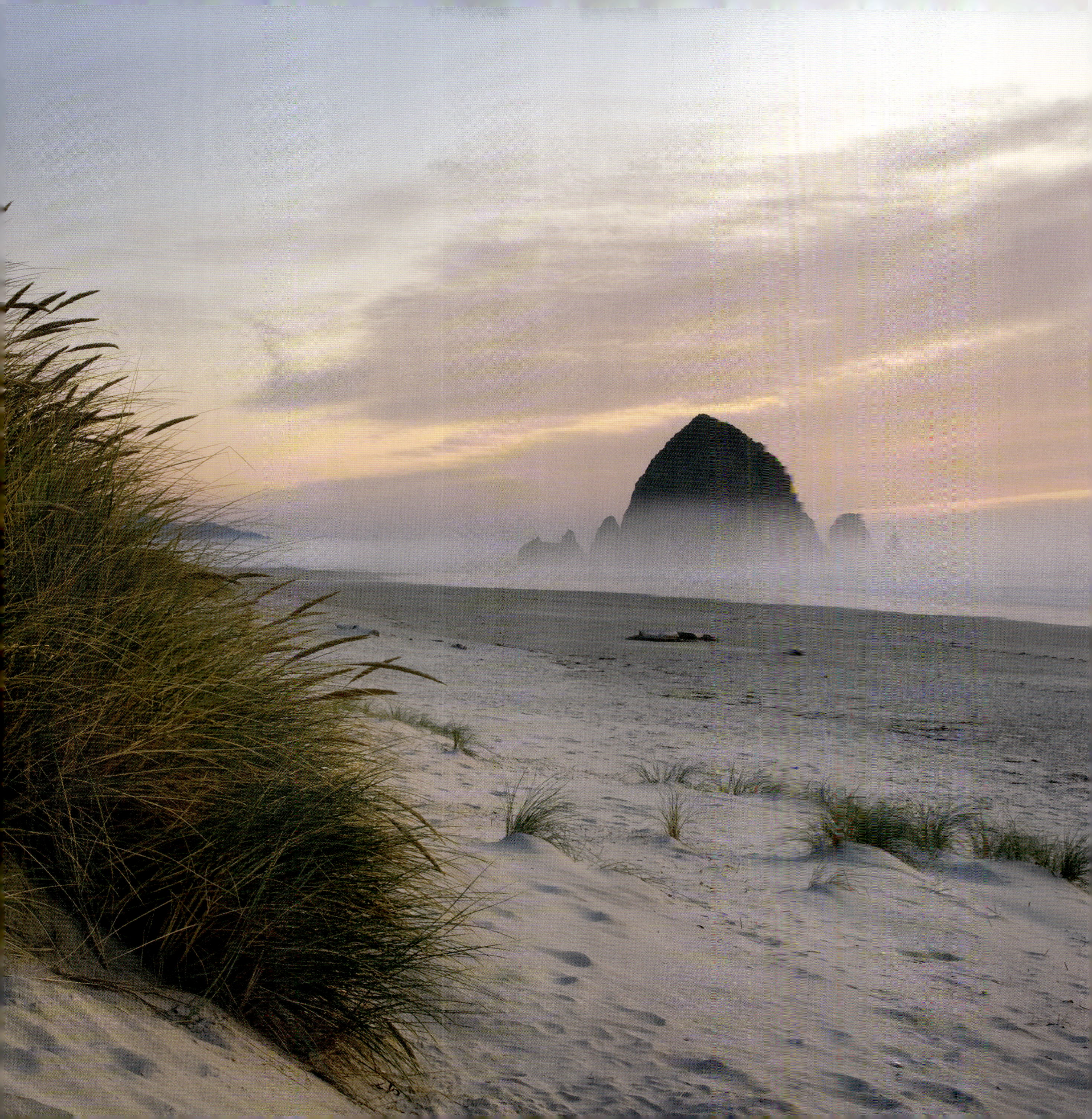

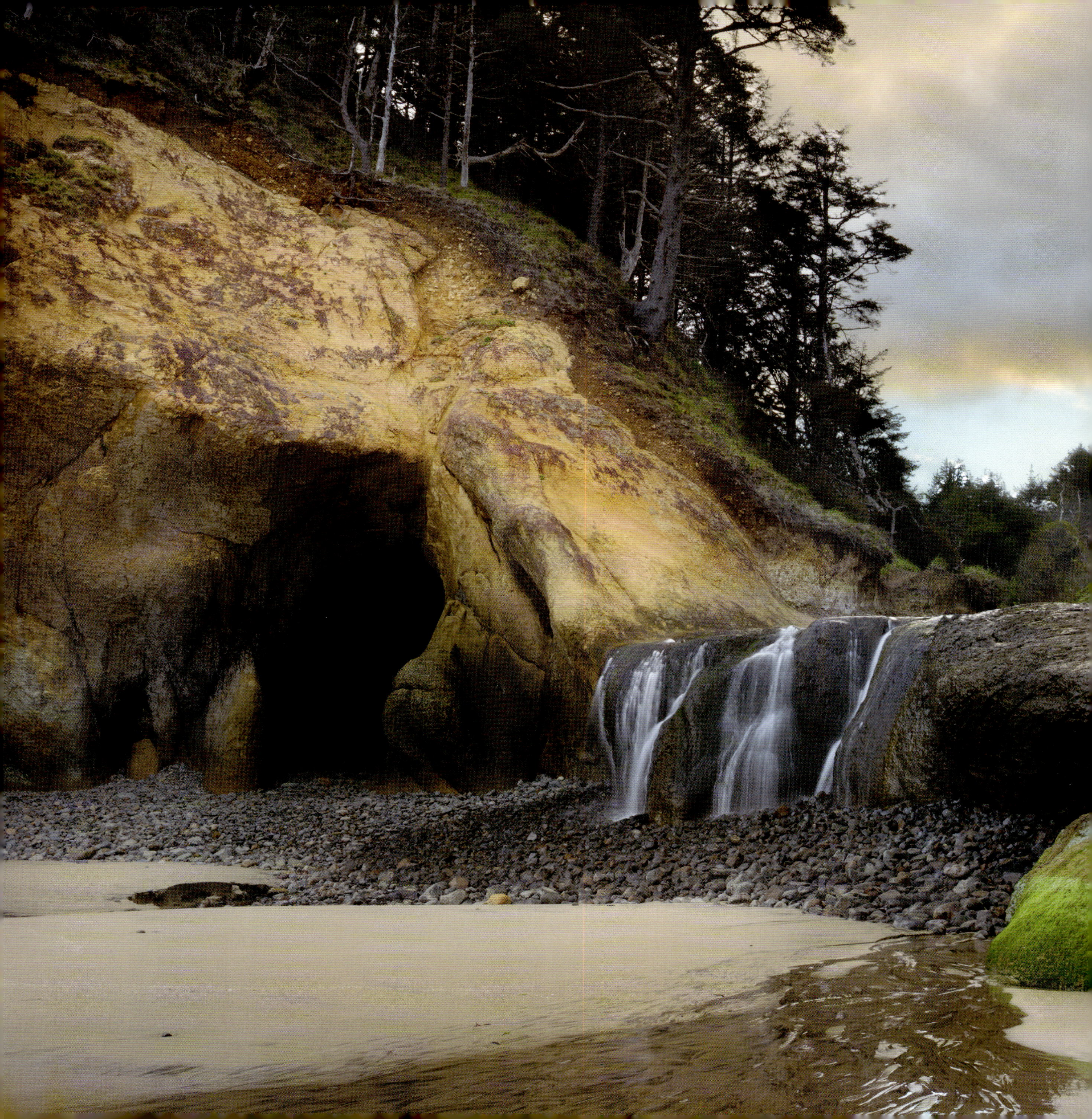

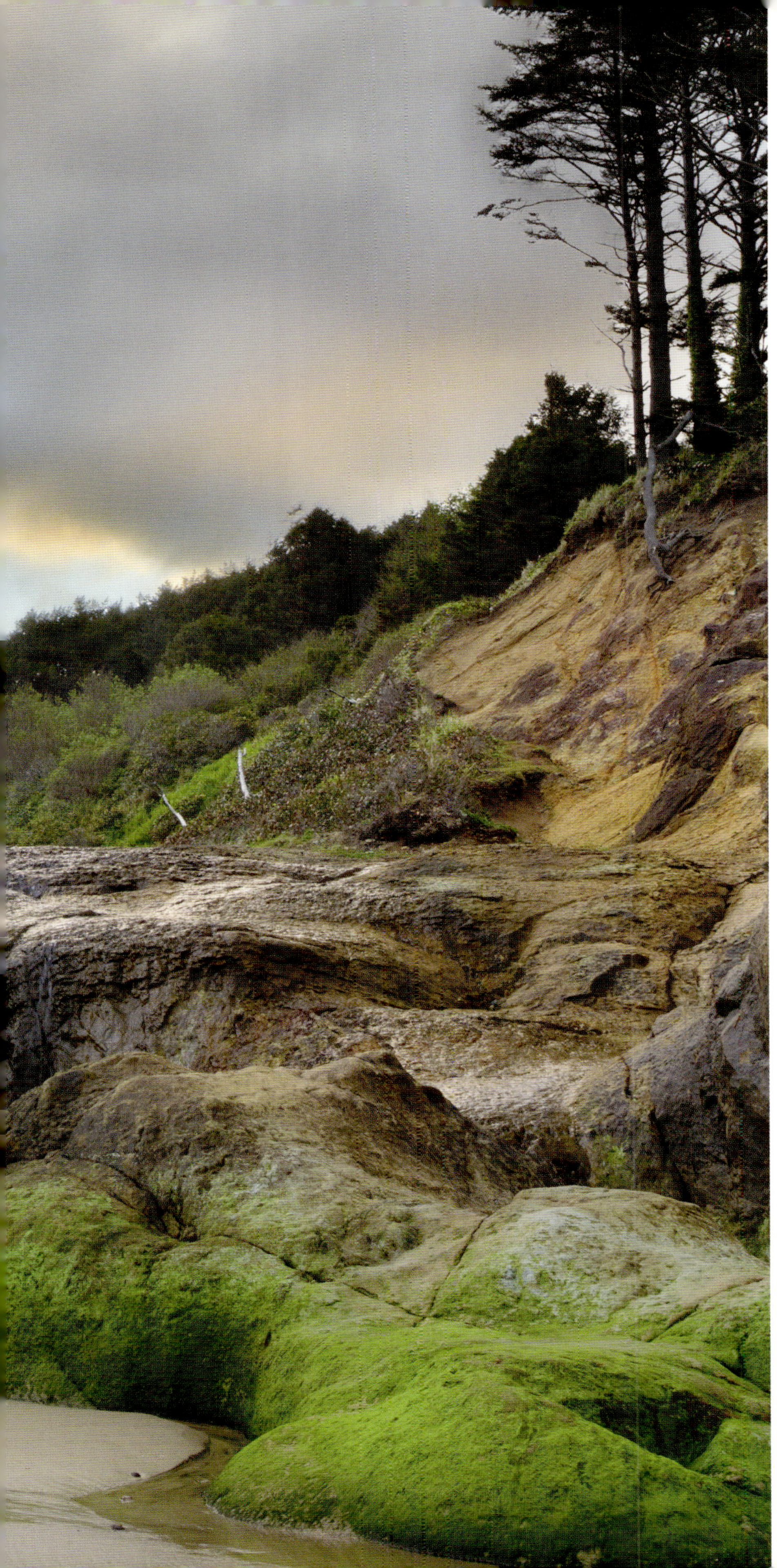

A small waterfall at Hug Point State Recreation Site at sunrise in spring.

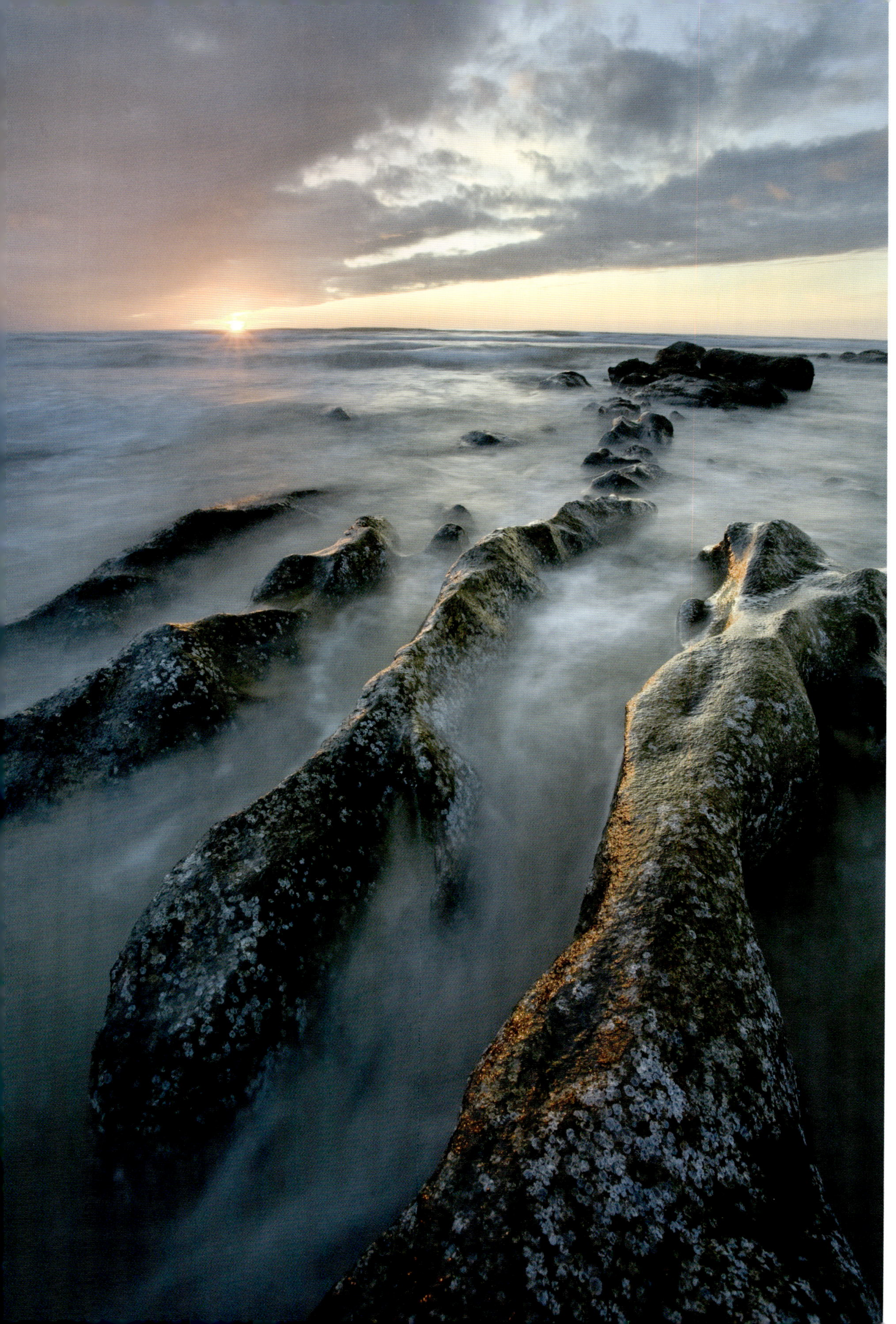

Unique parallel ridges of rock appear during certain phases of the tide at Arch Cape. ●

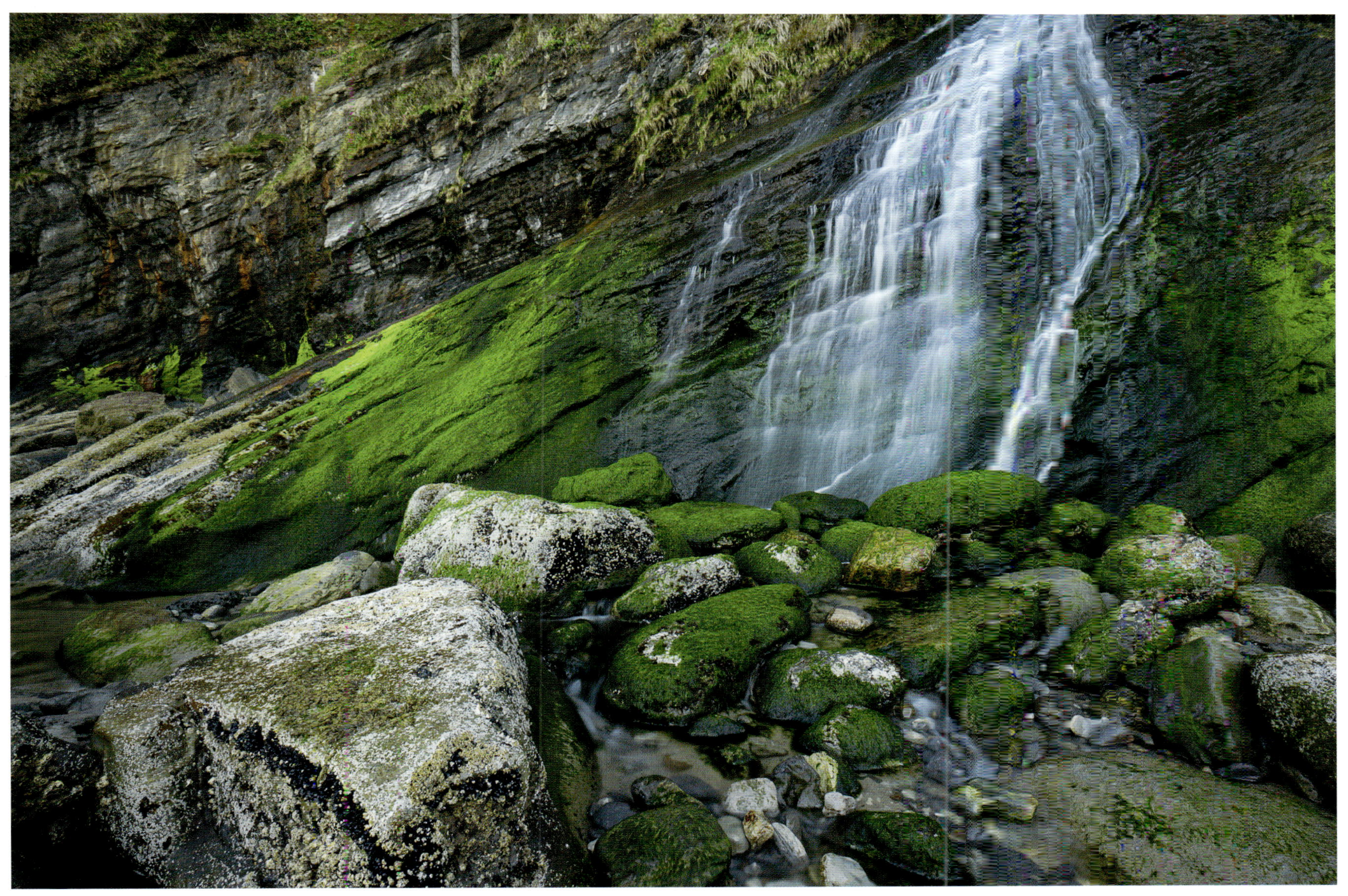

Vibrant moss surrounds the tumbling waters of Blumenthal Falls in Oswald West State Park. •

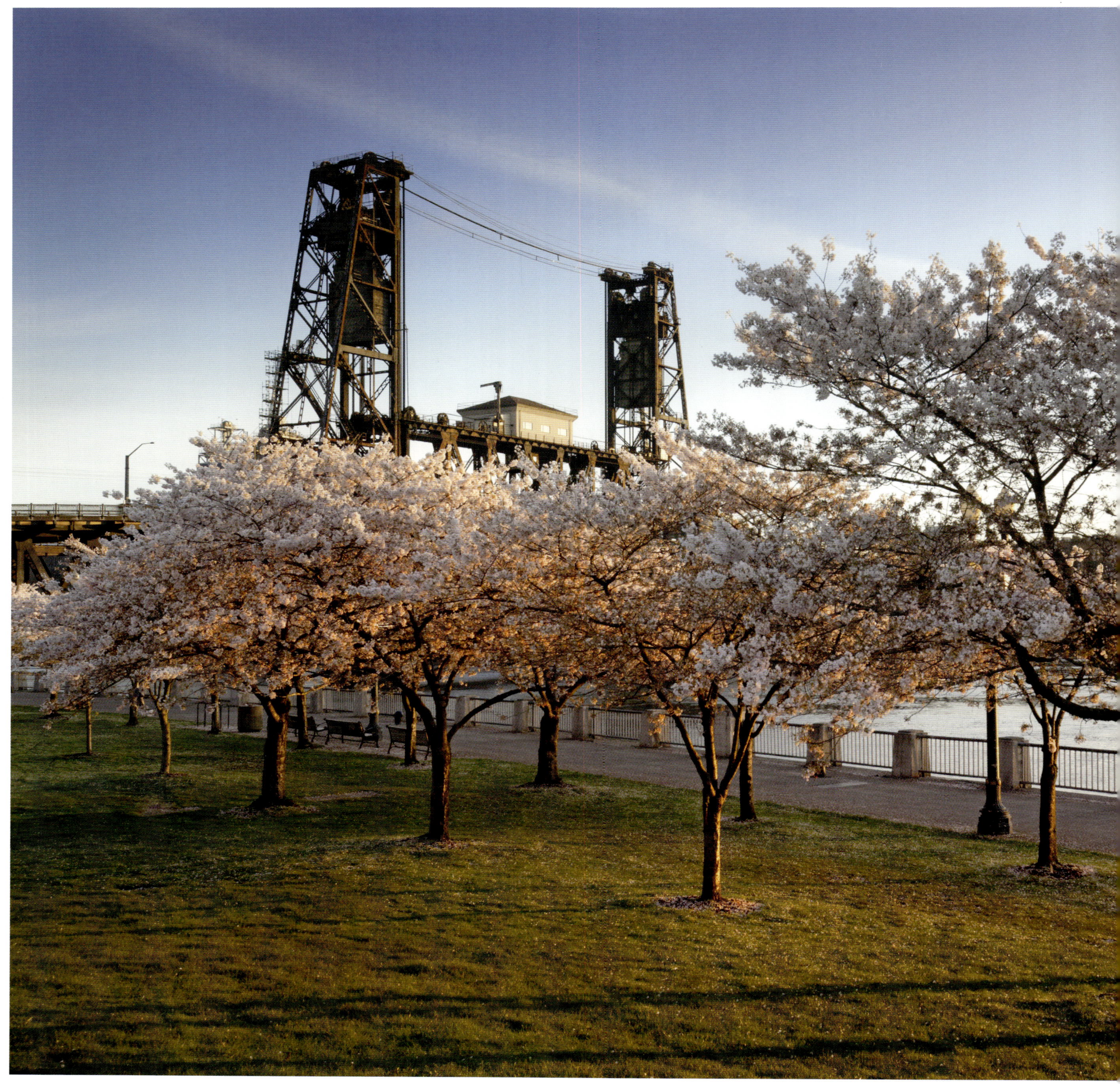

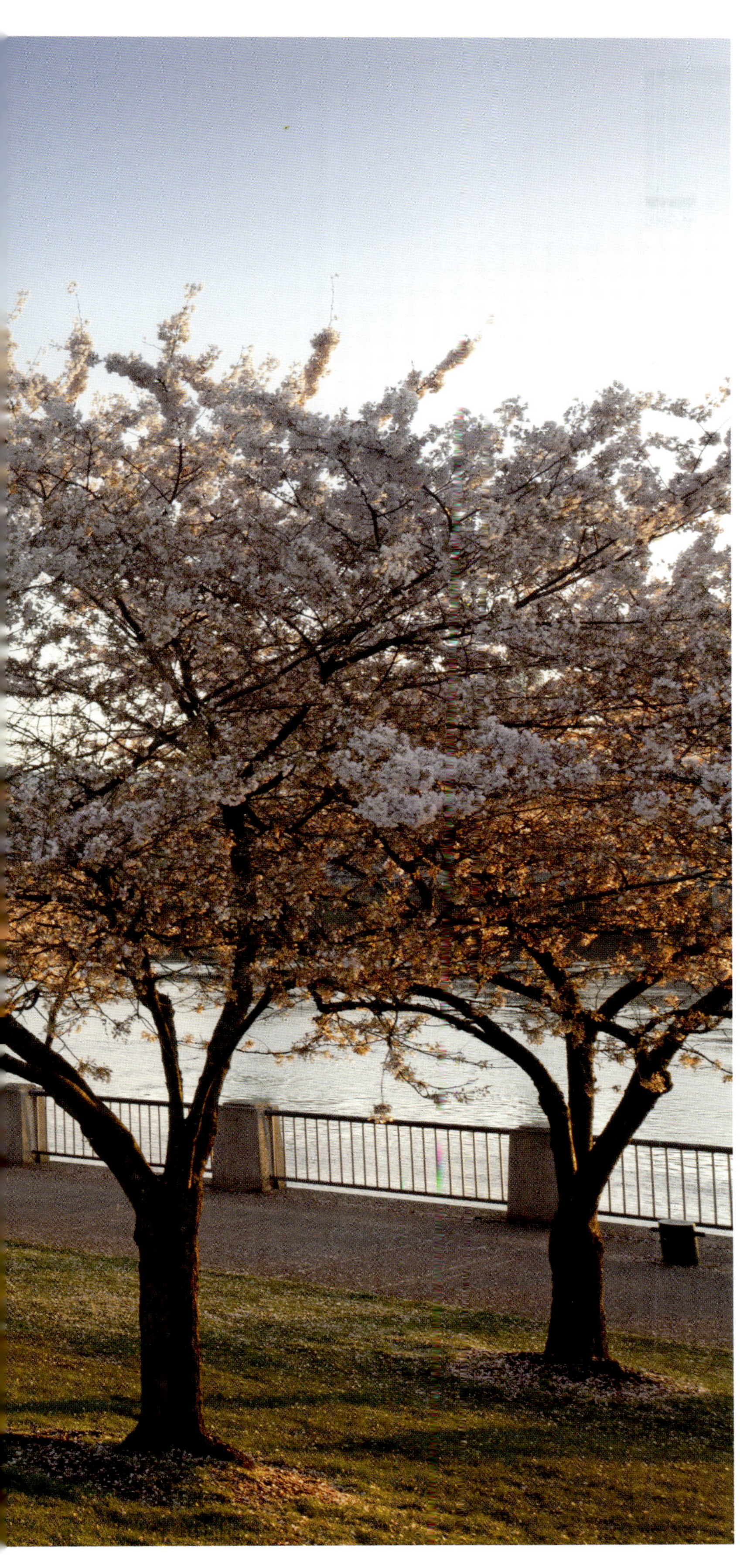

Cherry blossoms at sunrise along Tom
McCall Waterfront Park in Portland; the
Steel Bridge is in the background.

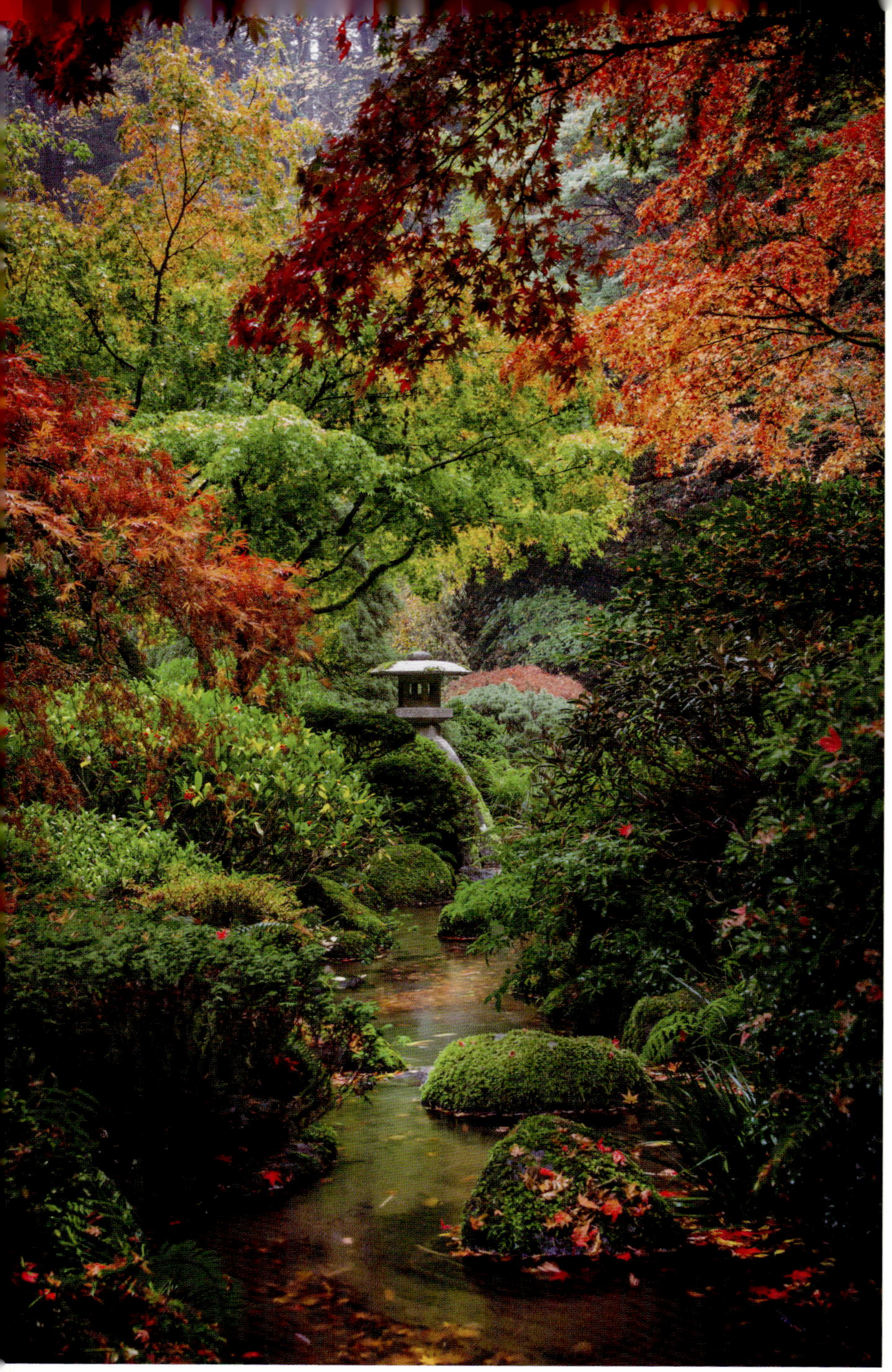

ABOVE Autumn reflections in a
small pond nestled inside the Portland
Japanese Garden. ●

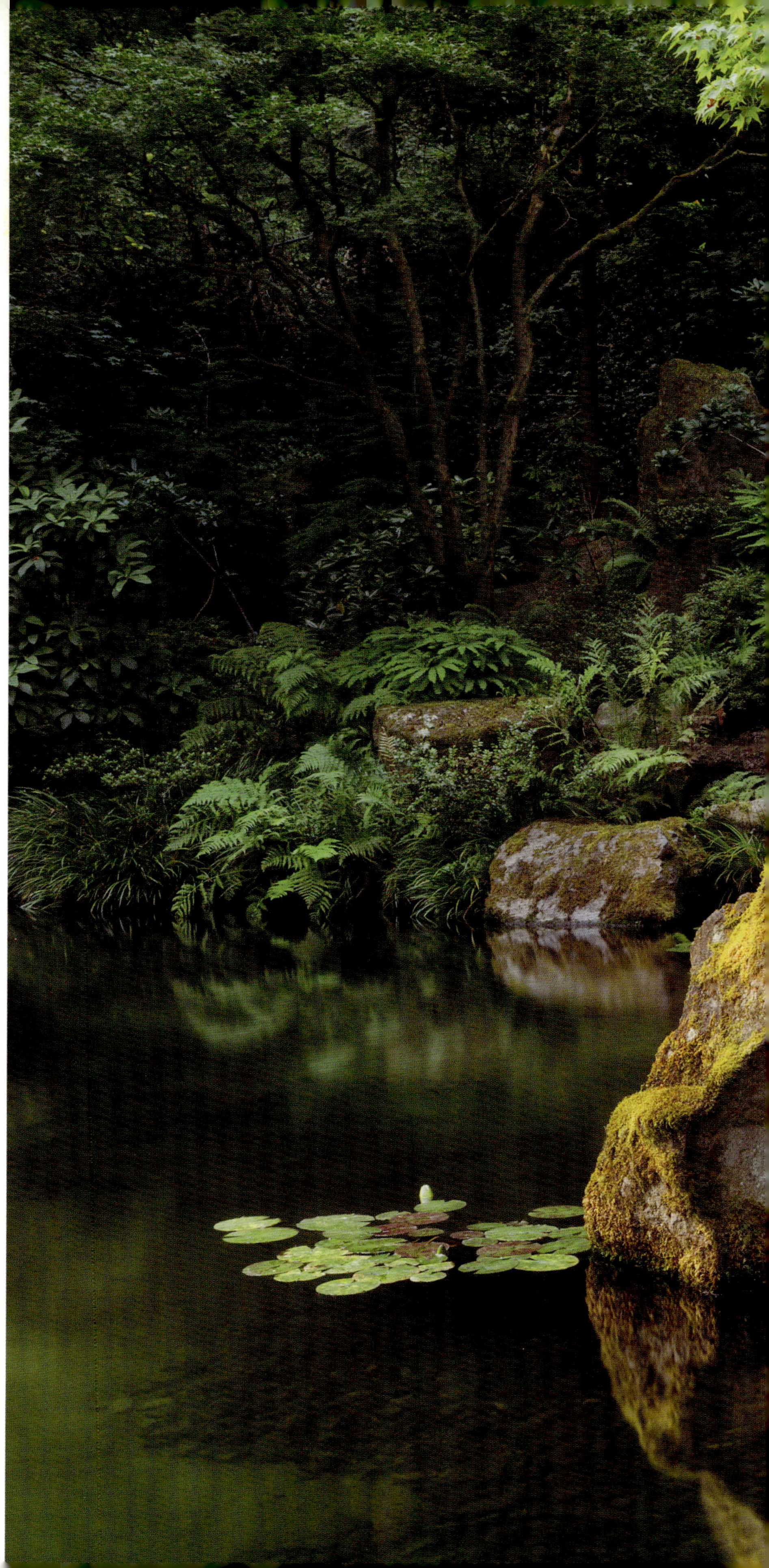

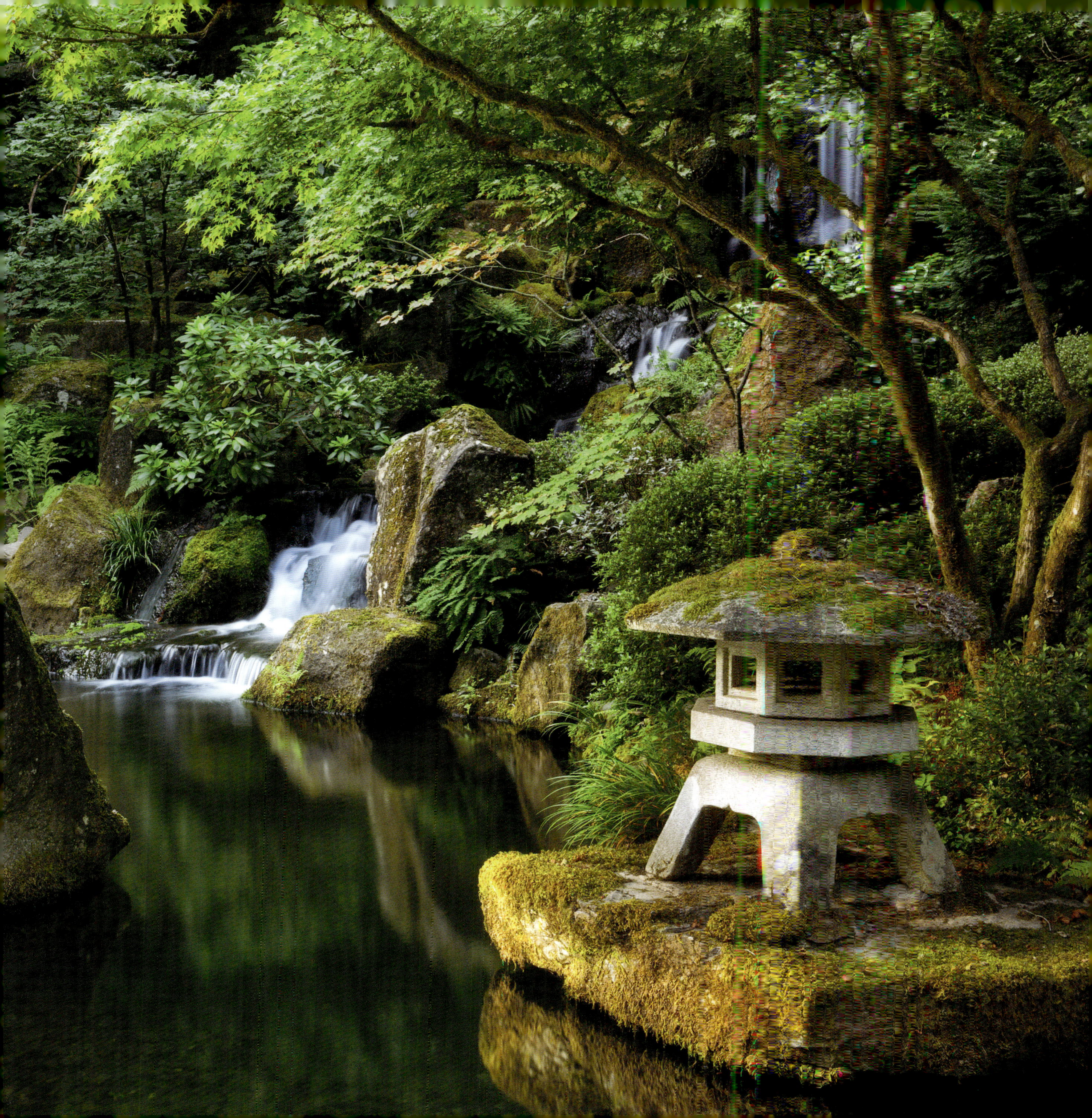

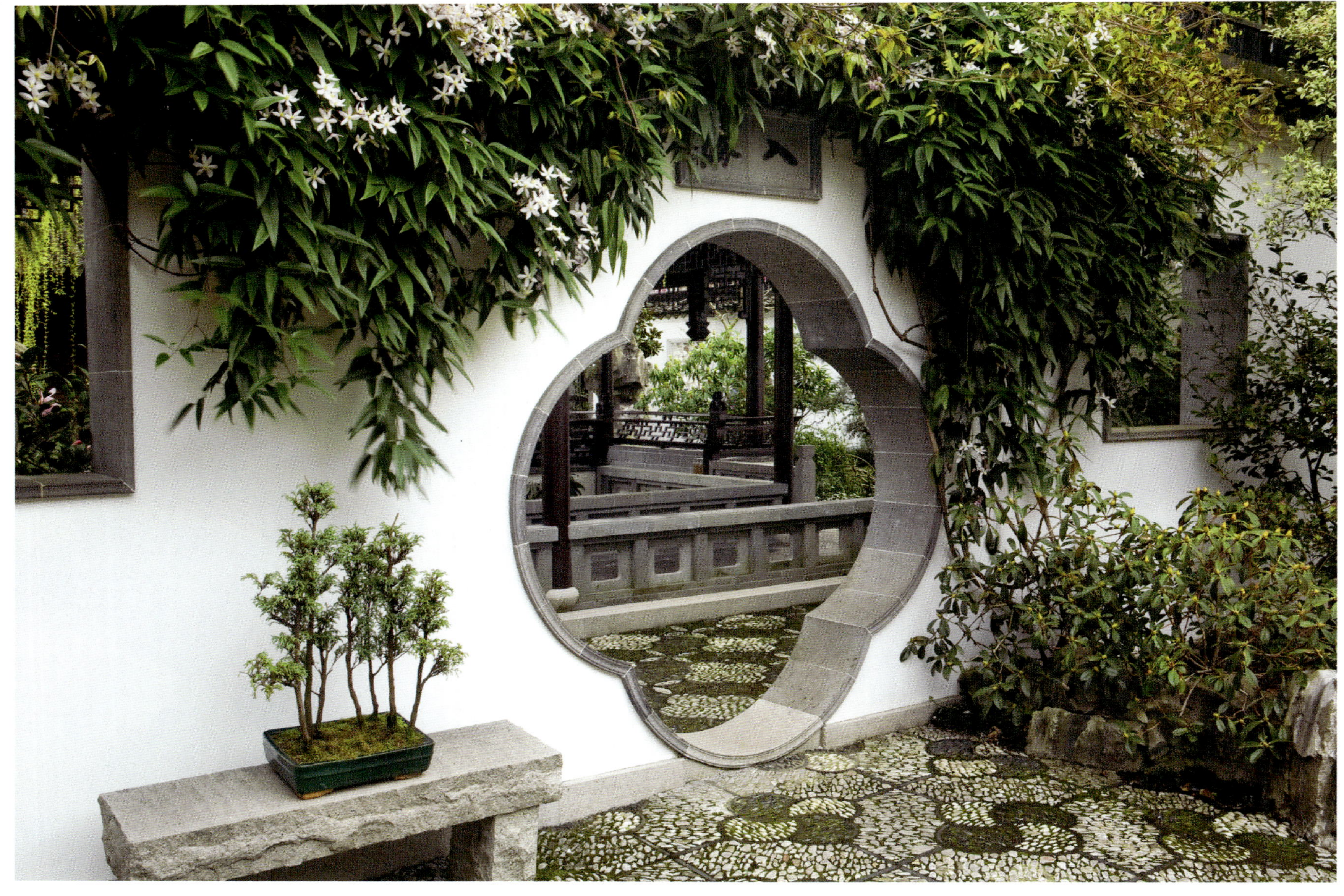

PREVIOUS PAGES Lush greens surround
the Snow Lantern and Heavenly Falls in
the Strolling Pond Garden at the Portland
Japanese Garden. •

ABOVE The Courtyard of
Tranquility at the Lan Su Chinese
Garden in Portland. •

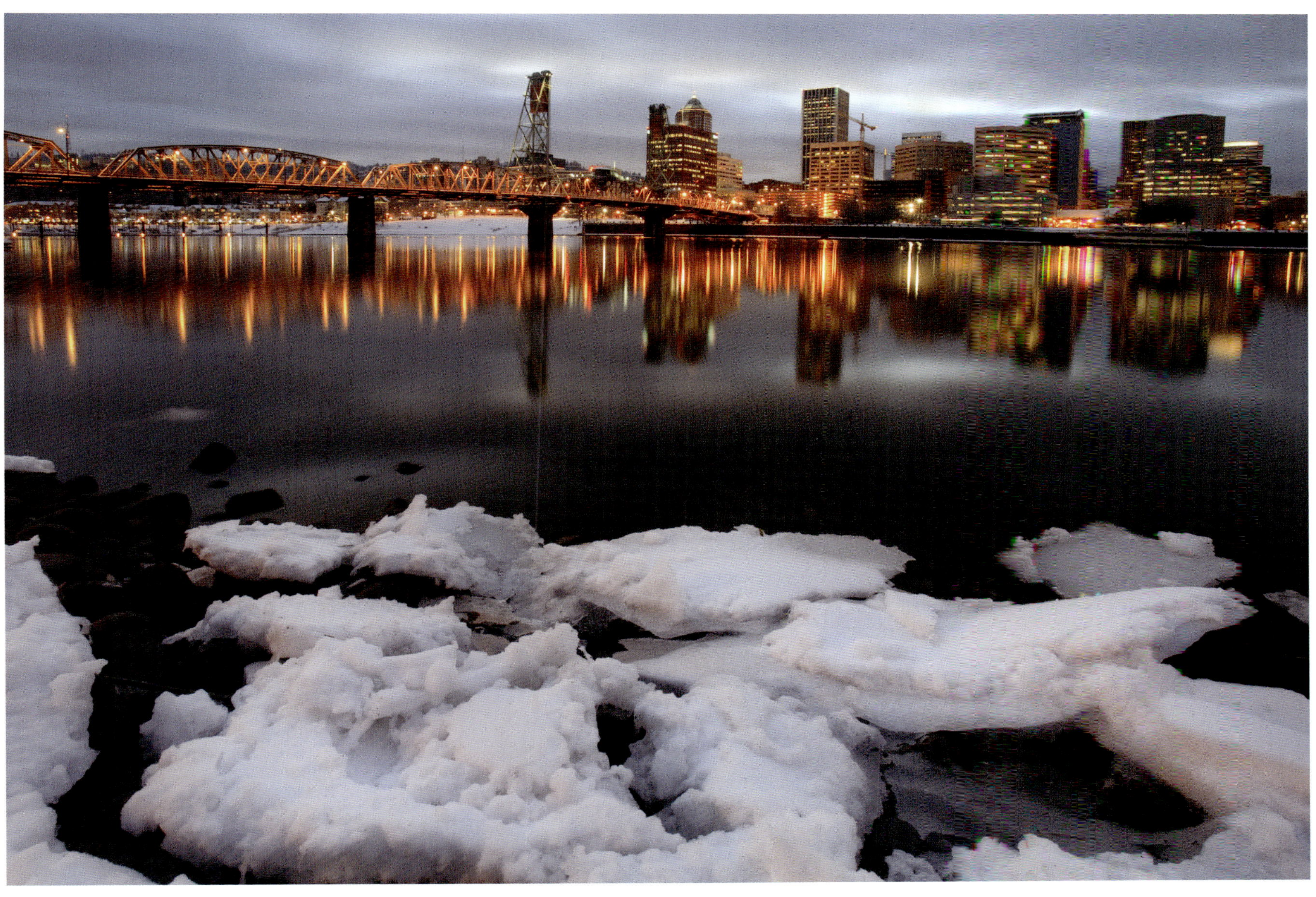

Downtown Portland and the Hawthorne
Bridge at sunset along the Willamette
River during a winter cold spell. •

Sunset at Crown Point in the Columbia
River Gorge. •

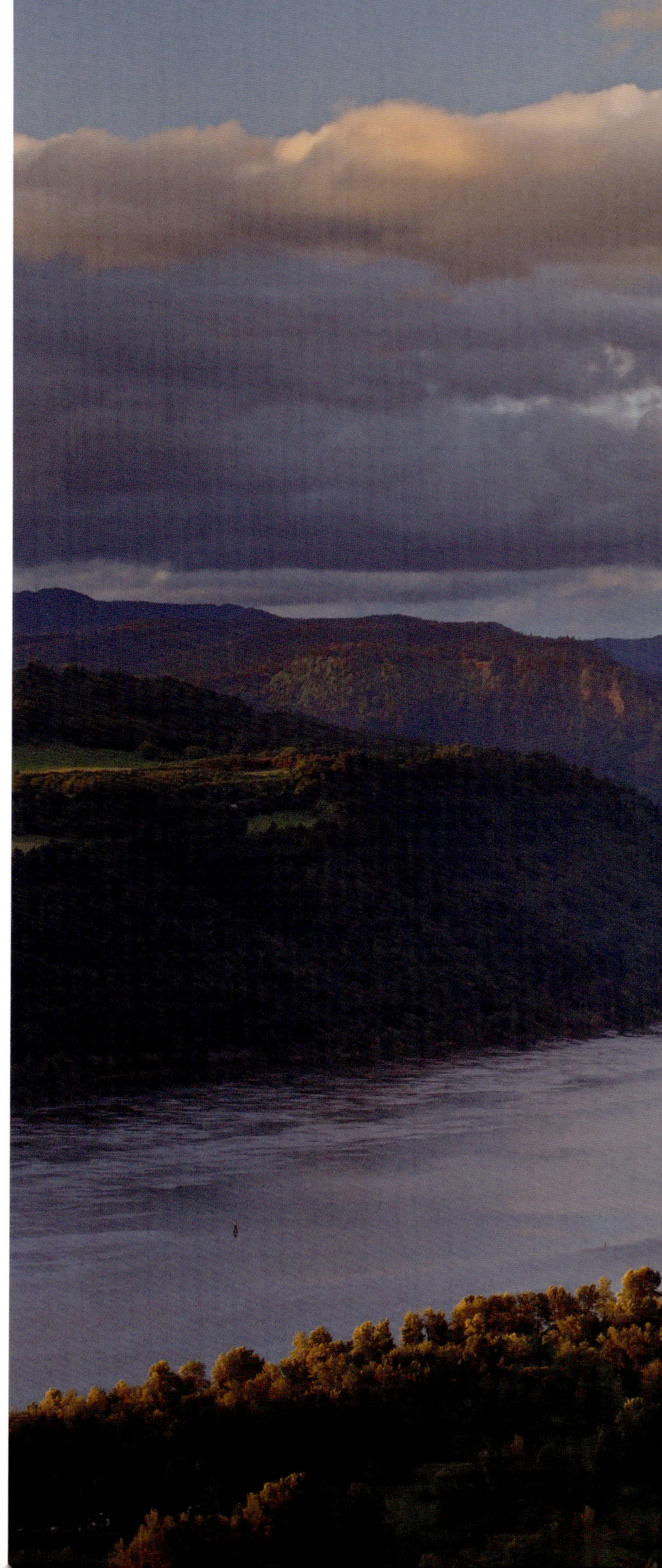

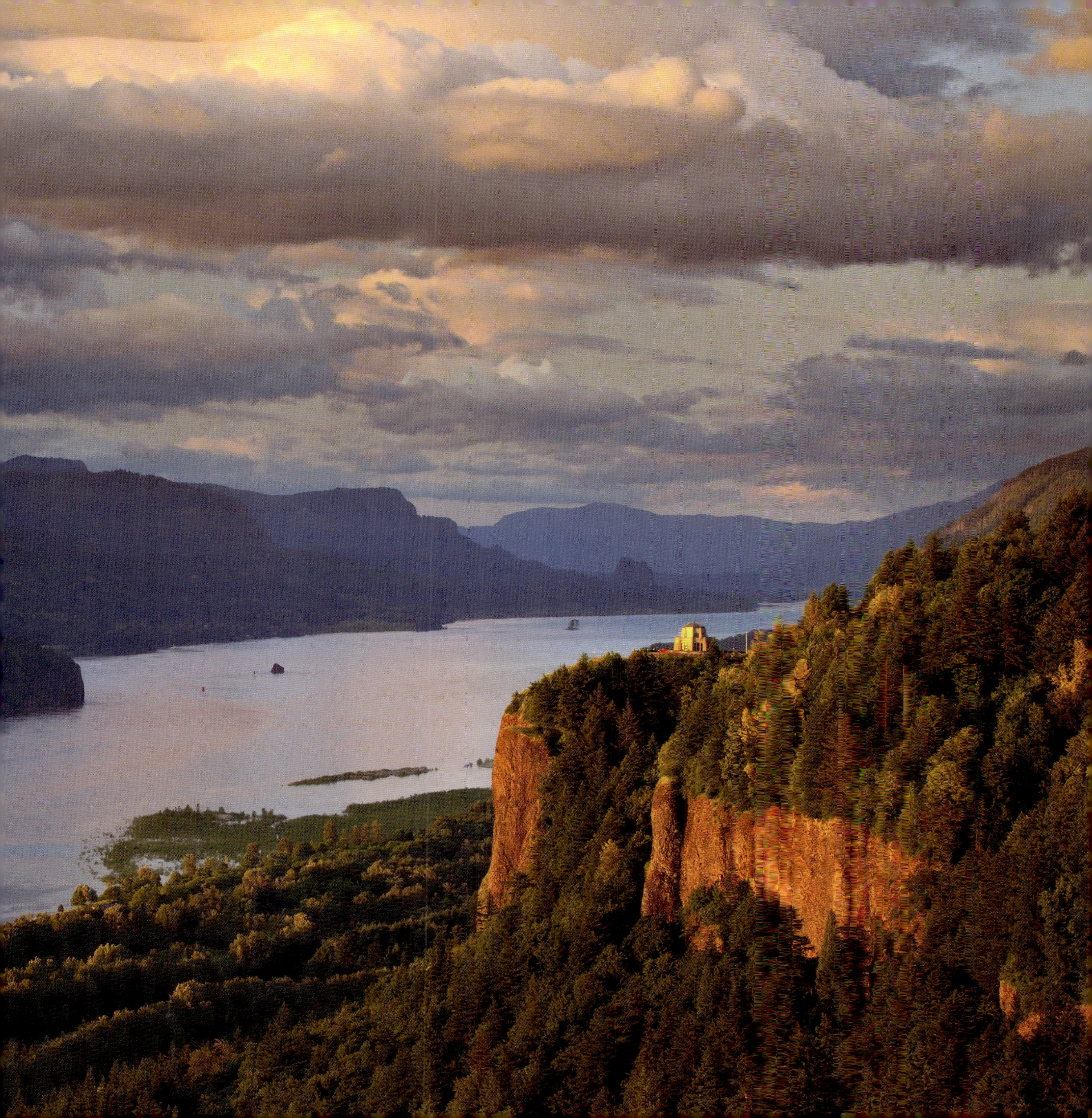

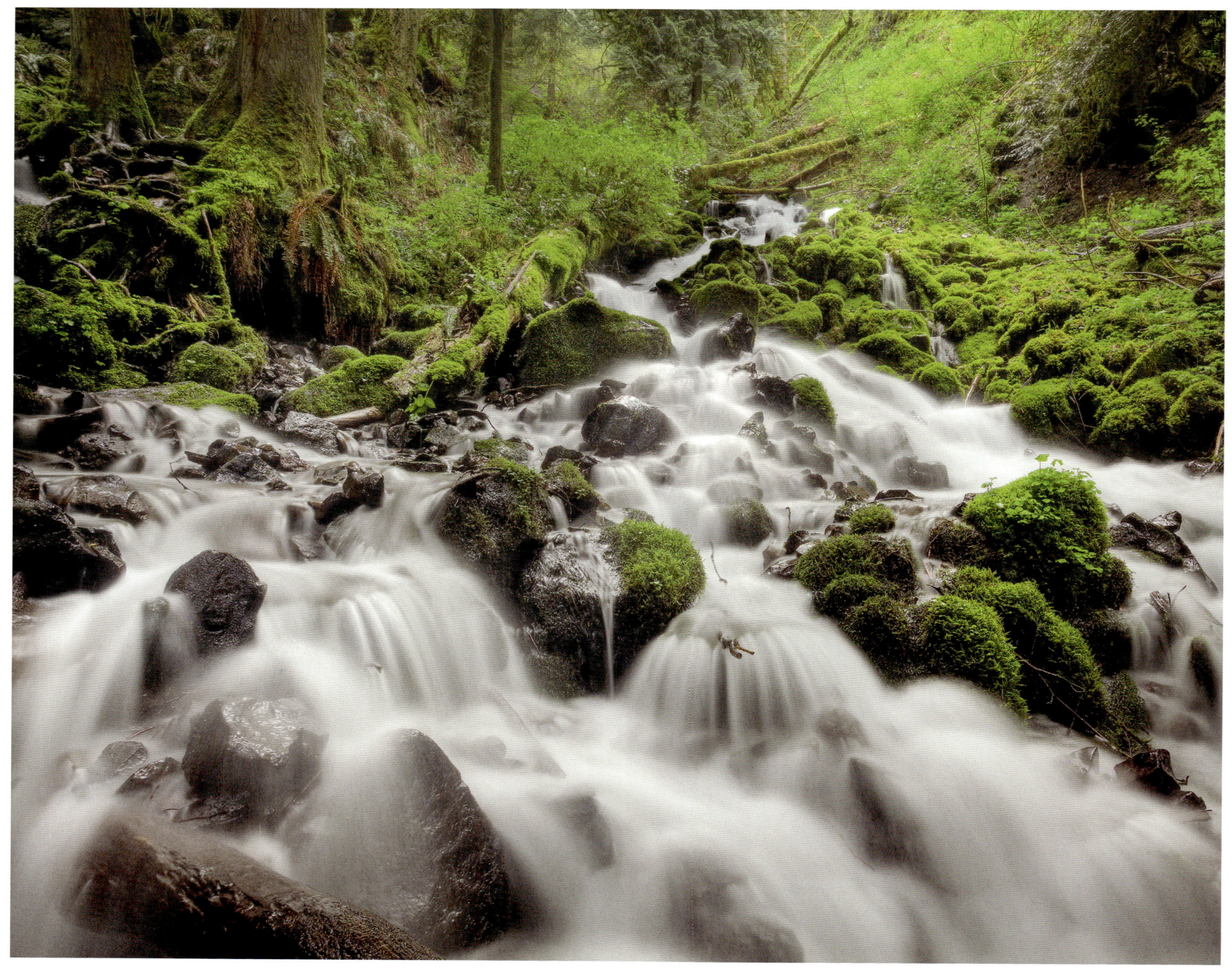

Fairy Falls, one of the many that can
be found in the stunning Columbia
River Gorge. •

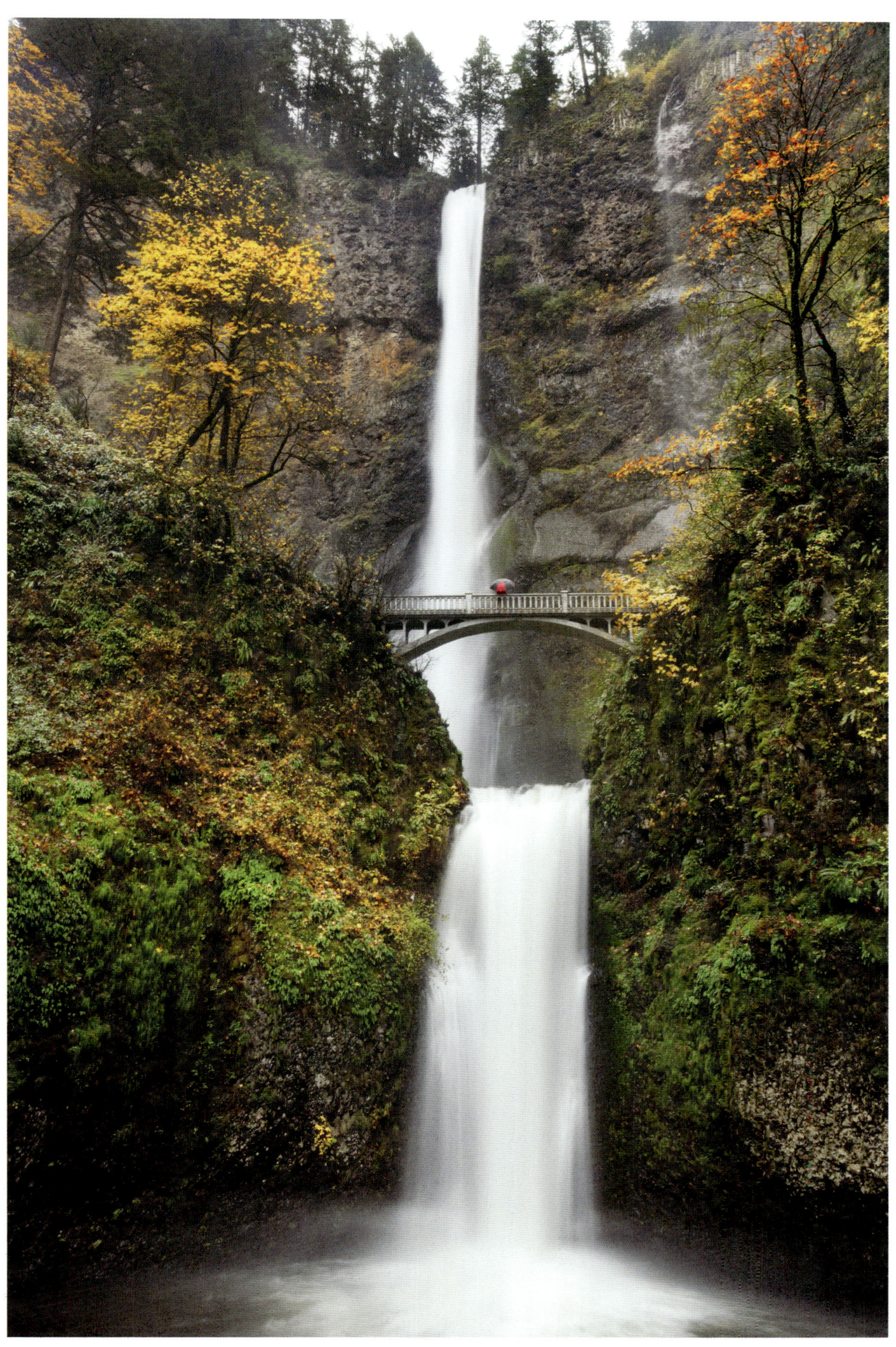

Multnomah Falls and Benson Bridge
during the colorful fall season.

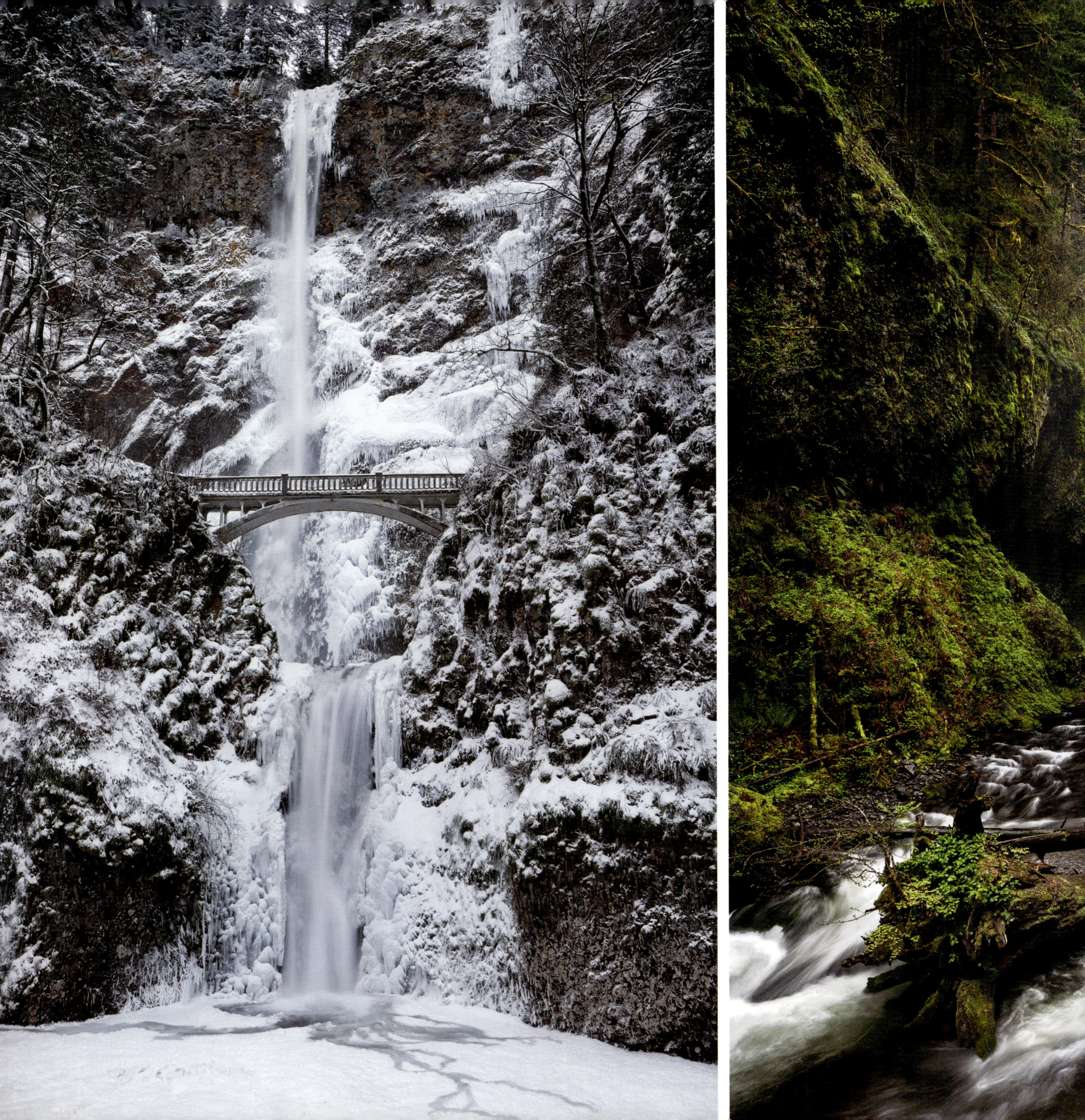

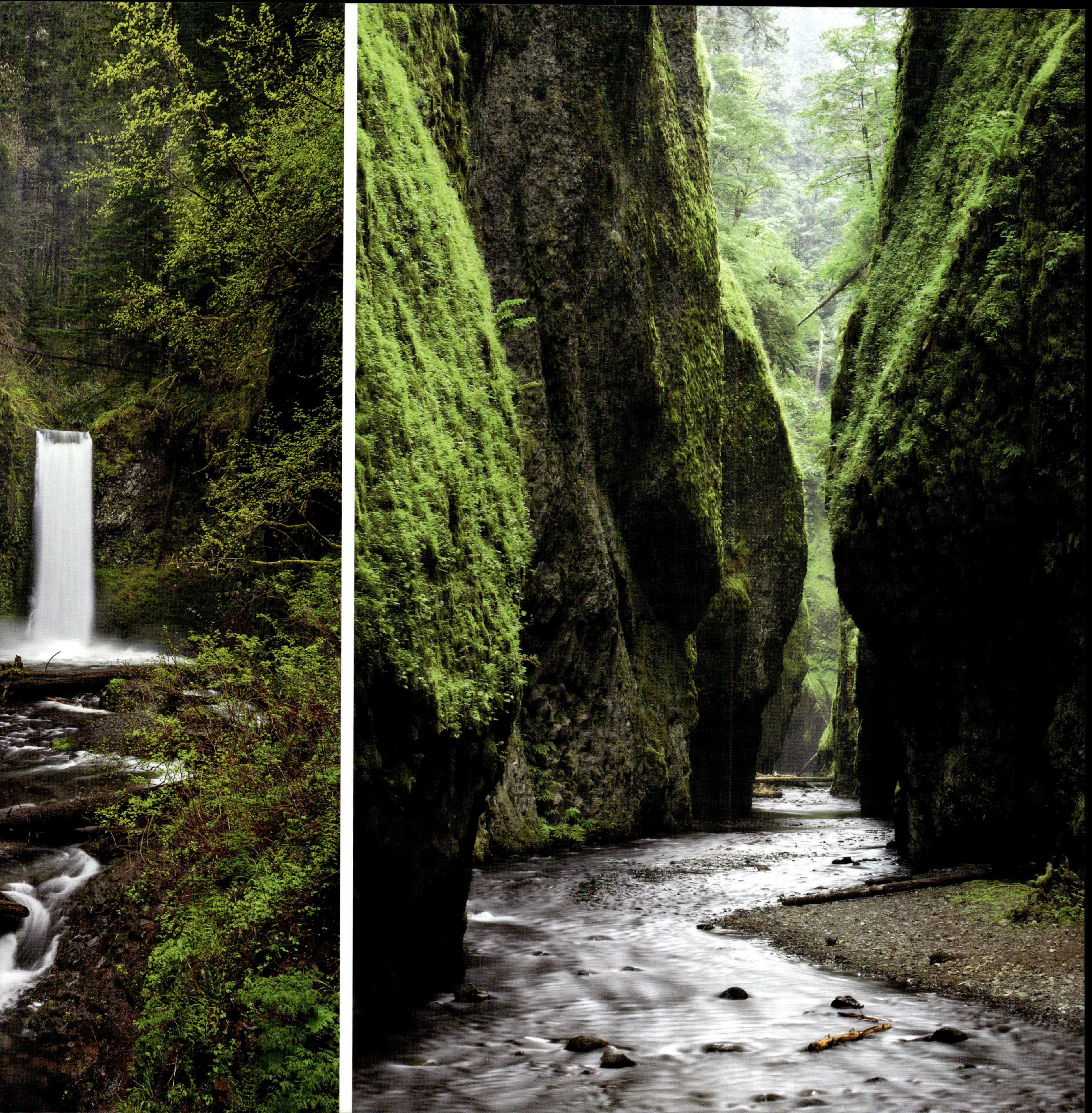

A partially frozen Multnomah Falls shows
off its winter beauty in the Columbia River
Gorge. • A mile above Multnomah Falls,
Multnomah Creek cascades 50 feet over
Wiesendanger Falls in the Columbia River
Gorge. • Oneonta Creek fills the narrow
slot canyon of Oneonta Gorge, formed
by a structural fault in the surrounding
volcanic basalt. •

  The hiking trail to Horsetail Falls
in the Columbia River Gorge passes
under a cliff, providing views of the water
from behind. •

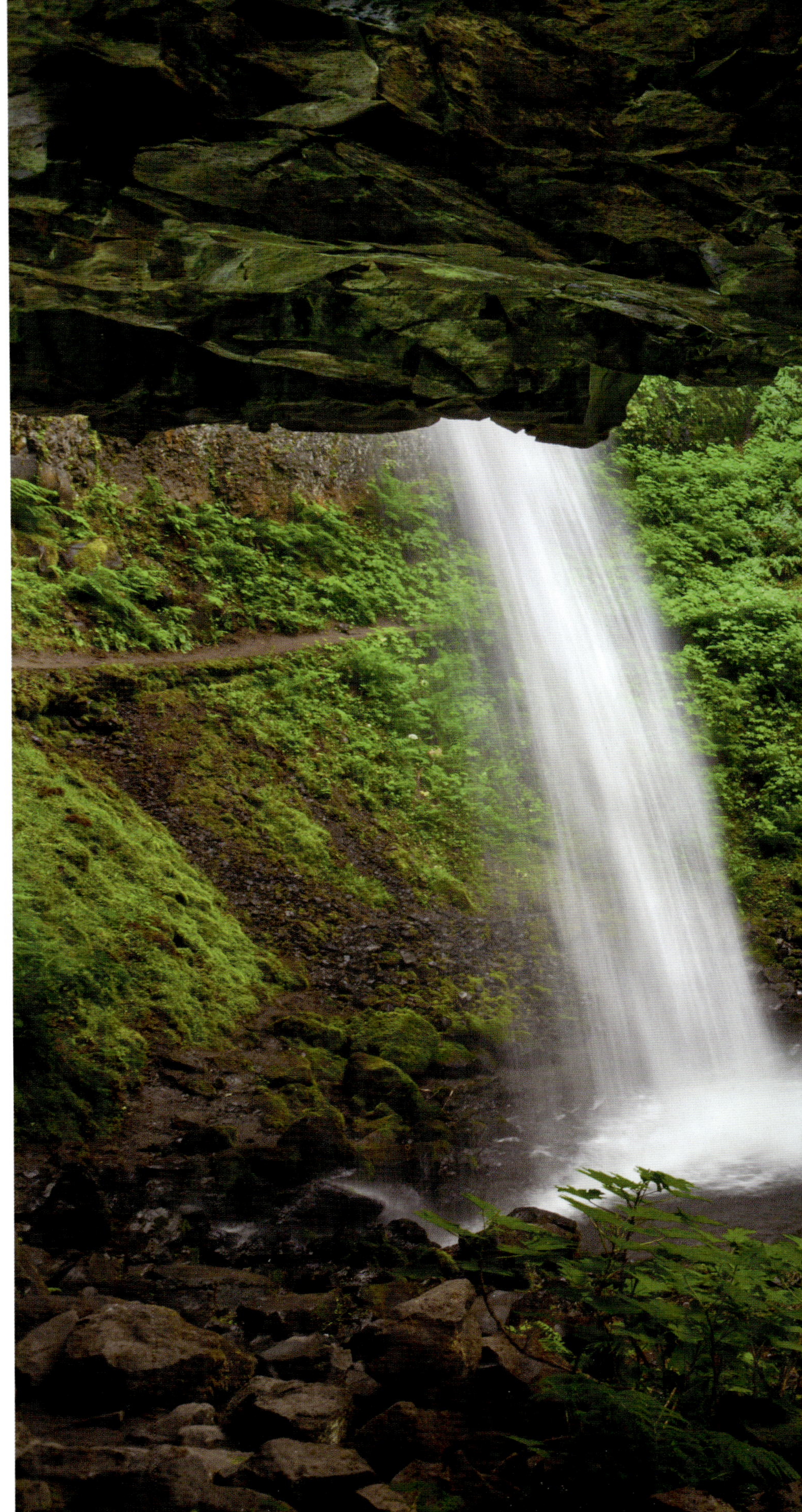

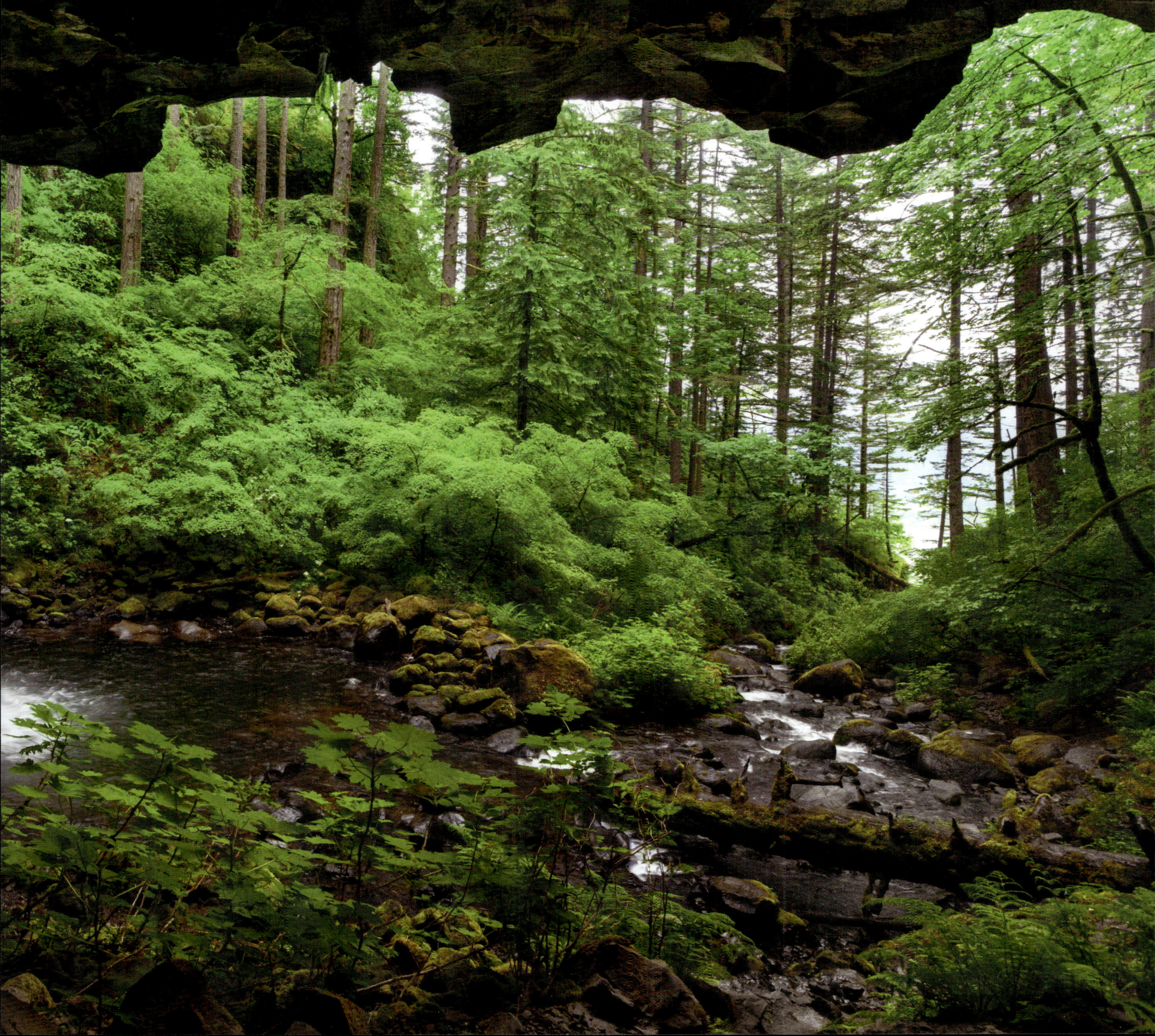

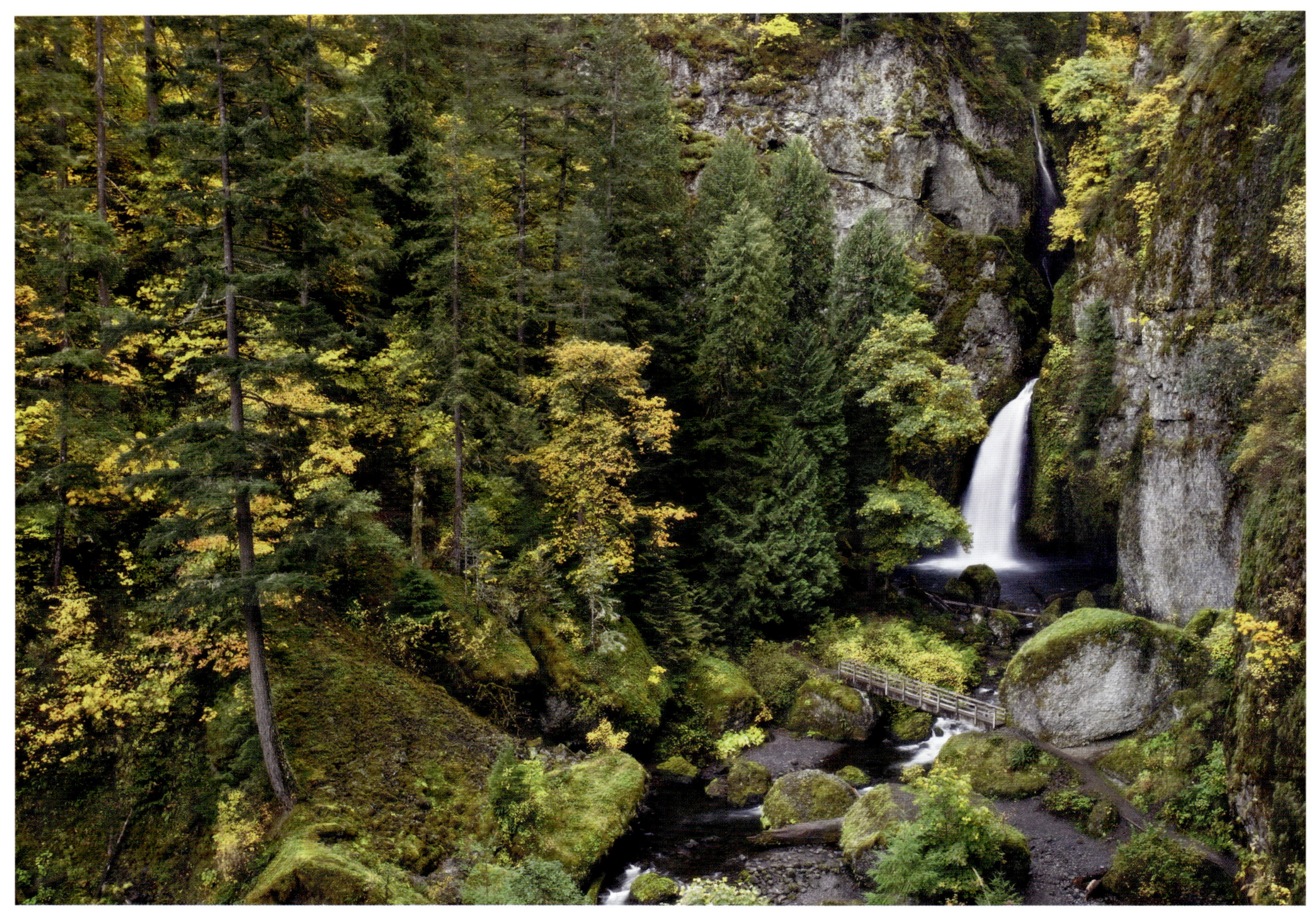

Wahclella Falls, in the Columbia River
Gorge, during the peak of fall color. •

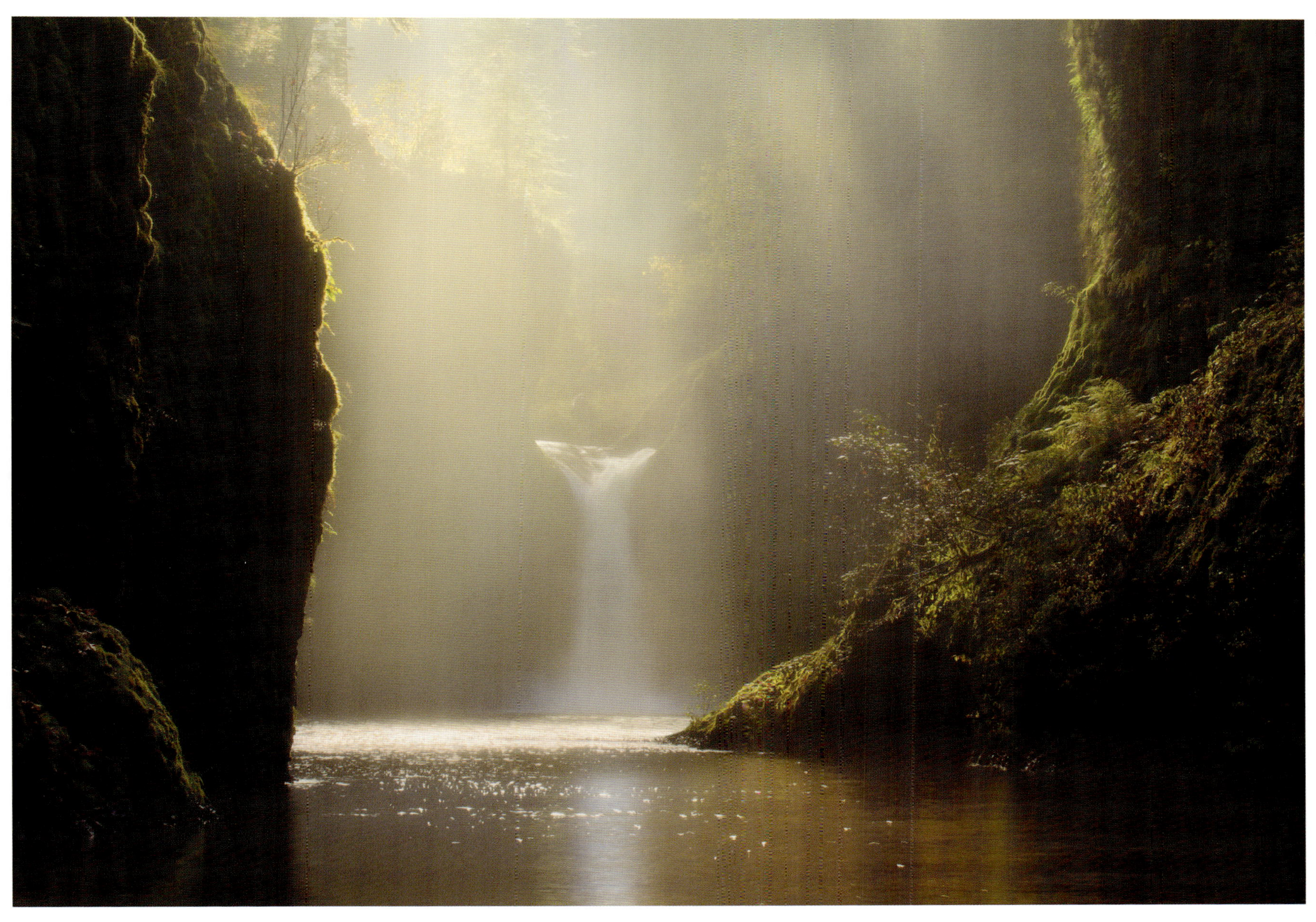

Punch Bowl Falls, in the Columbia River
Gorge, just after a misty sunrise. •

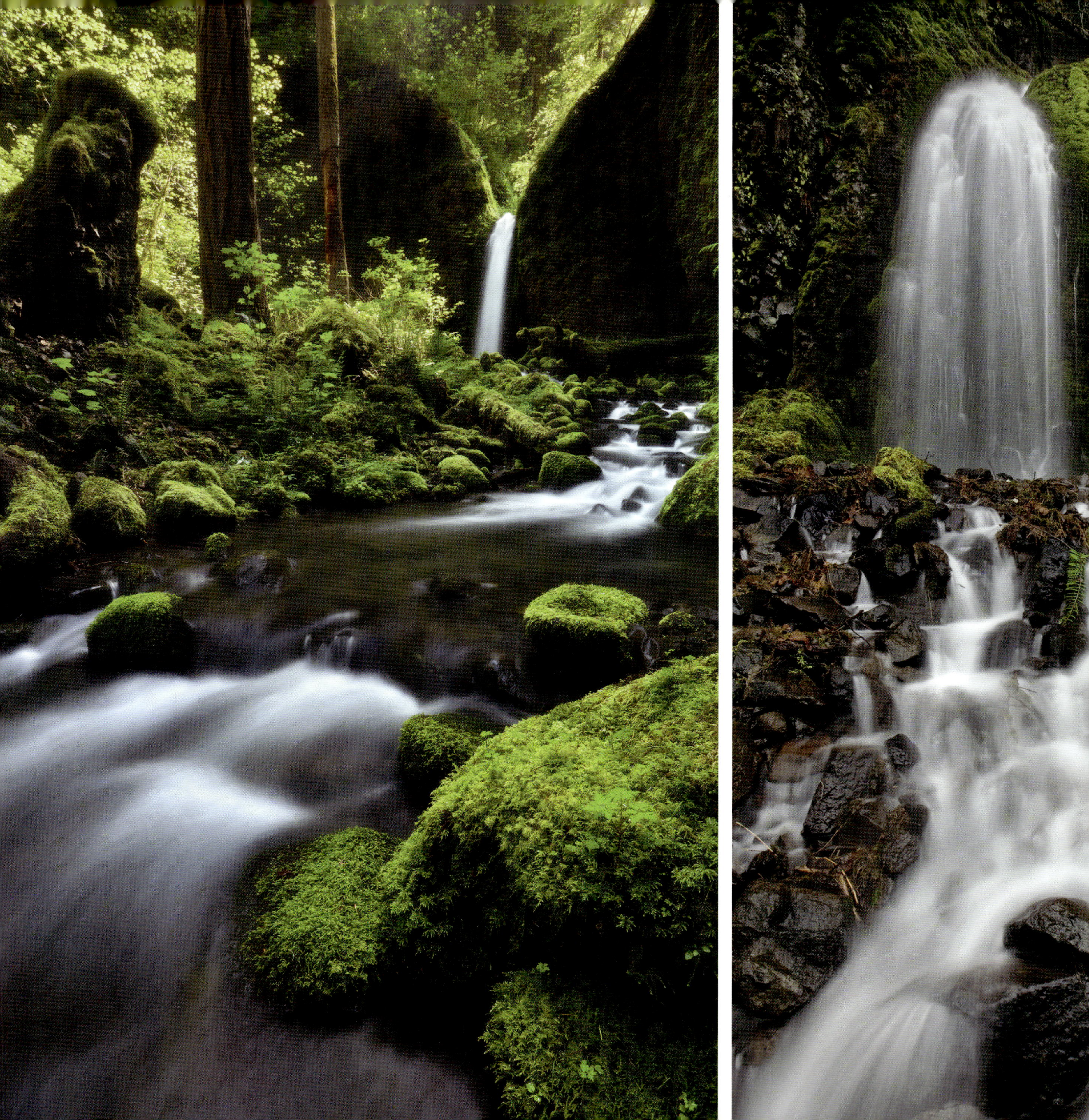

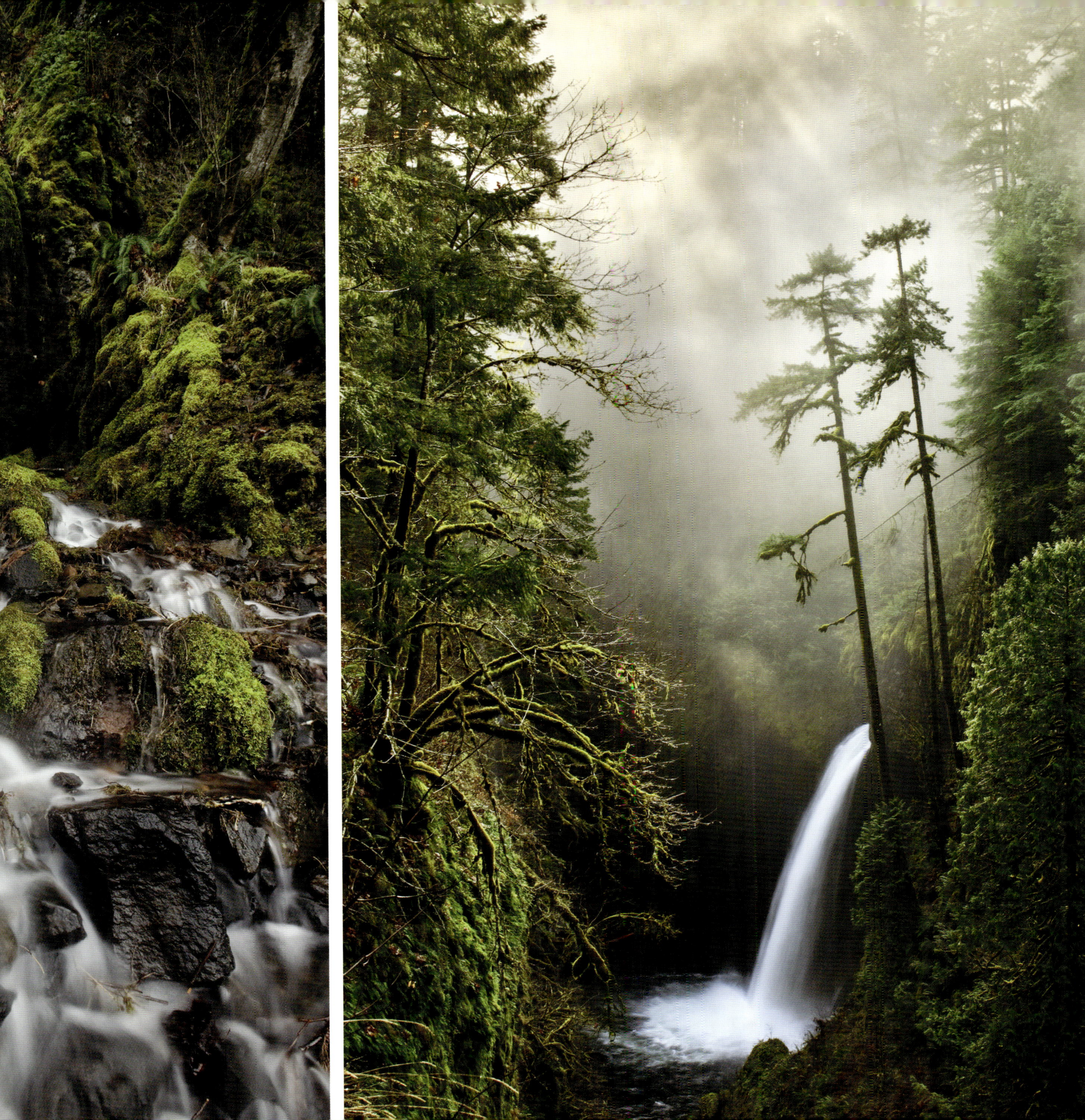

PREVIOUS PAGES, LEFT TO RIGHT
Ruckel Creek flowing through lush
spring greens in a secluded canyon. •
The waters of Lancaster Falls fan out
over lush green mosses in the Columbia
River Gorge. • Metlako Falls in the
Columbia River Gorge, before the
devastating Eagle Creek Fire of 2017. •

RIGHT   The base of Cabin Creek Falls
in the Columbia River Gorge. •

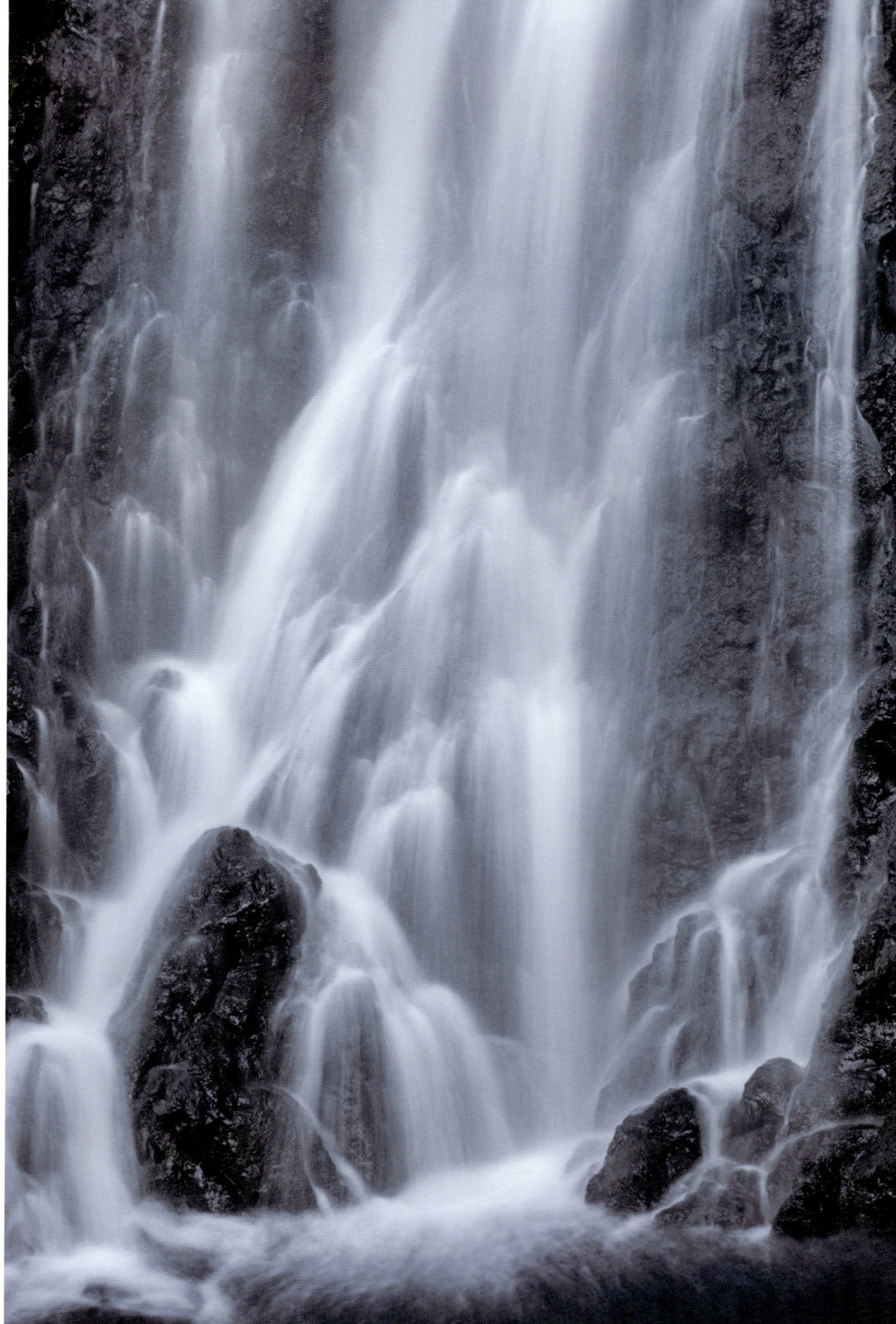

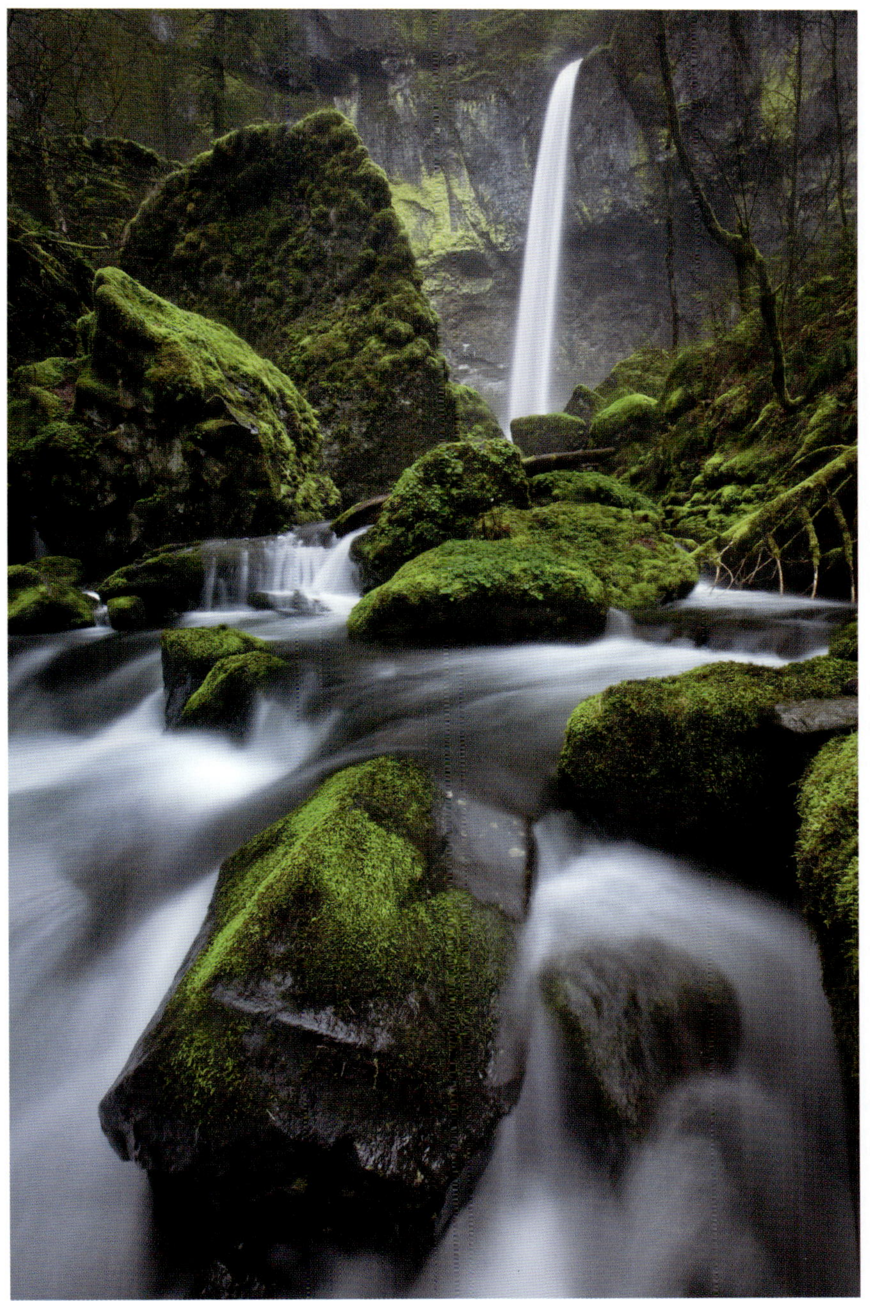

Elowah Falls, plunging its 213 feet
smoothly in early spring. •

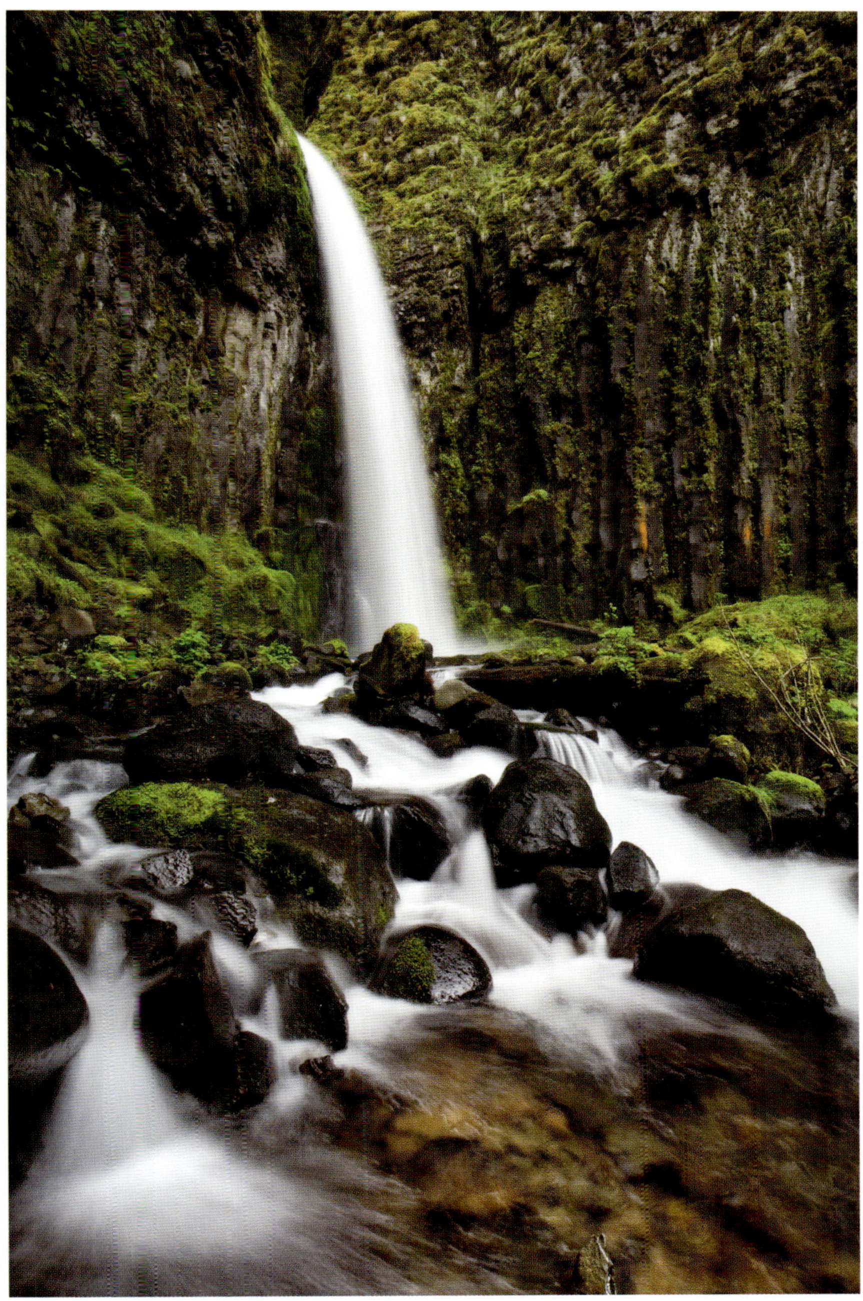

Dry Creek Falls looking anything but as
it accommodates the spring melt. •

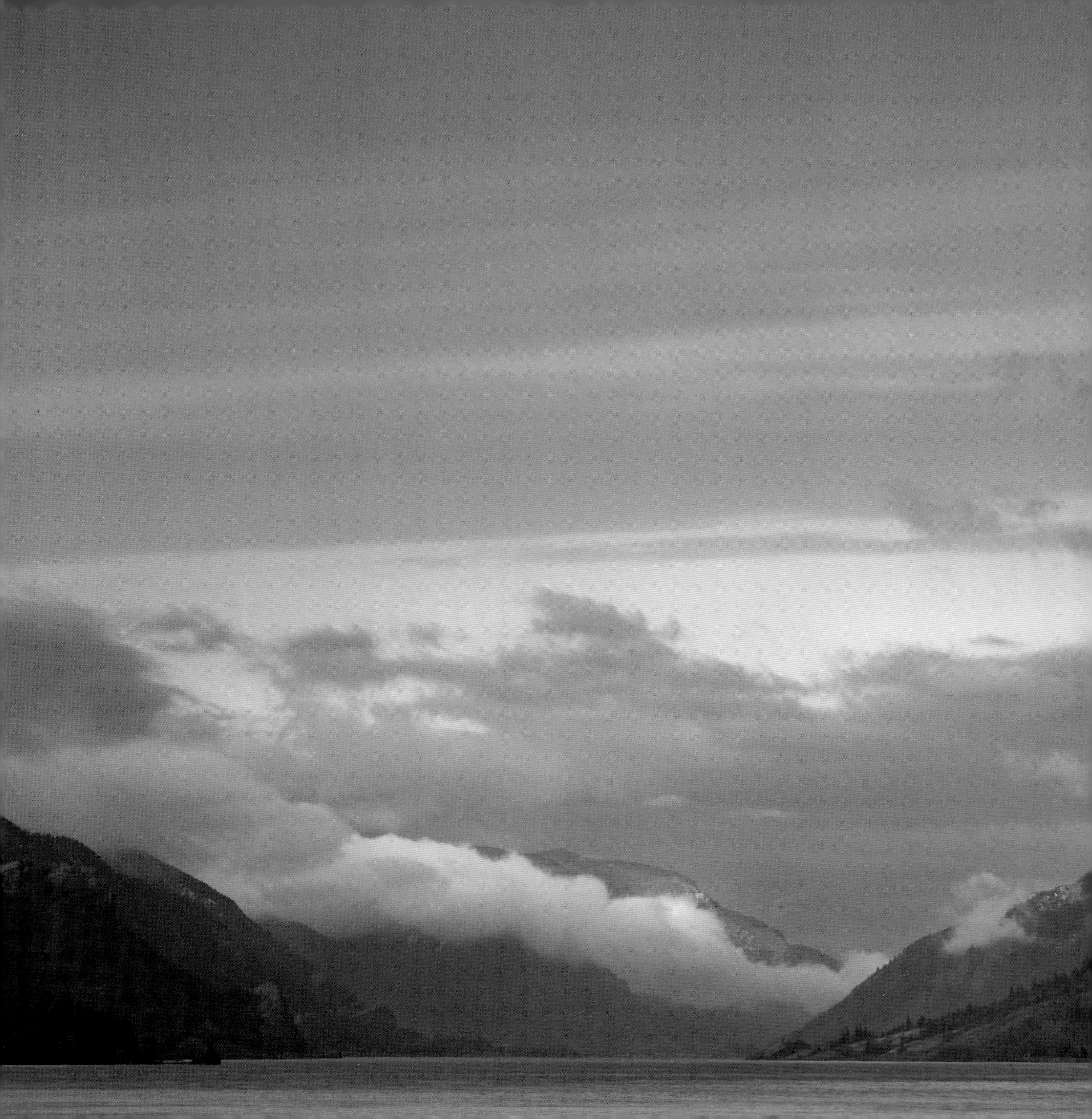

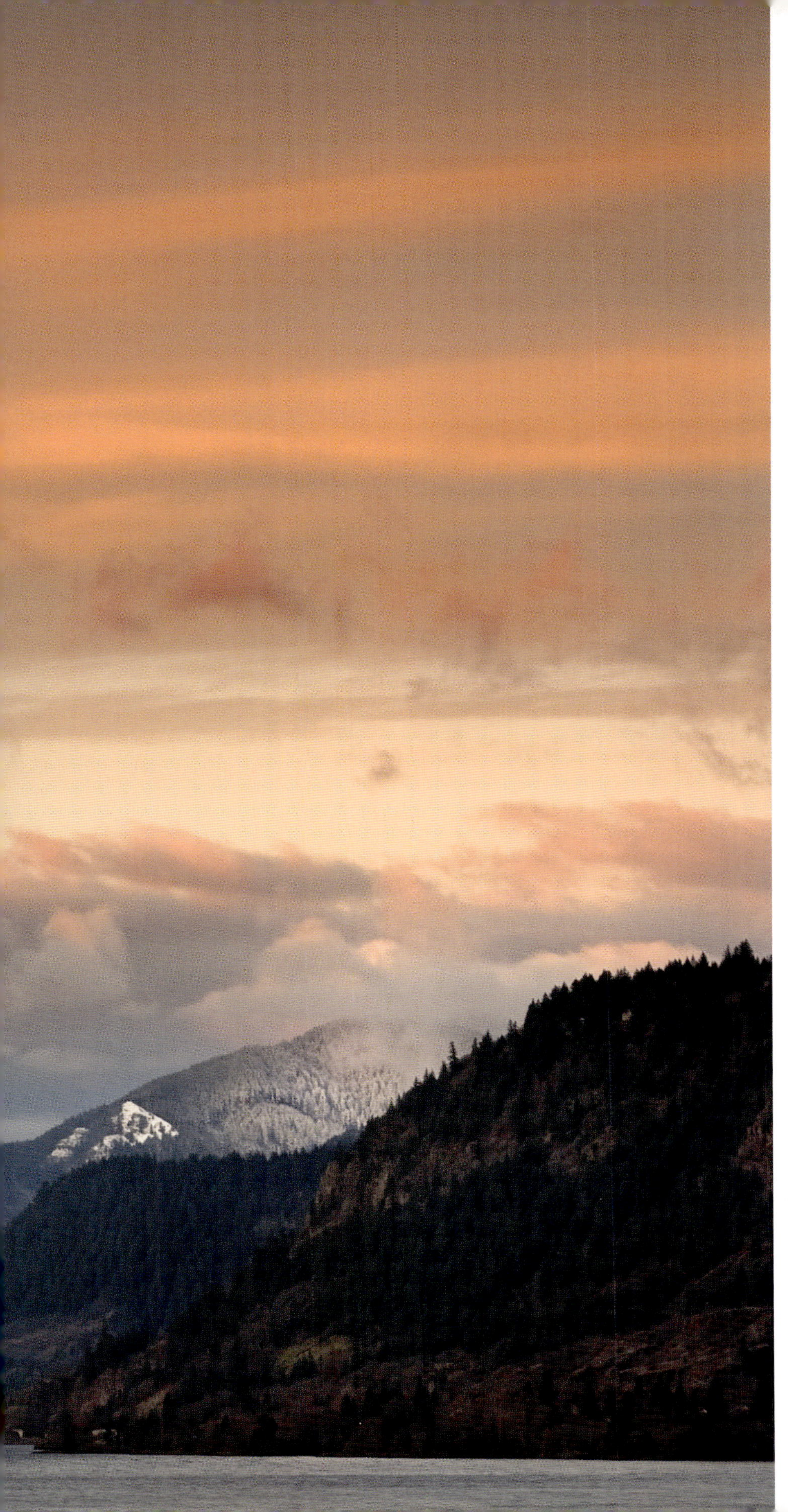

The pastel colors of sunrise hover
over the eastern end of the Columbia
River Gorge. •

Fruit tree blossoms fill the Hood River
Valley in spring; majestic Mount Hood
presides above. •

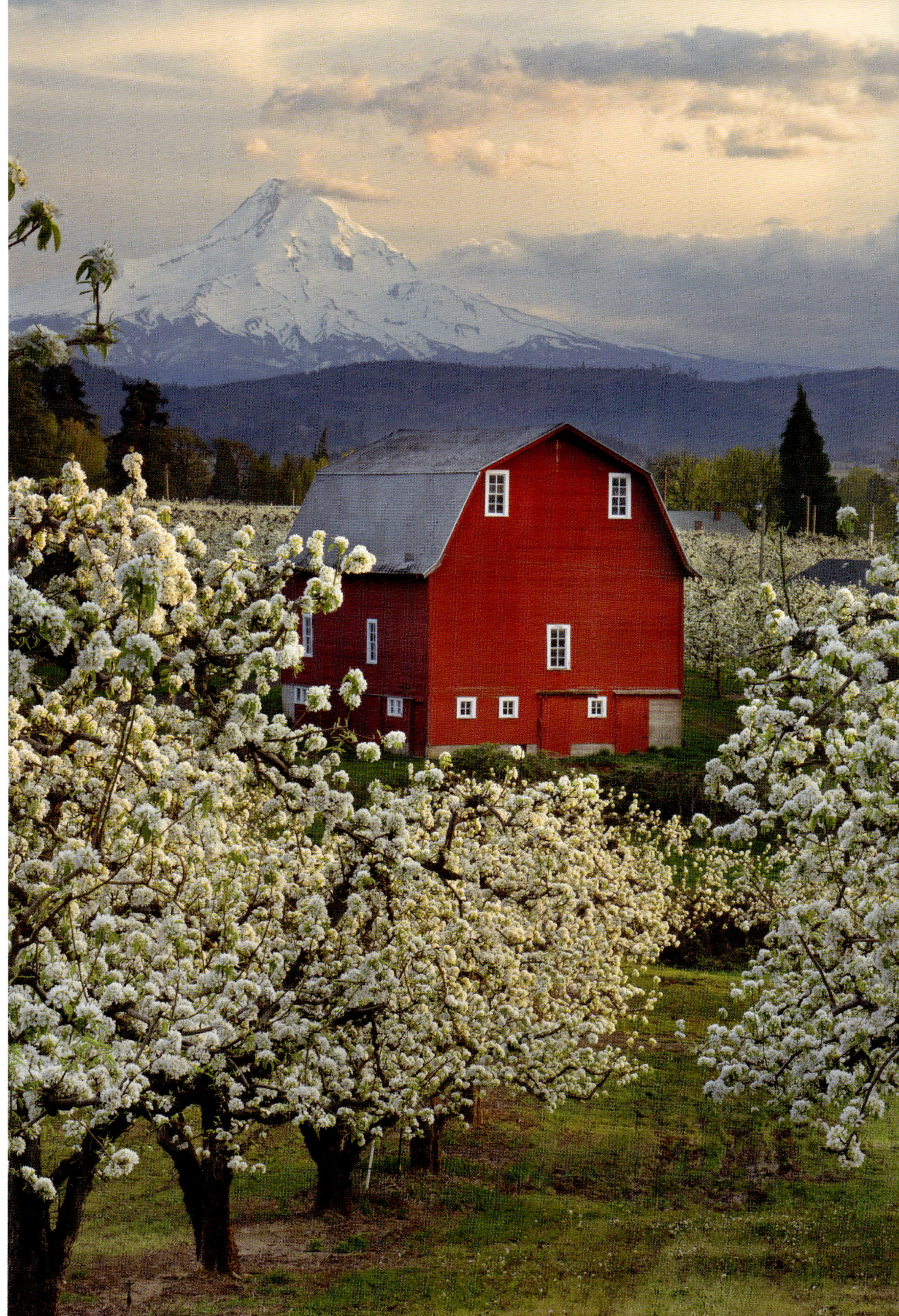

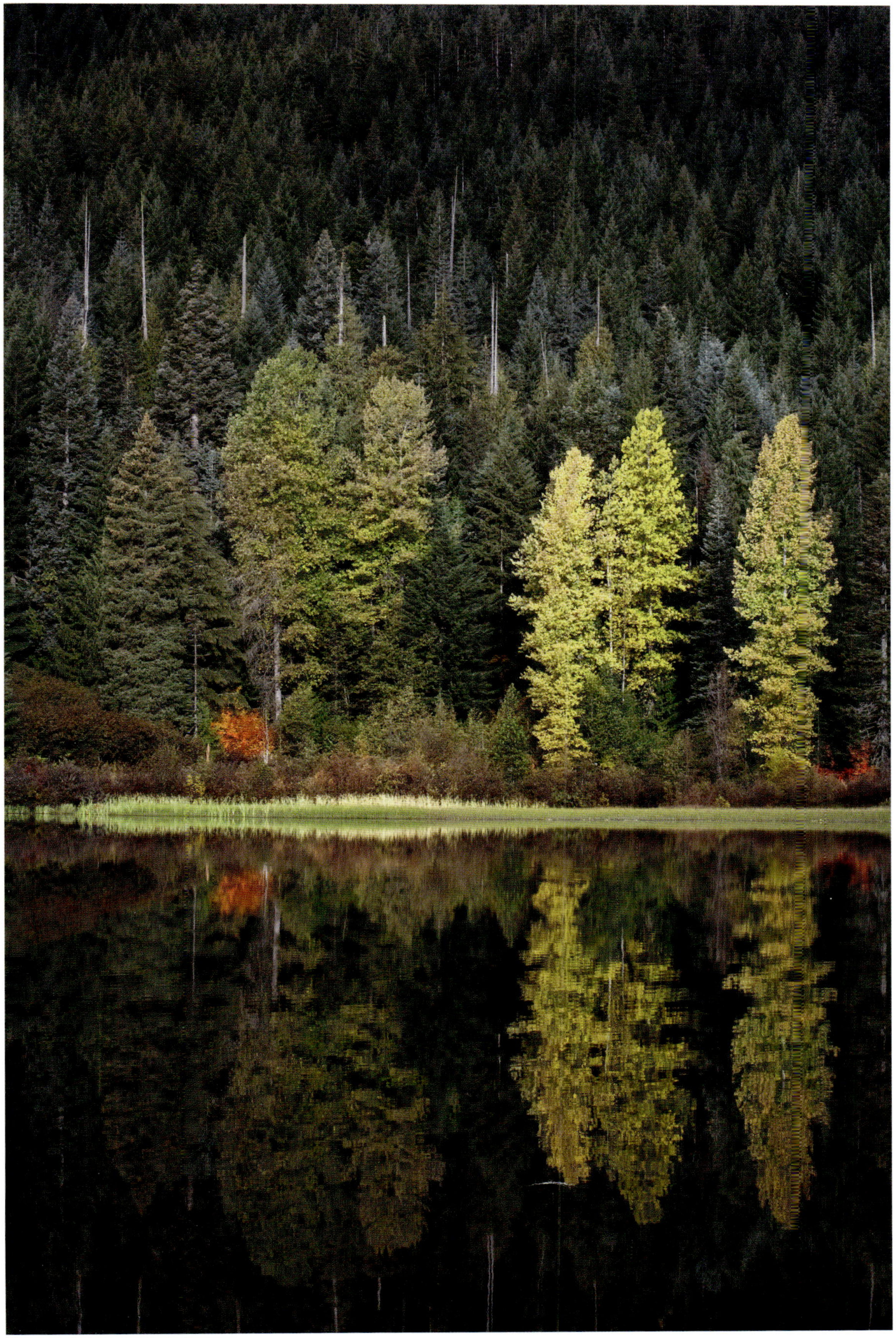

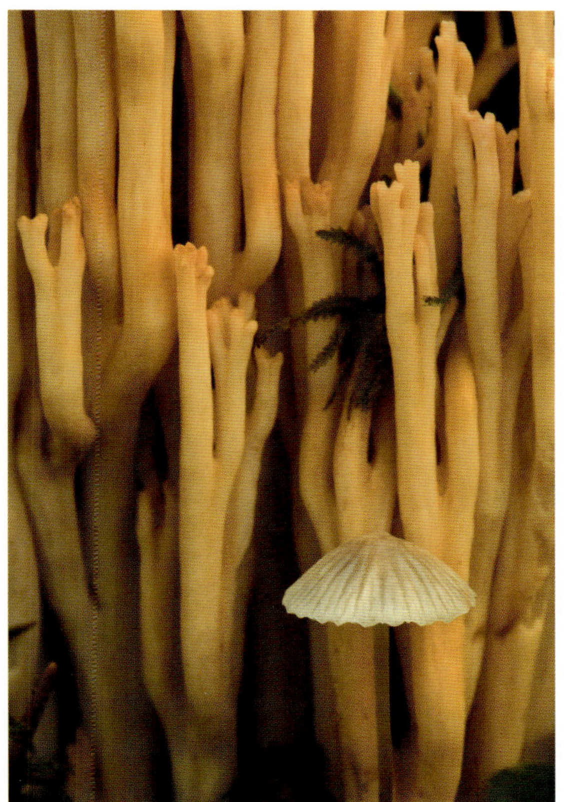

ABOVE A variety of coral mushrooms
grow throughout the Columbia River
Gorge. •

LEFT The fall colors of deciduous trees
pop against the conifer colors along the
shore of Trillium Lake in the Mount Hood
National Forest. •

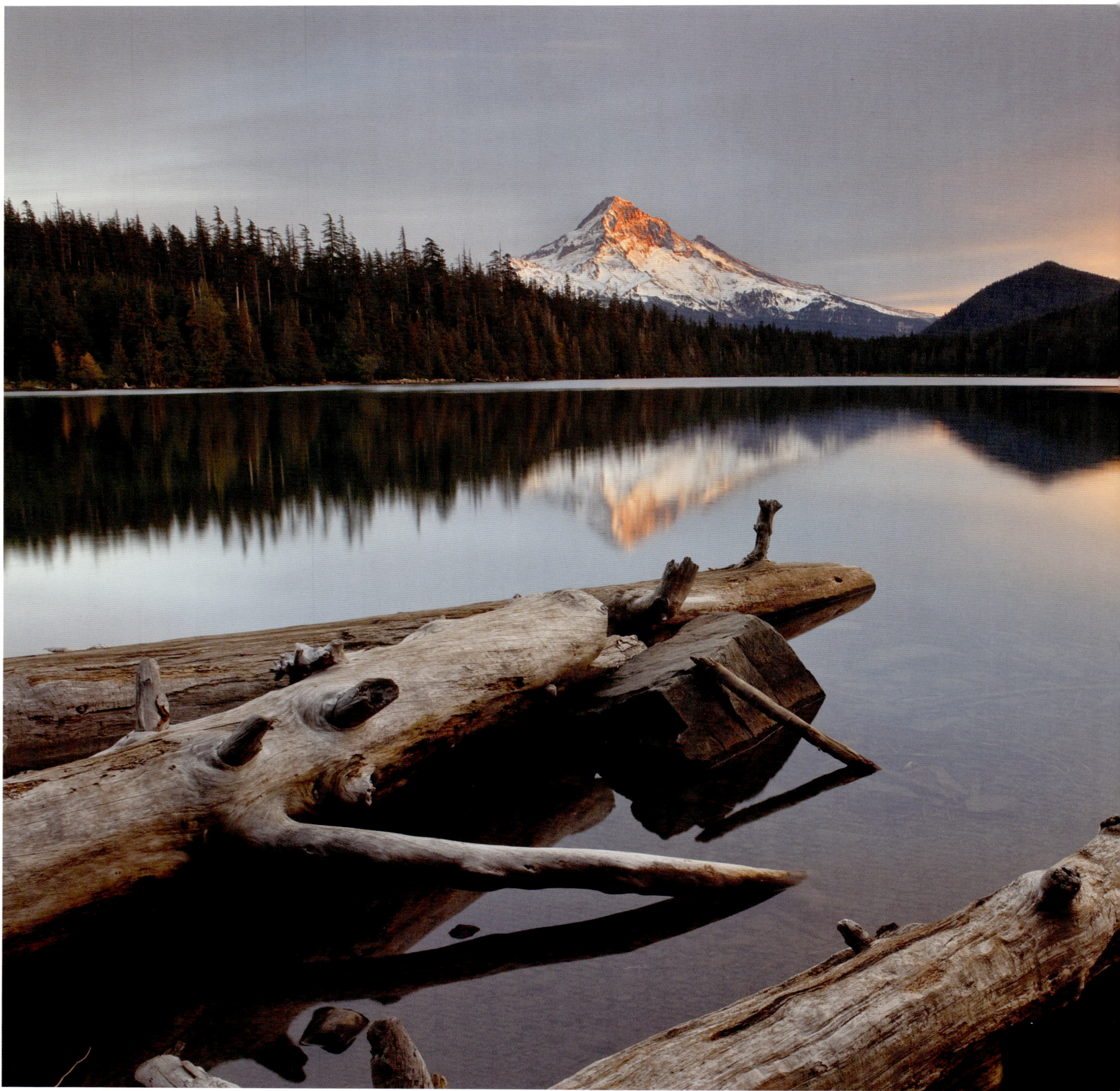

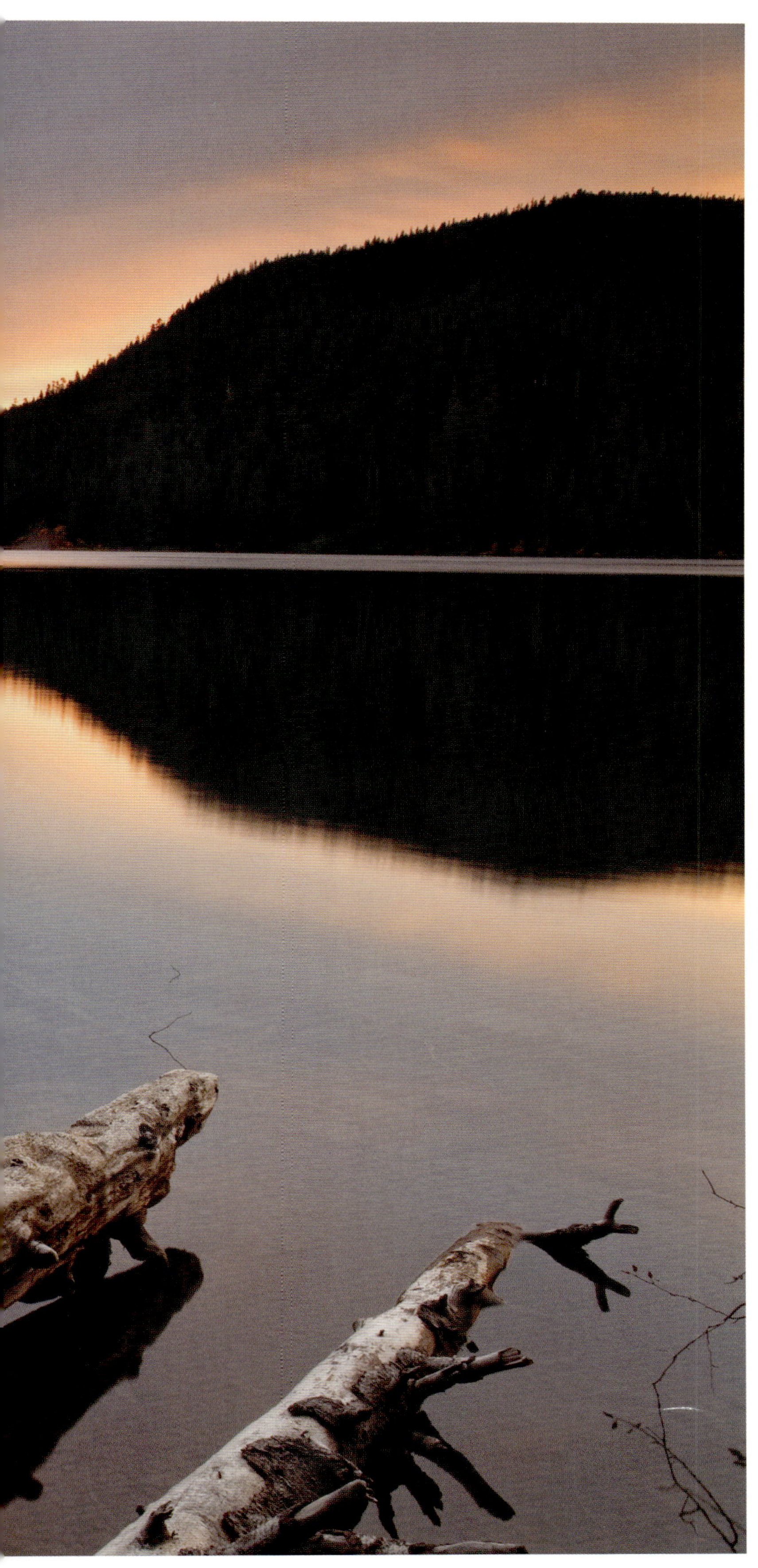

Mount Hood reflected in the beautiful waters of Lost Lake in the Mount Hood National Forest. ●

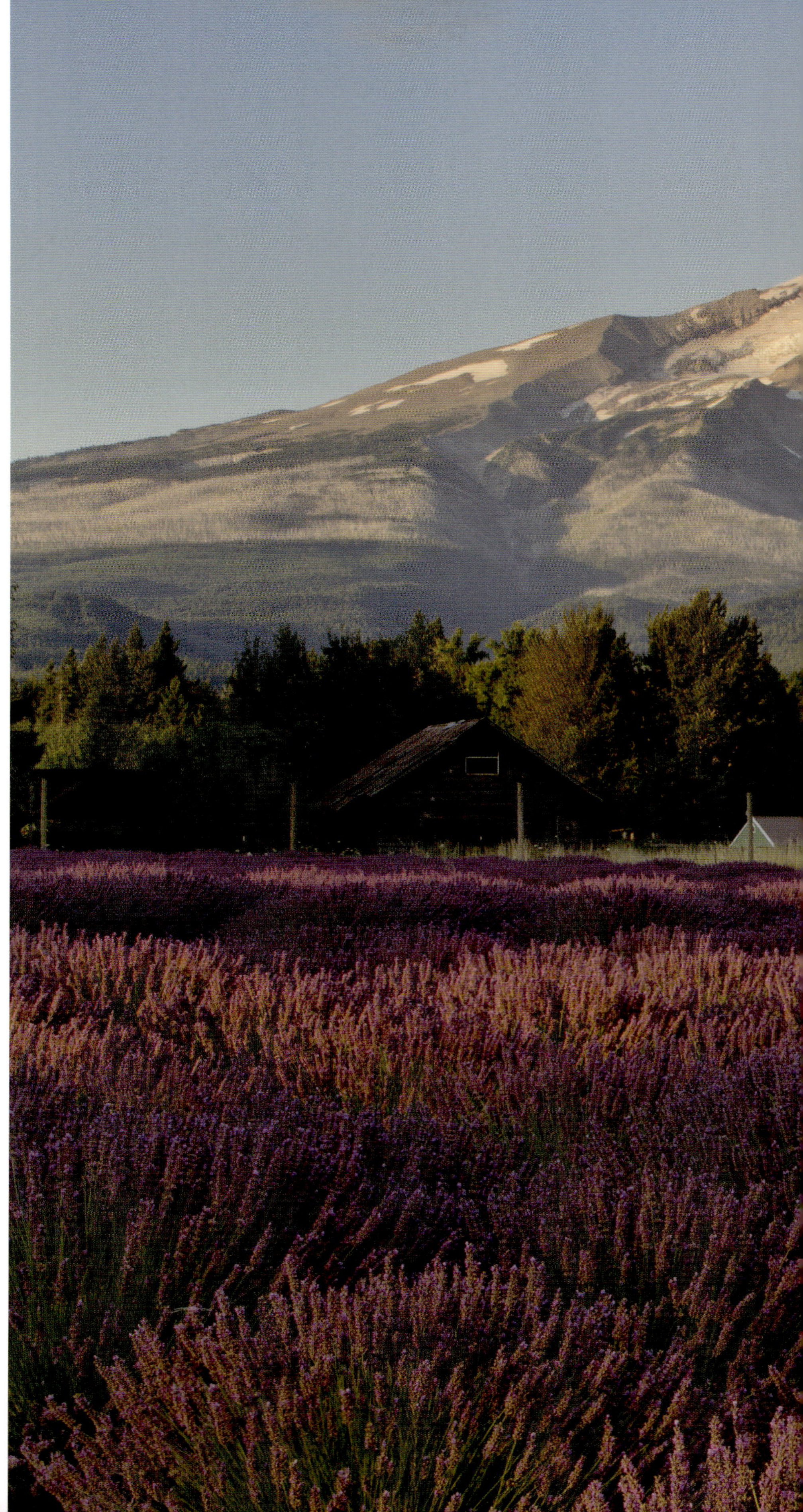

Fields of blooms in August at Lavender Valley, a farm near Hood River. •

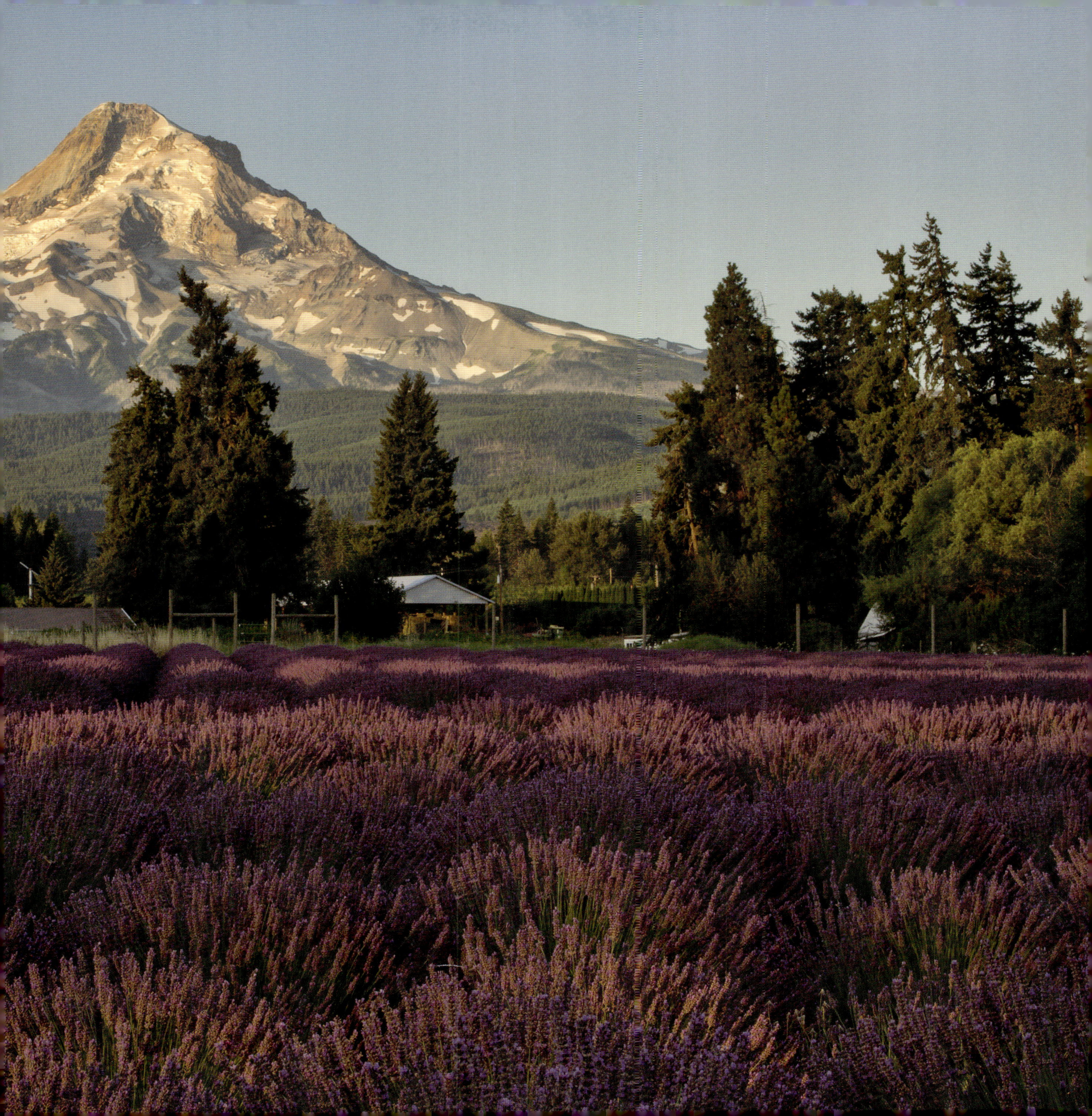

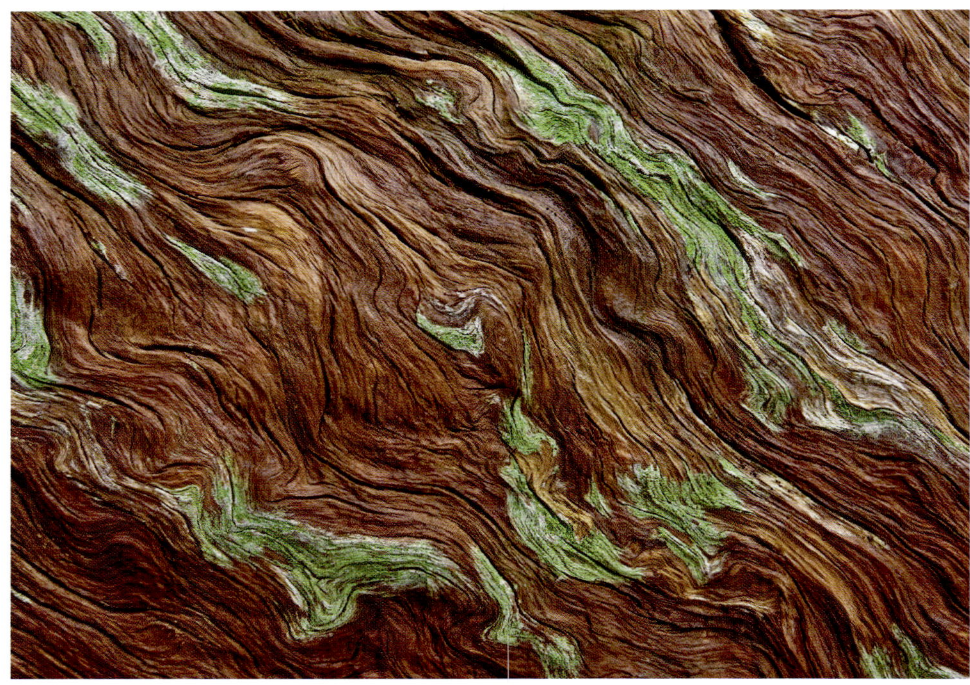

ABOVE   Intricate whorls on a fallen tree
the in Mount Hood National Forest.   •

RIGHT   Elk Meadows, a popular hiking
trail in the Mount Hood National Forest,
during fall.   •

OPPOSITE   Pristine winter conditions
and dreamy midmorning light on
Mount Hood.   •

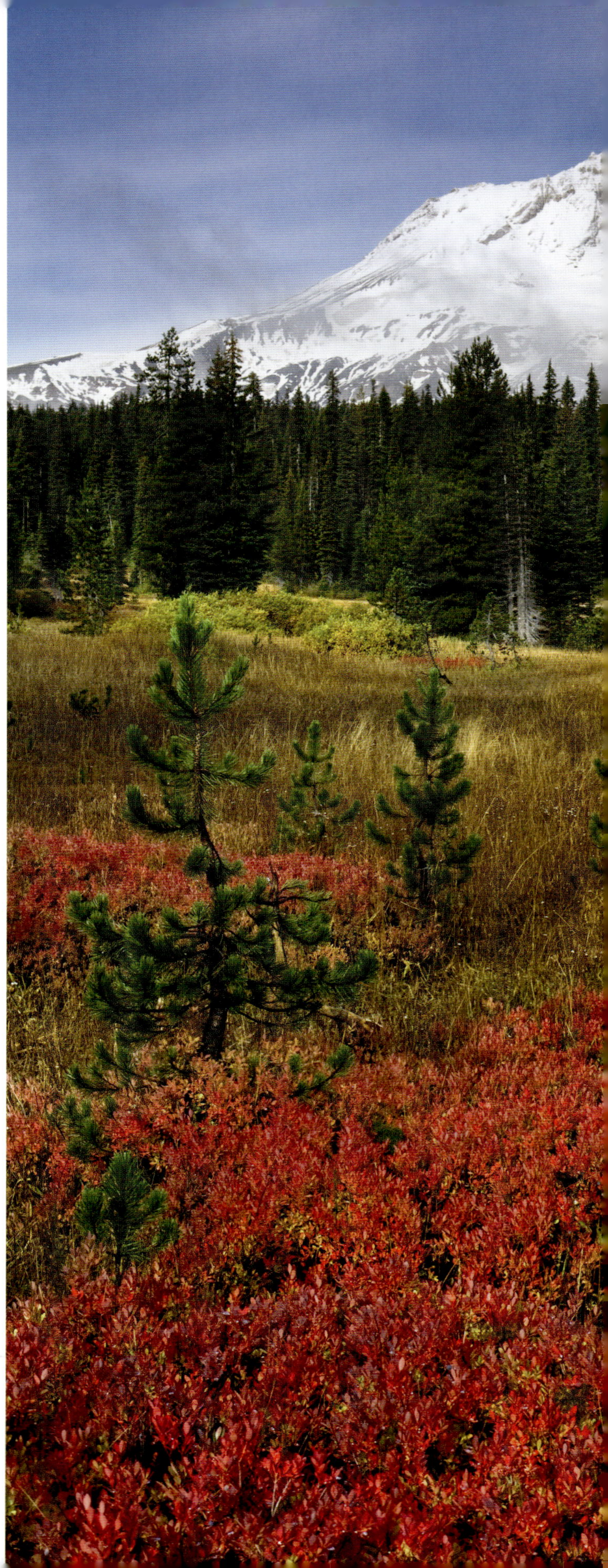

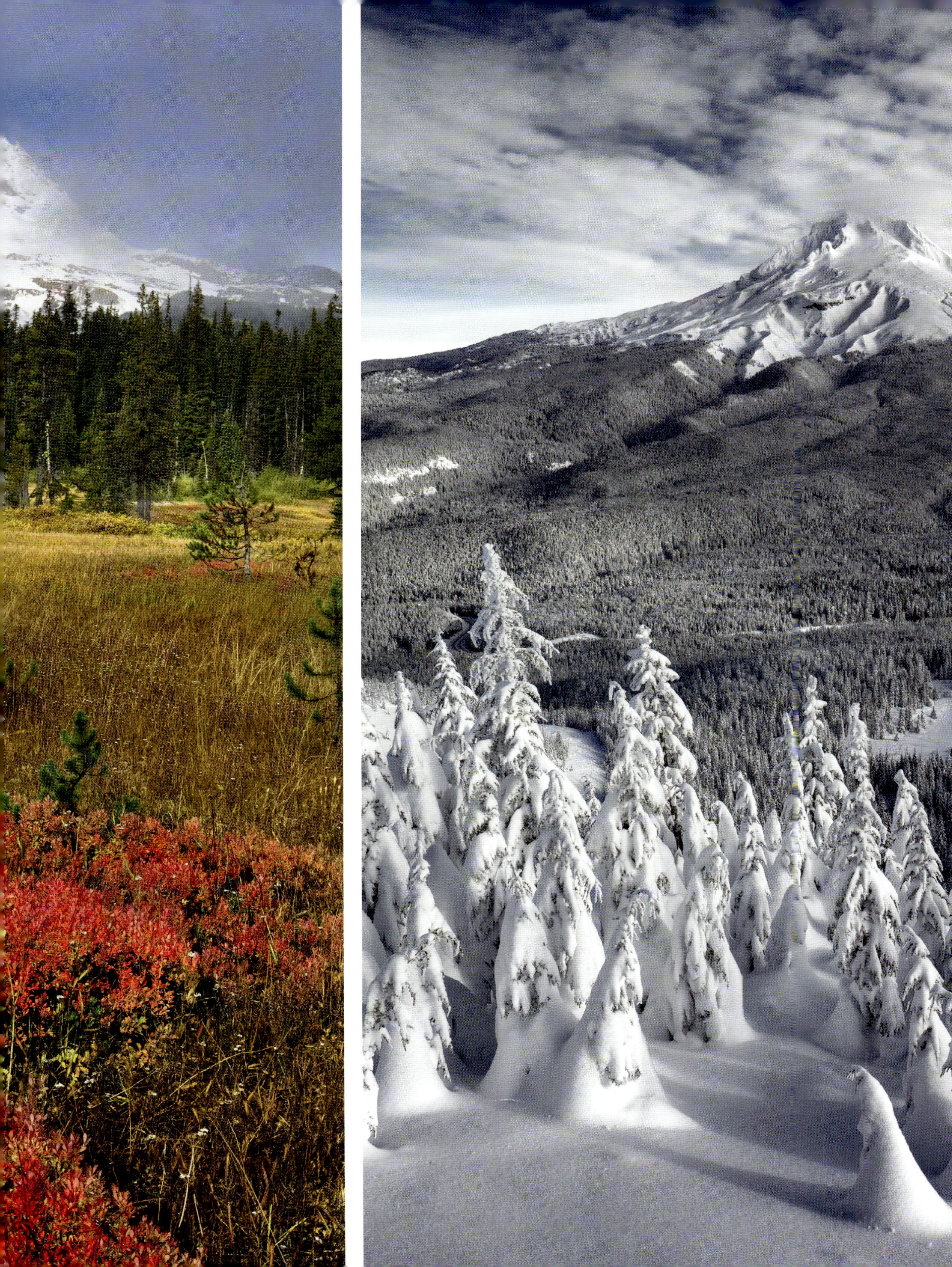

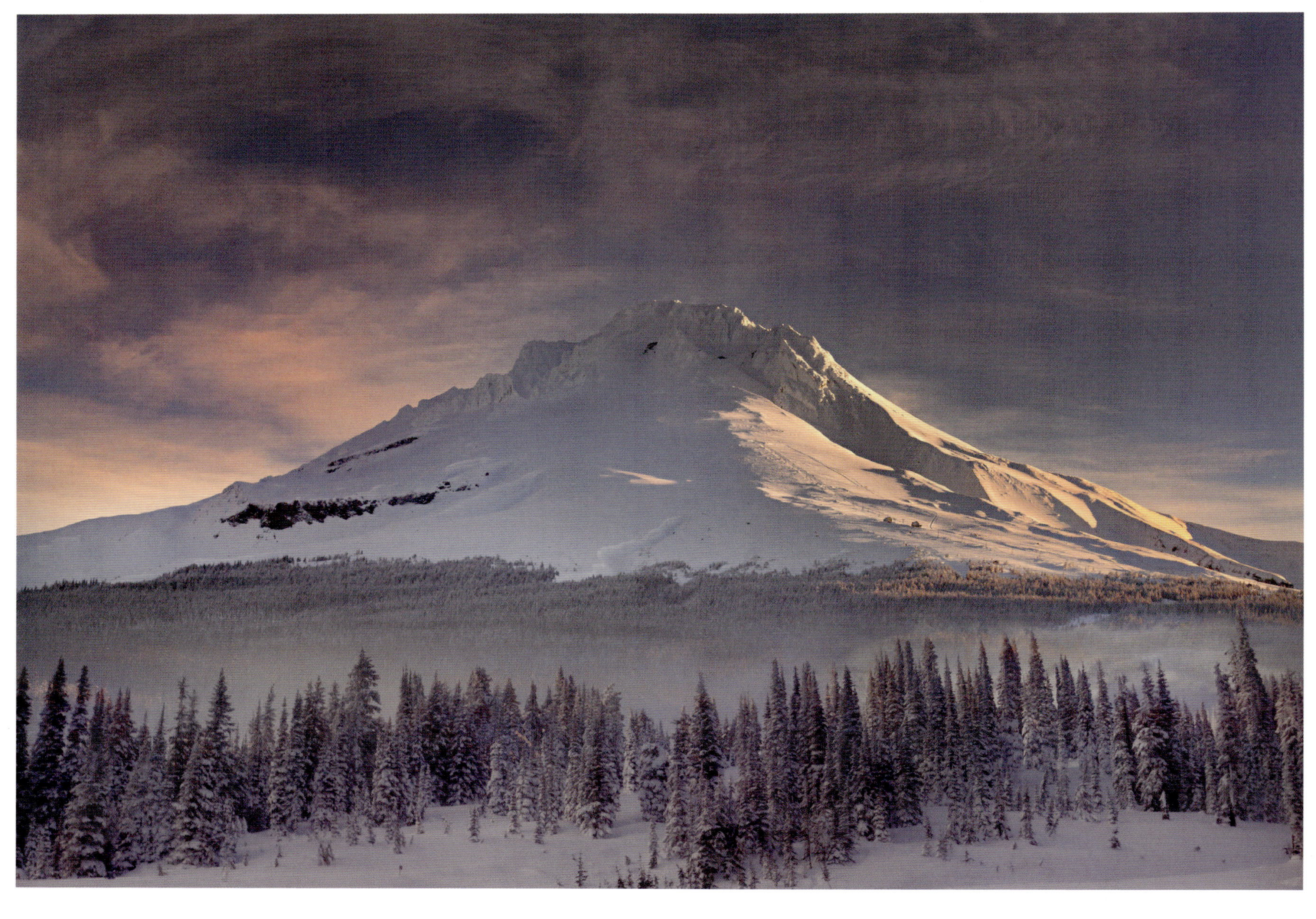

A cold winter sunrise in the valley below
snow-blanketed Mount Hood. ●

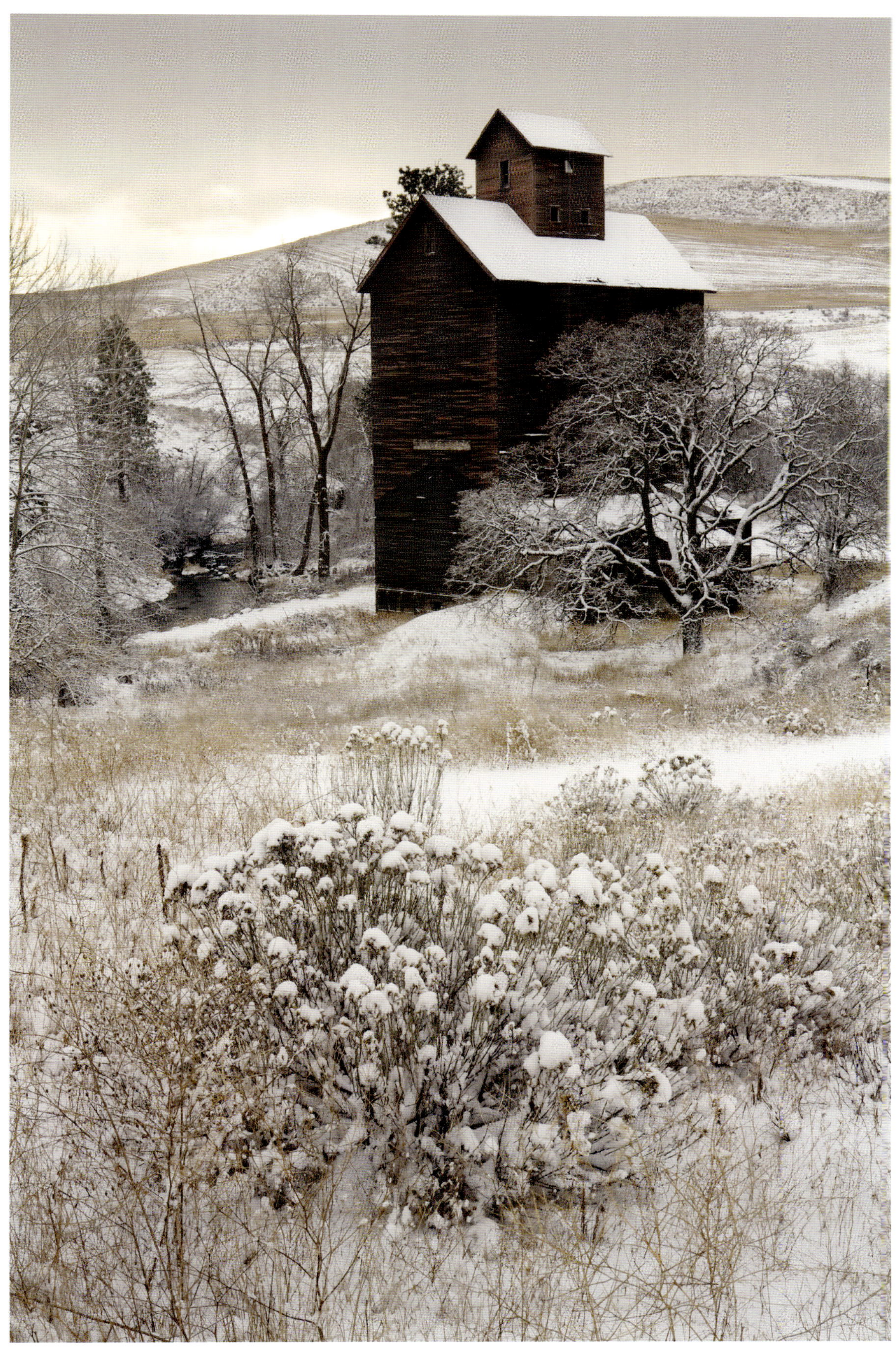

An old granary from a bygone era still stands on a winter's day near the town of Boyd. •

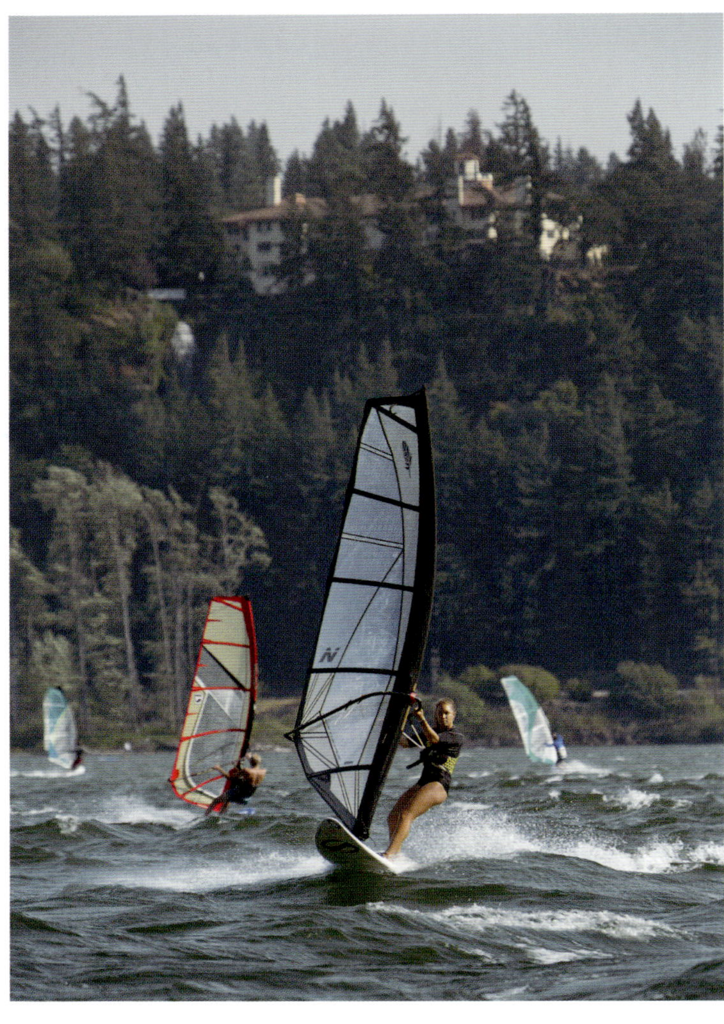

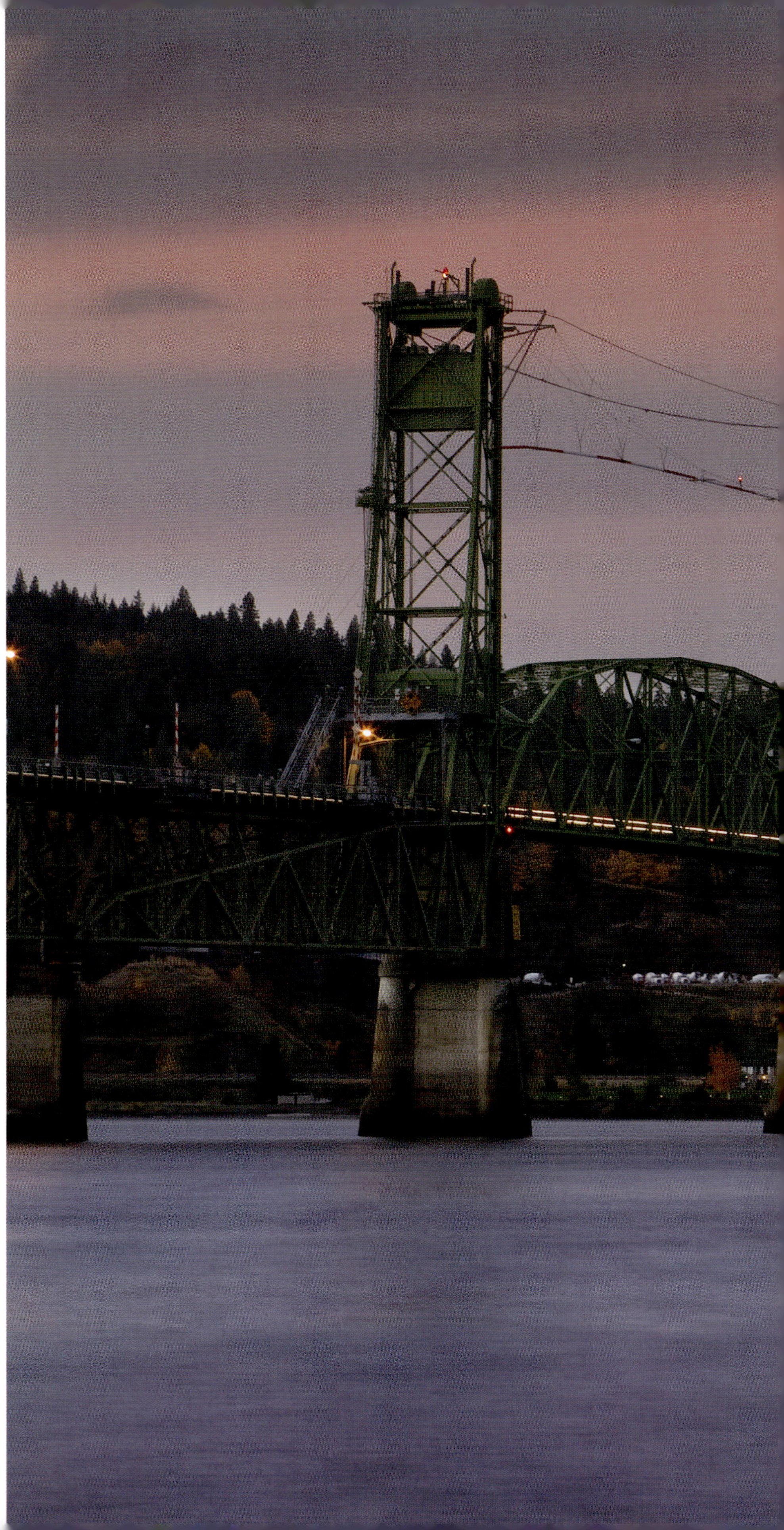

ABOVE Windsurfers enjoy a summer
day on the Columbia near the town of
Hood River. •

RIGHT Eastern dawn light
illuminates Mount Hood and
the Hood River Bridge. •

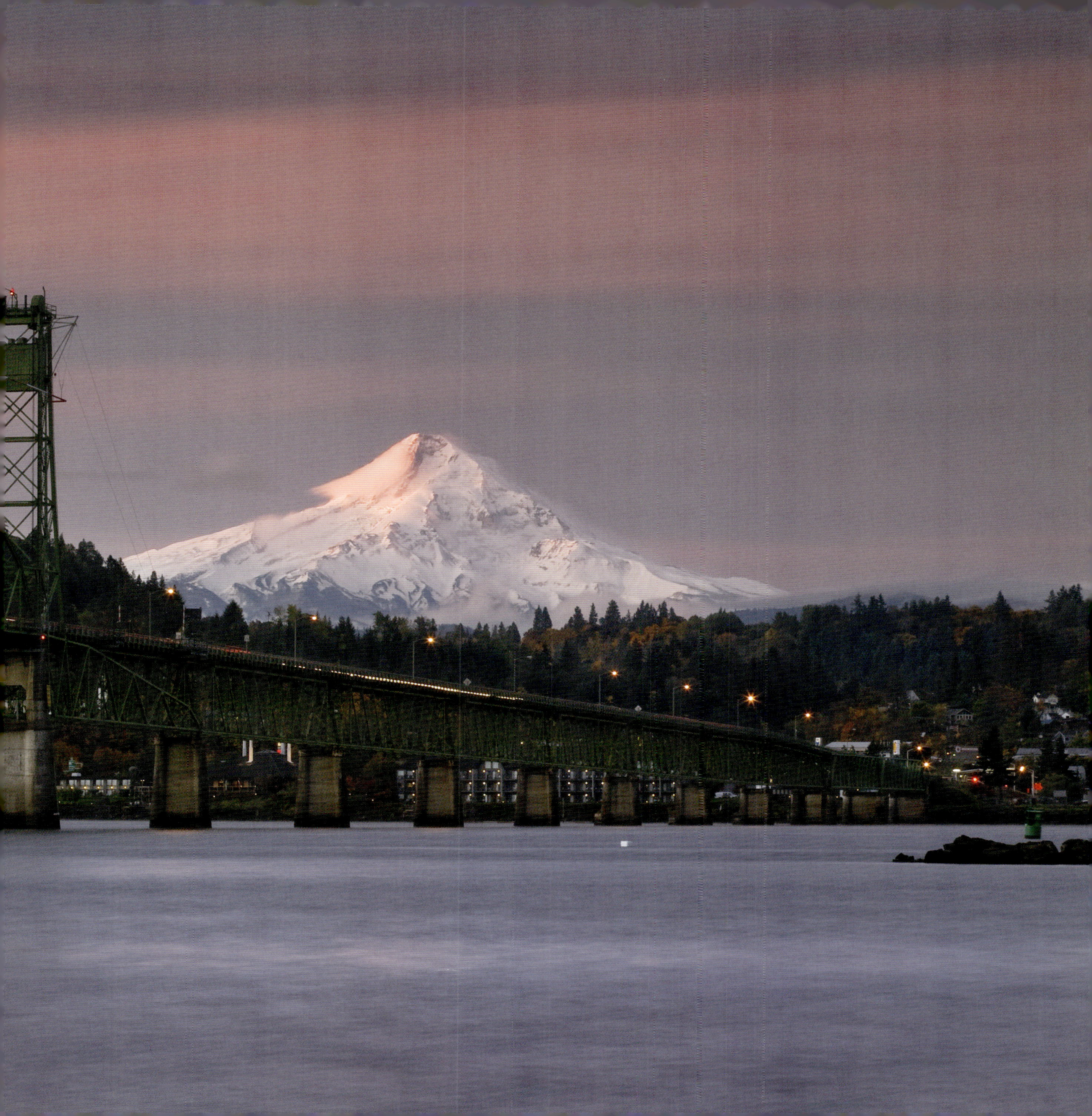

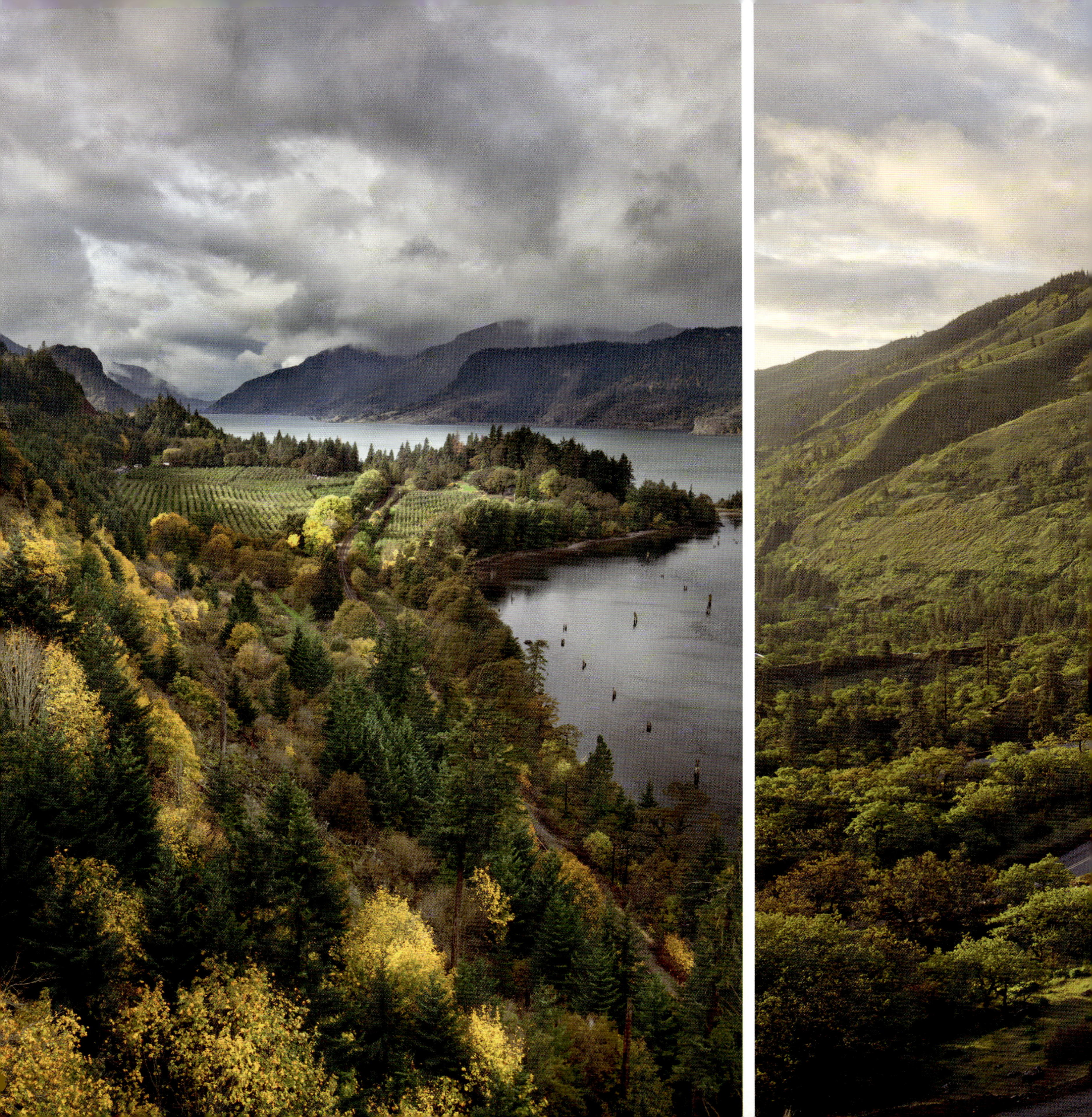

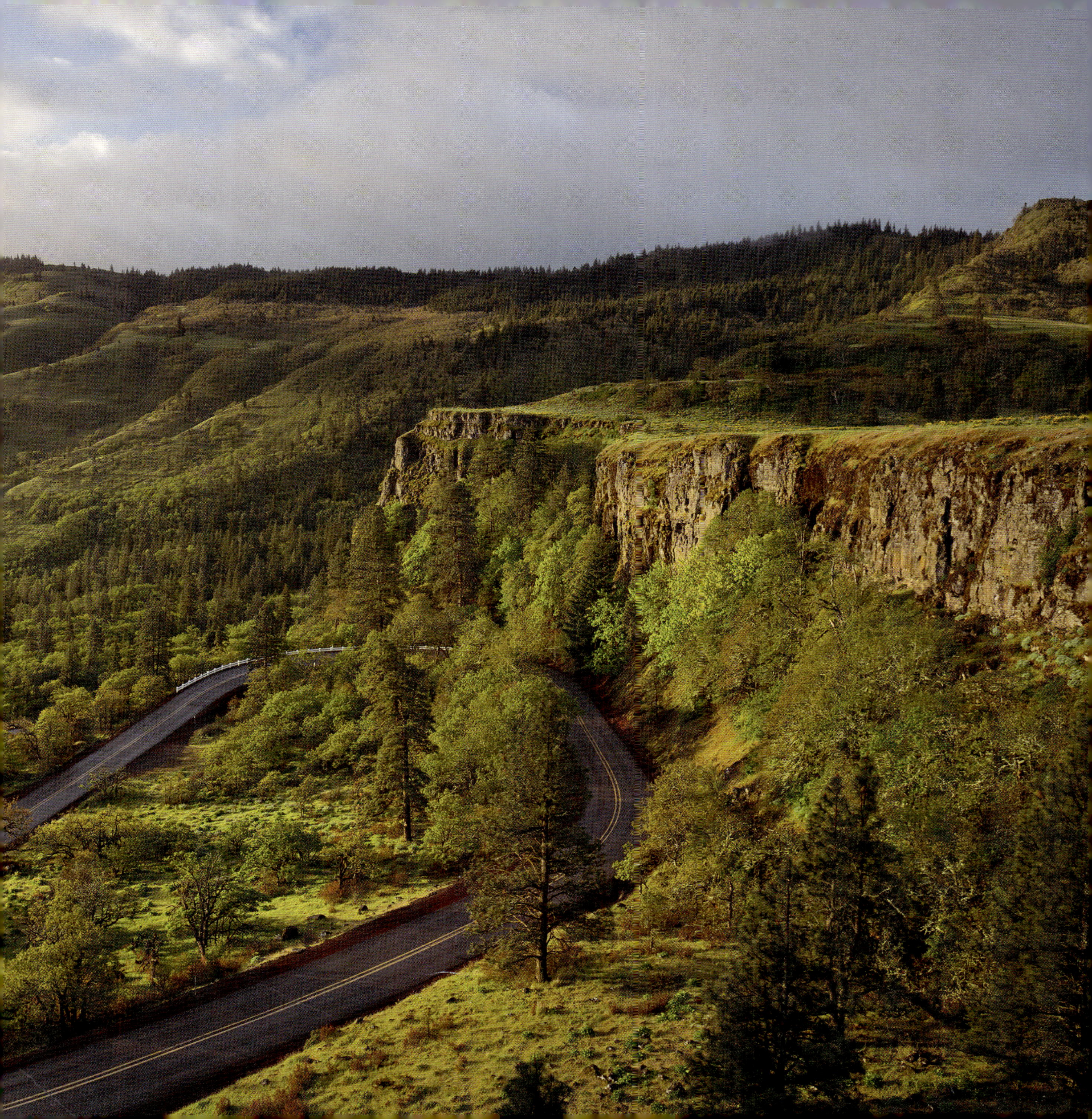

PREVIOUS PAGES, LEFT
A view of the Columbia River from Hood River during the peak of fall color. ●

PREVIOUS PAGES, RIGHT
The scenic Columbia River Highway winds down from the Rowena Crest Viewpoint. ●

RIGHT Fields of balsamroot and lupine cover the Rowena Plateau in spring. ●

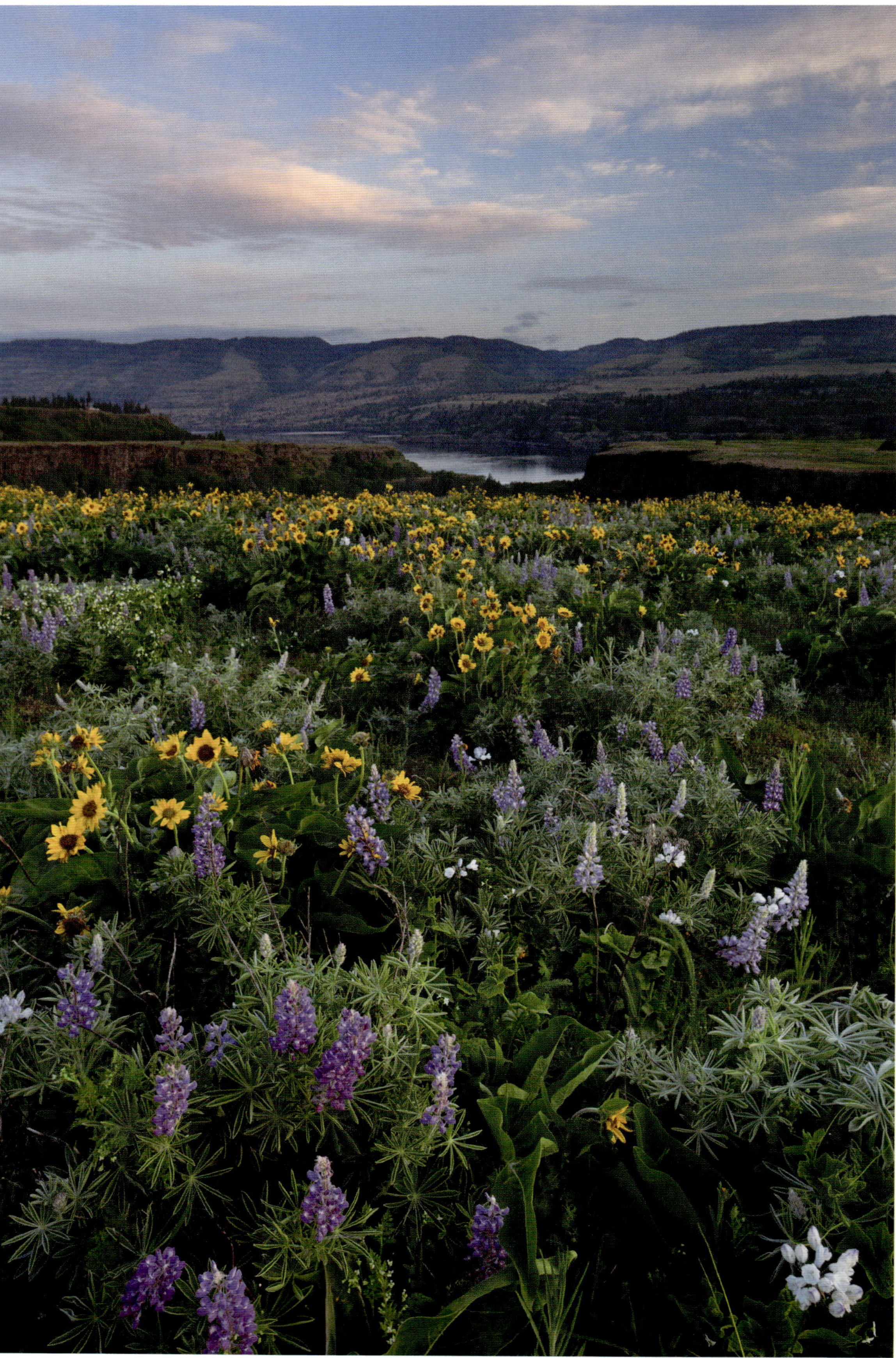

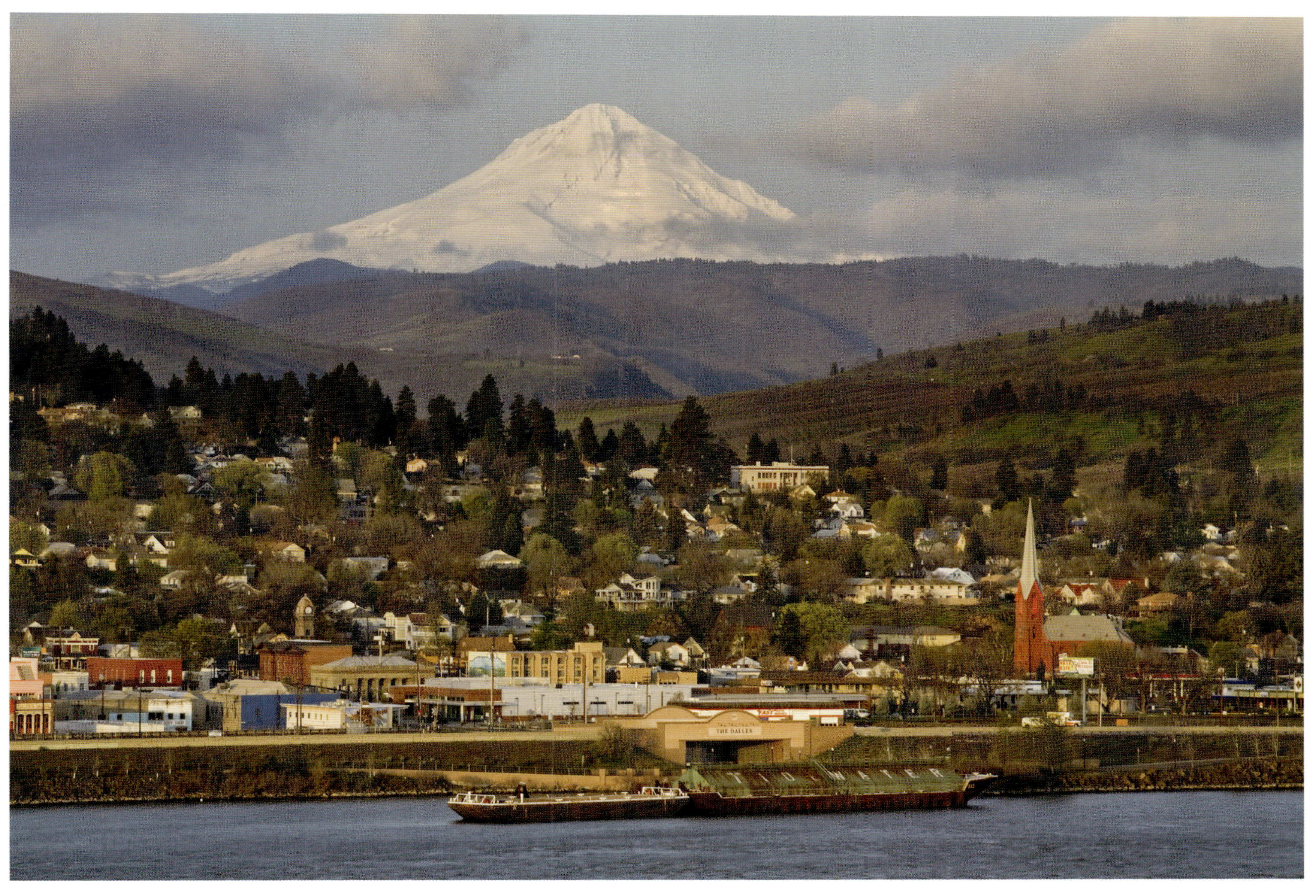

Mount Hood rises over the town of The
Dalles at the eastern end of the Columbia
River Gorge. •

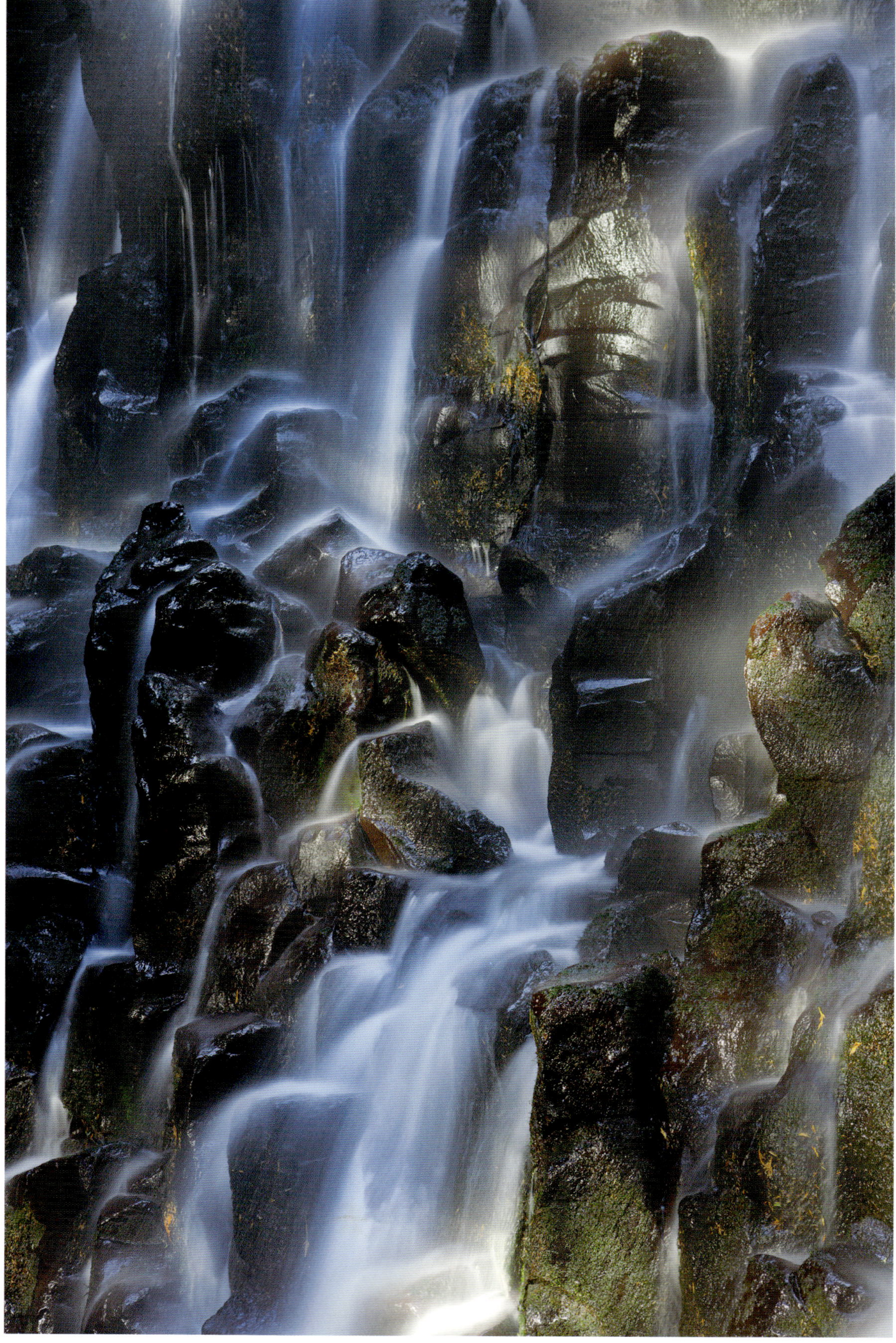

Columnar basalt creates intriguing patterns in the flow of Ramona Falls in the Mount Hood National Forest. •

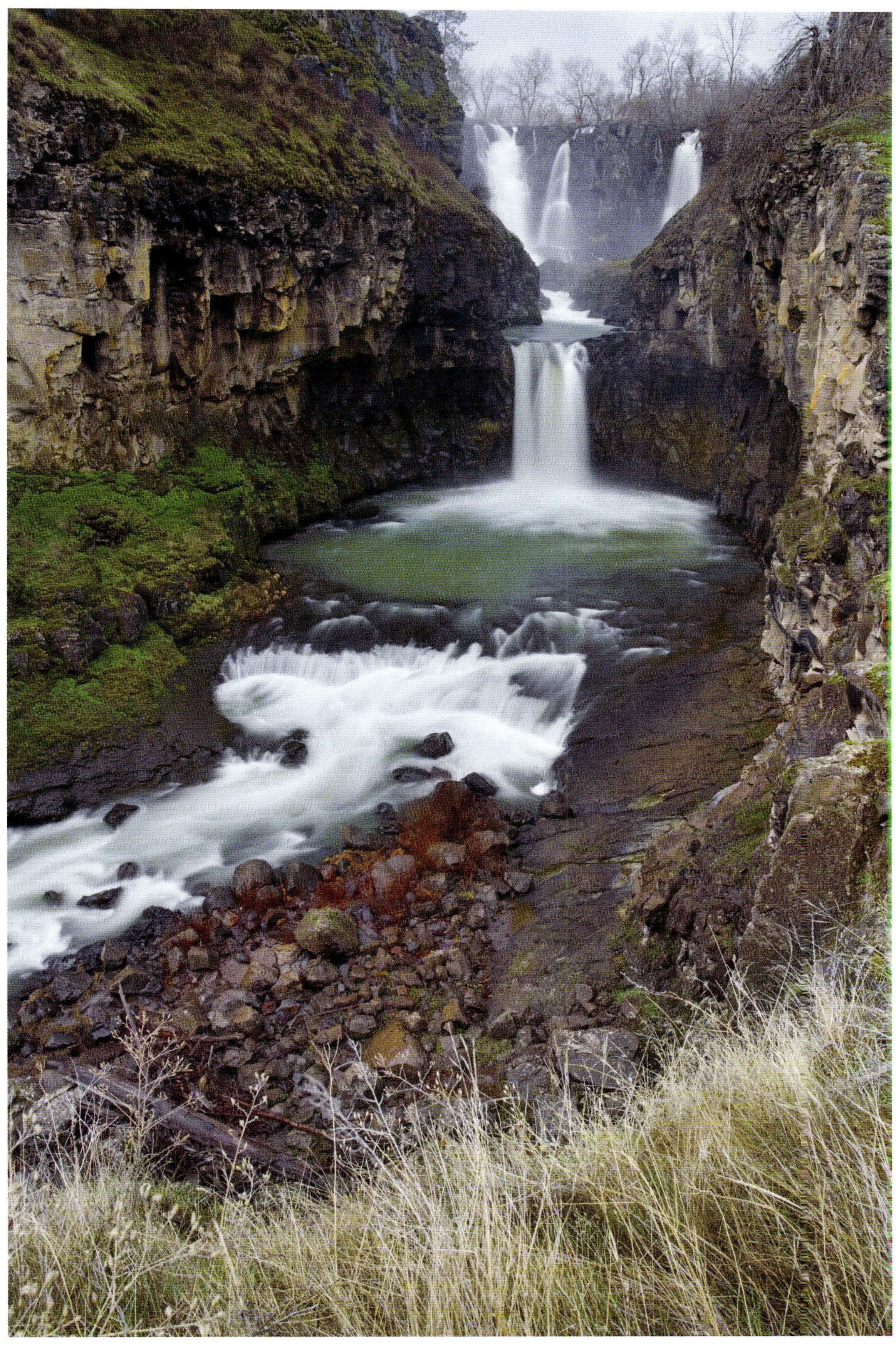

White River Falls plunging 90 feet over a basalt shelf during winter. ●

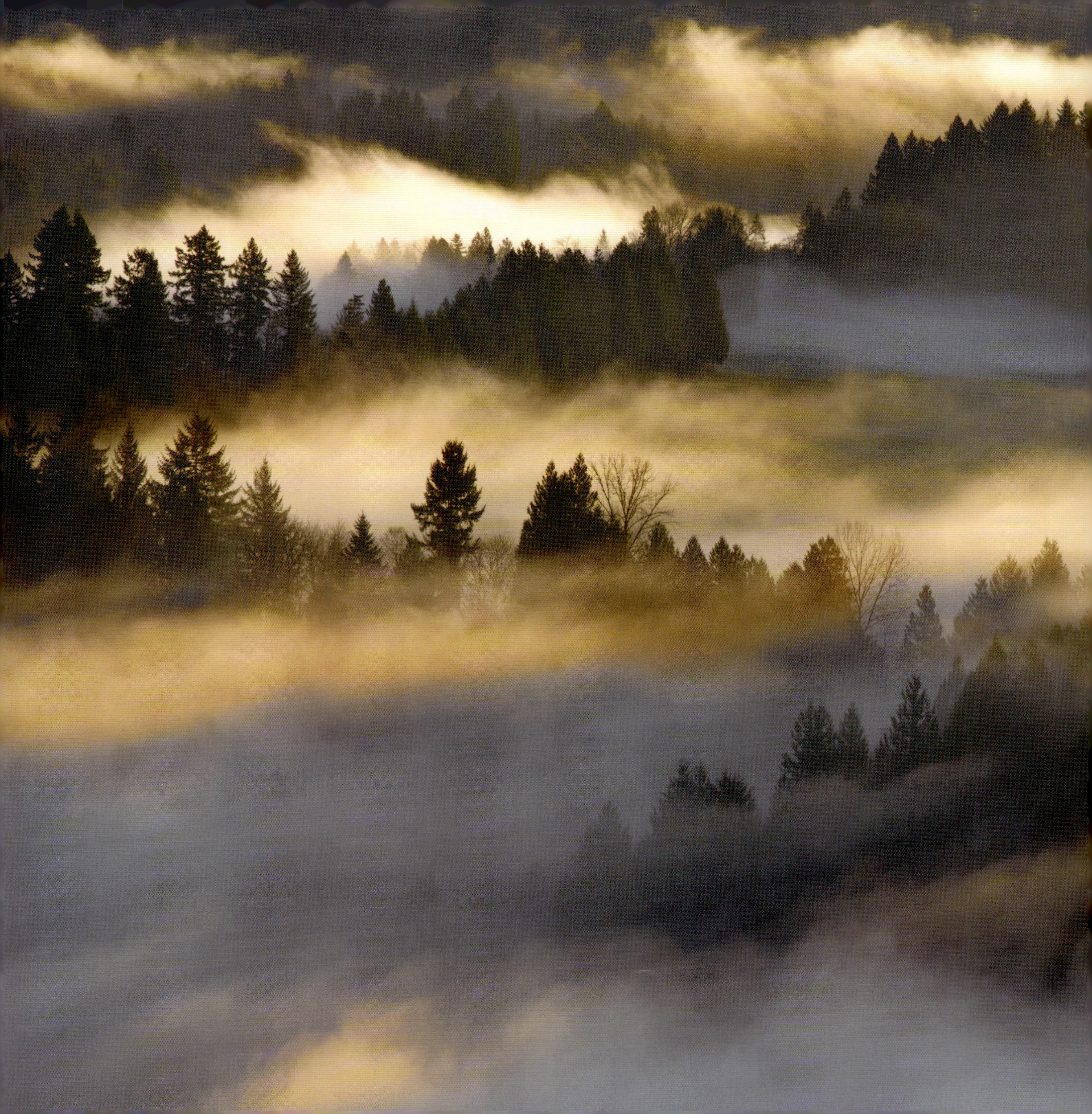

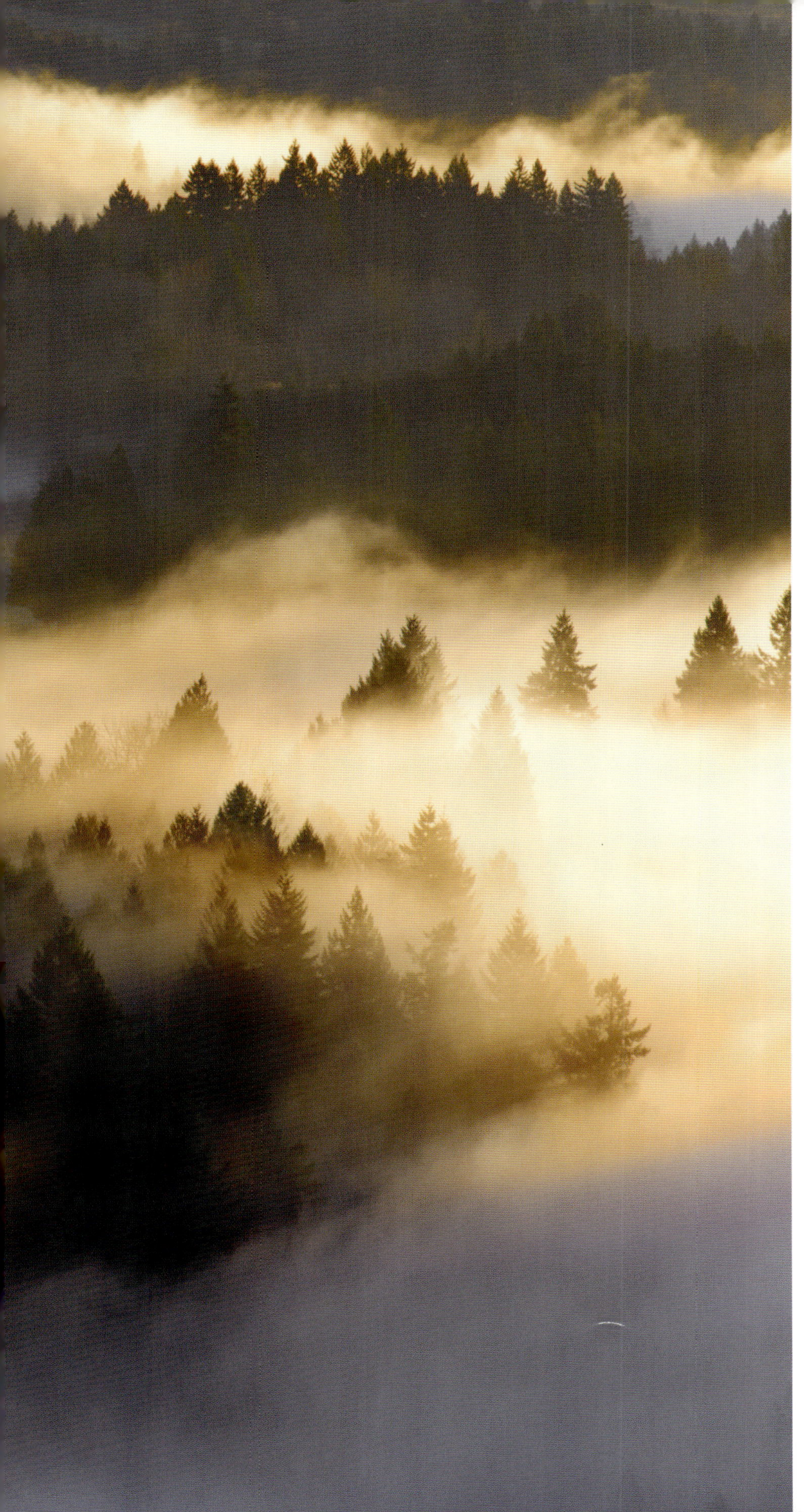

Forest and farmland seen from a viewpoint in the town of Sandy, just above the Sandy River, at sunrise during winter. •

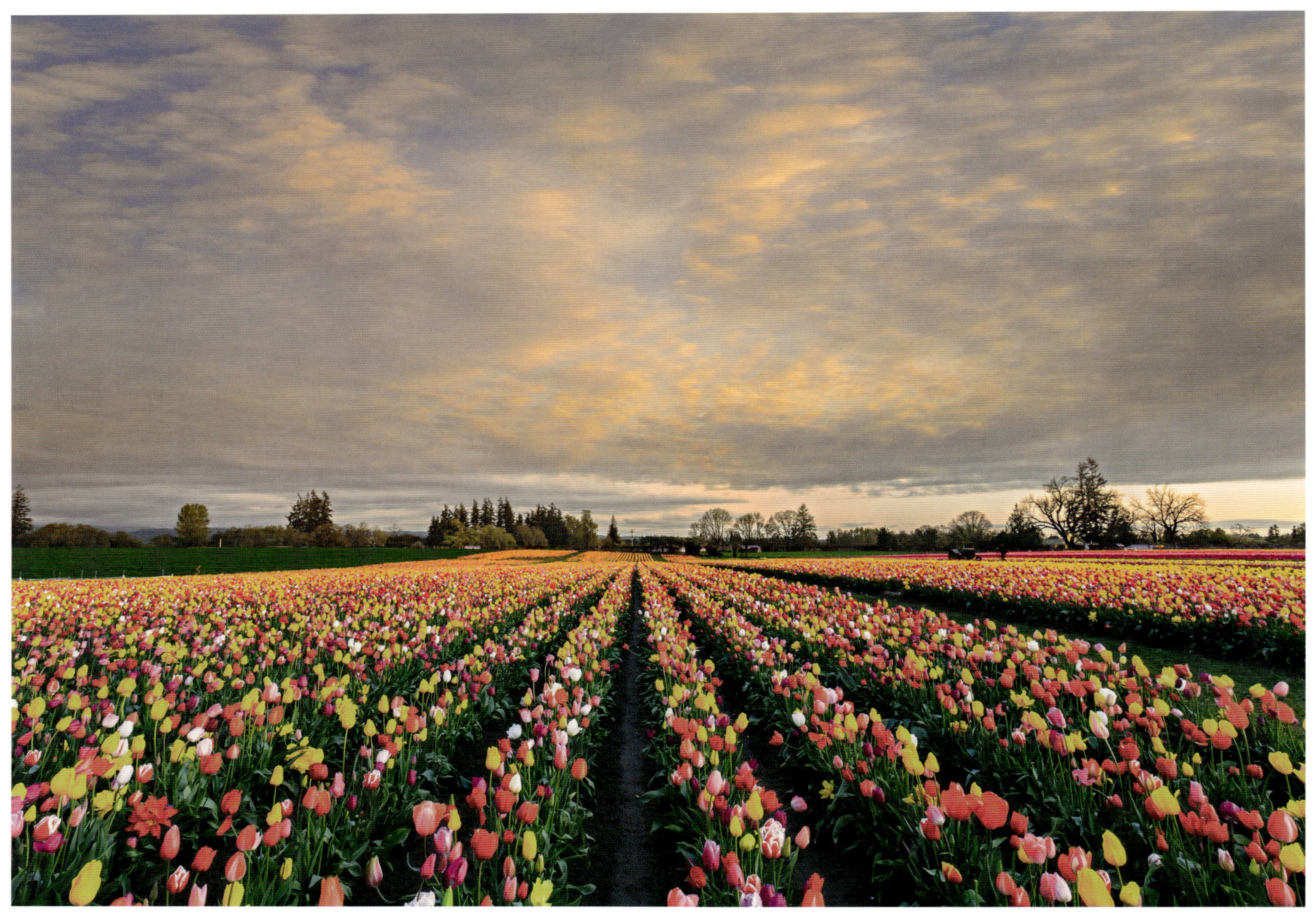

Rows of spring tulips converge toward
an April evening sunset at Wooden Shoe
Tulip Farm in Woodburn. •

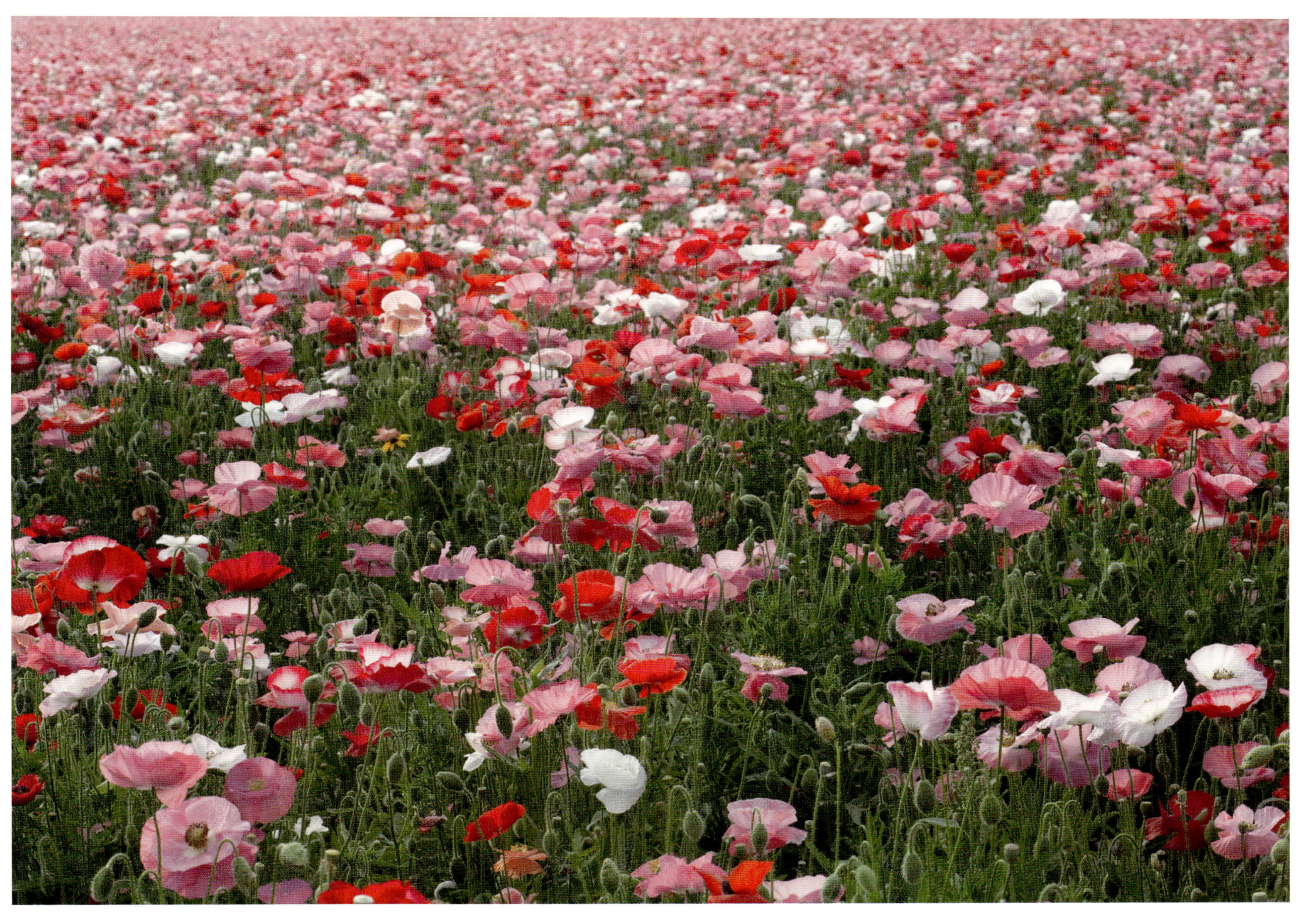

A colorful field of poppies blooms near
the town of Mount Angel in July. •

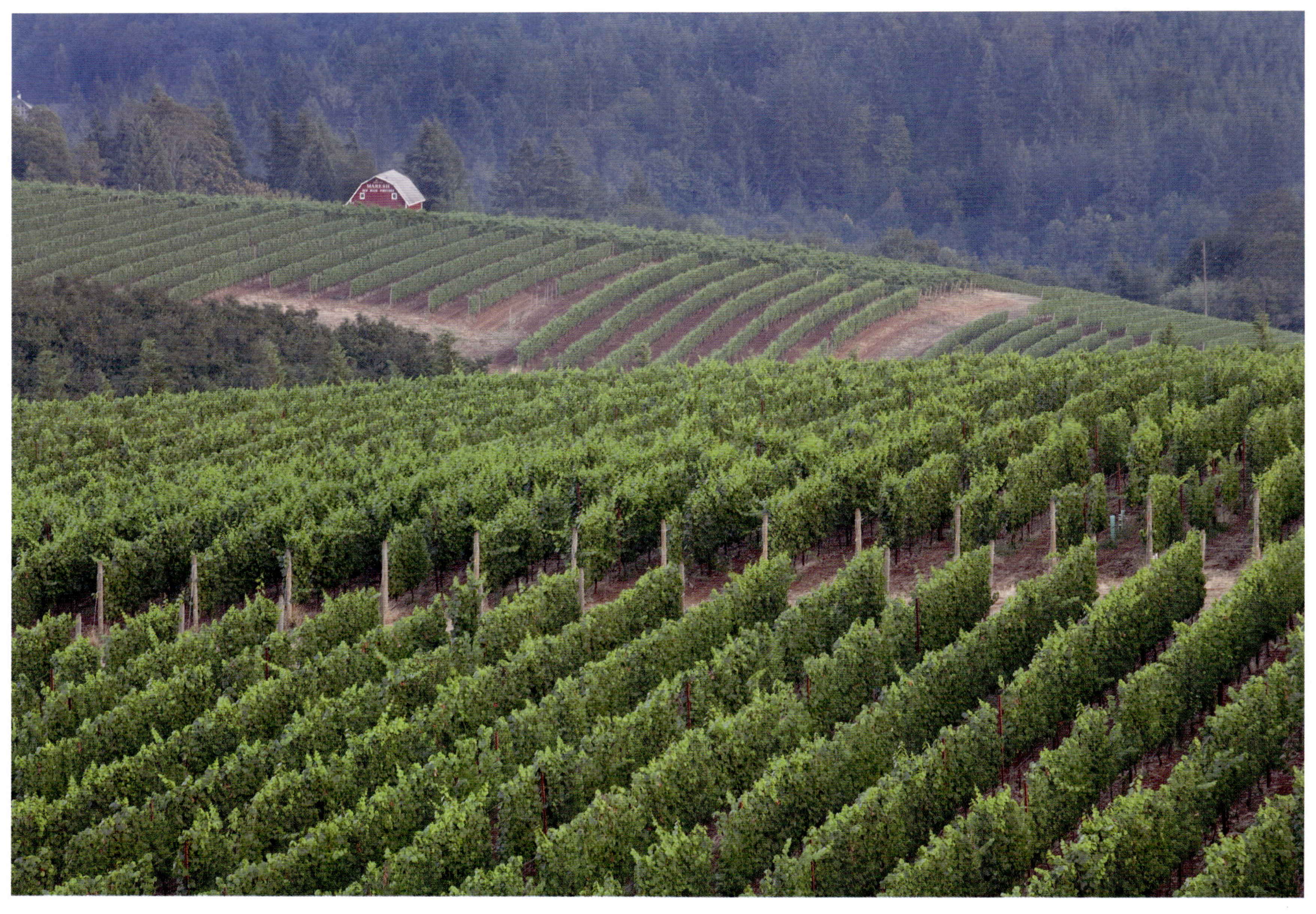

ABOVE Acres of vineyards fill the landscape near the town of Dundee. •

RIGHT Rays of morning light awaken the forest of Cascade Head, along the central coast. •

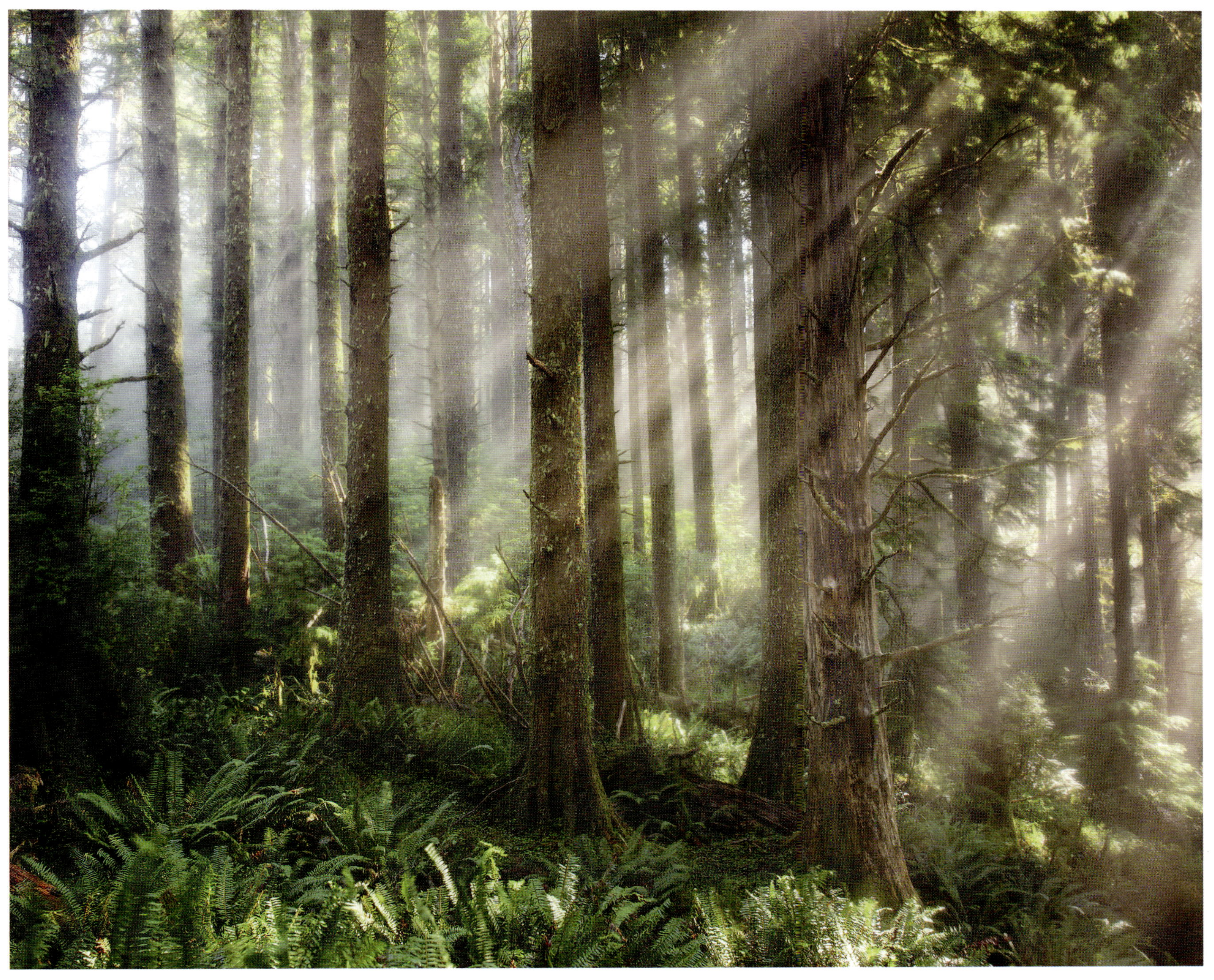

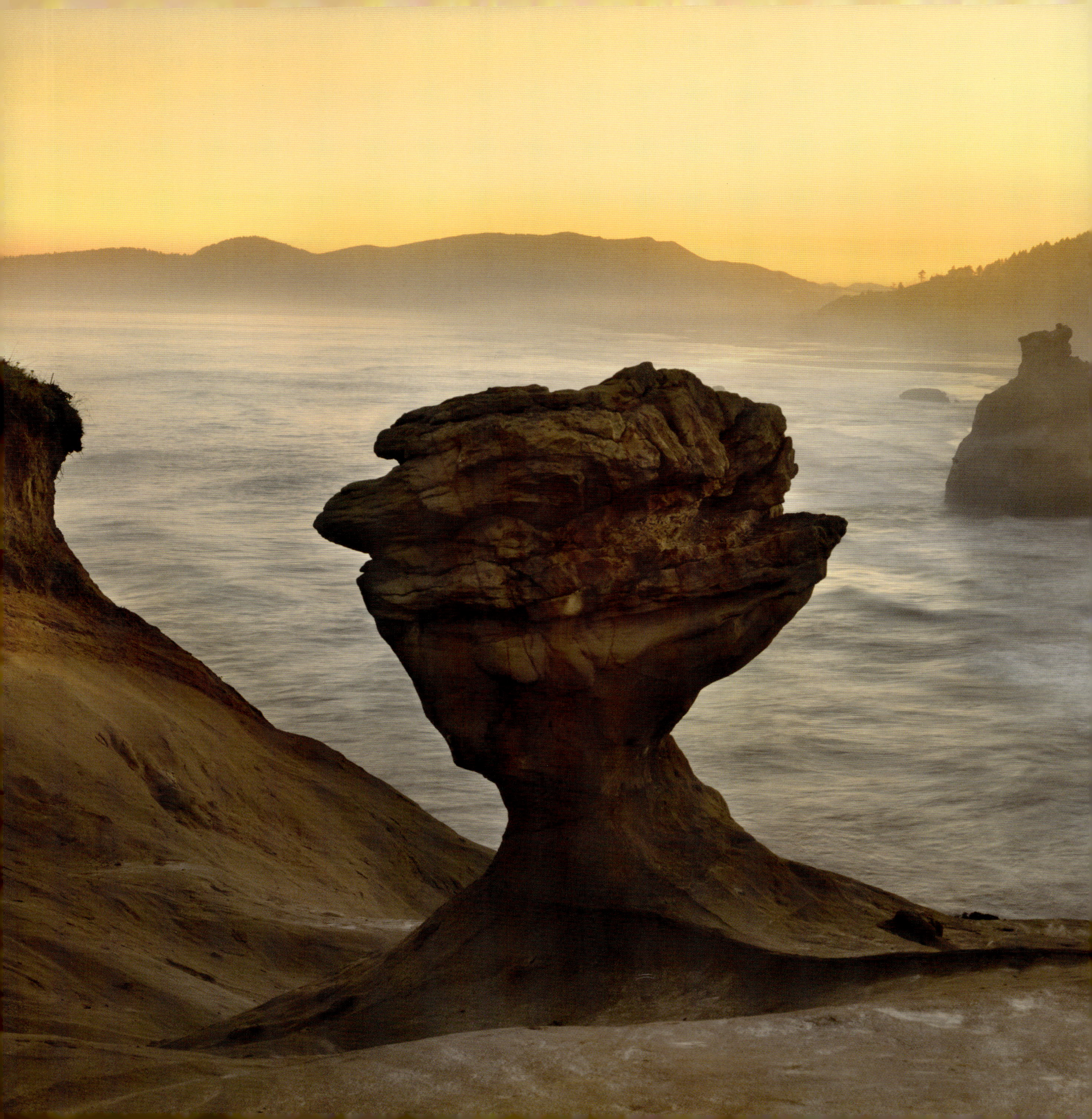

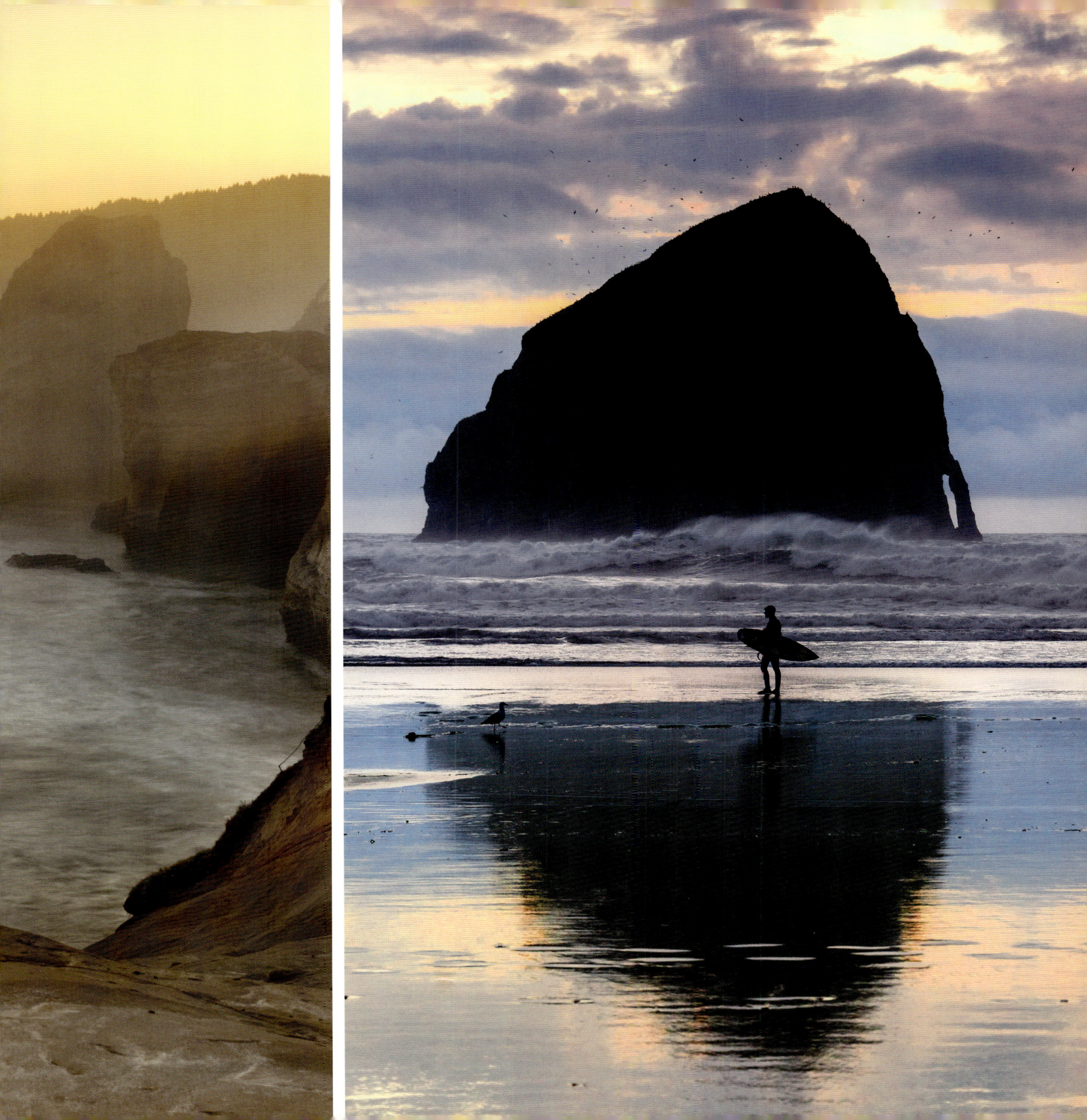

PREVIOUS PAGES, LEFT A sandstone hoodoo at Cape Kiwanda, near Pacific City, at sunrise. •

PREVIOUS PAGES, RIGHT Sunset casts warm pastels over a lone surfer passing in front of Chief Kiawanda Rock. •

RIGHT Visitors atop Cape Kiwanda's sandstone viewpoint provide a staggering sense of scale for the height of the cliffs and the size of the waves. •

OPPOSITE Misty sunset clouds breach the shore cliffs and archway along the back side of Cape Kiwanda. •

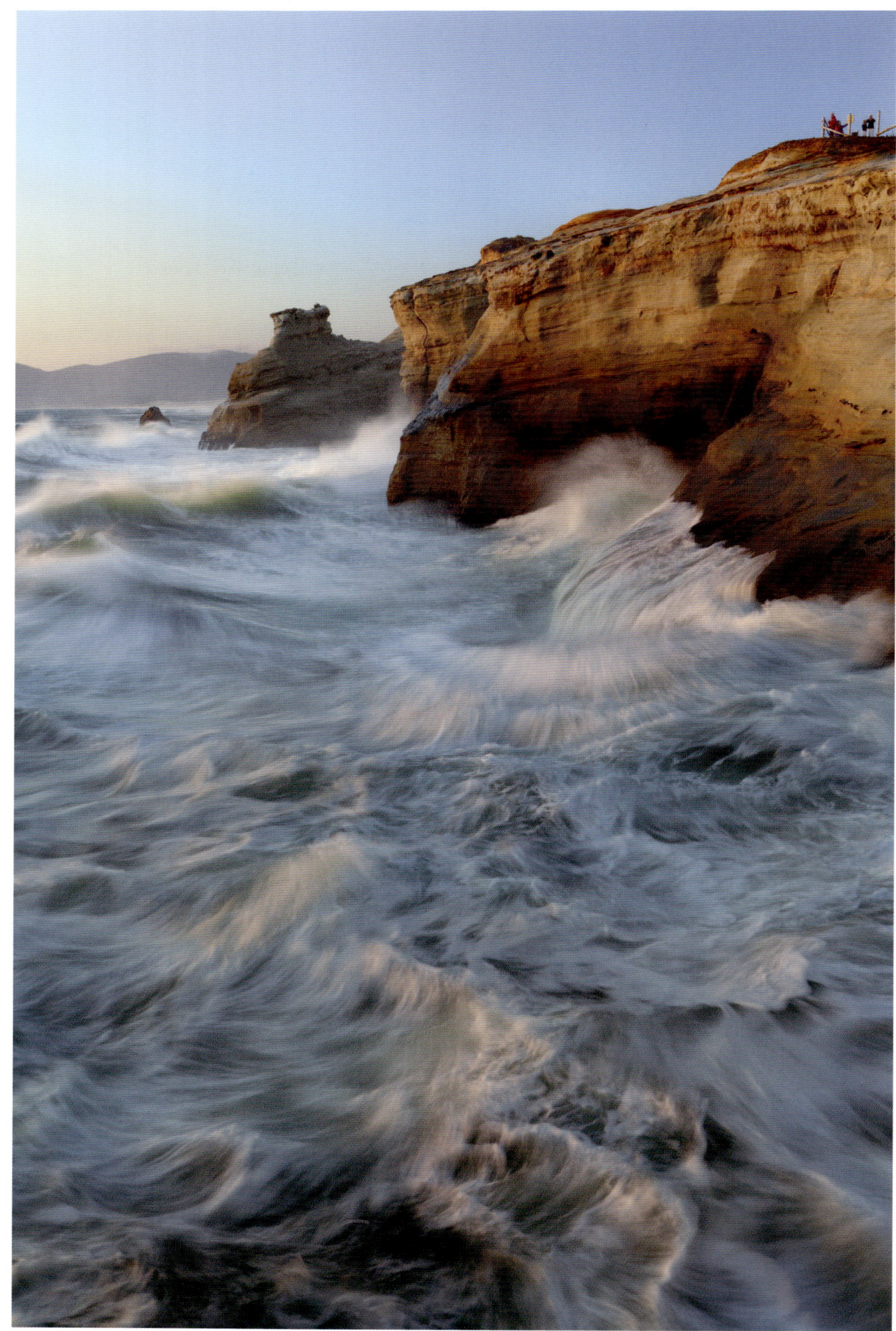

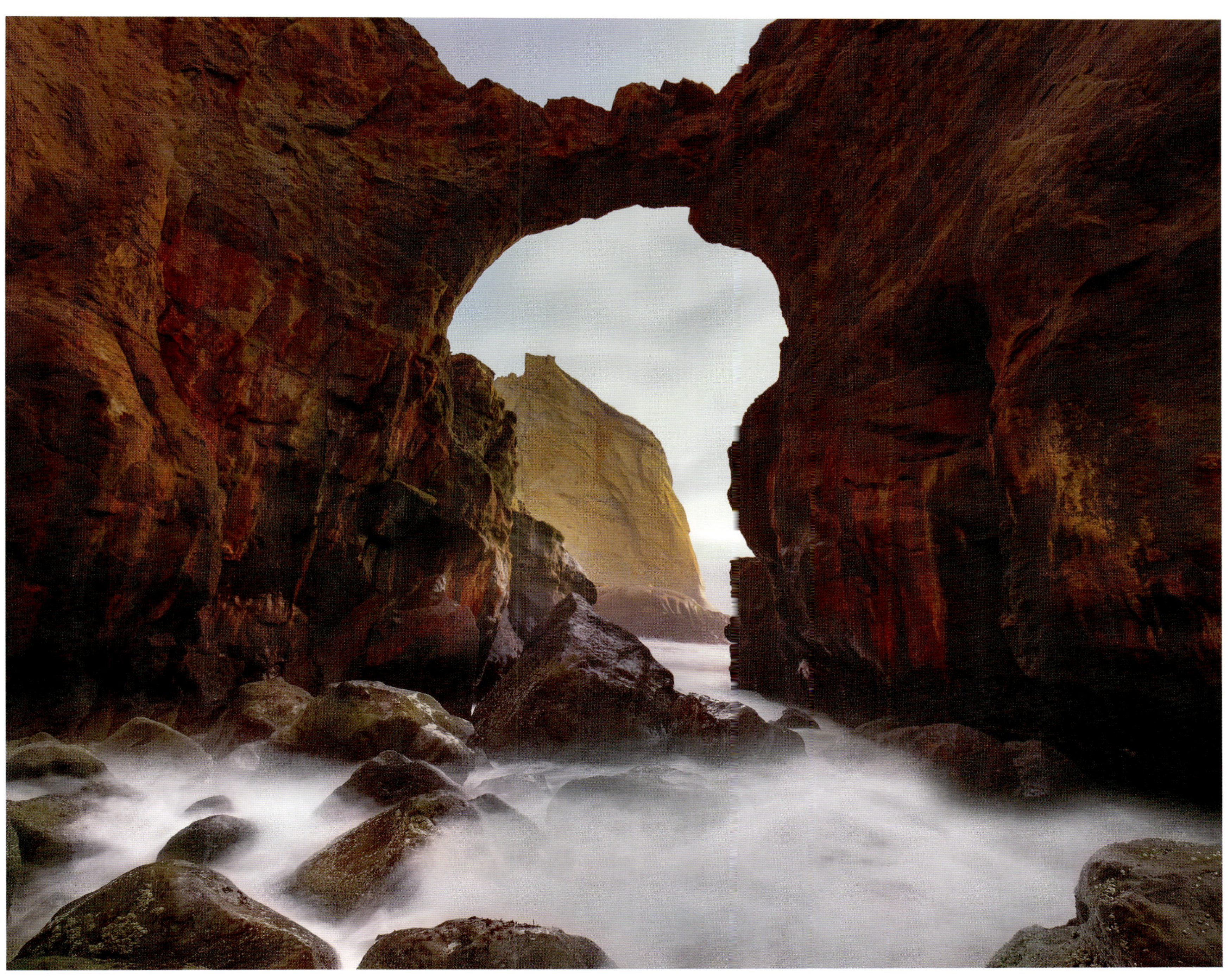

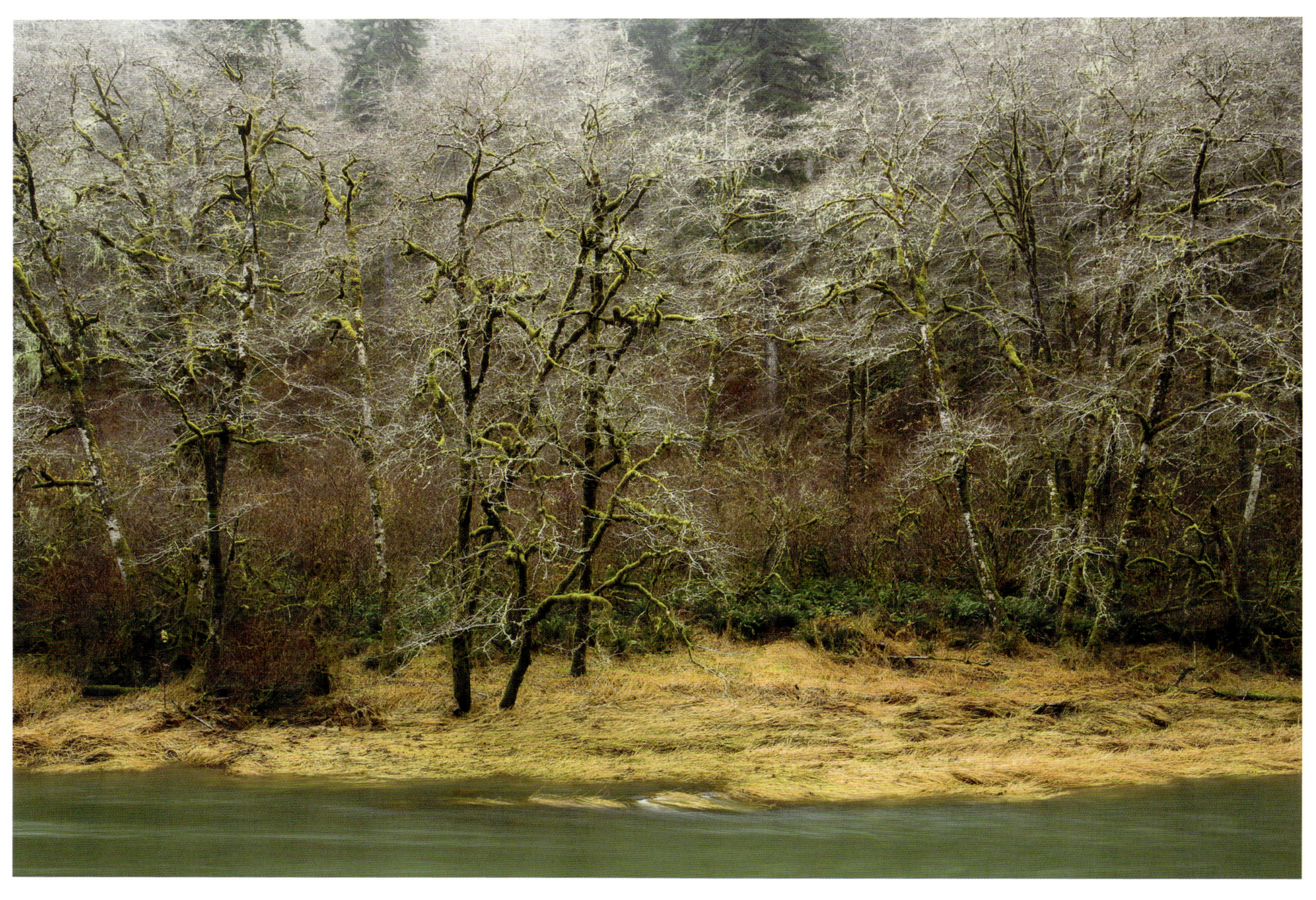

The Nestucca River flows by reeds
and stark winter stands of alder near
the central coast. •

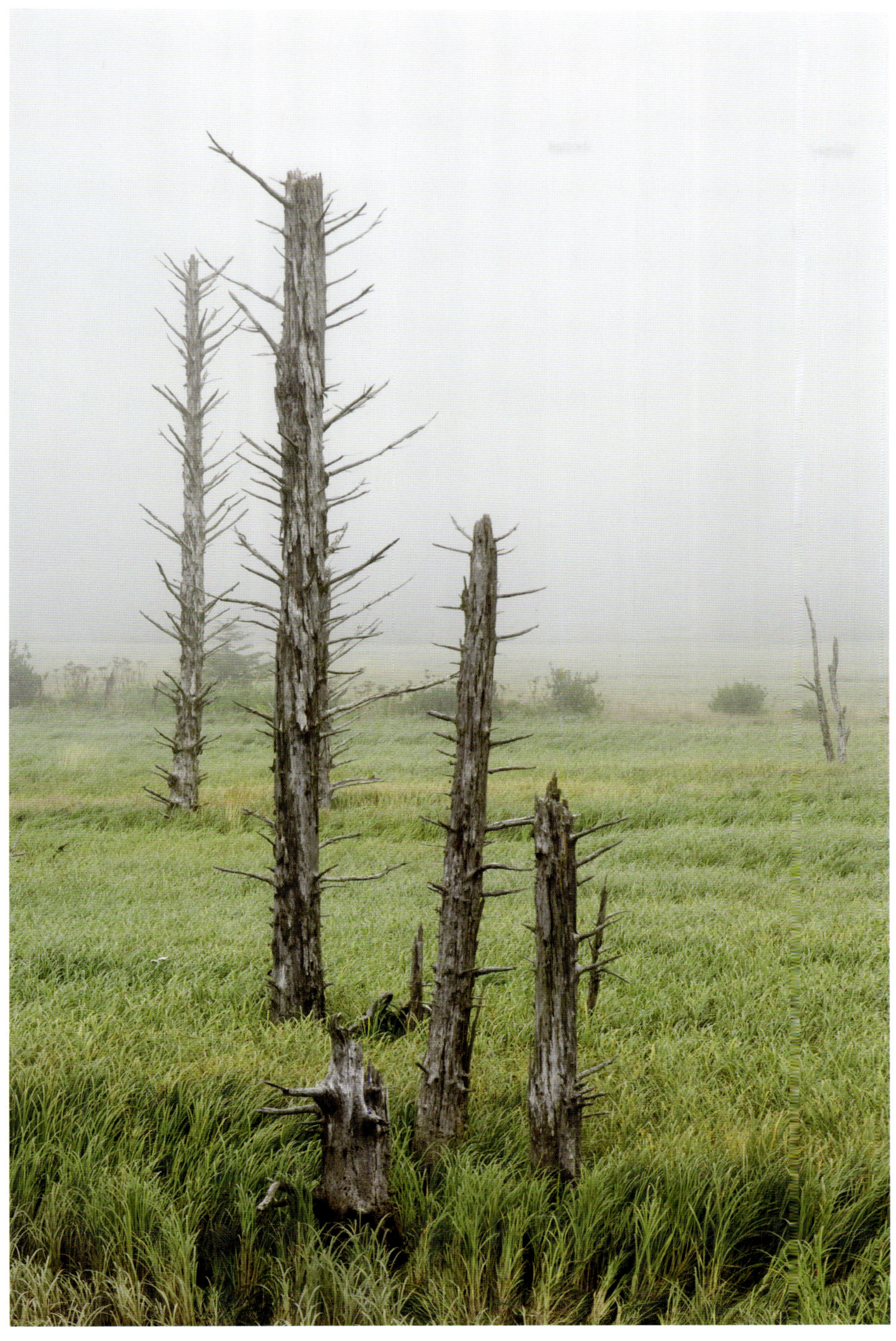

Salt-starched trees at Siletz Bay National Wildlife Refuge, near Lincoln City. ●

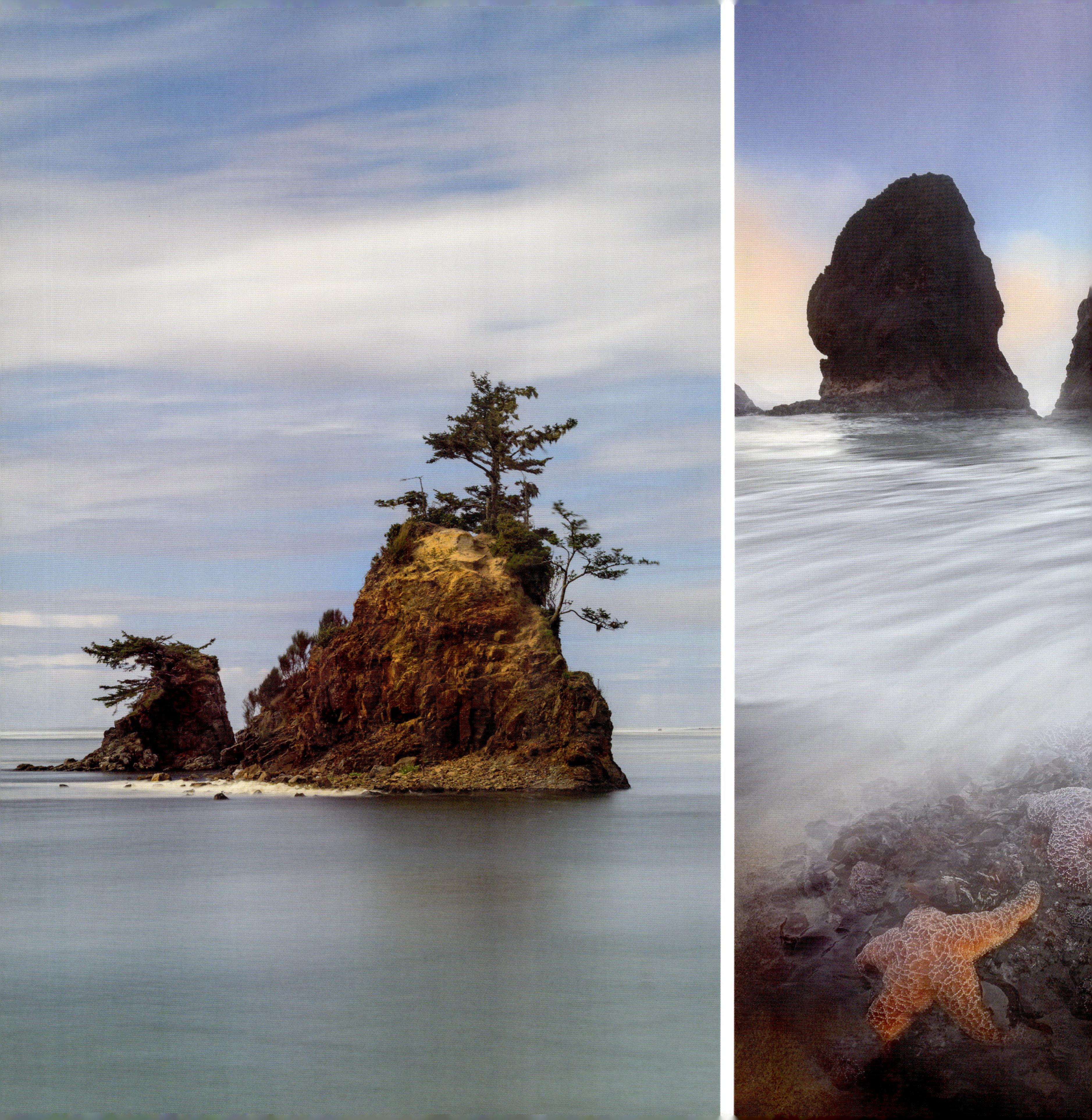

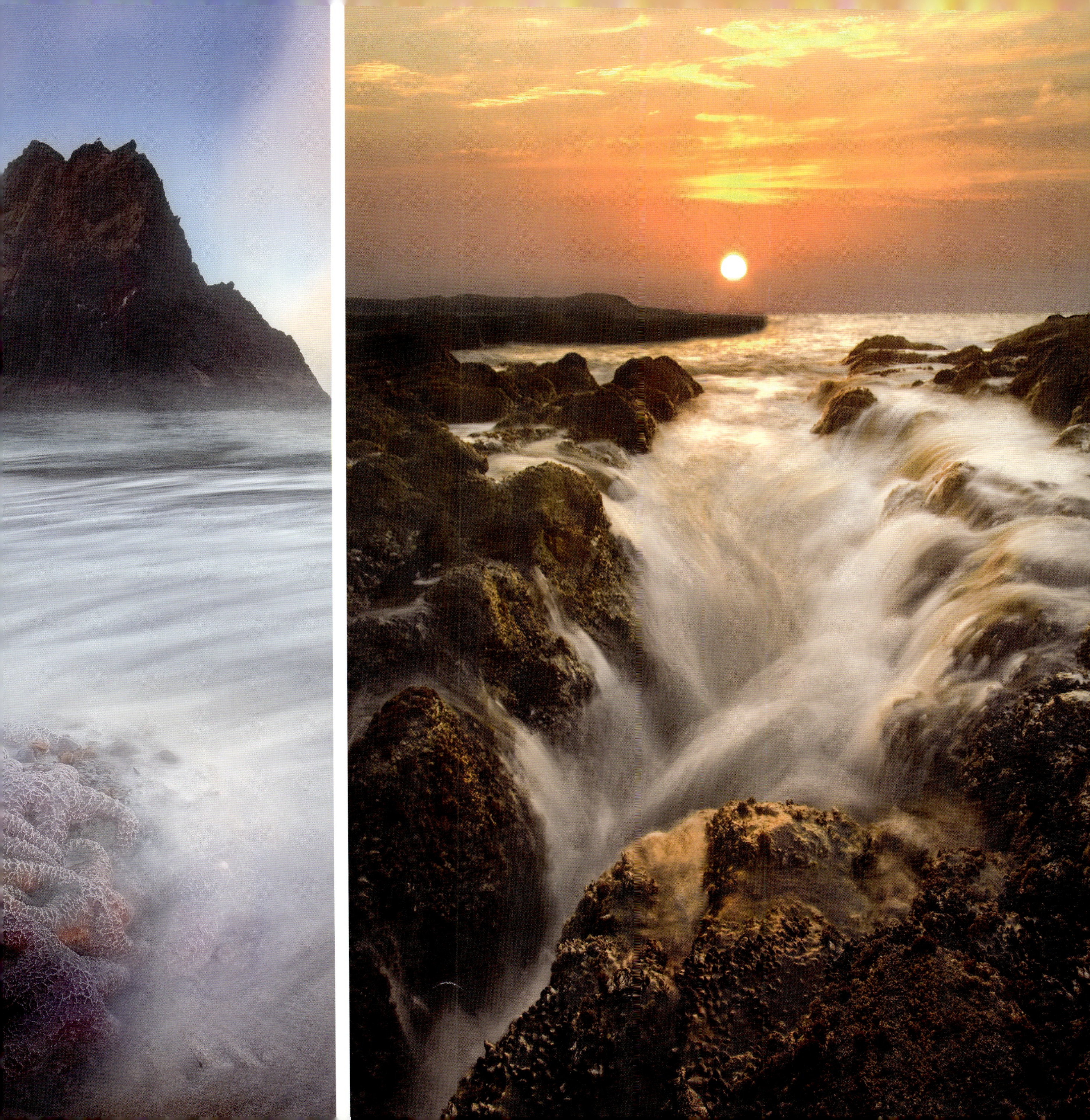

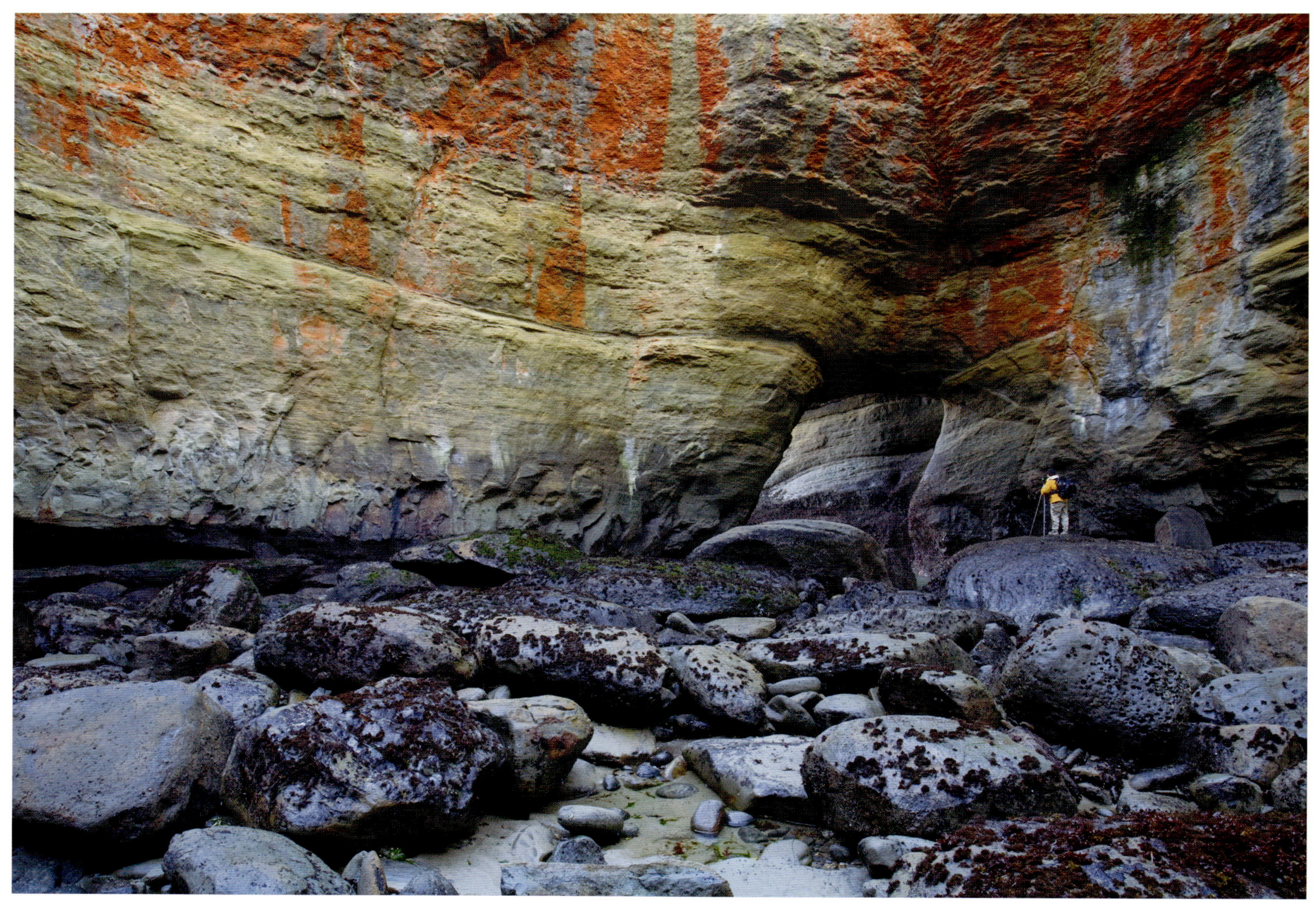

PREVIOUS PAGES, LEFT TO RIGHT
Late-afternoon light casts the crags of
sea stacks in jagged relief at Three Capes,
near Lincoln City. • Starfish cling to the
shore rocks as high tide returns to Lincoln
Beach. • Deep channels direct crashing
waves along the shores of Depoe Bay at
sunset. •

ABOVE Kevin McNeal photographing
inside of Devils Punchbowl State Natural
Area during a very low tide. •

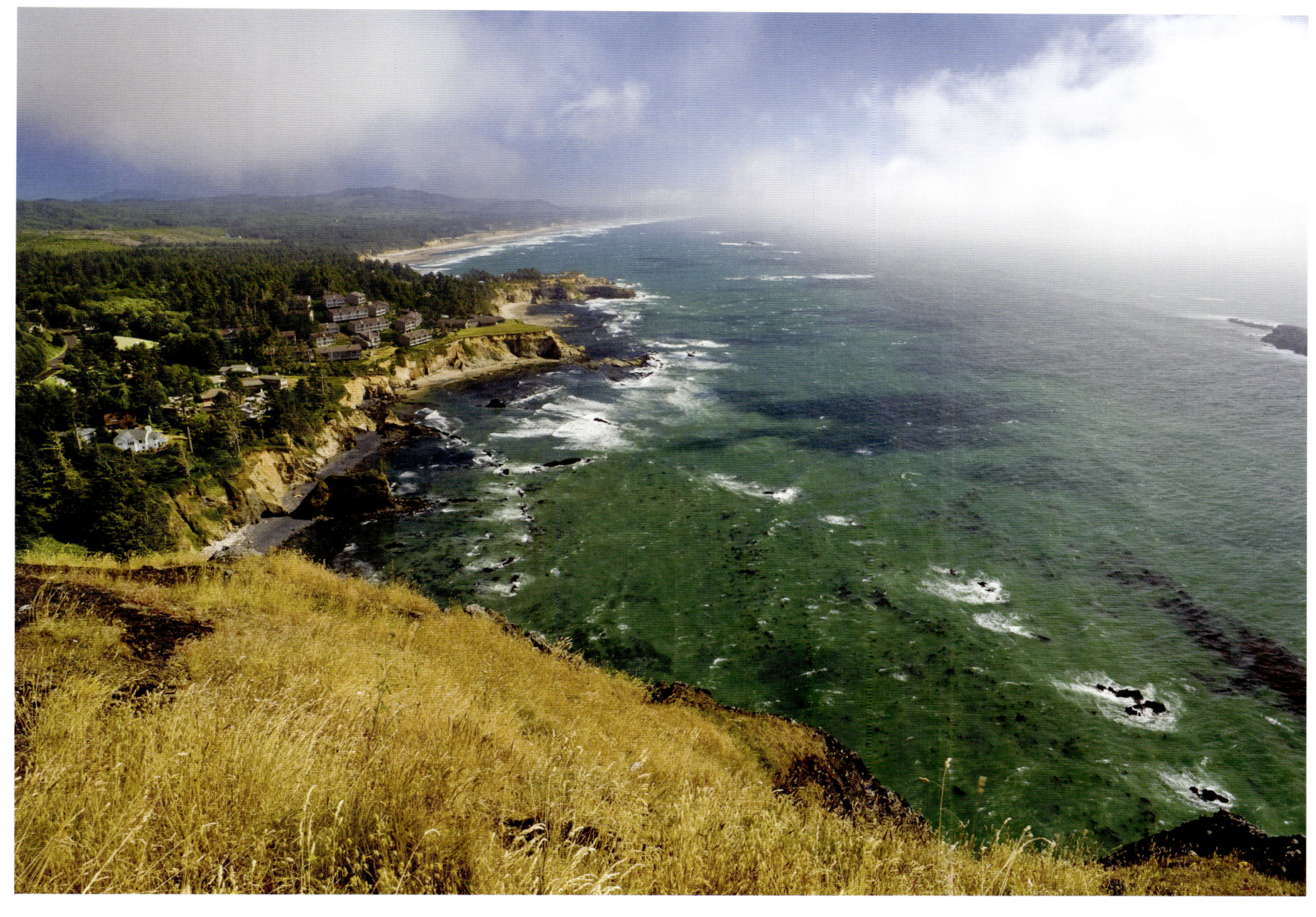

View to the south toward Otter Rock
from the Cape Foulweather overlook
in summer. •

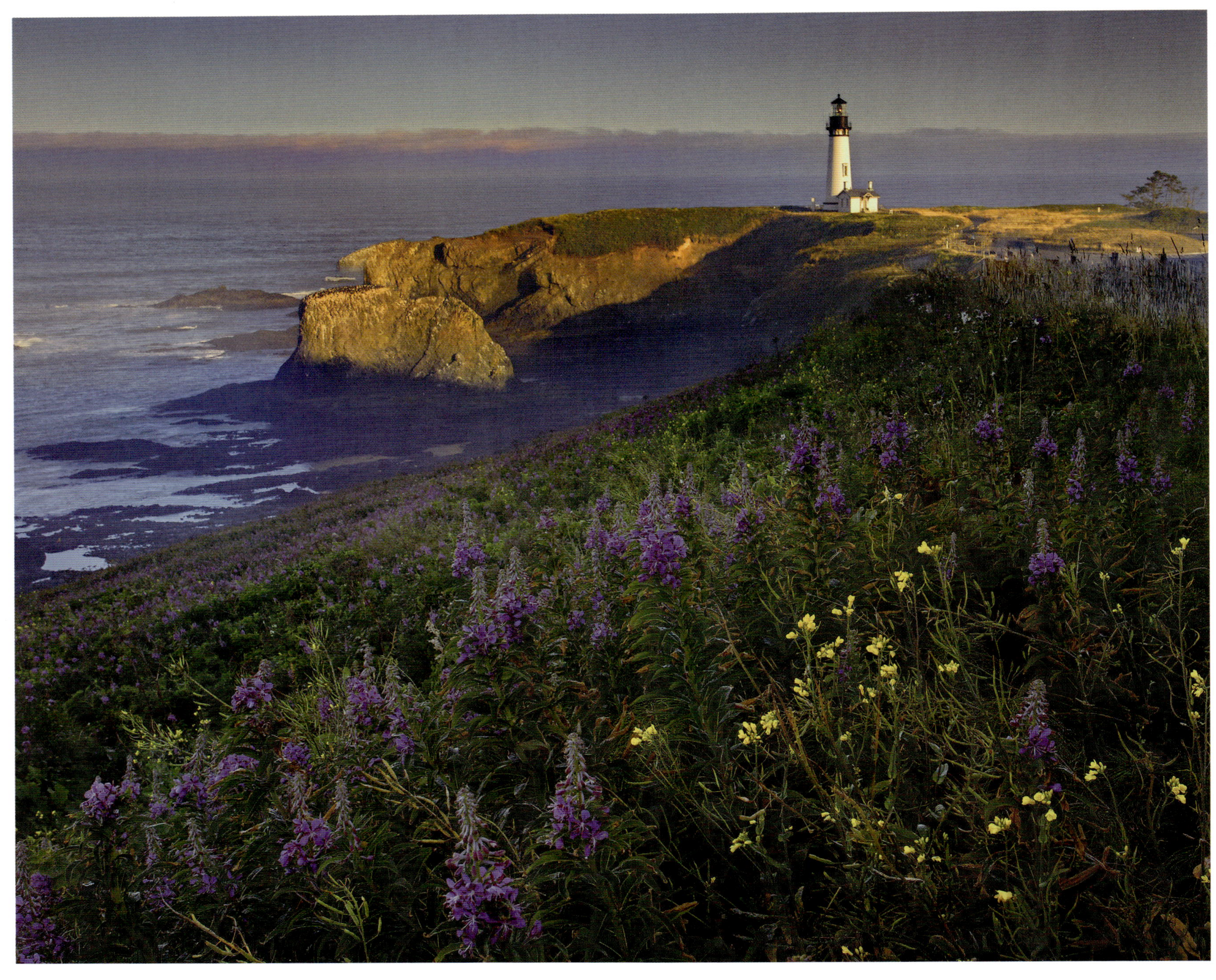

Summer flowers line the hillsides at
Yaquina Head Lighthouse near Newport
along the central coast. •

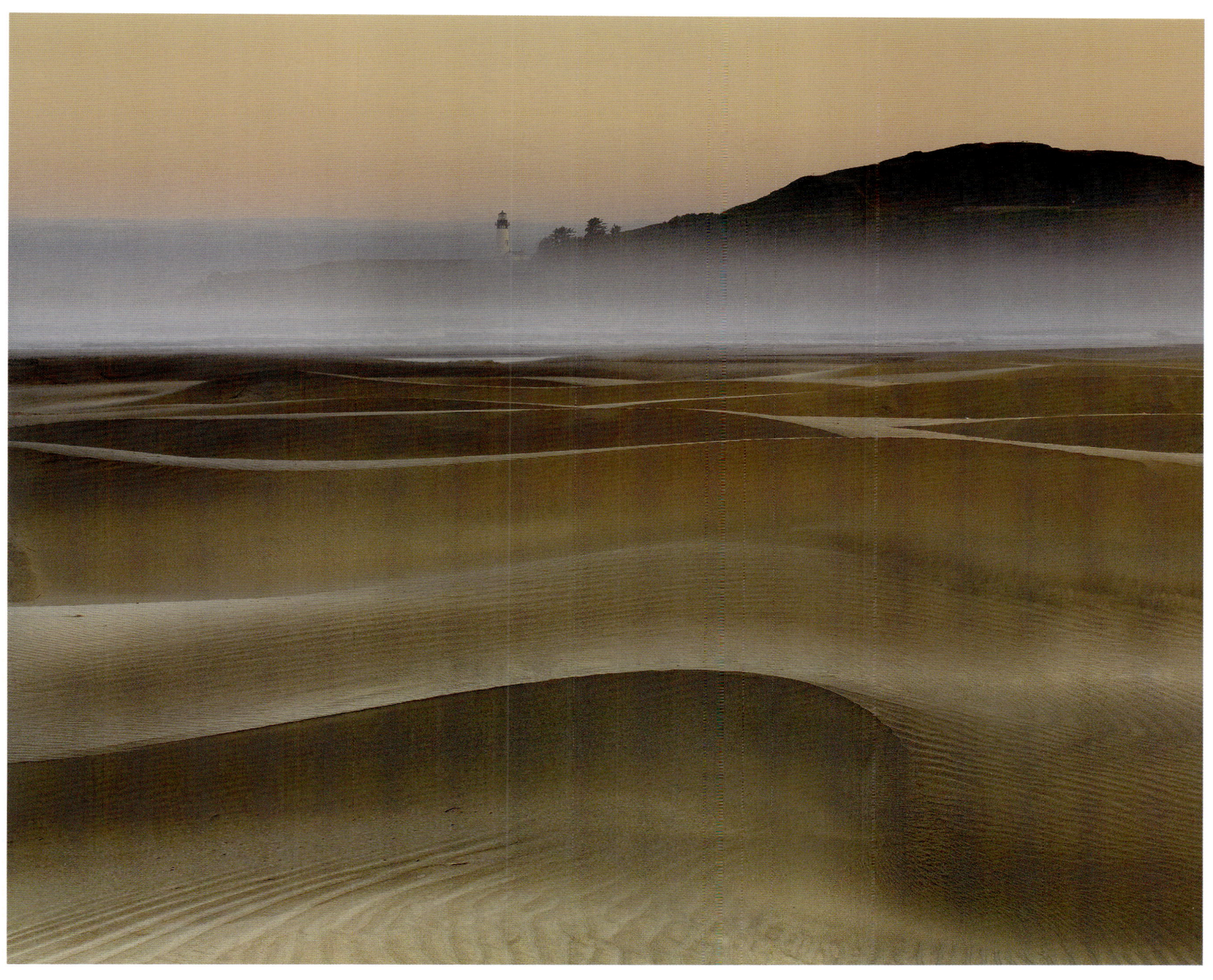

Low-lying mist hovers above
the patterned sand dunes that shape
Agate Beach, near Newport.

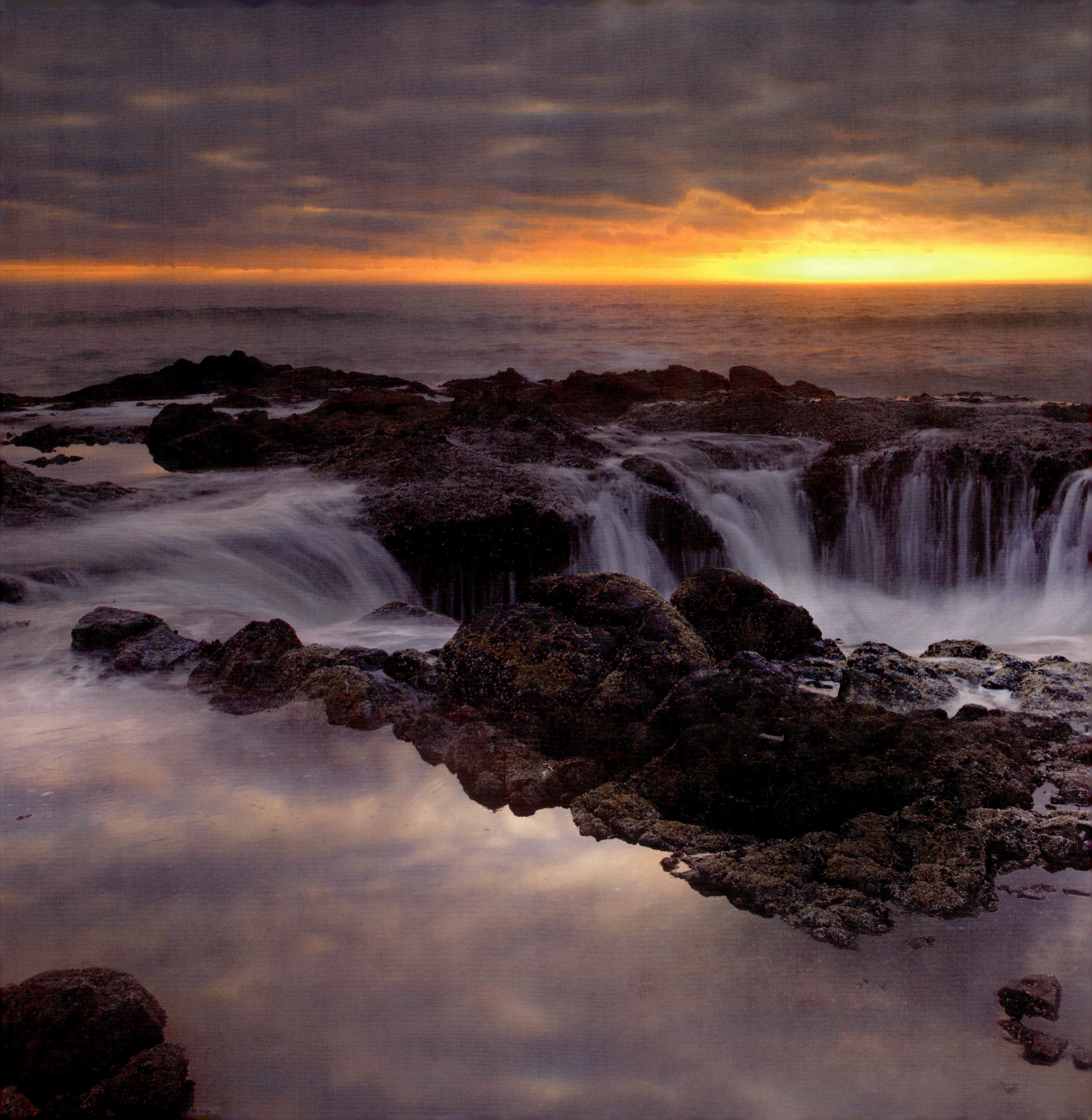

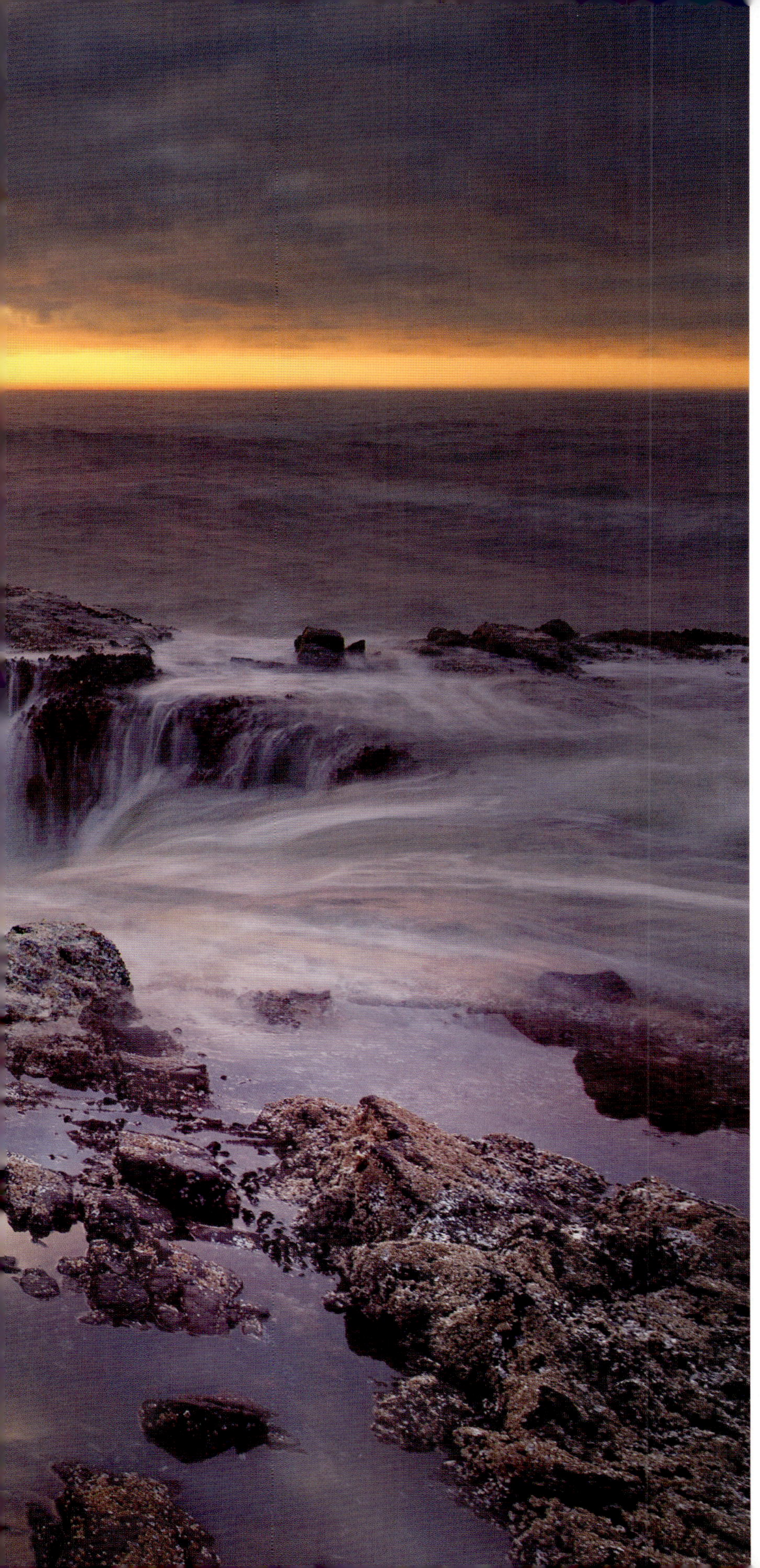

Warm colors and dramatic clouds fill
the sky above the iconic Thor's Well,
near Yachats. •

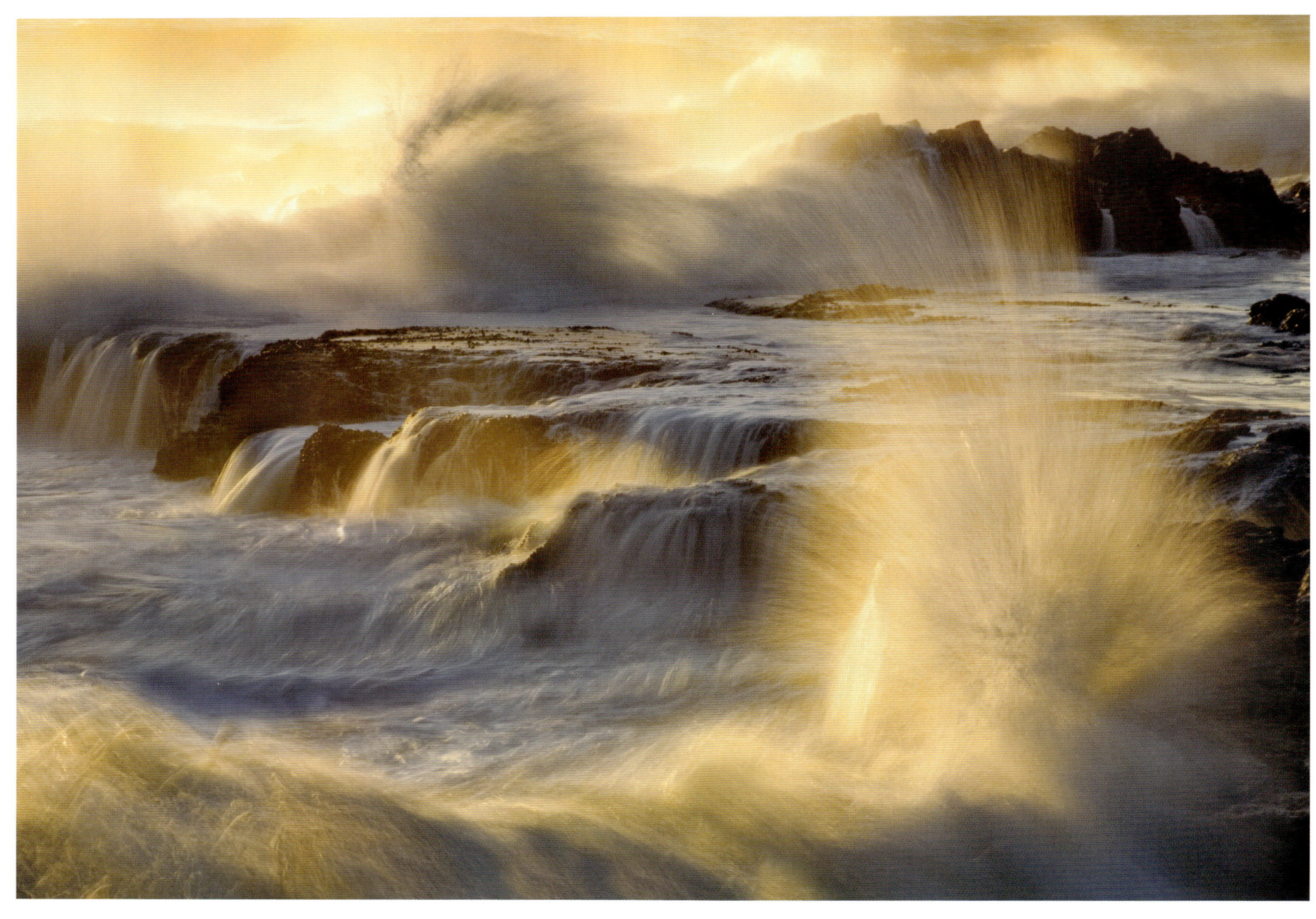

Waves crashing against the rocky shore in
Yachats, along the central coast. •

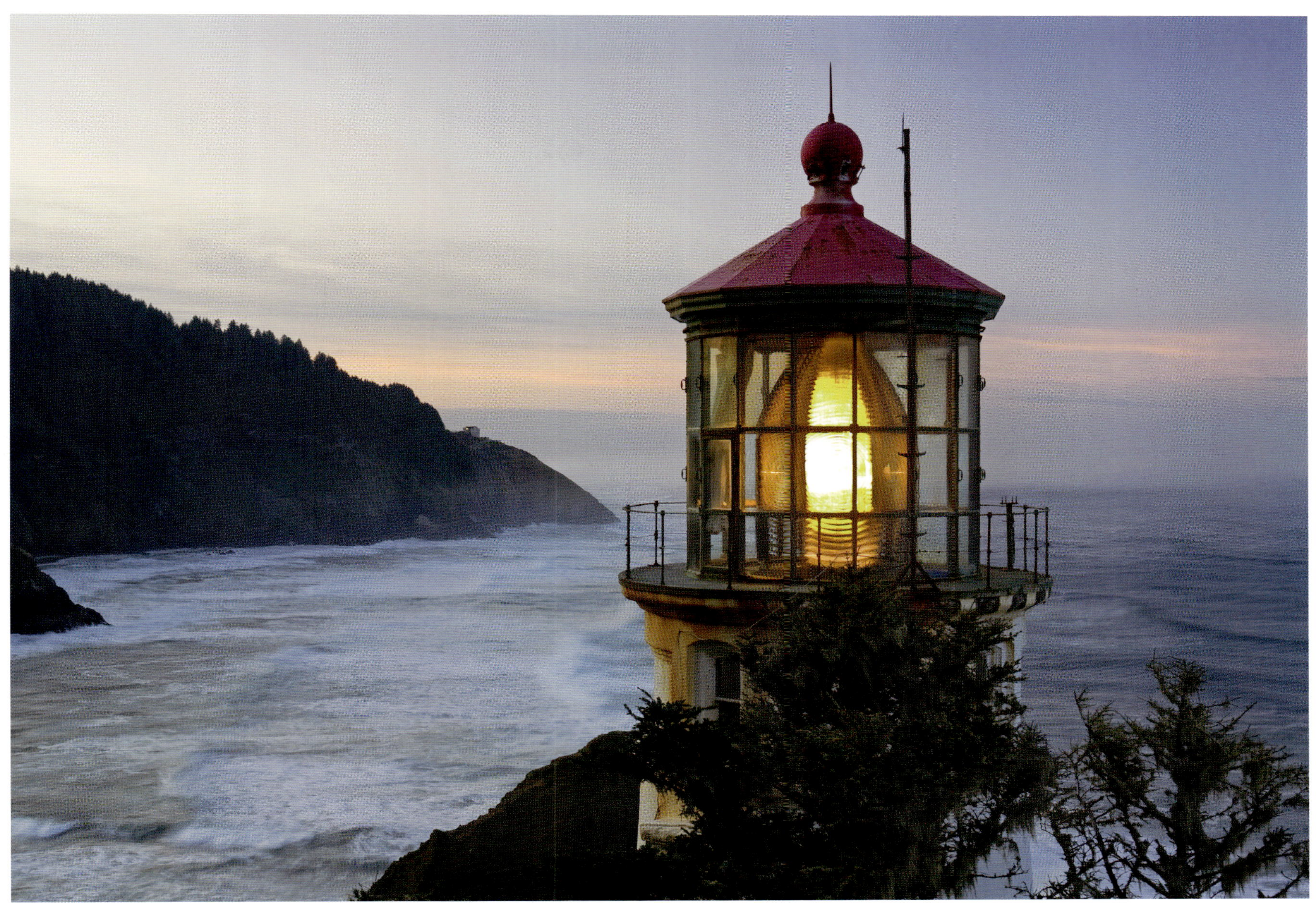

The Heceta Head Lighthouse
still acts as a beacon along the rugged
central coast. •

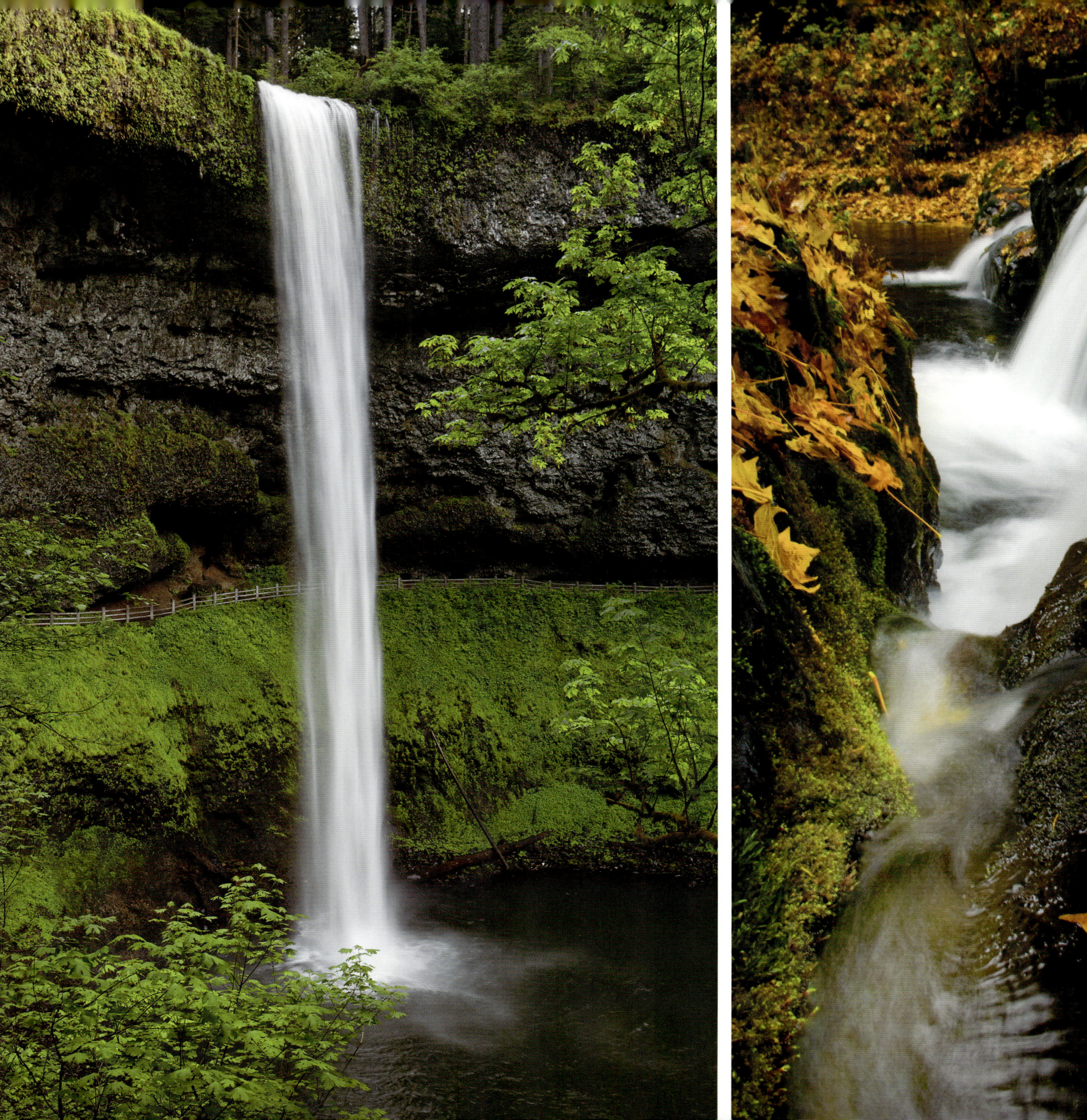

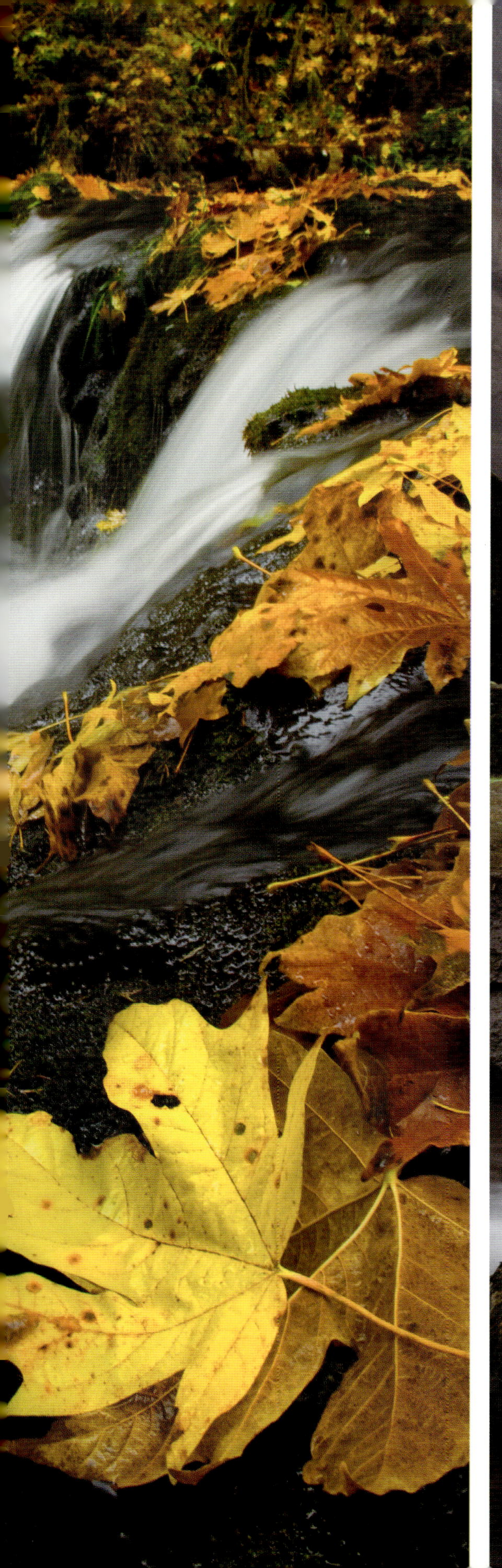

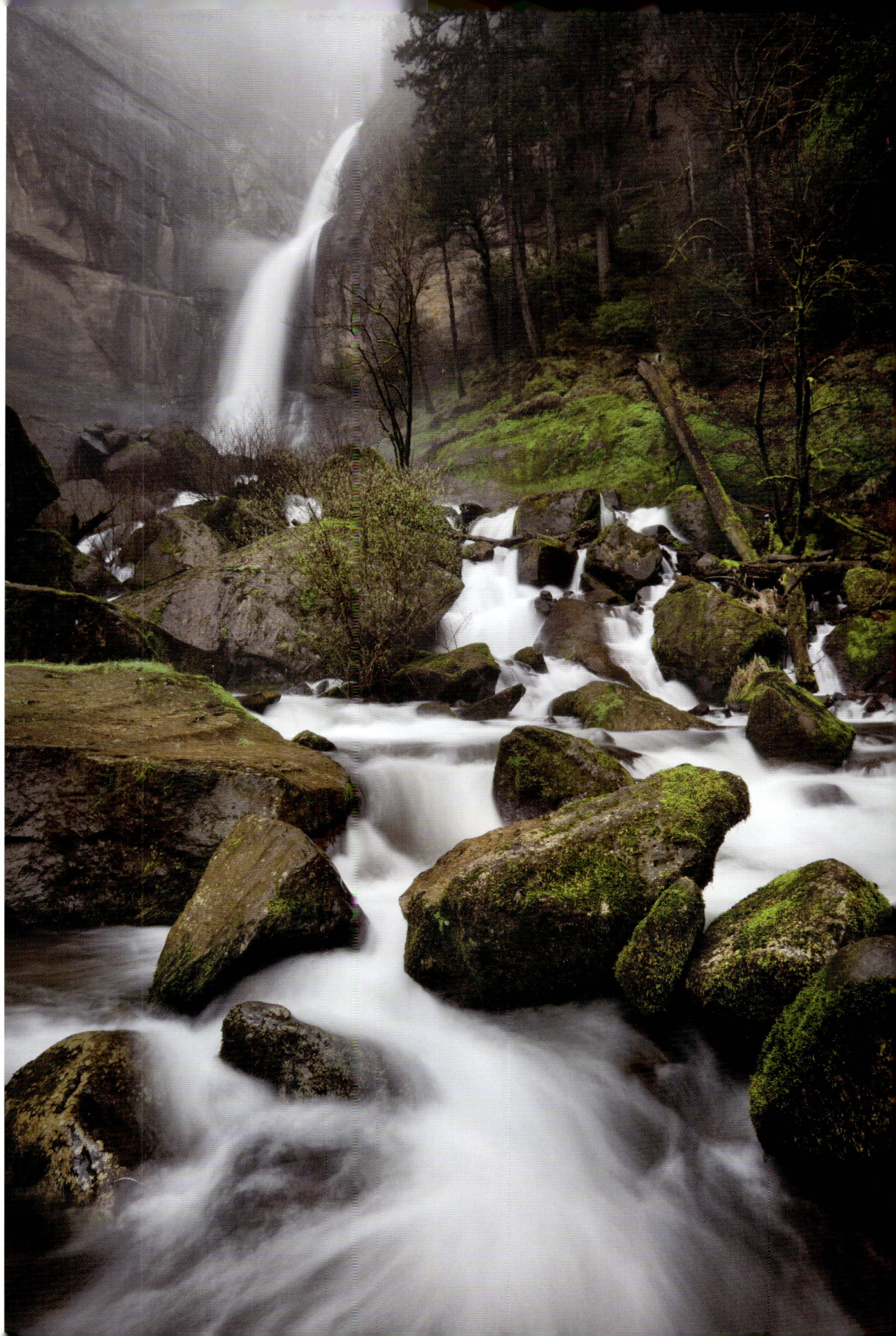

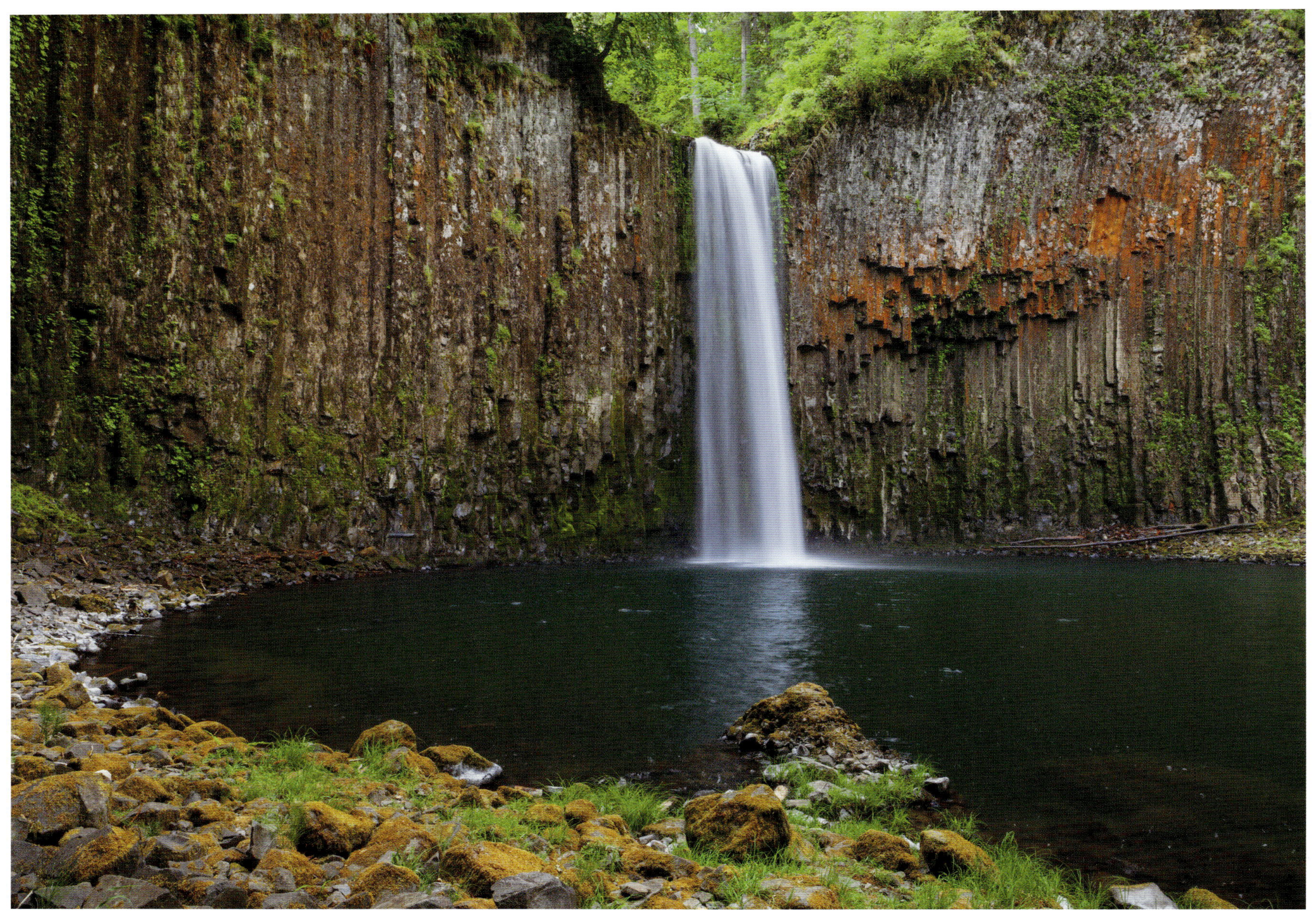

PREVIOUS PAGES, LEFT TO RIGHT
New spring greens surround South Falls at
Silver Falls State Park. • Autumn maples
add extra dimension to the waterfalls at
Silver Falls State Park. • Golden Falls,
in the Coast Range, plummets in a two-
tiered drop from a height of over 100 feet
before joining Glenn Creek as it flows
toward the Pacific Ocean. •

ABOVE Columnar basalt forms
a dramatic backdrop to Abiqua Falls. •

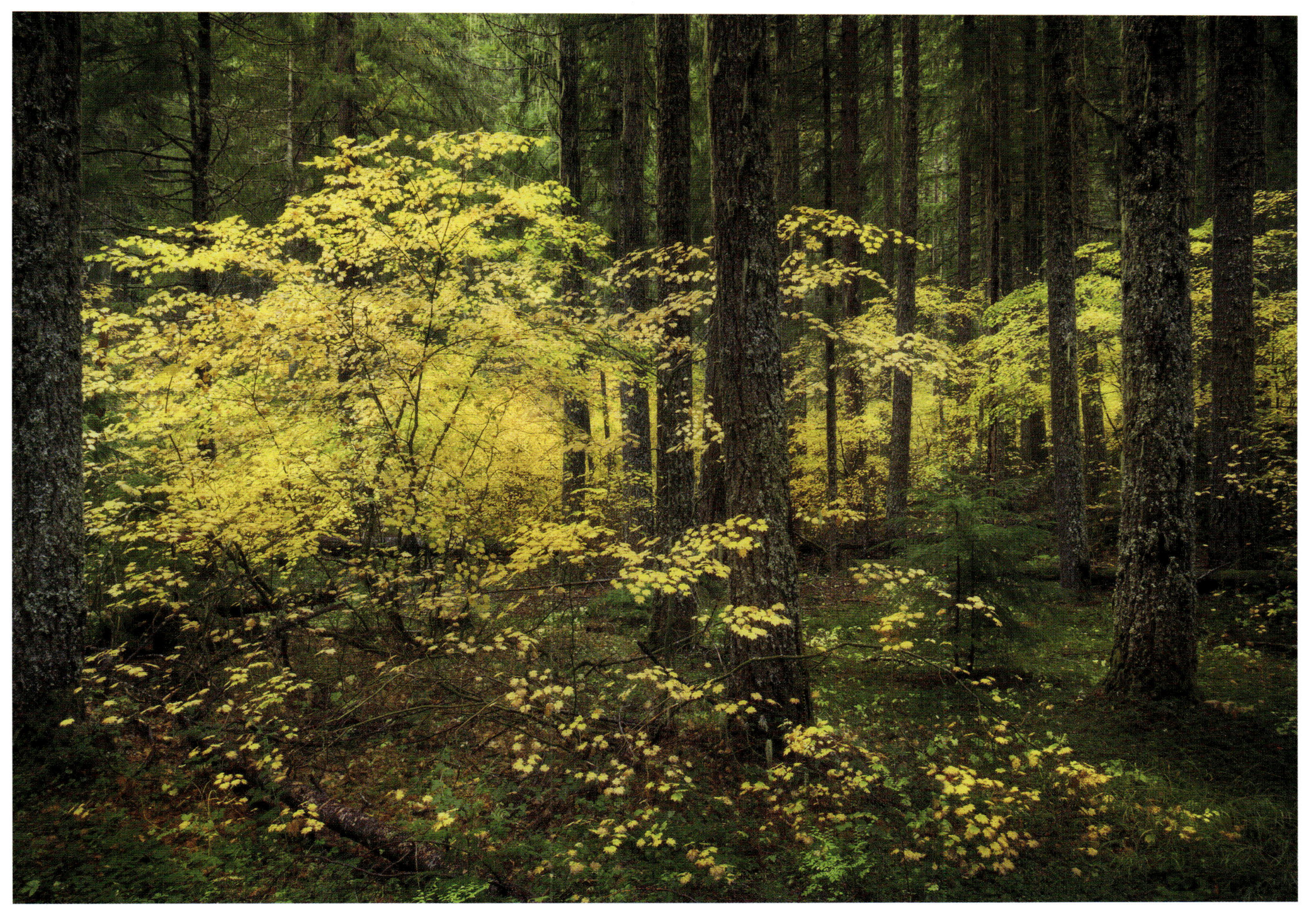

In autumn, vine maples illuminate the understory of the Willamette National Forest near McKenzie Pass. •

Koosah Falls flows vibrantly through
the Willamette National Forest in late
spring. ●

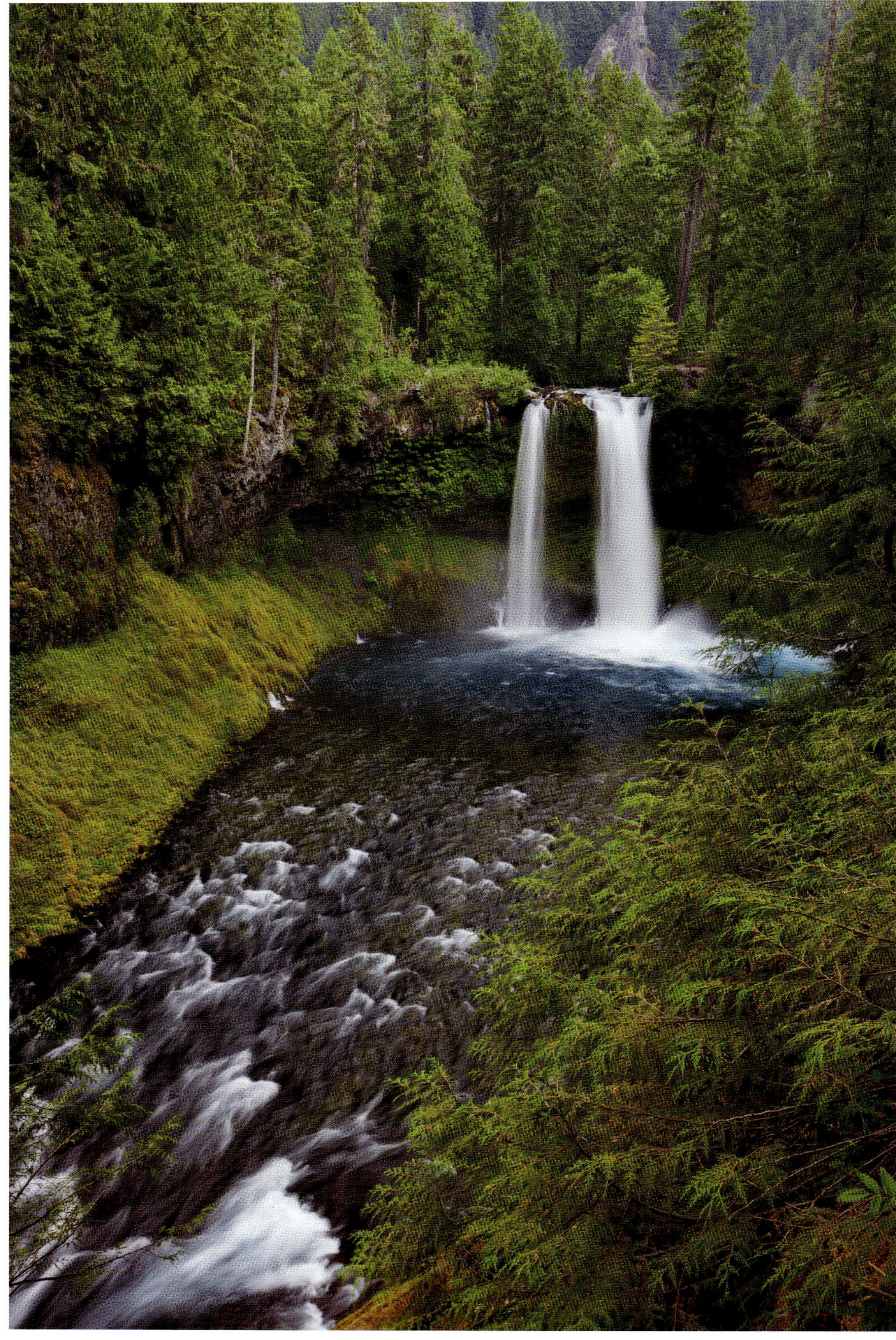

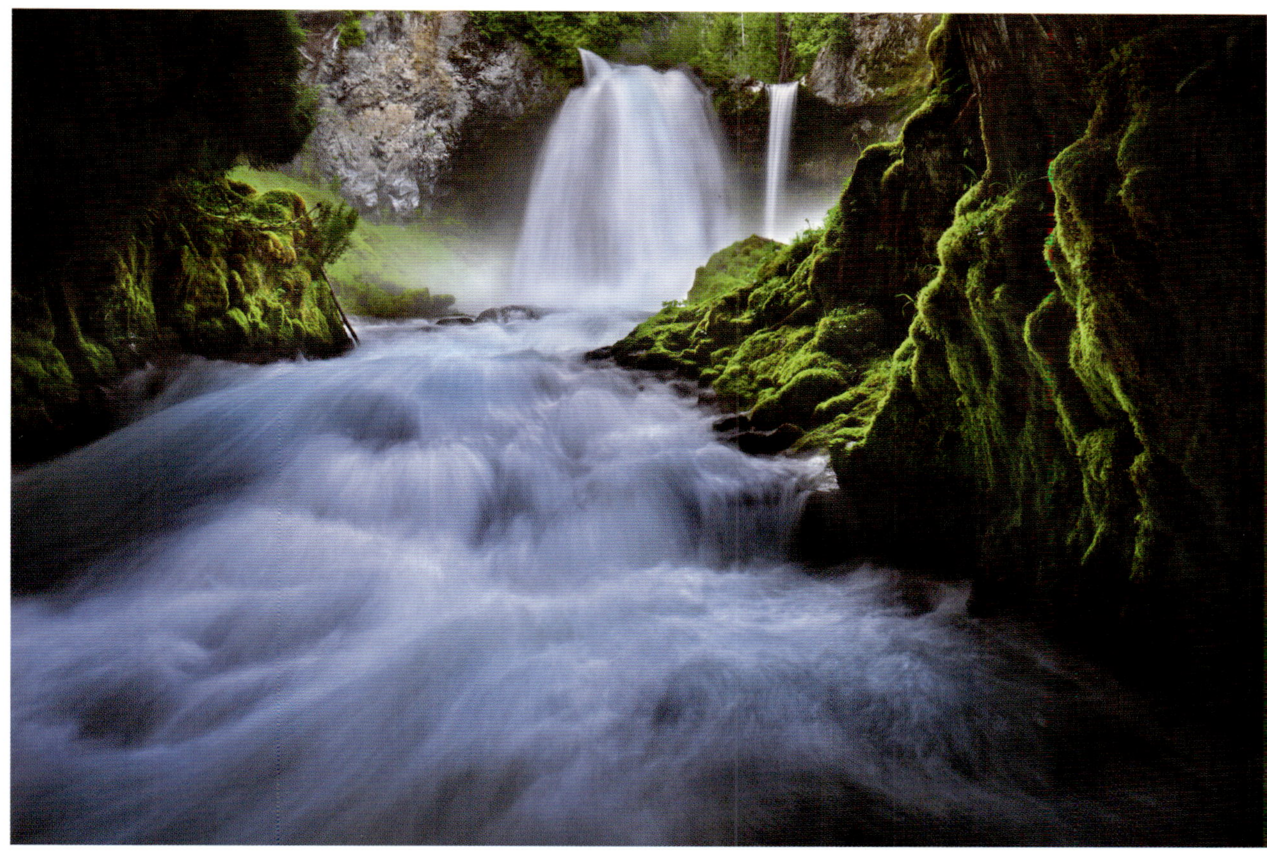

Spring snow melt causes the McKenzie River to flow swiftly over Sahalie Falls. •

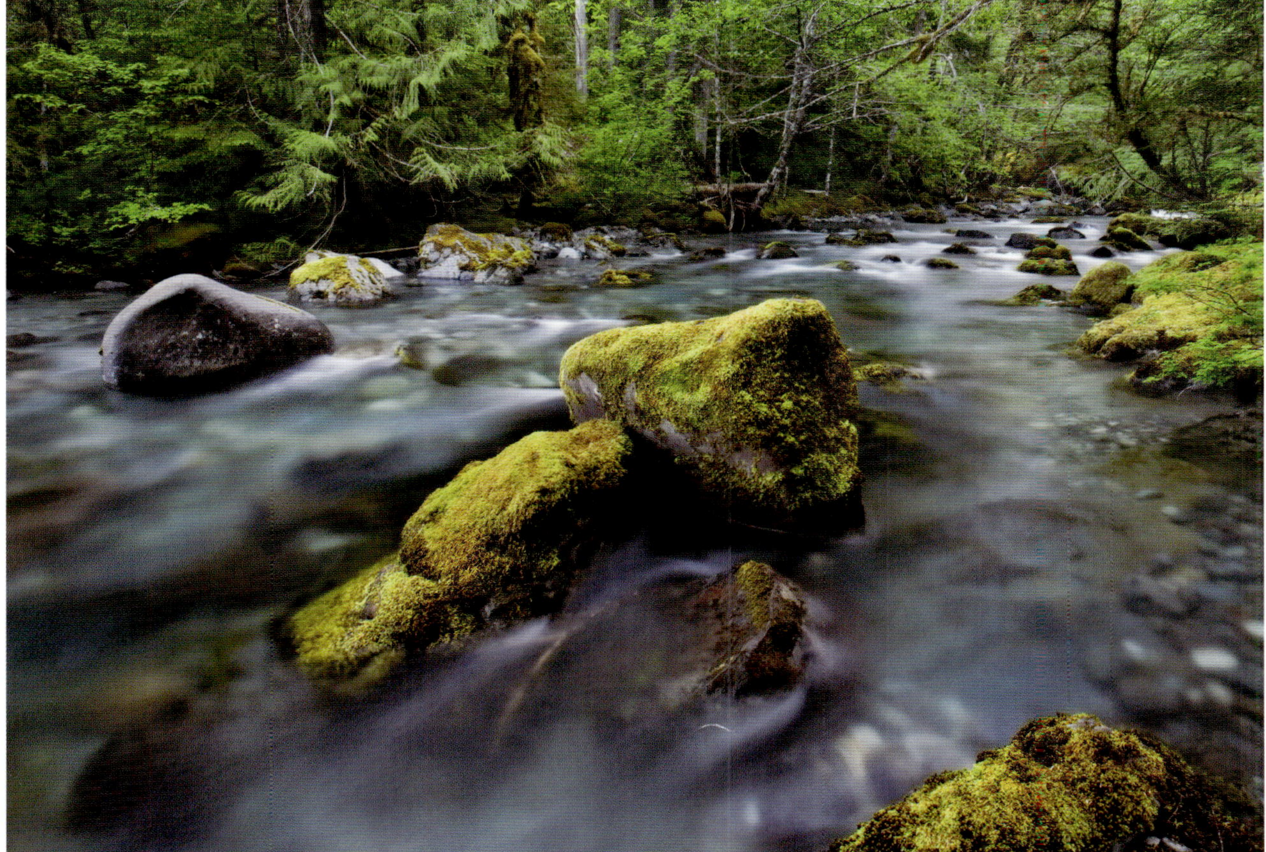

The Little North Santiam River in the Opal Creek Wilderness runs turquoise during summer. •

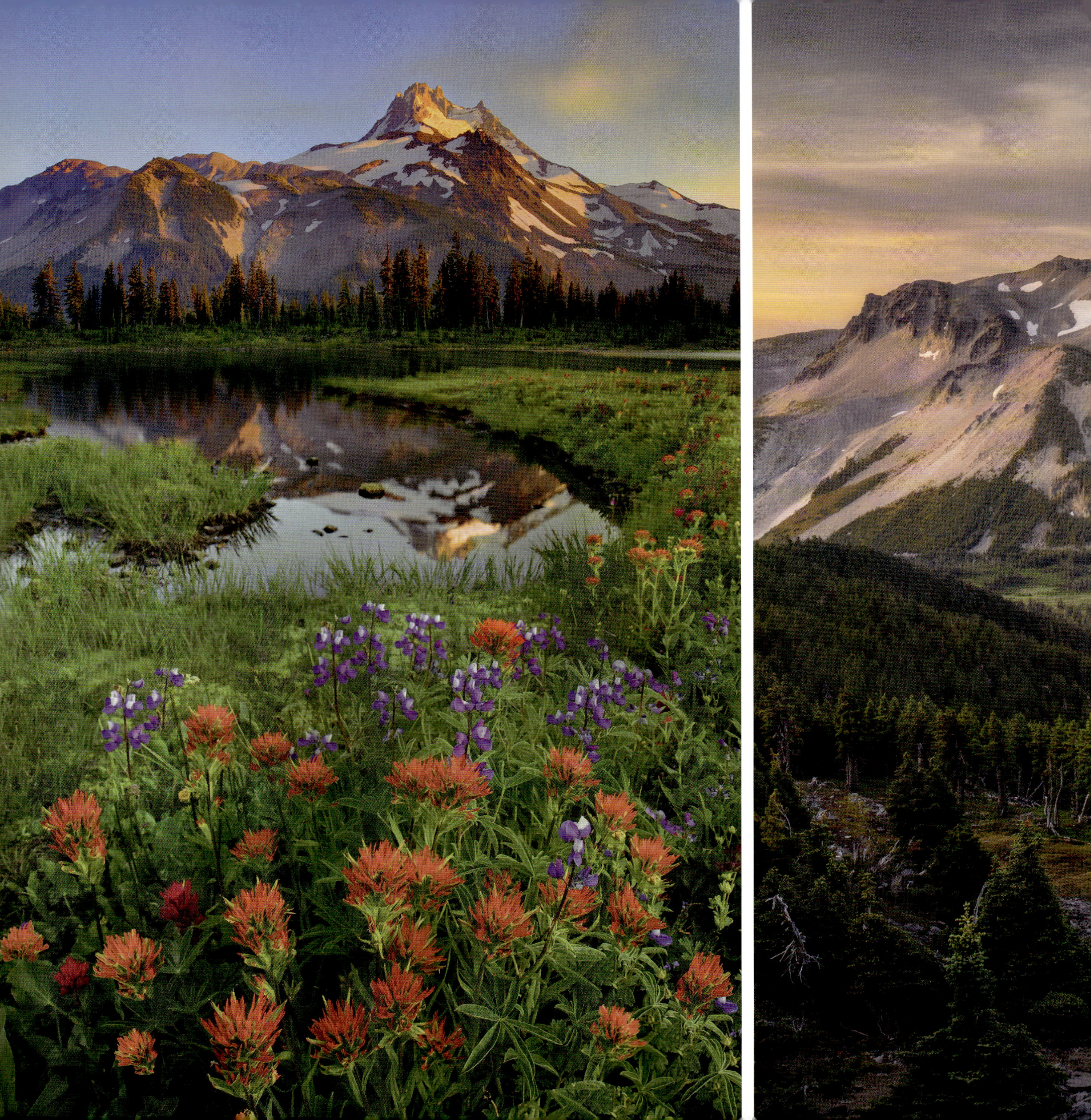

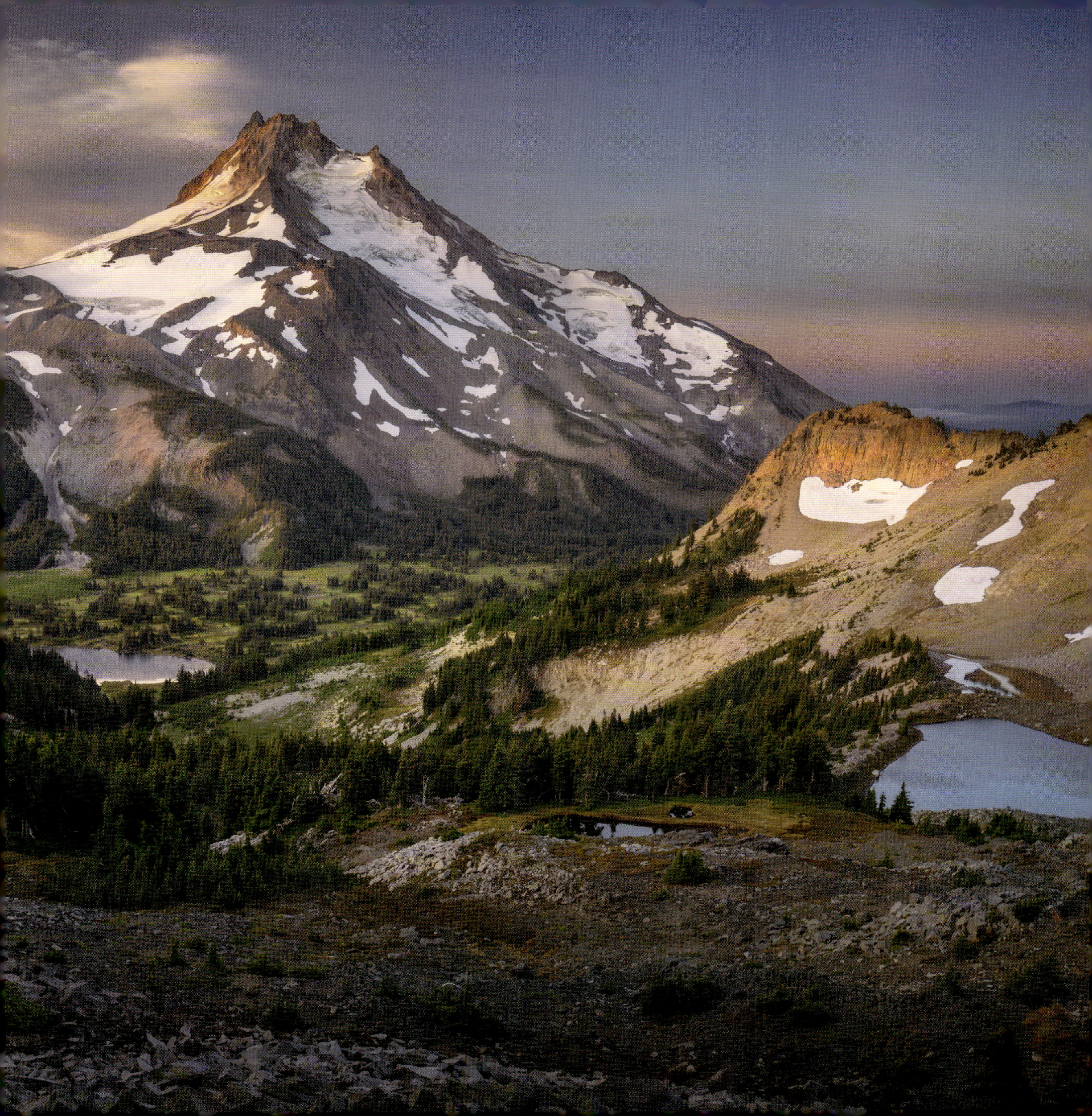

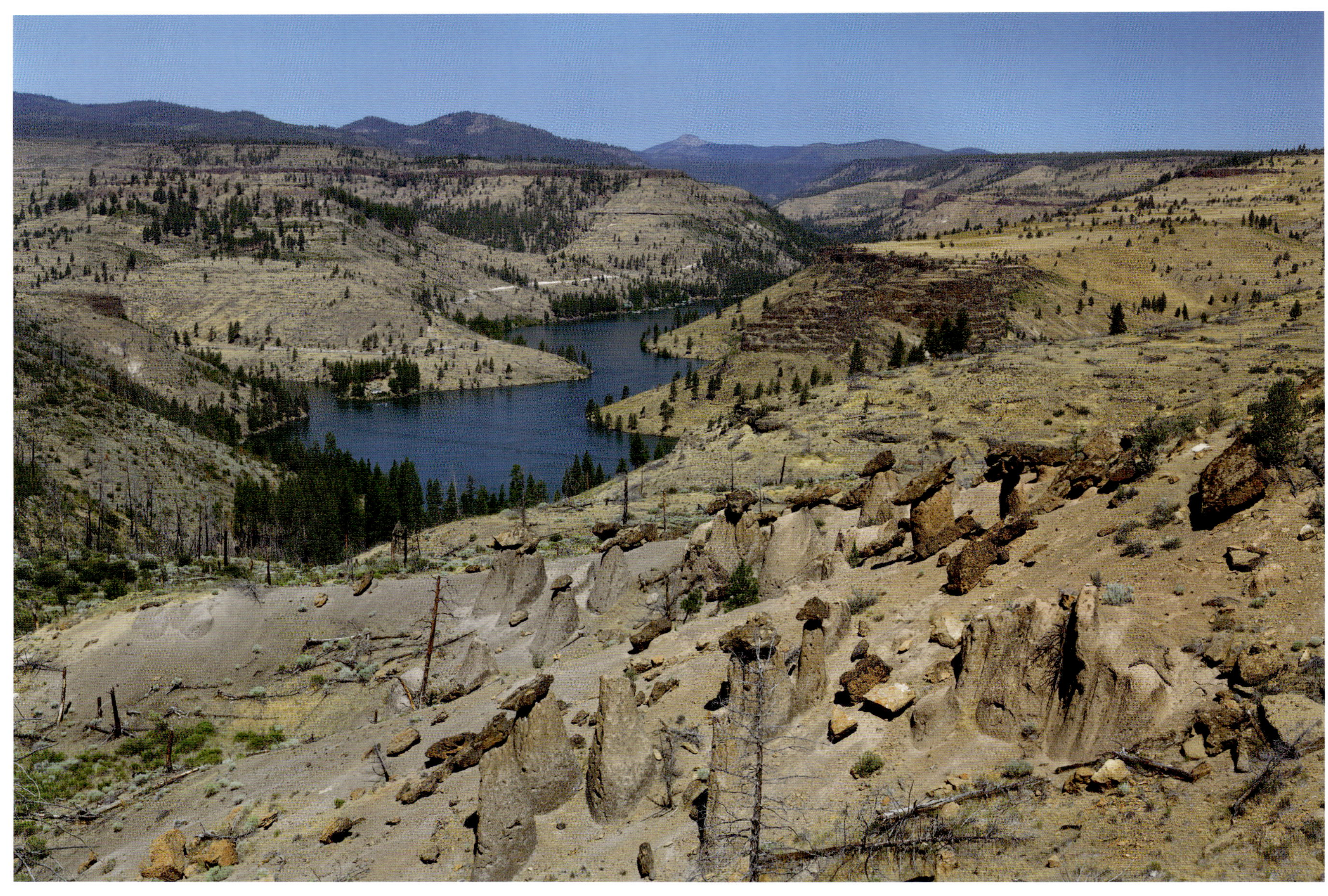

PREVIOUS PAGES Wildflowers, including
species of *Castilleja* and *Lupinus,* fill
the Mount Jefferson Wilderness Area in
summer. • The first rays of August
morning sunshine reach the 10,495-foot
peak of Mount Jefferson, the second-
highest mountain in Oregon. •

ABOVE The Metolius Balancing Rocks,
near Lake Billy Chinook, were only
revealed when a wildfire burned down
the surrounding forest in 2003. •

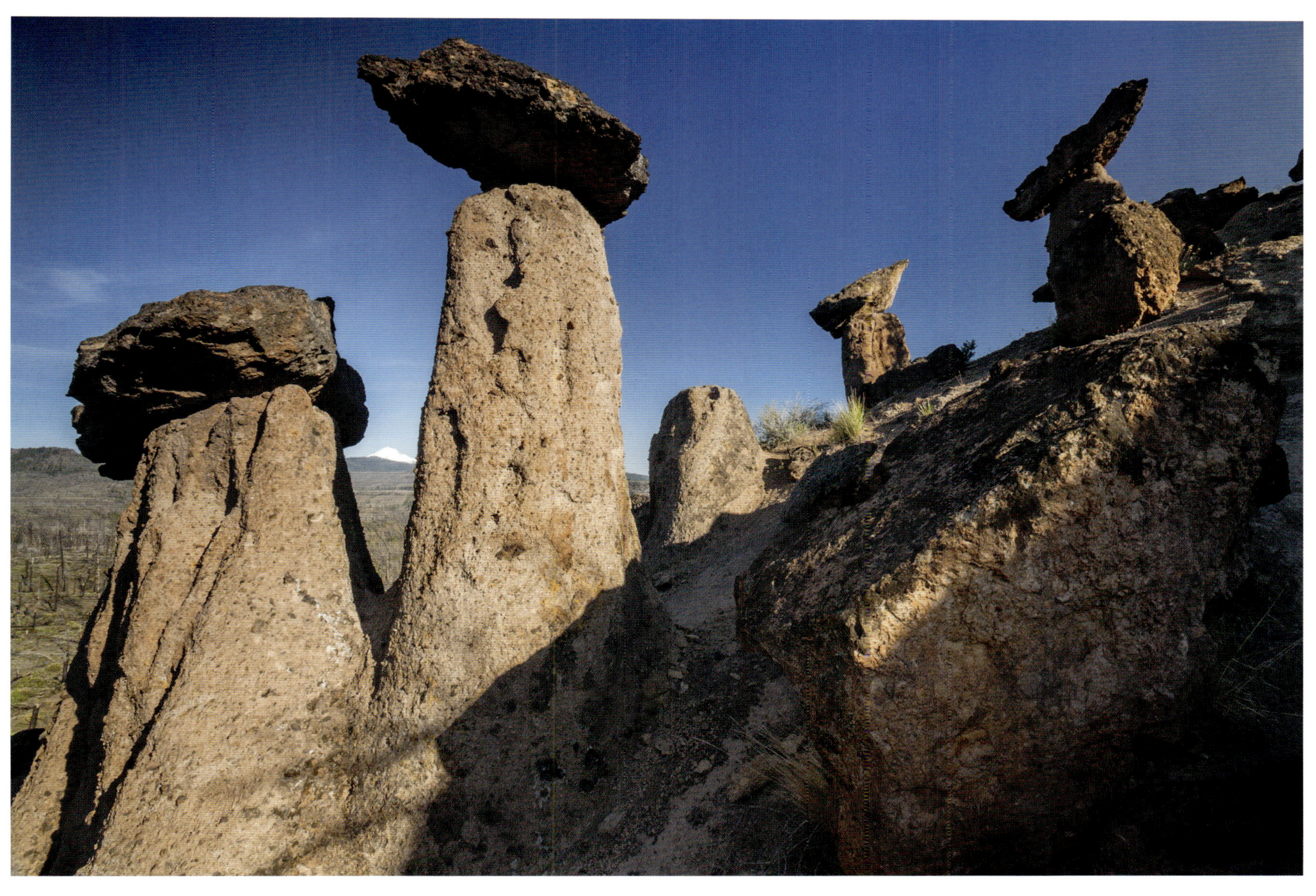

The Oregon HooDoos are remnants of a lava flow that rested on softer material below, which erodes at a faster rate. Mount Jefferson, in the distance, is also part of the region's volcanic legacy. •

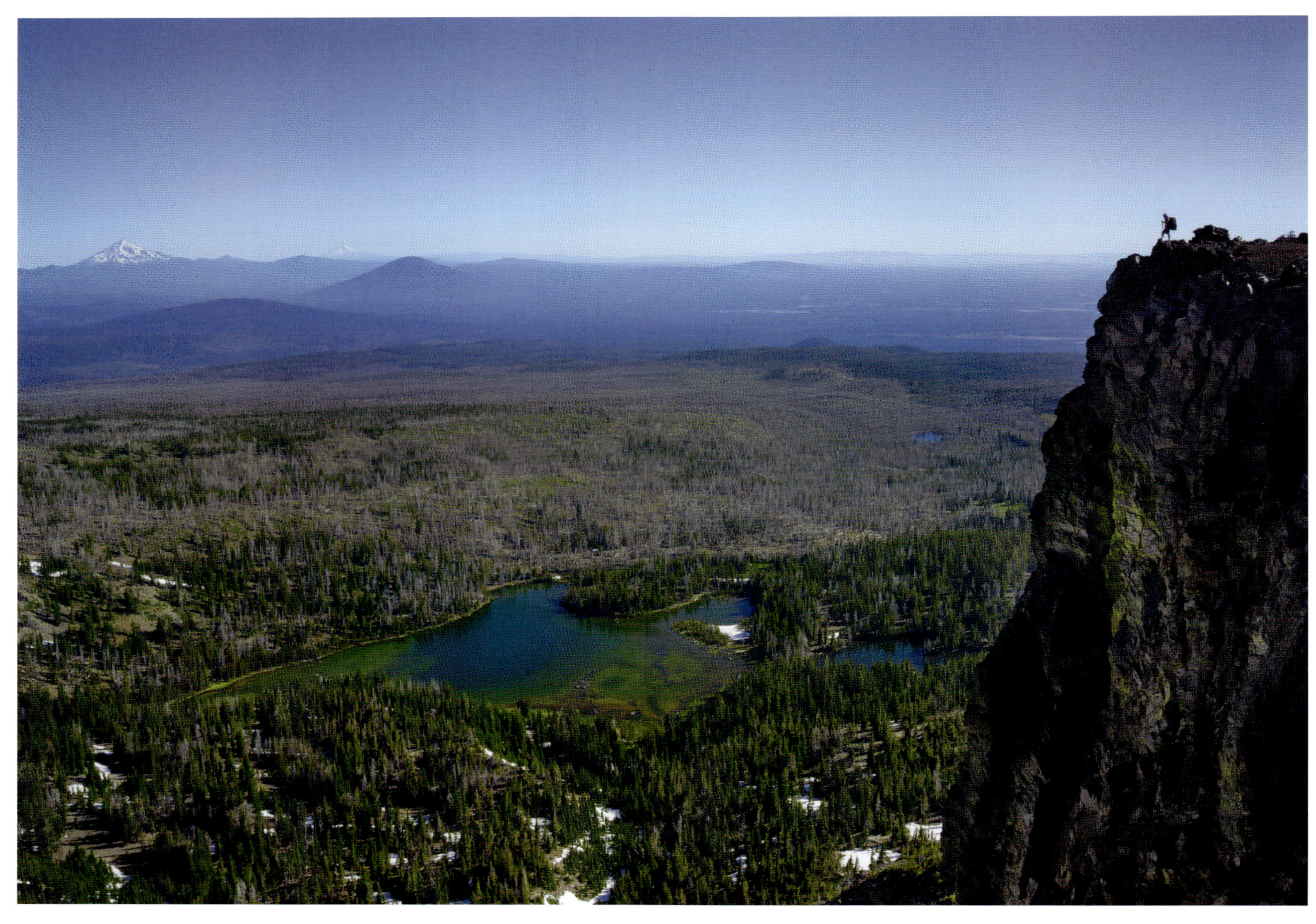

A backpacker stands near the edge of
a cliff along Tam McArthur Rim in the
Three Sisters Wilderness above Little
Three Creek Lake. ●

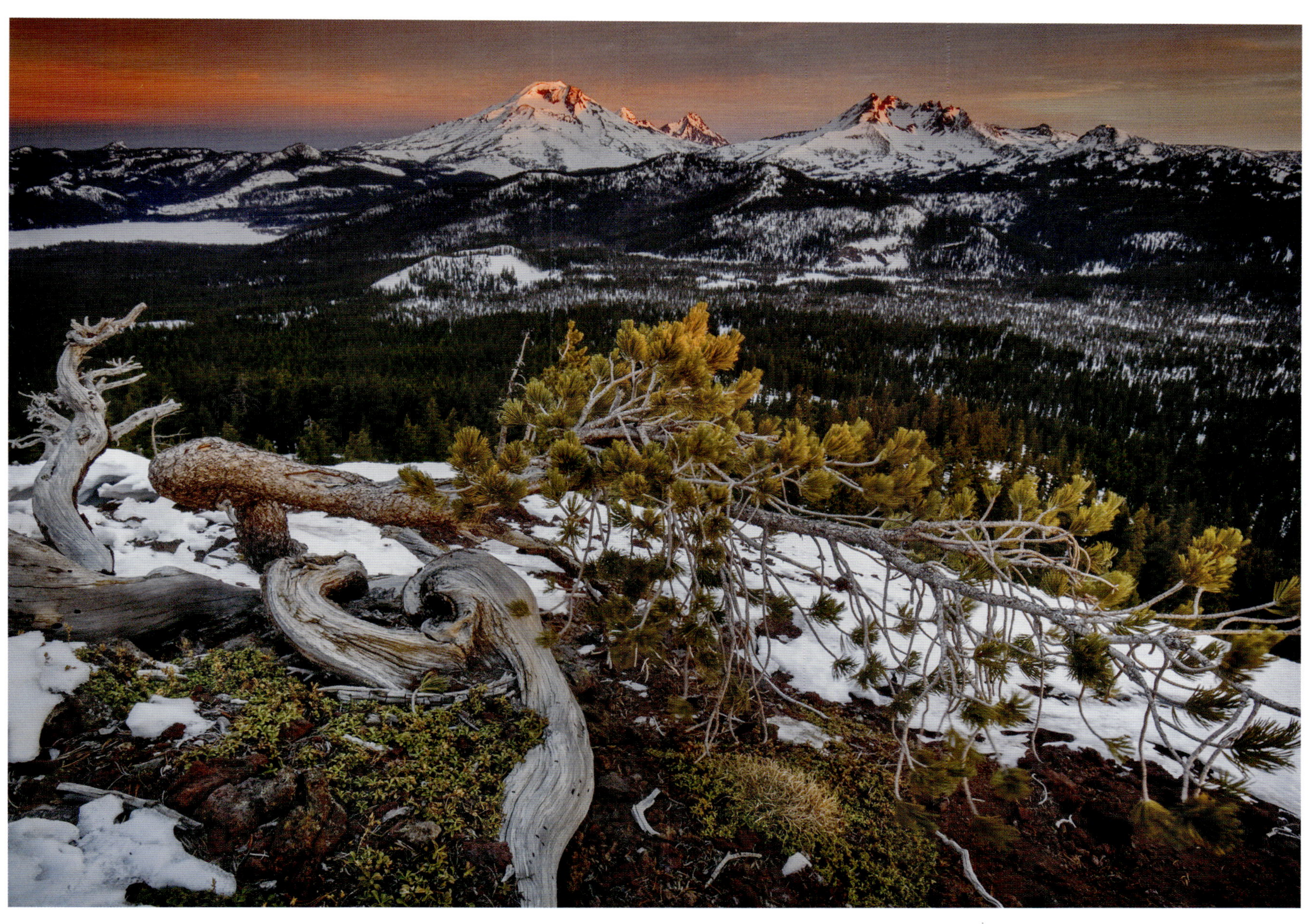

Sunrise just catching the tops of the
Three Sisters in the Cascade Range on
a cold winter morning. •

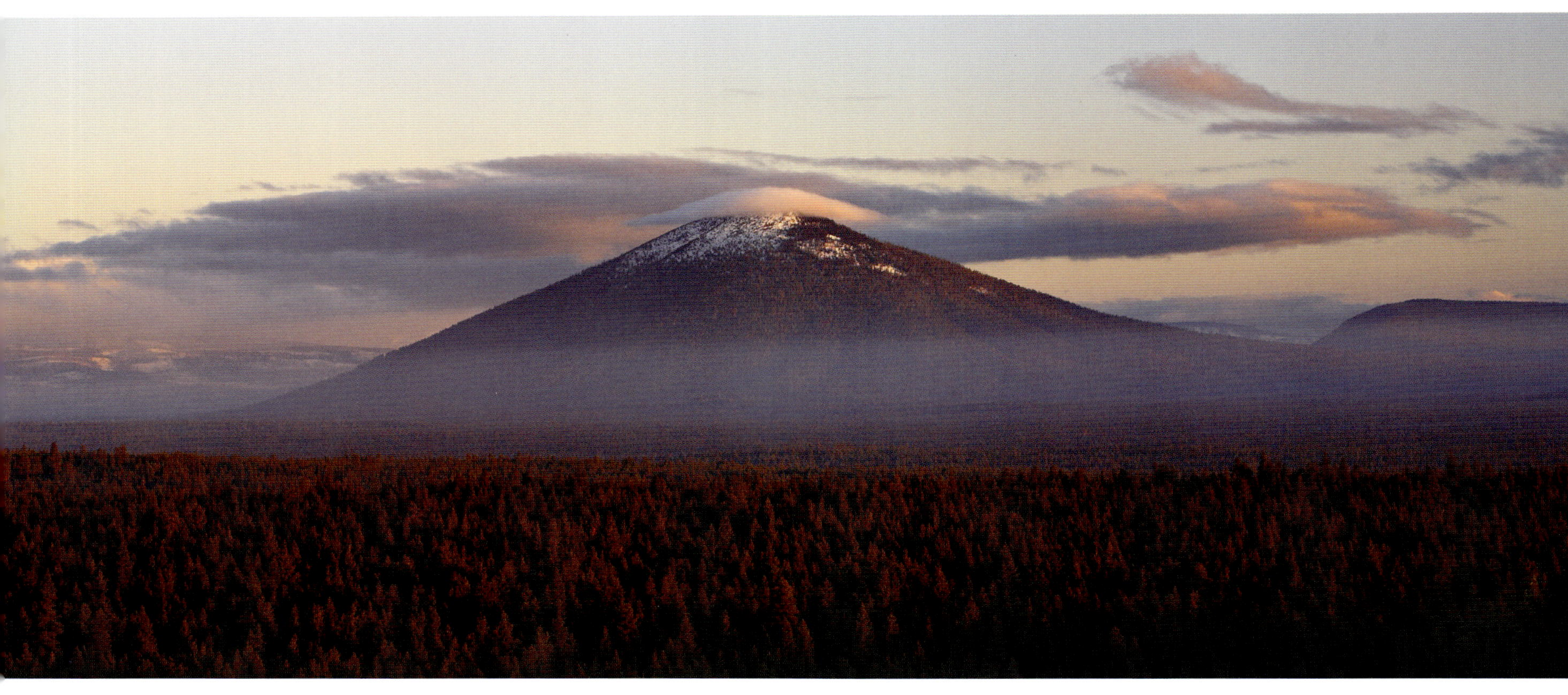

Black Butte, an extinct stratovolcano,
wears a lenticular cloud cap at sunrise on
a February morning. ●

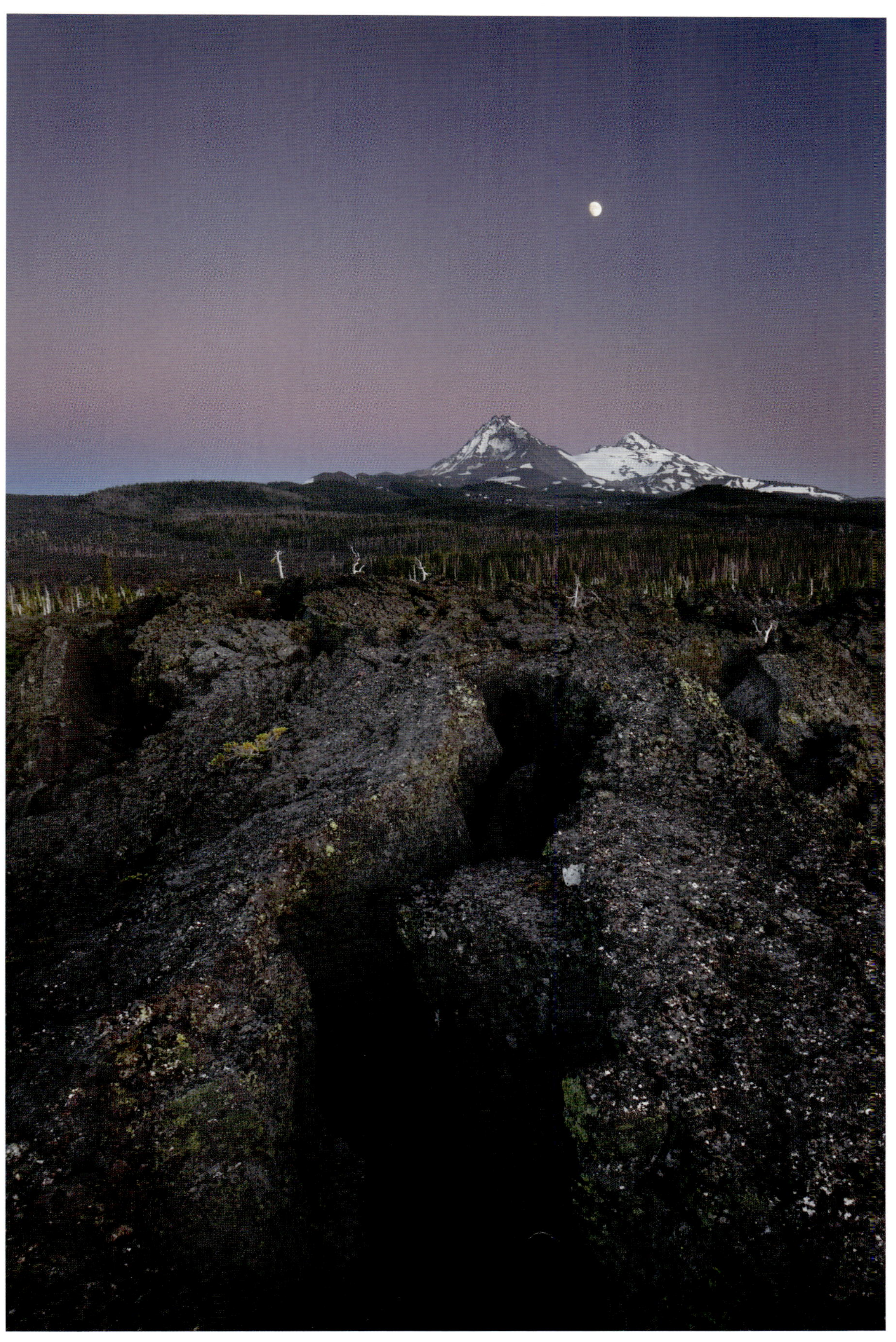

Moonrise, twilight, and cracked basalt lava flows converge at McKenzie Pass near the North and Middle Sisters. ●

During the summer months, kayakers enjoy Sparks Lake in the Deschutes National Forest. ●

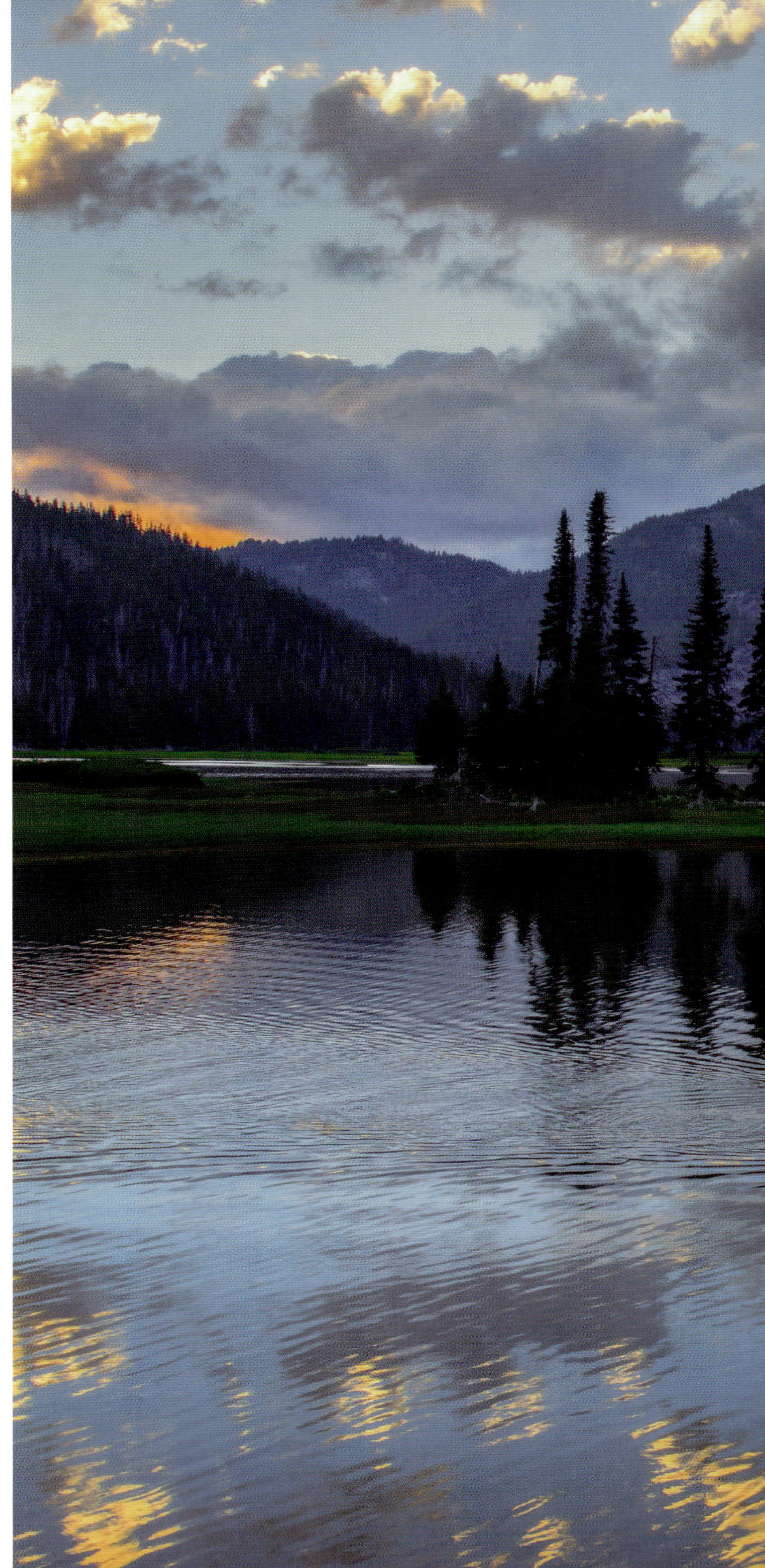

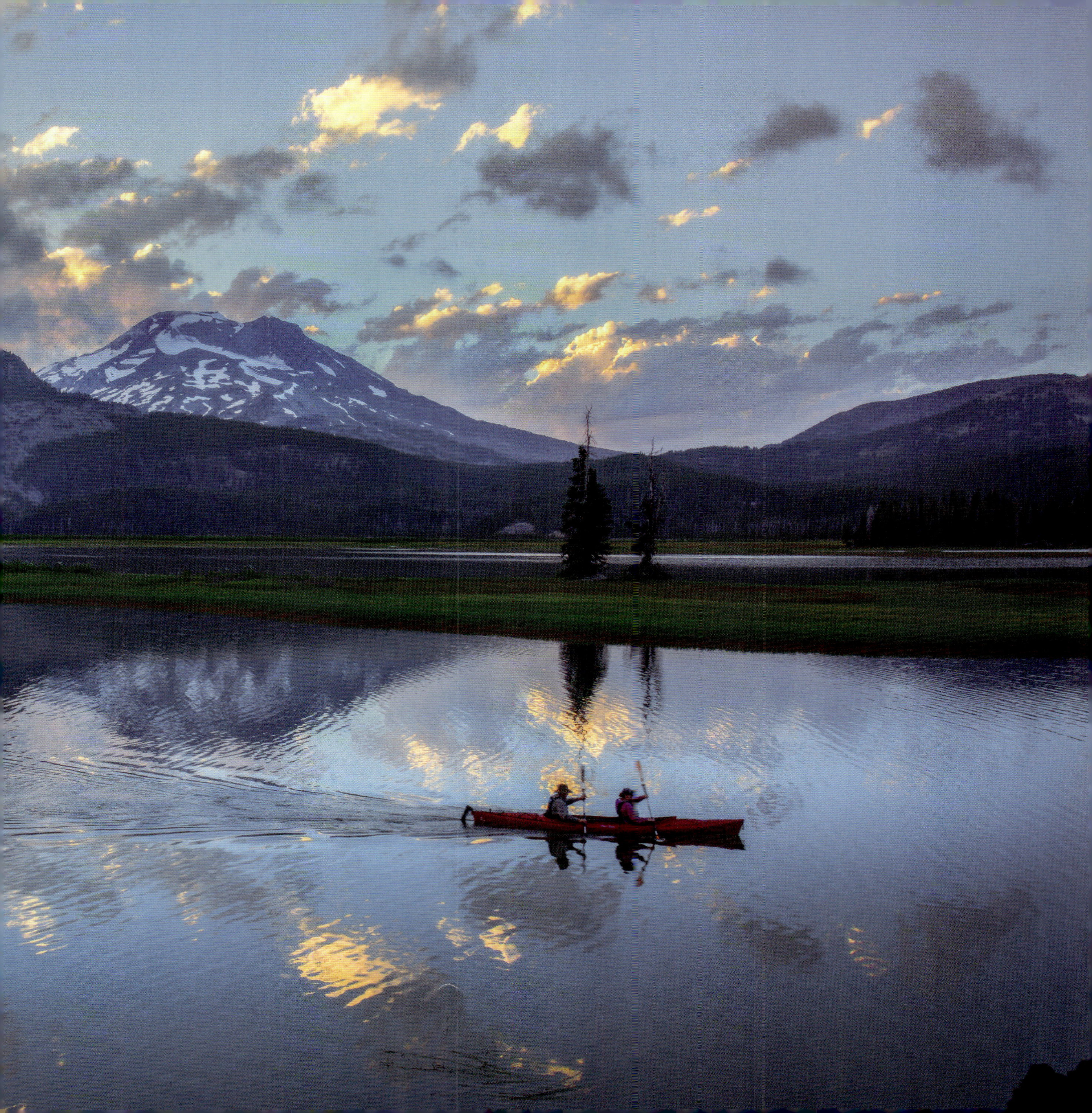

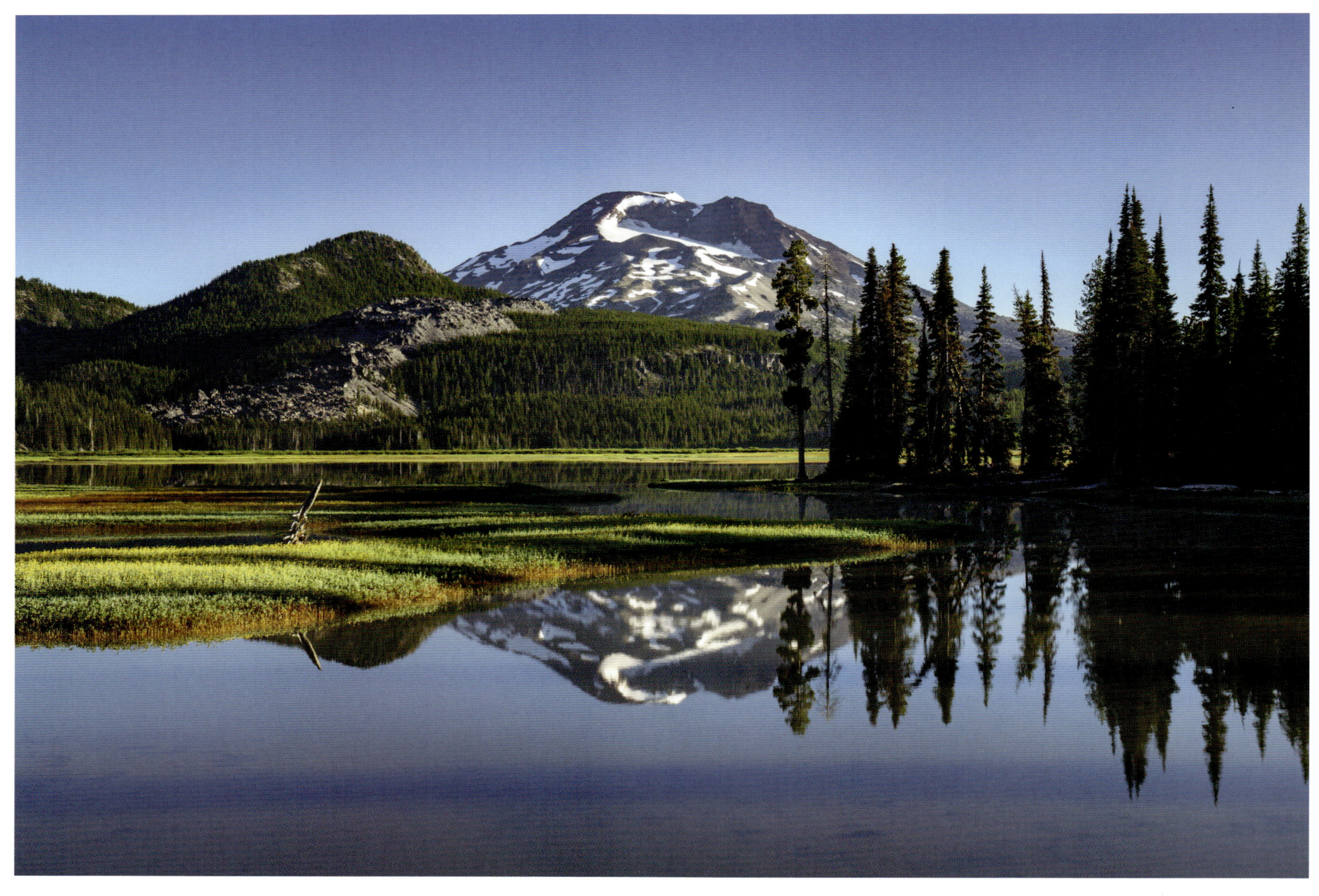

ABOVE   The South Sister mirrored in the pristine morning waters or Sparks Lake. •

RIGHT   No Name Lake flowing into a small stream during summer in the Three Sisters Wilderness, with Broken Top in the background. •

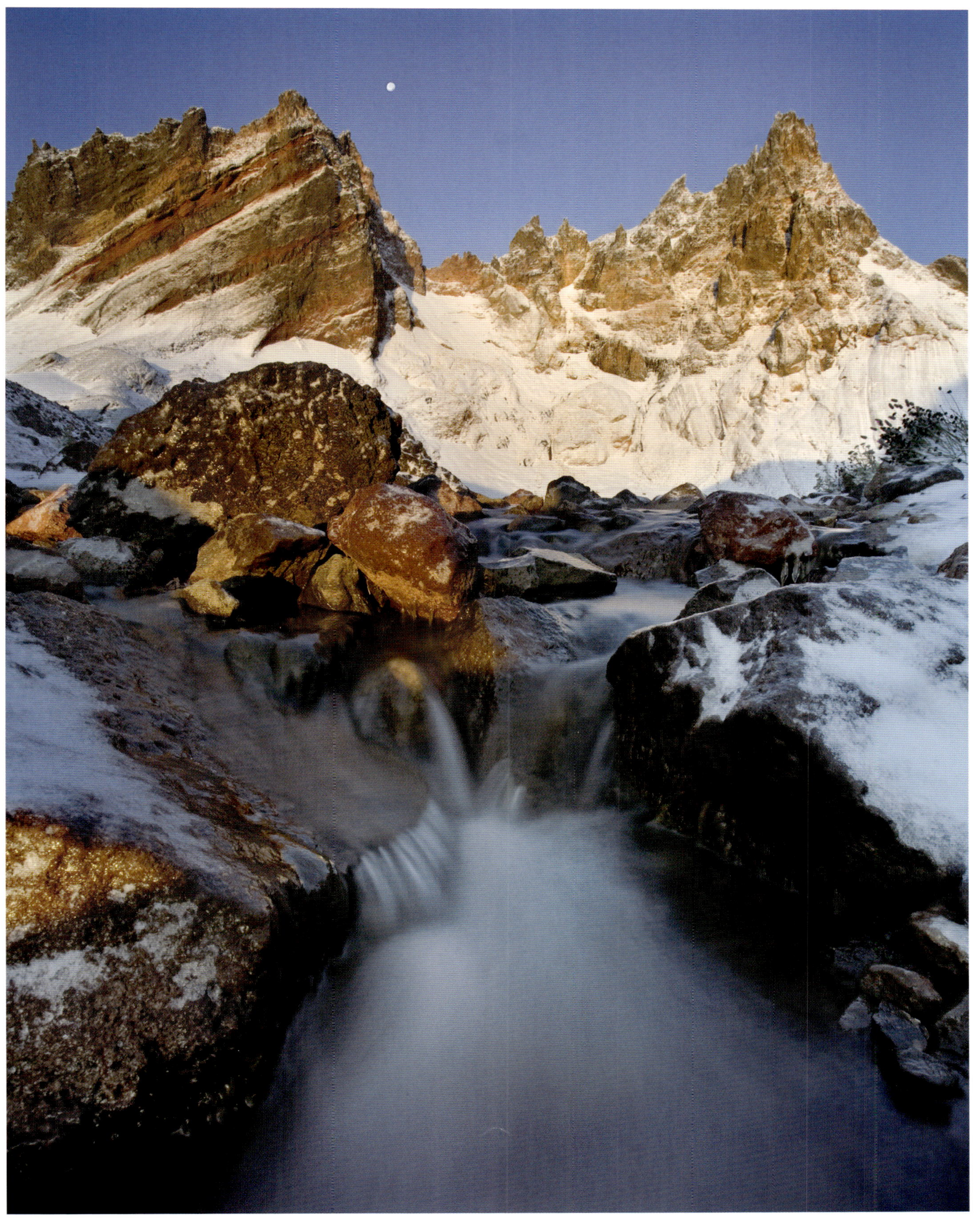

A clearing winter storm reveals a pristine
blanket of snow on the landscape around
the Three Sisters and Broken Top. •

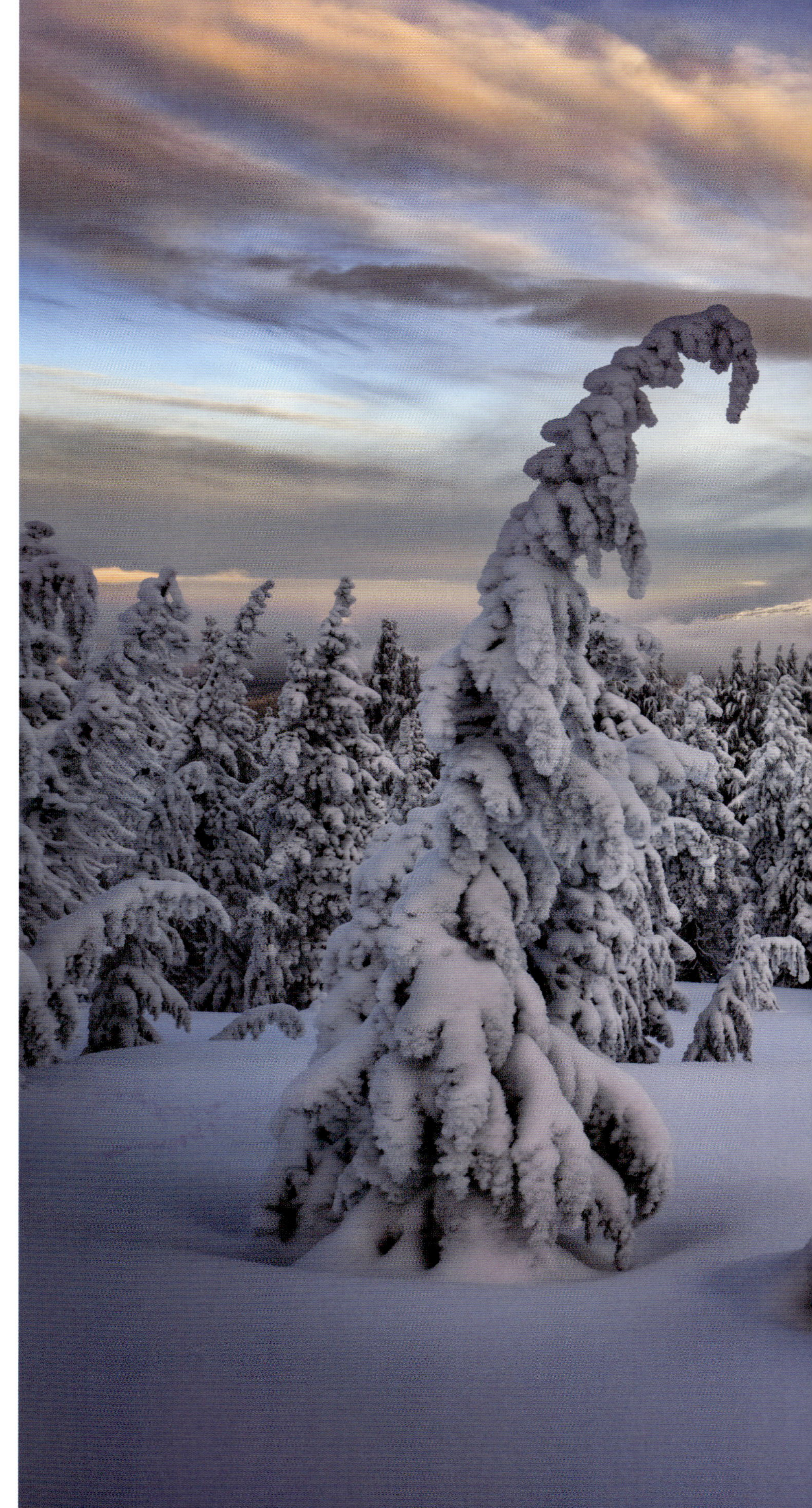

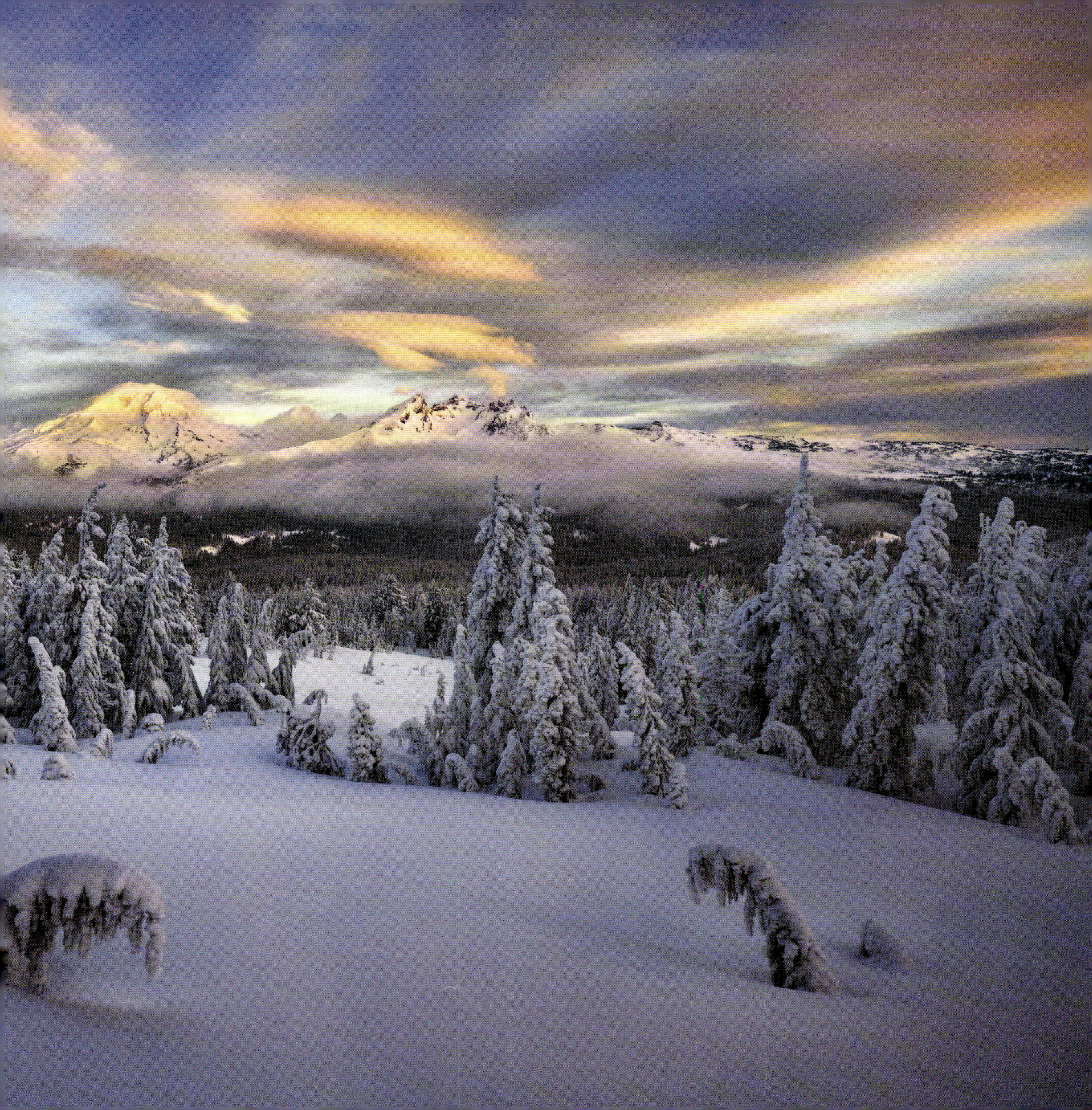

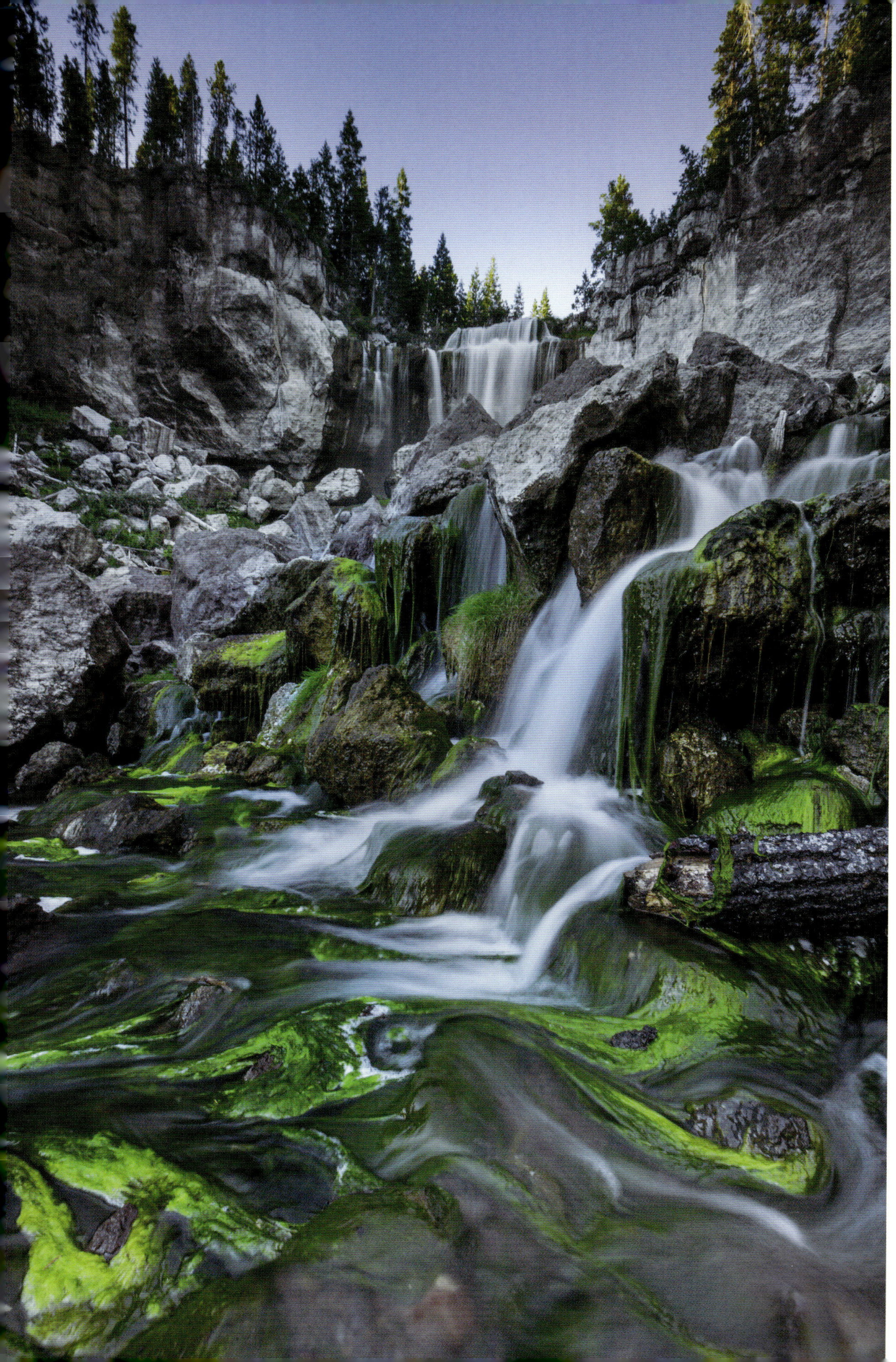

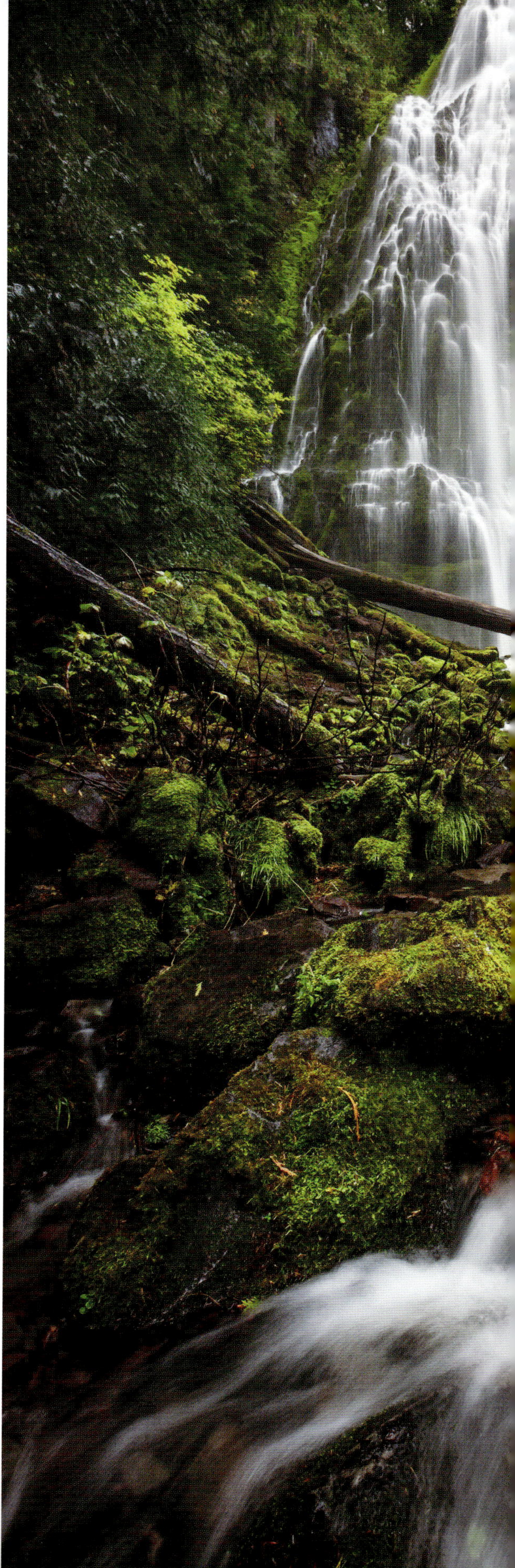

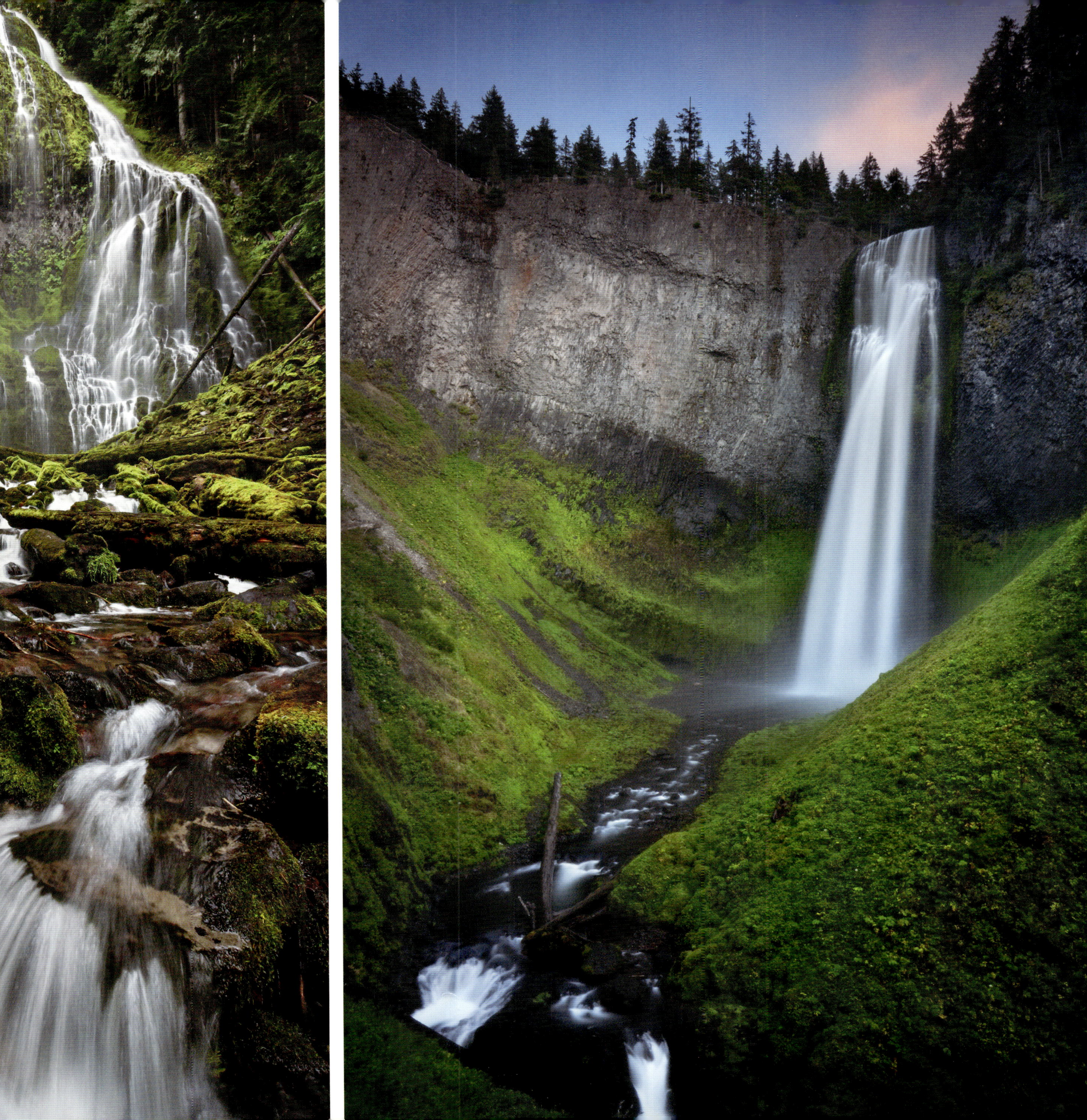

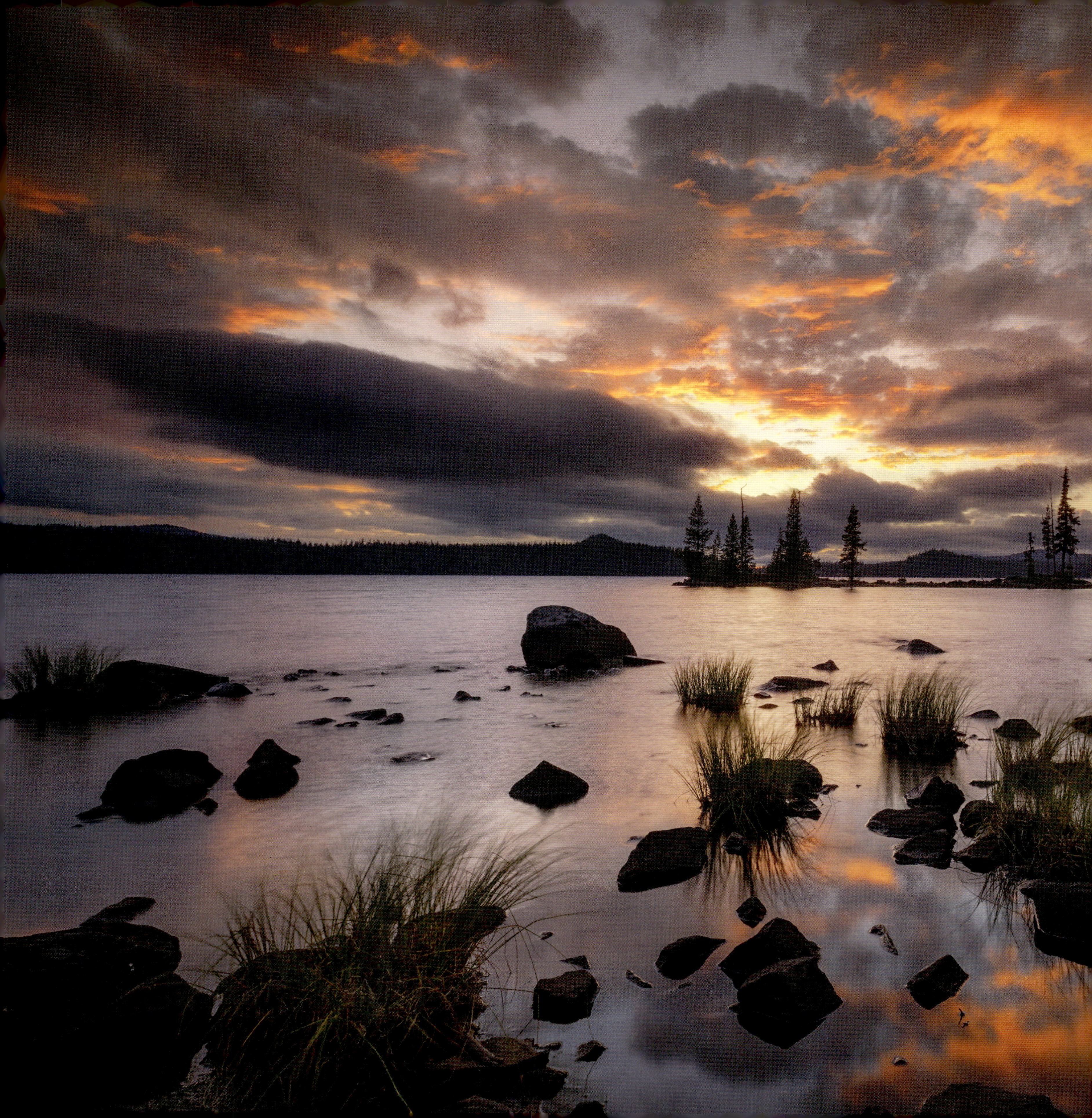

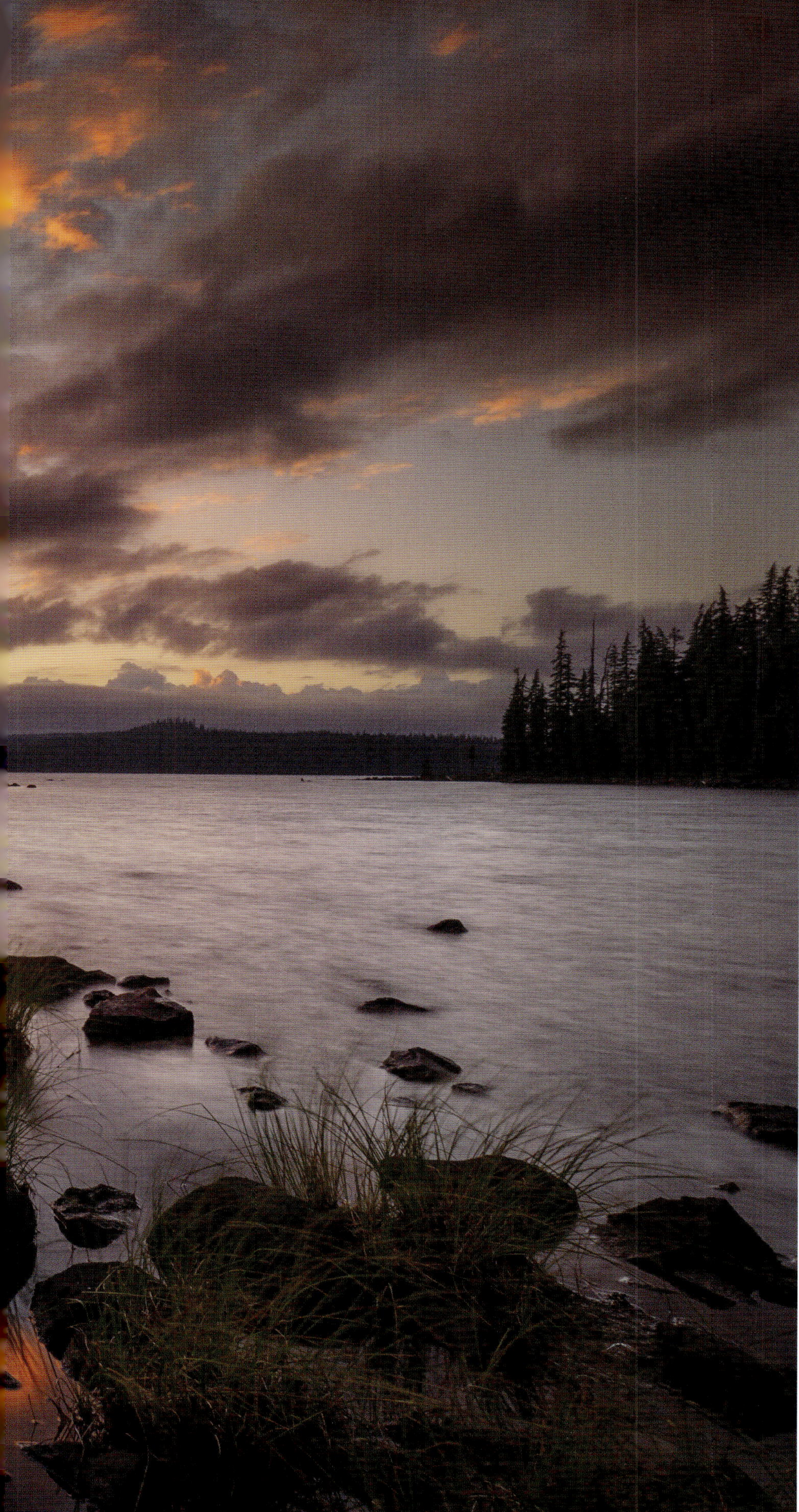

PREVIOUS PAGES, LEFT TO RIGHT
View from the base of Paulina
Creek Falls which falls over 80 feet
over volcanic rocks near the town of
La Pine. • Proxy Falls, a cascade-
and-plunge waterfall in the Willamette
National Forest that drops 226 feet into
a deep canyon. • Salt Creek Falls, near
Willamette Pass, runs through a deep
canyon carved by glaciers and drops 286
feet, making it the third-highest waterfall
in Oregon. •

LEFT   A late-summer sunset blazes
over Waldo Lake—the second-
deepest lake in Oregon. •

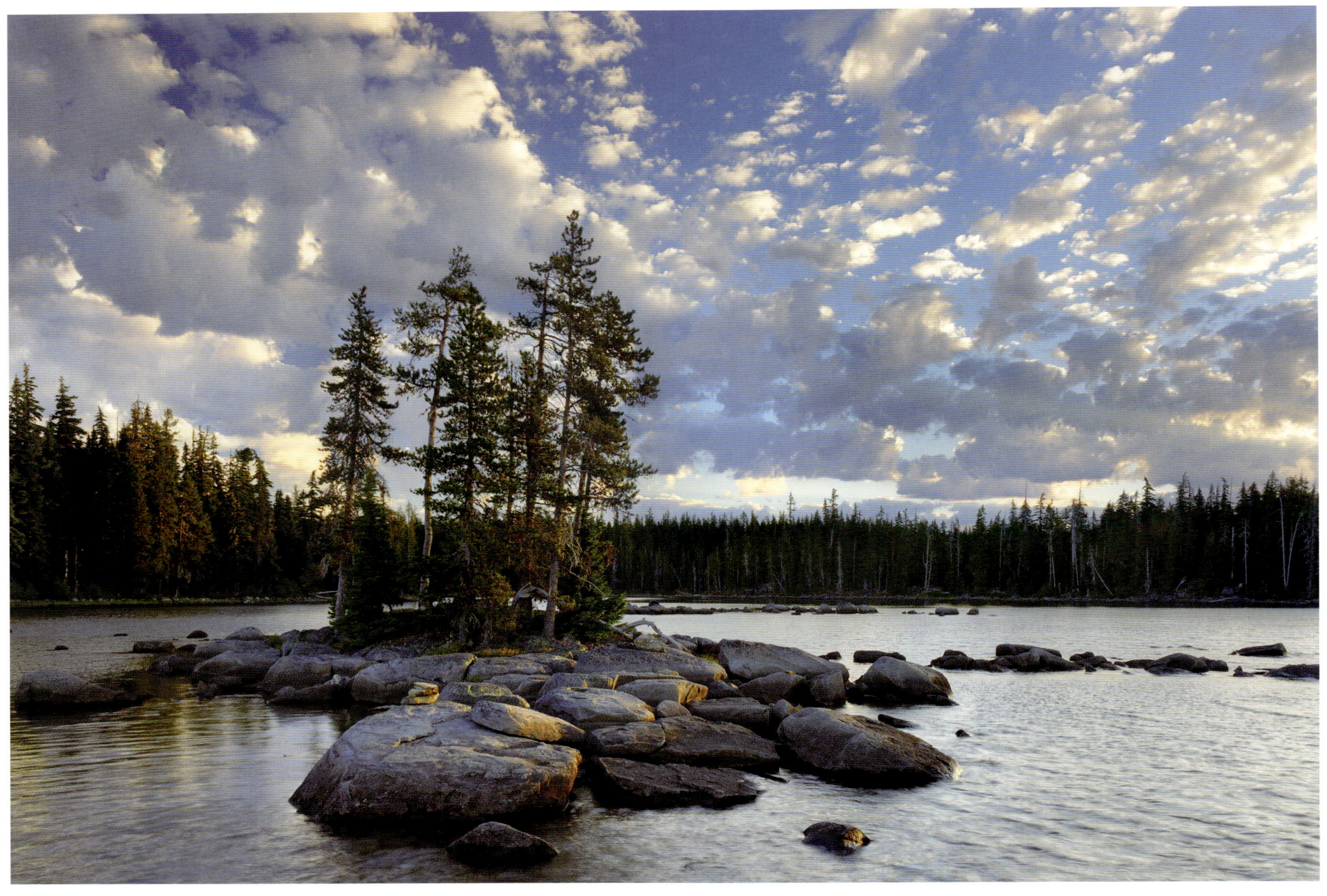

ABOVE Sunrise on one of the many small islands along the shores of Waldo Lake, so clear that on a sunny day visibility extends 120 feet into its depths. •

RIGHT Sunrise over Todd Lake and Mount Bachelor, blanketed by fresh snow. •

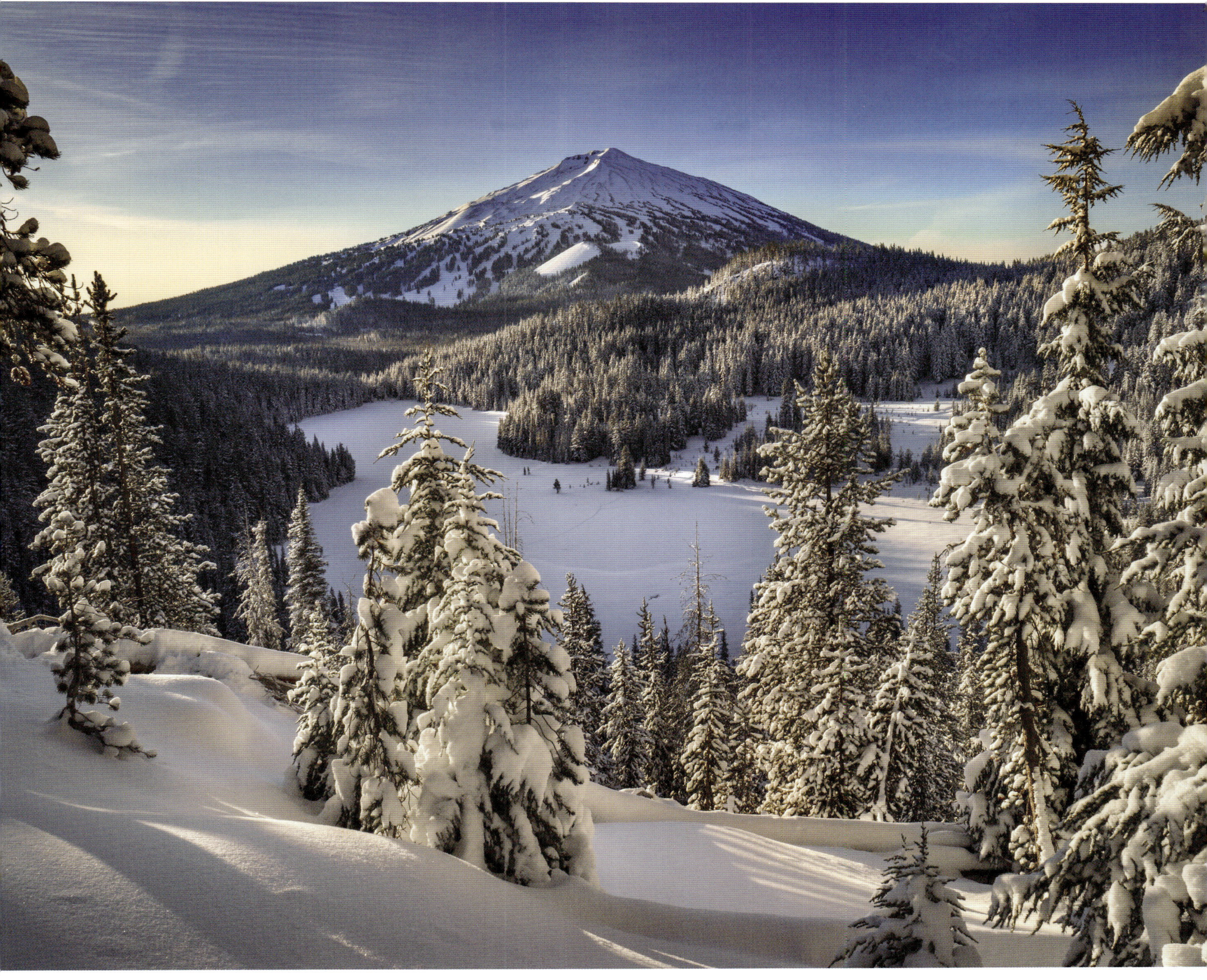

The waters of the Deschutes River
shoot through a cataract at Dillon Falls
near Bend. ●

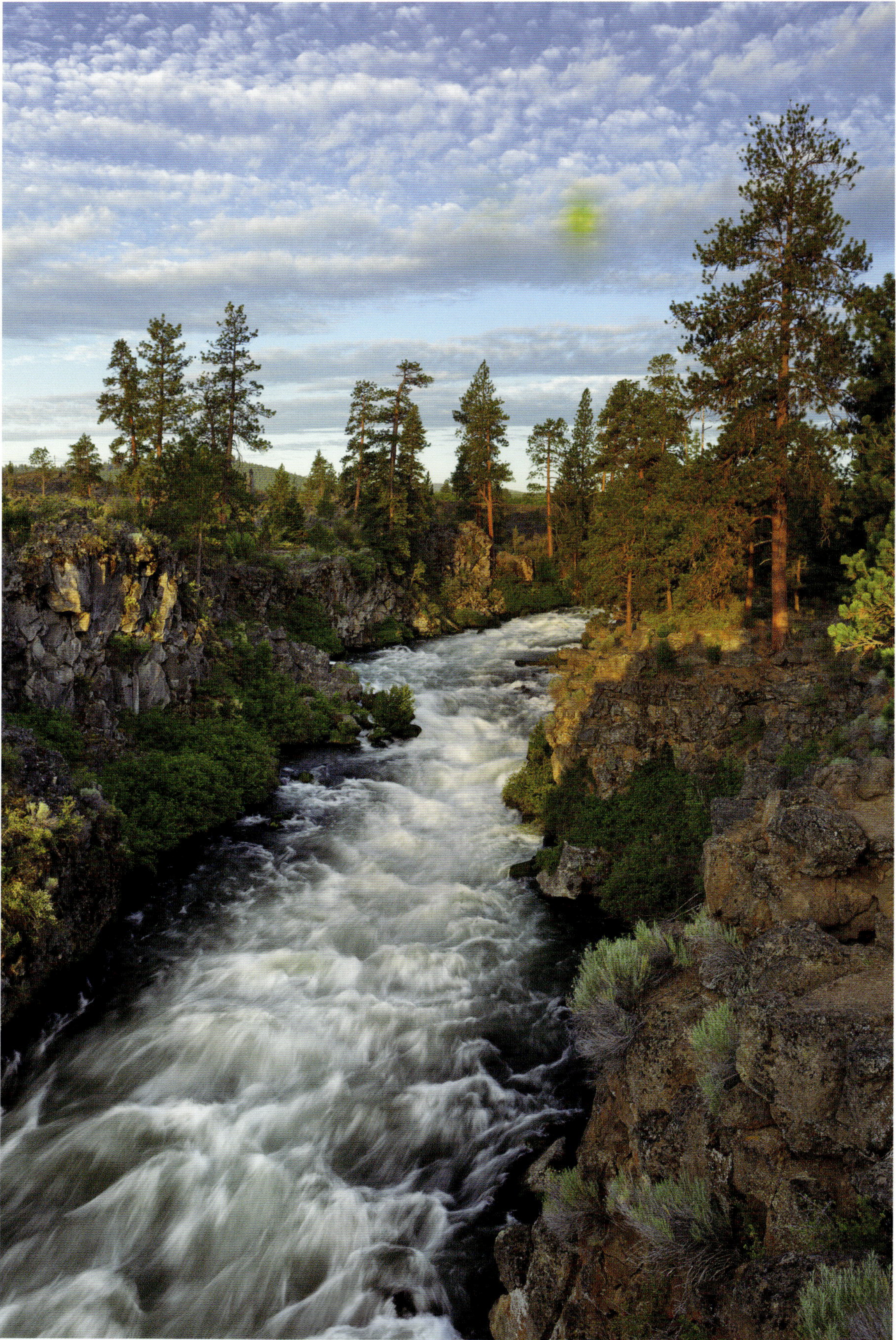

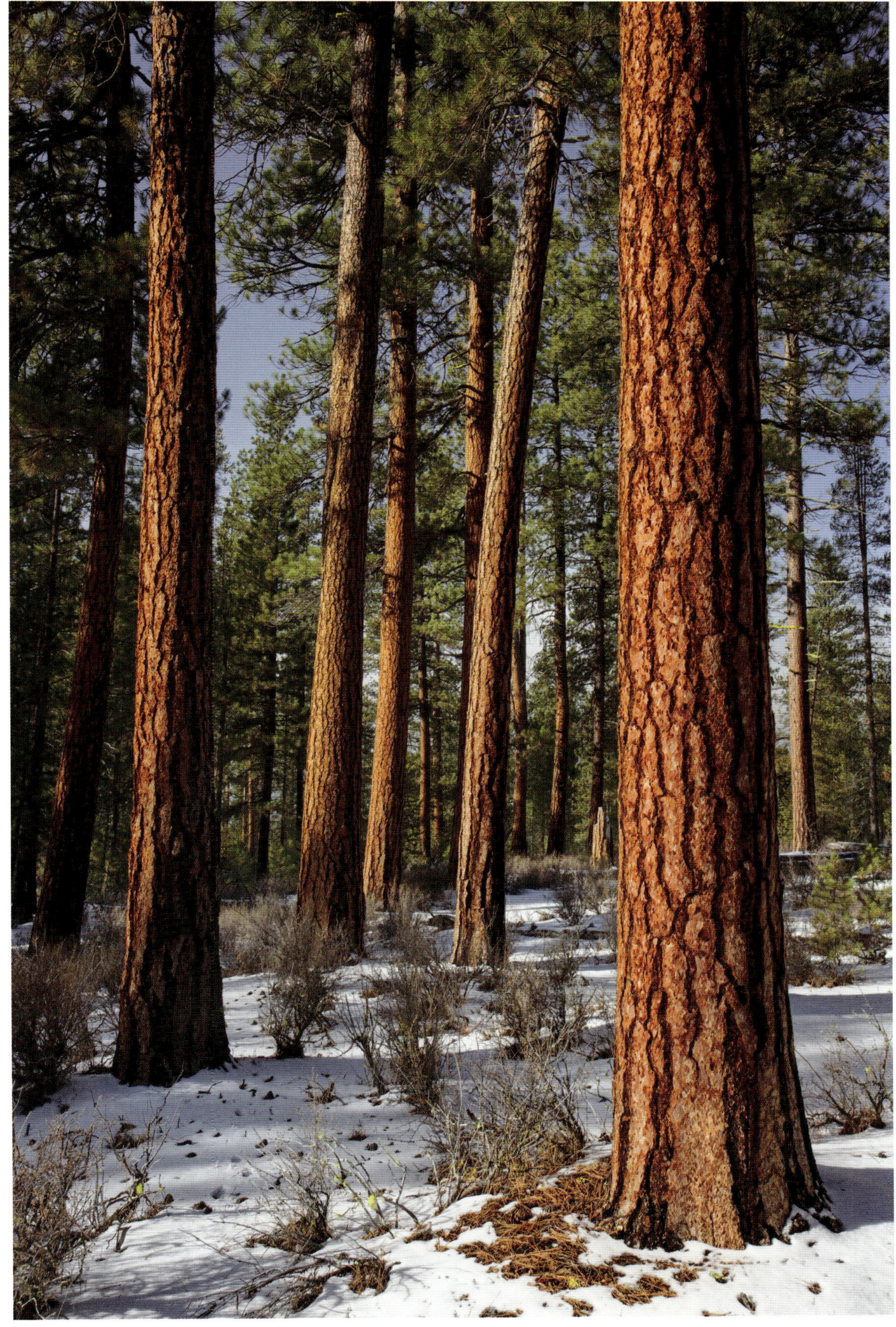

Ponderosa pines, identifiable by their tall straight trunks, orange-red bark, and bright green needles, grow on the eastern slopes of the Cascade Range. •

Various types of paintbrush (*Castilleja* spp.) grow among the grasses at the Hart Mountain National Antelope Refuge in the southeast part of the state. •

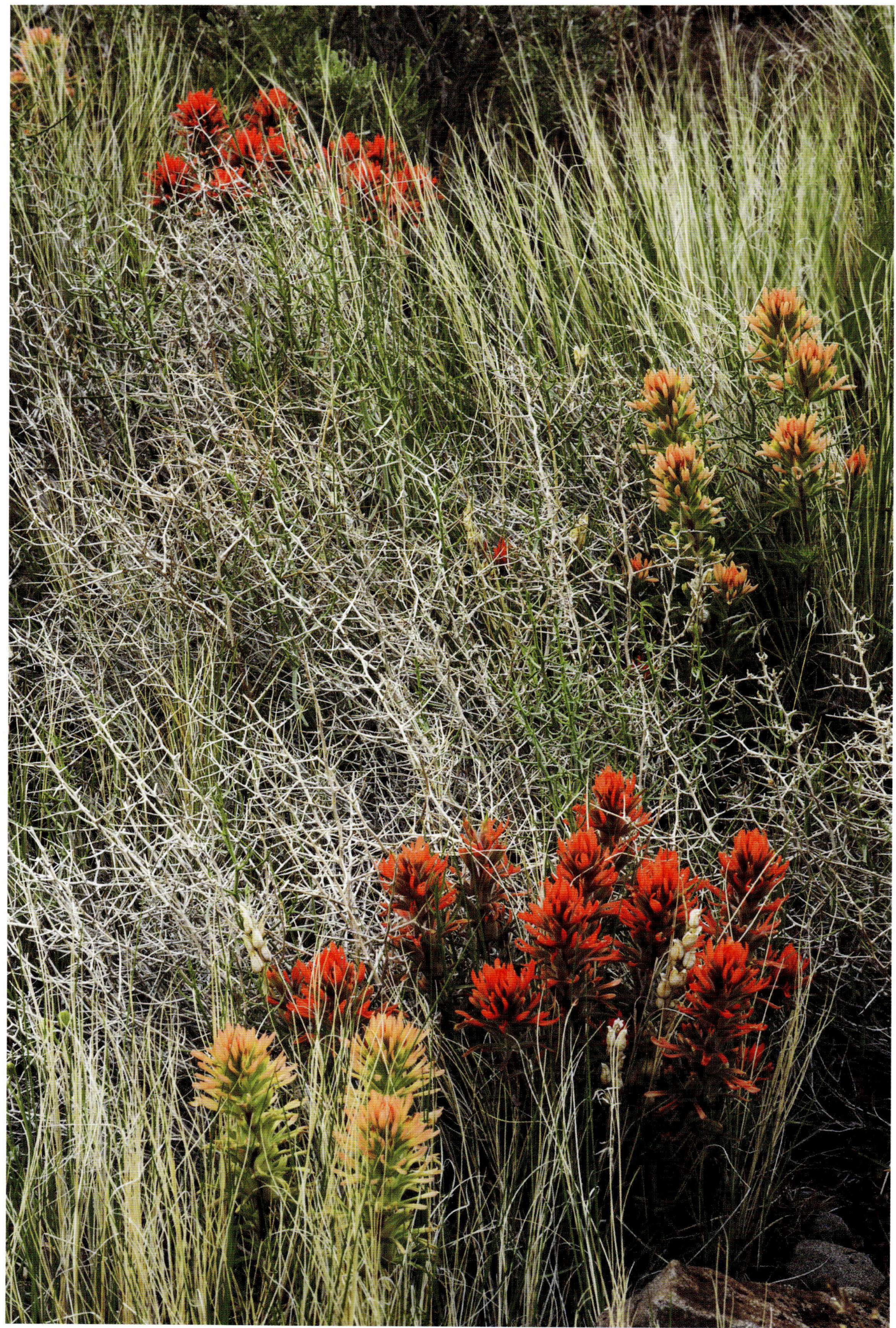

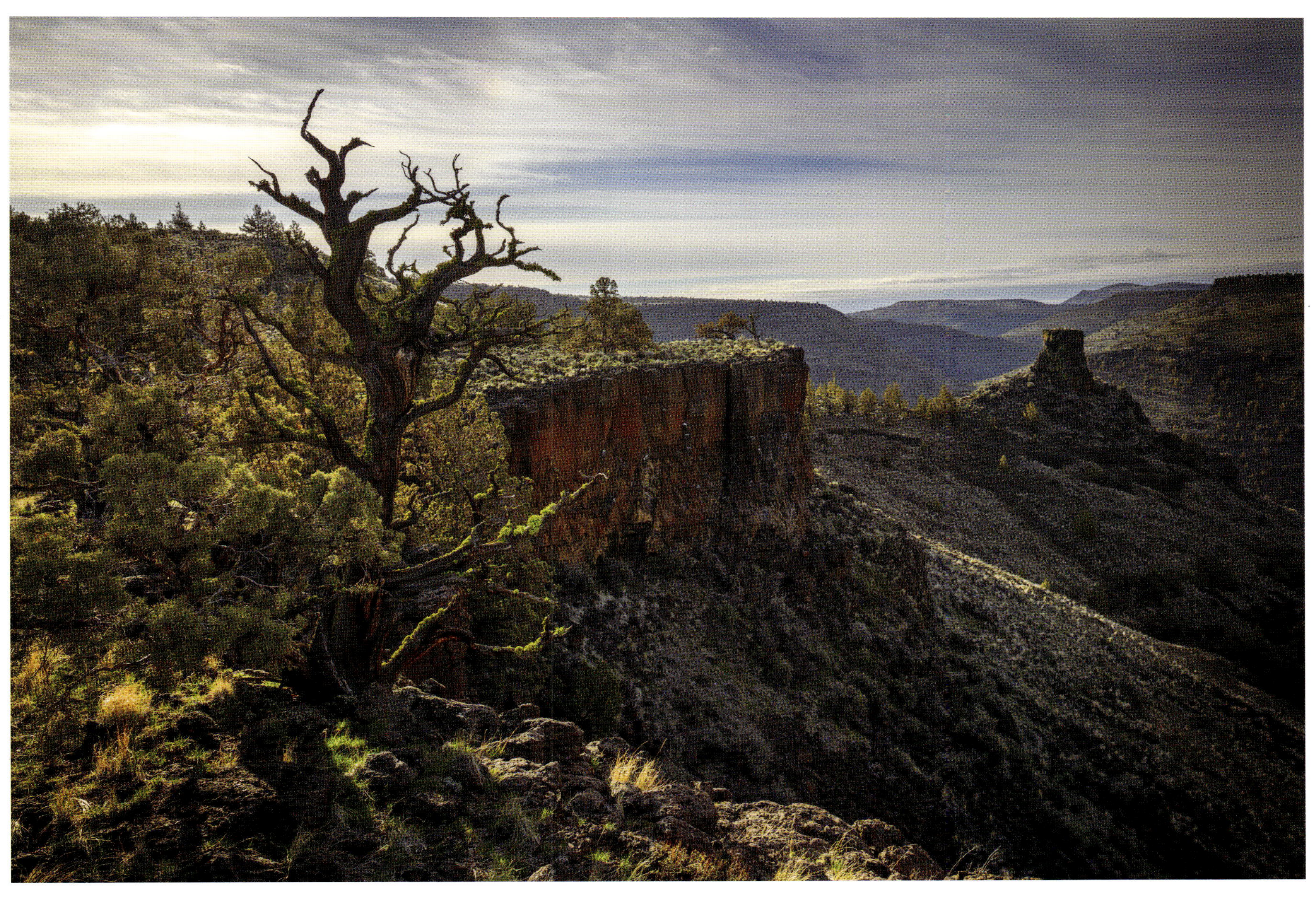

An ancient juniper tree, basalt cliffs,
and Chimney Rock look out over the
canyon of the Lower Crooked Wild
and Scenic River. •

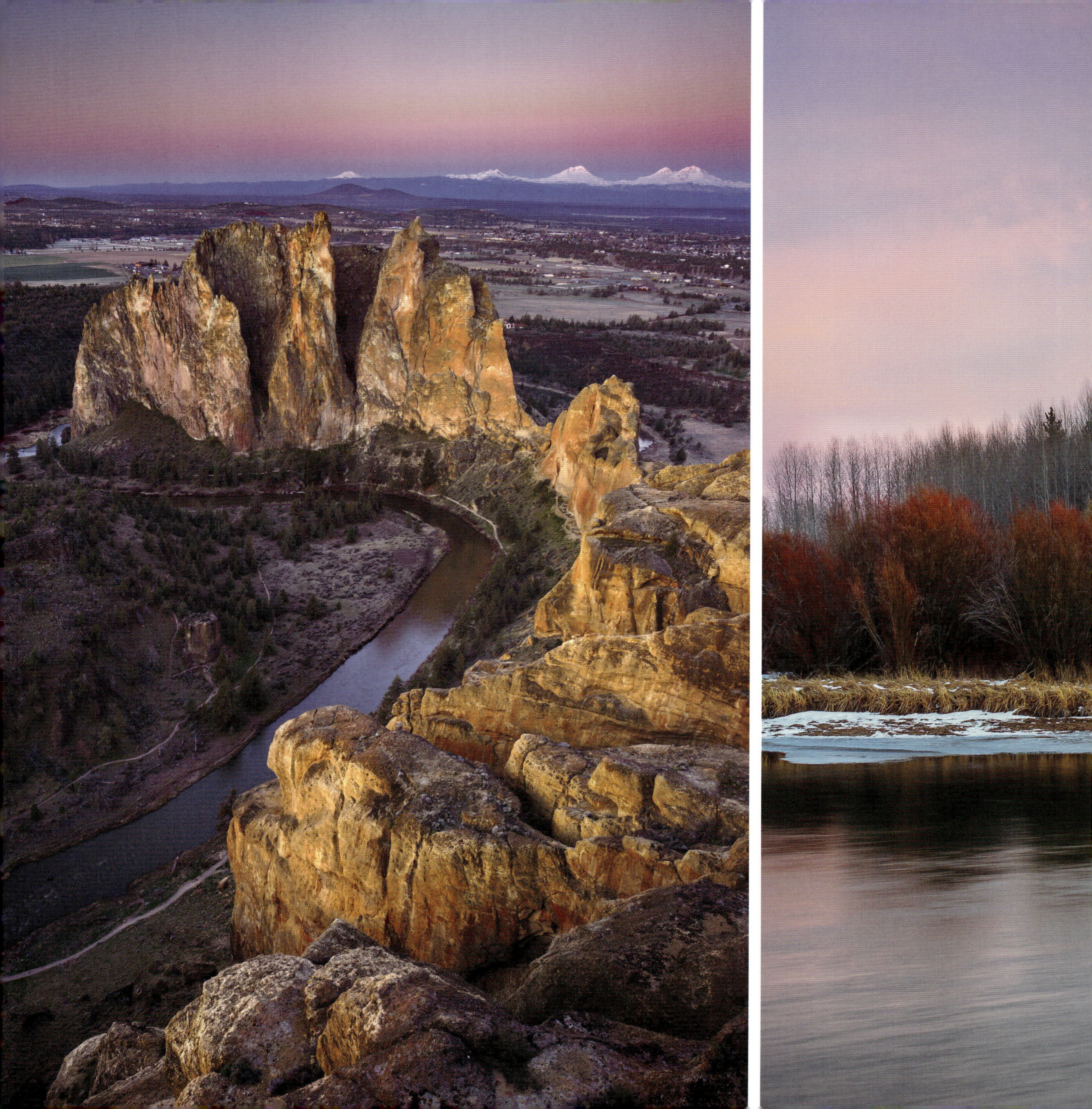

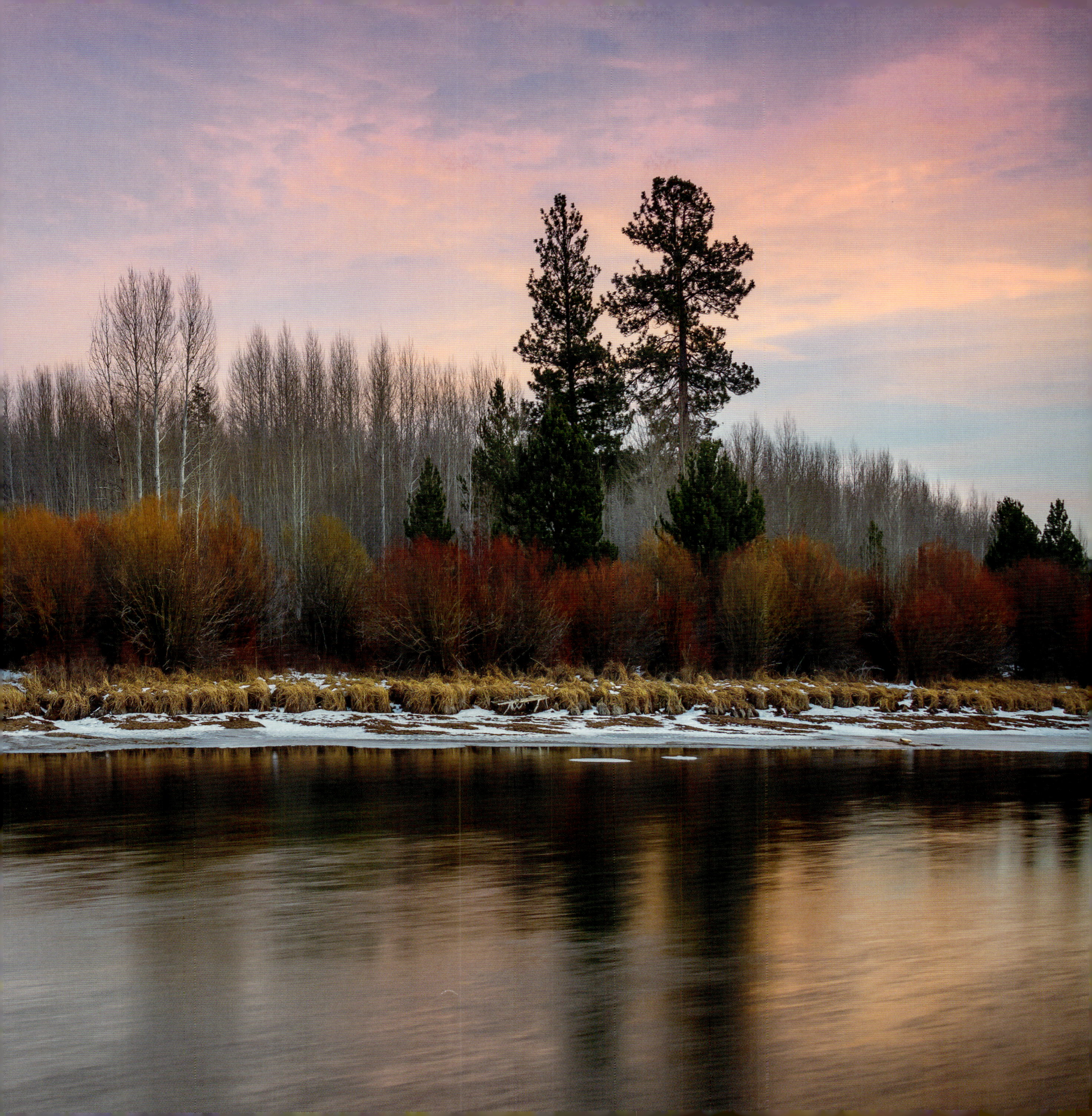

PREVIOUS PAGES, LEFT
A bird's-eye view at sunrise from one of the tallest pinnacles in Smith Rock State Park with the Three Sisters, Broken Top, and Mount Bachelor glowing in the background and the town of Terrebonne in between. •

PREVIOUS PAGES, RIGHT
Fall colors line the riverbank of the Deschutes River at twilight. •

RIGHT   The Crooked River winds its way around Smith Rock at sunset. •

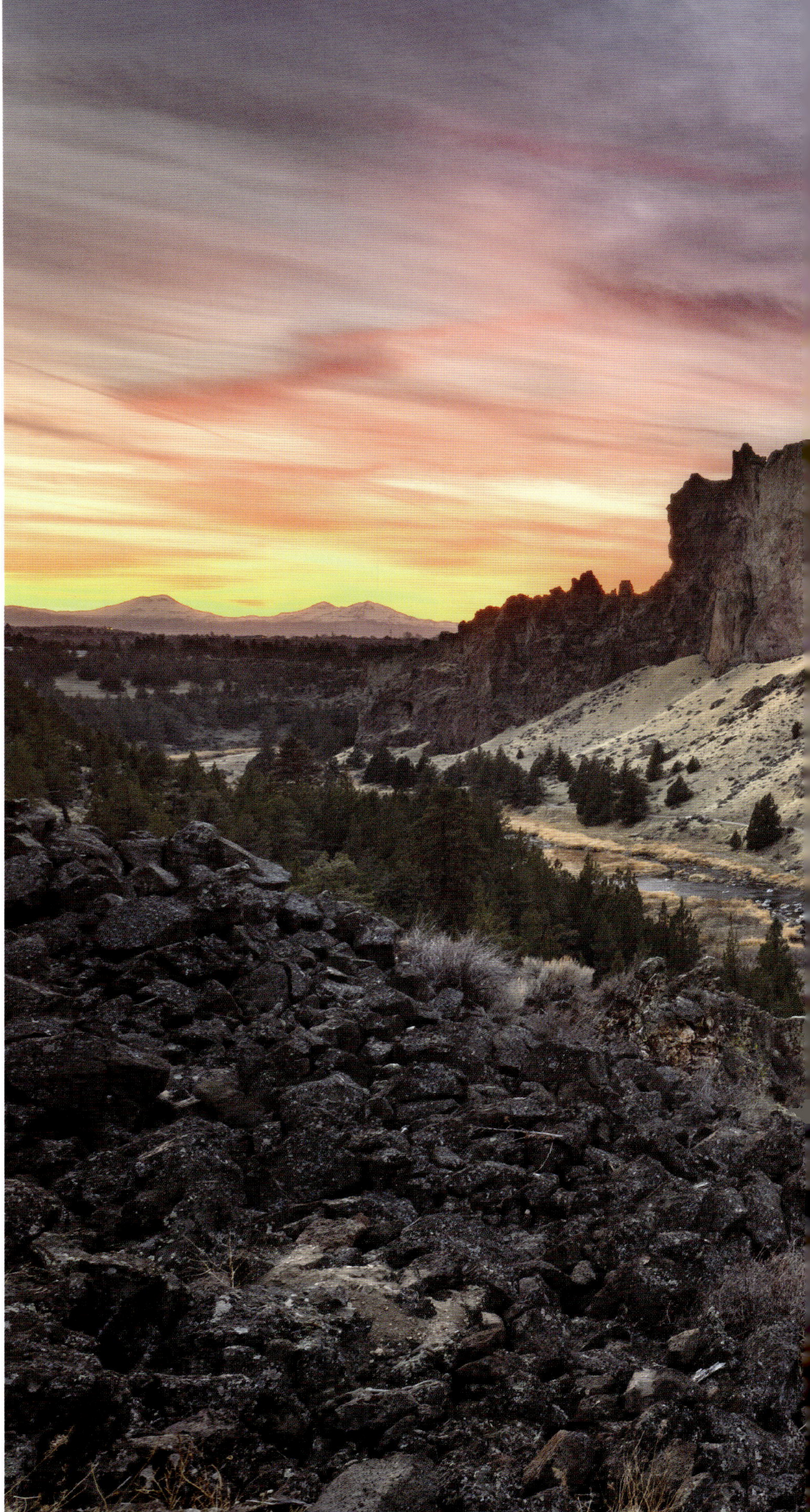

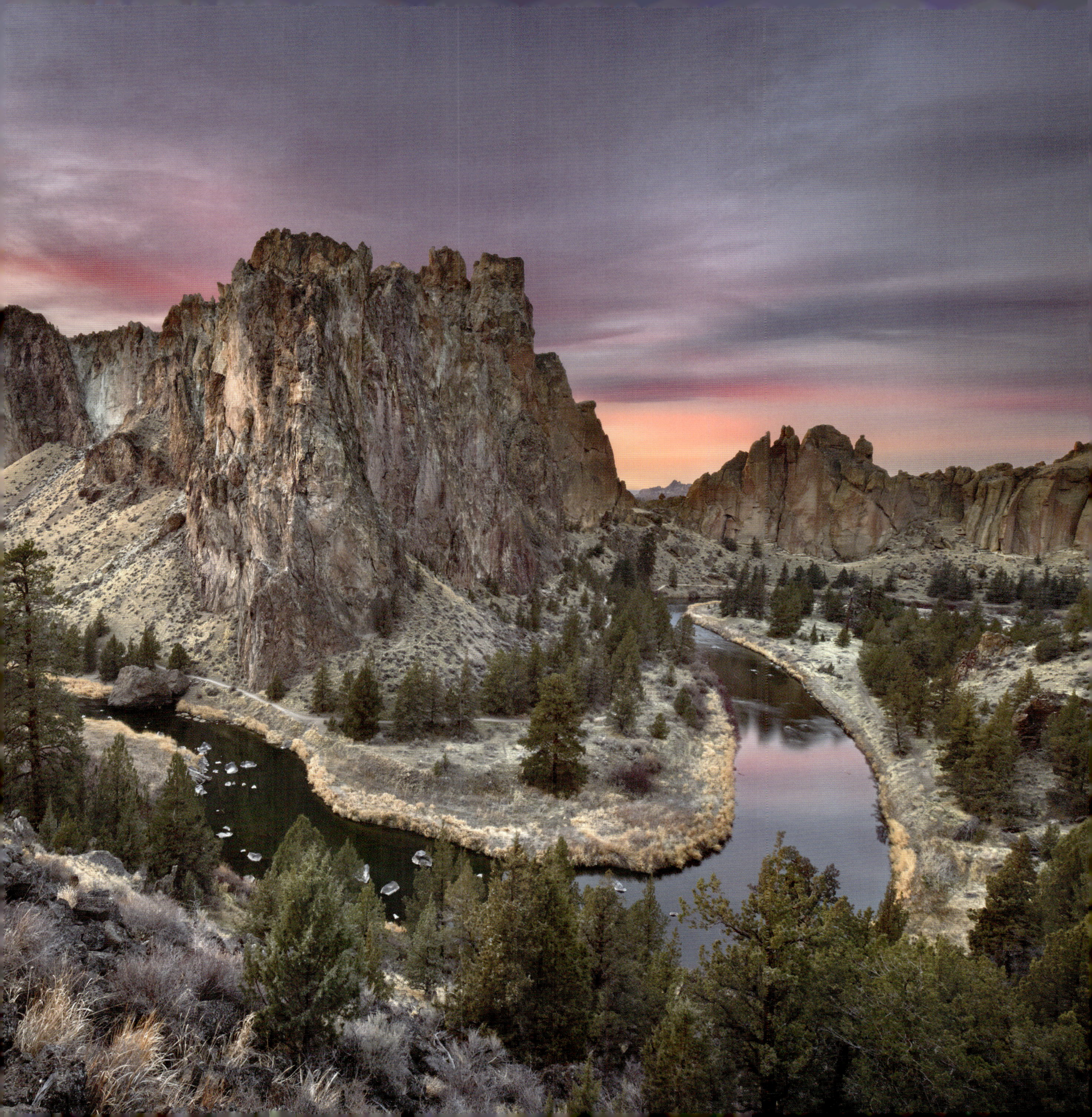

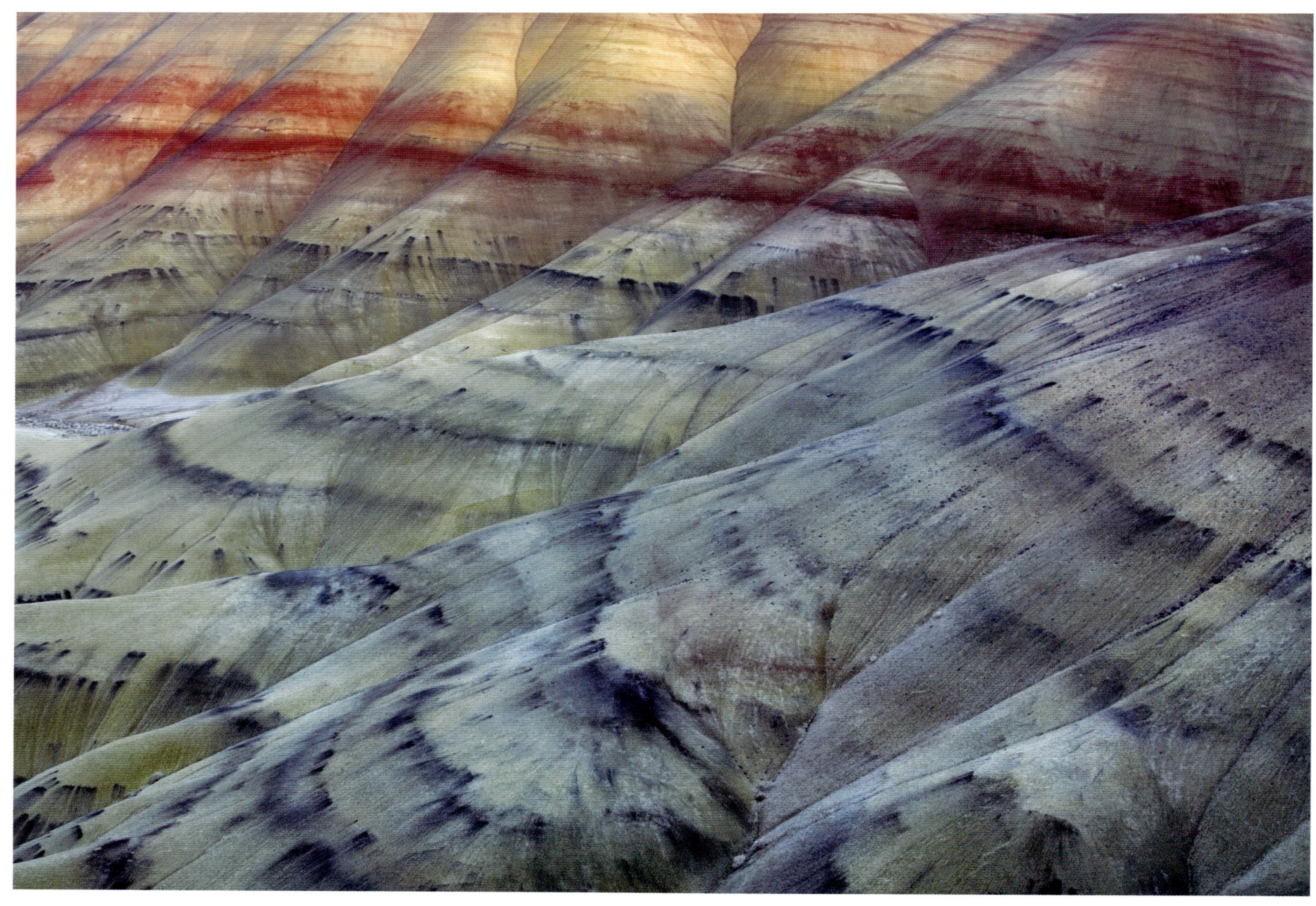

The Painted Hills in the John Day Fossil
Beds National Monument are famous for
their stratifications of yellows, golds, reds,
and blacks. •

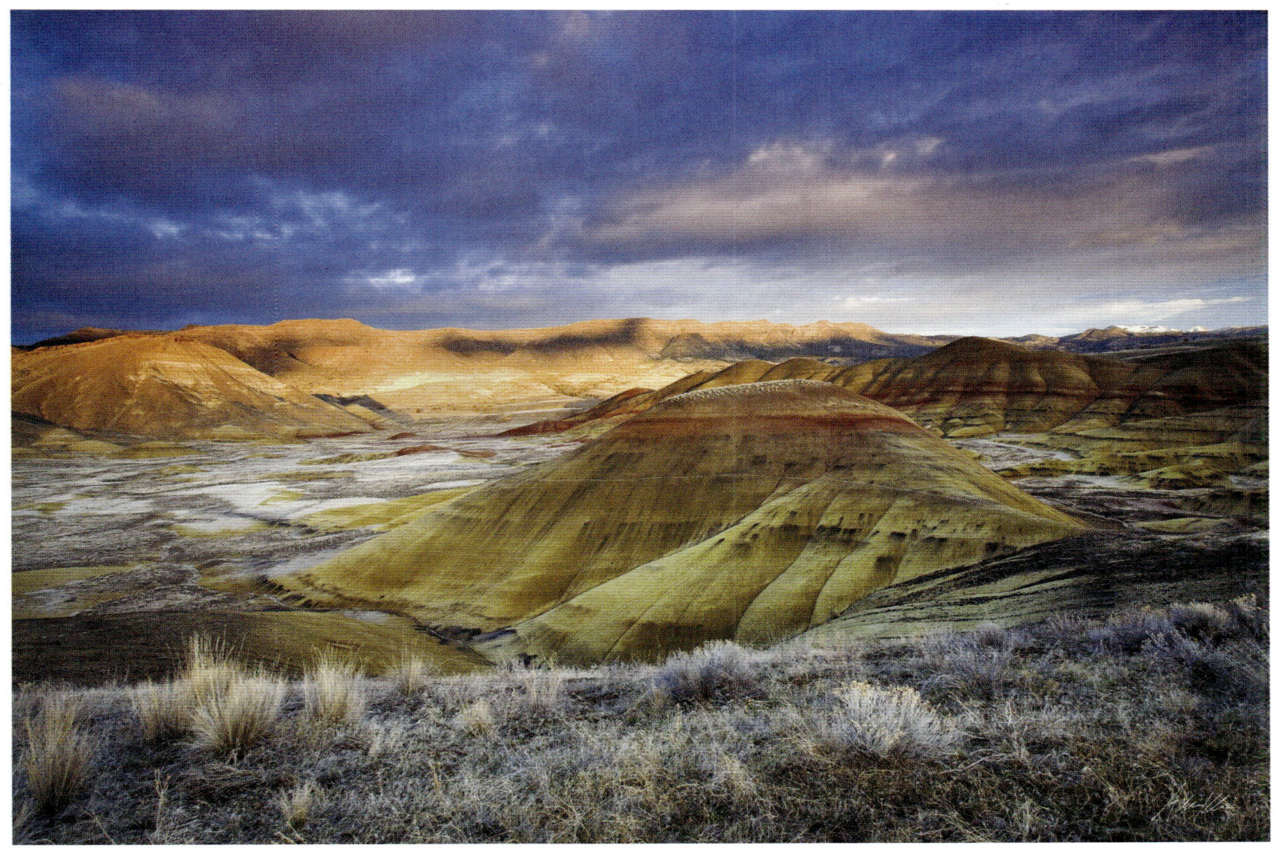

Shifting light can have a profound effect on the appearance of the Painted Hills.

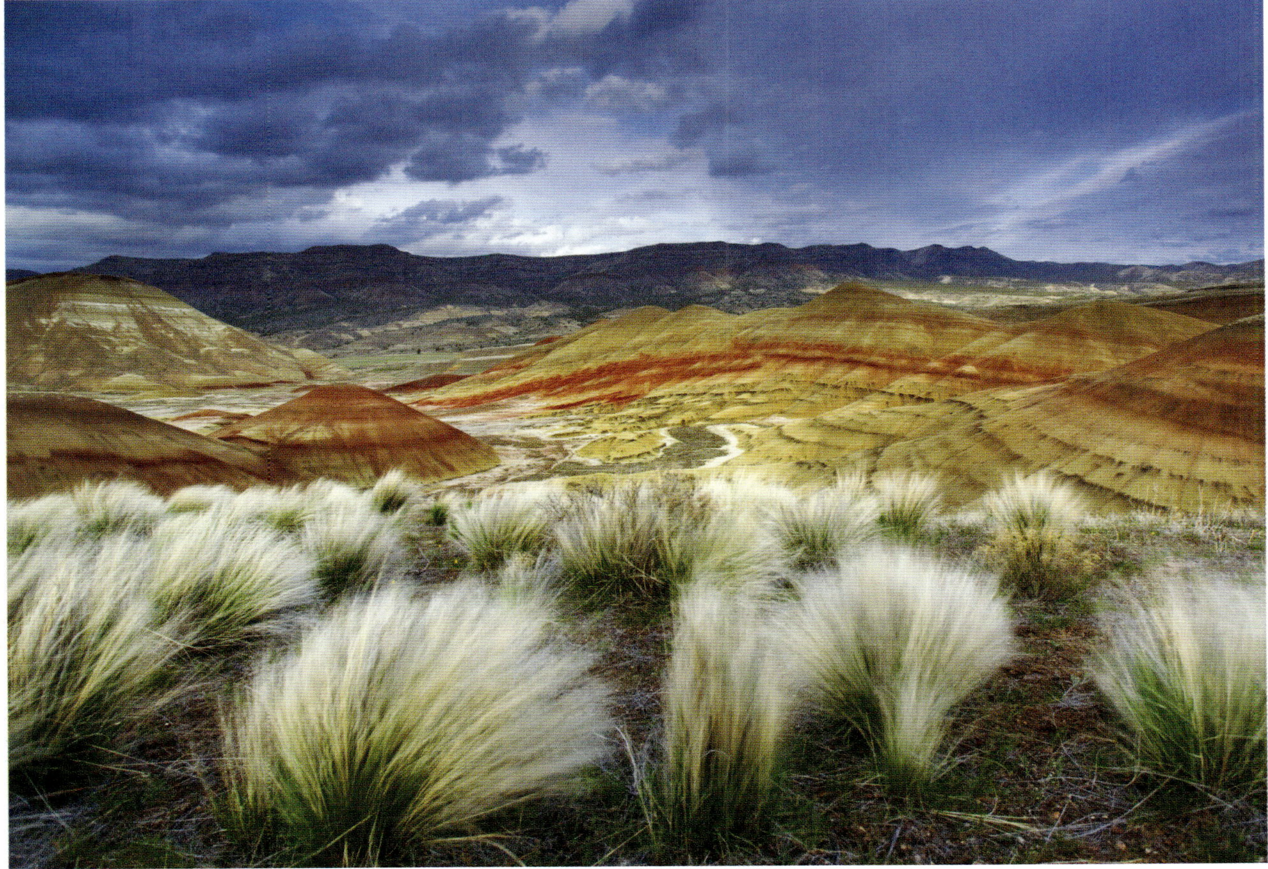

The hills' colored bands serve as a visual record of changes in climate over time.

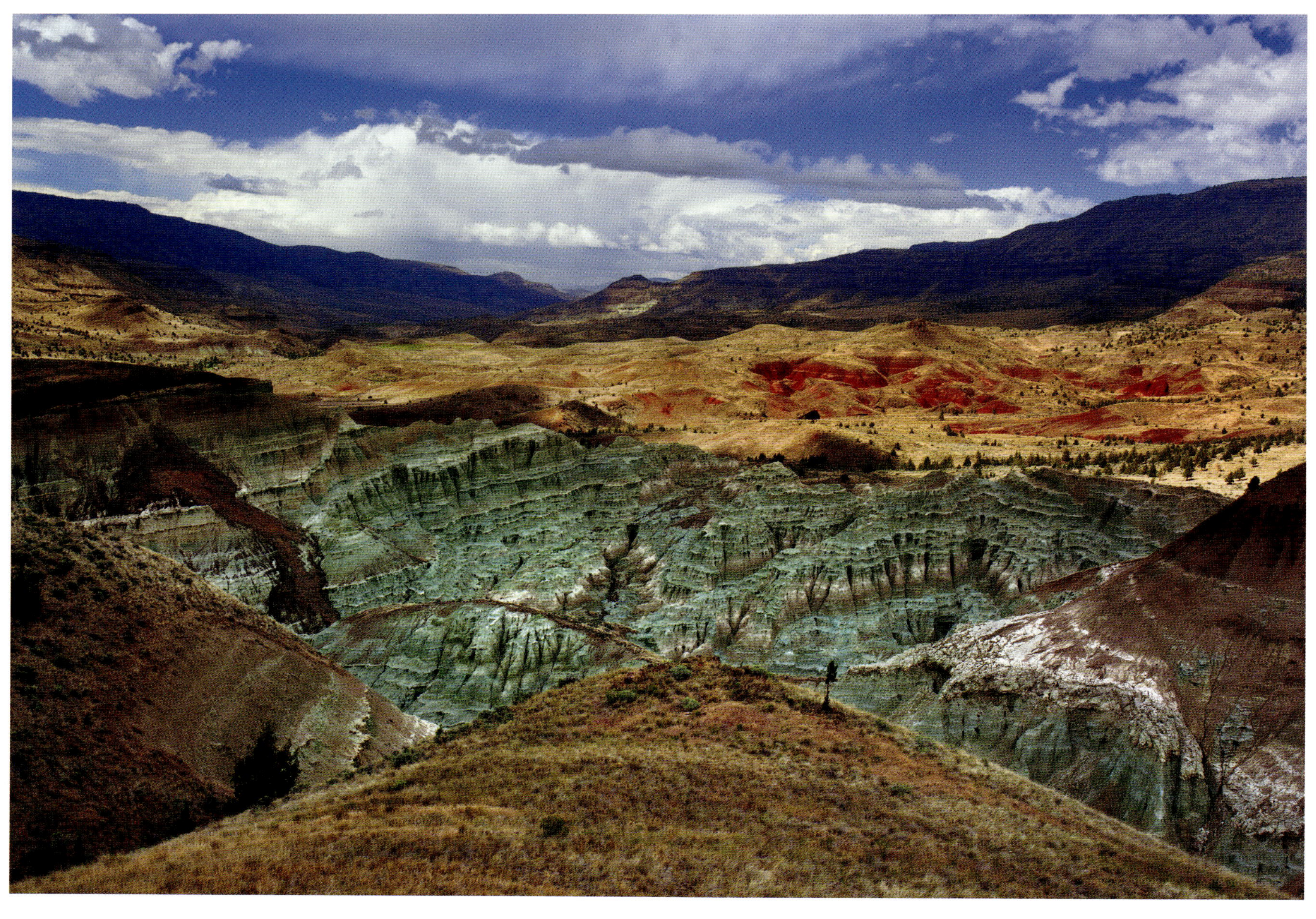

View from the Blue Basin Overlook Trail in the John Day Fossil Beds National Monument, Sheep Rock Unit. •

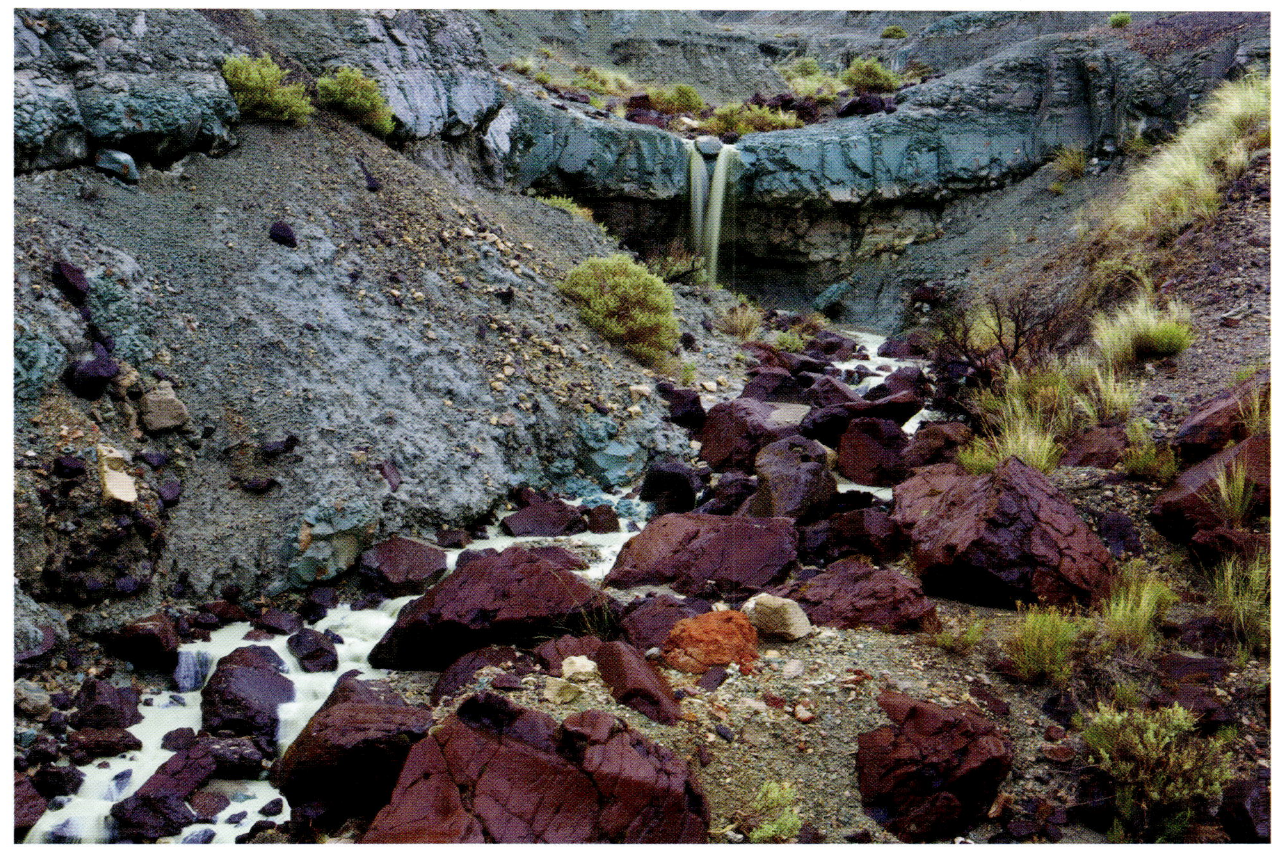

Water flows blue-green after a rainstorm over the Island in Time Trail, part of the Sheep Rock Unit. •

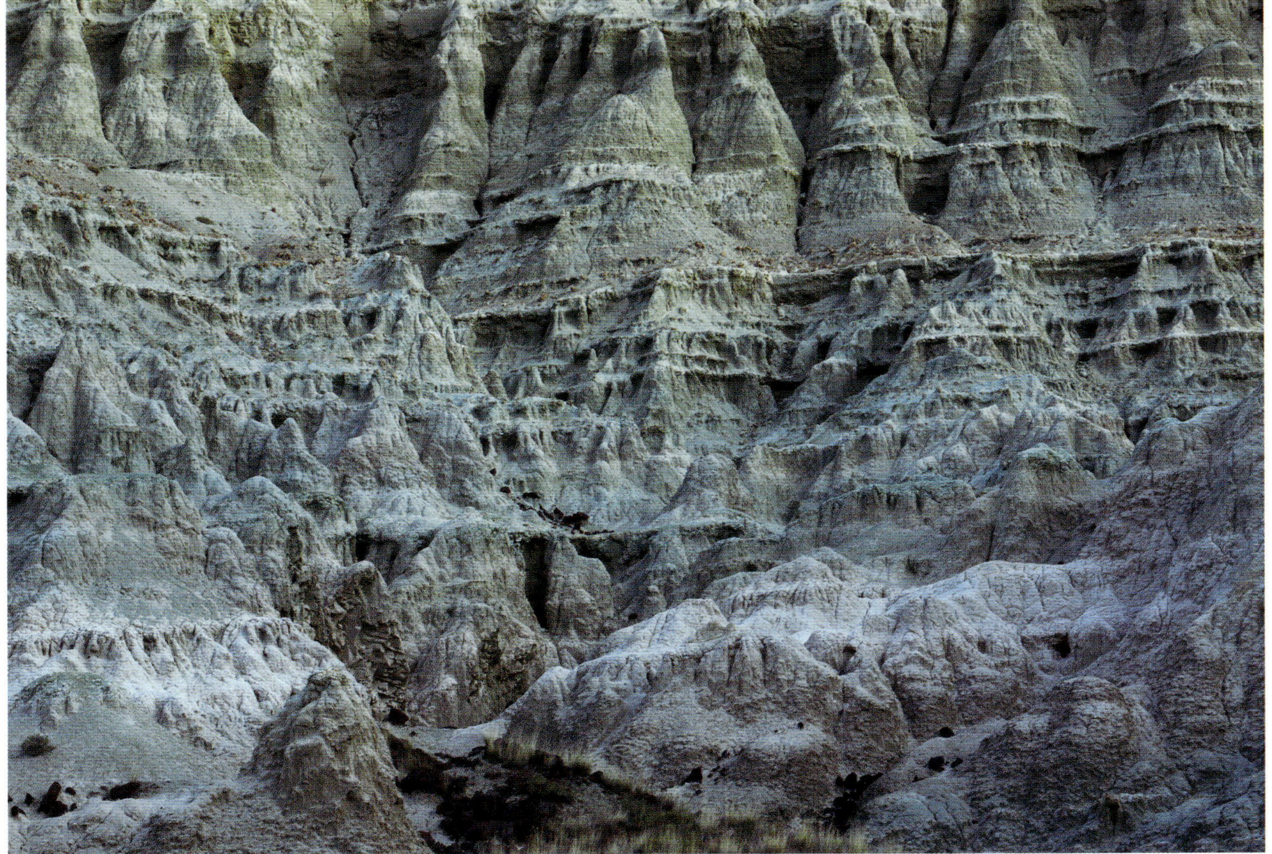

The Island in Time Trail takes you to the blue-green claystone of the John Day Formation. The color is caused by weathering of the mineral celadonite. •

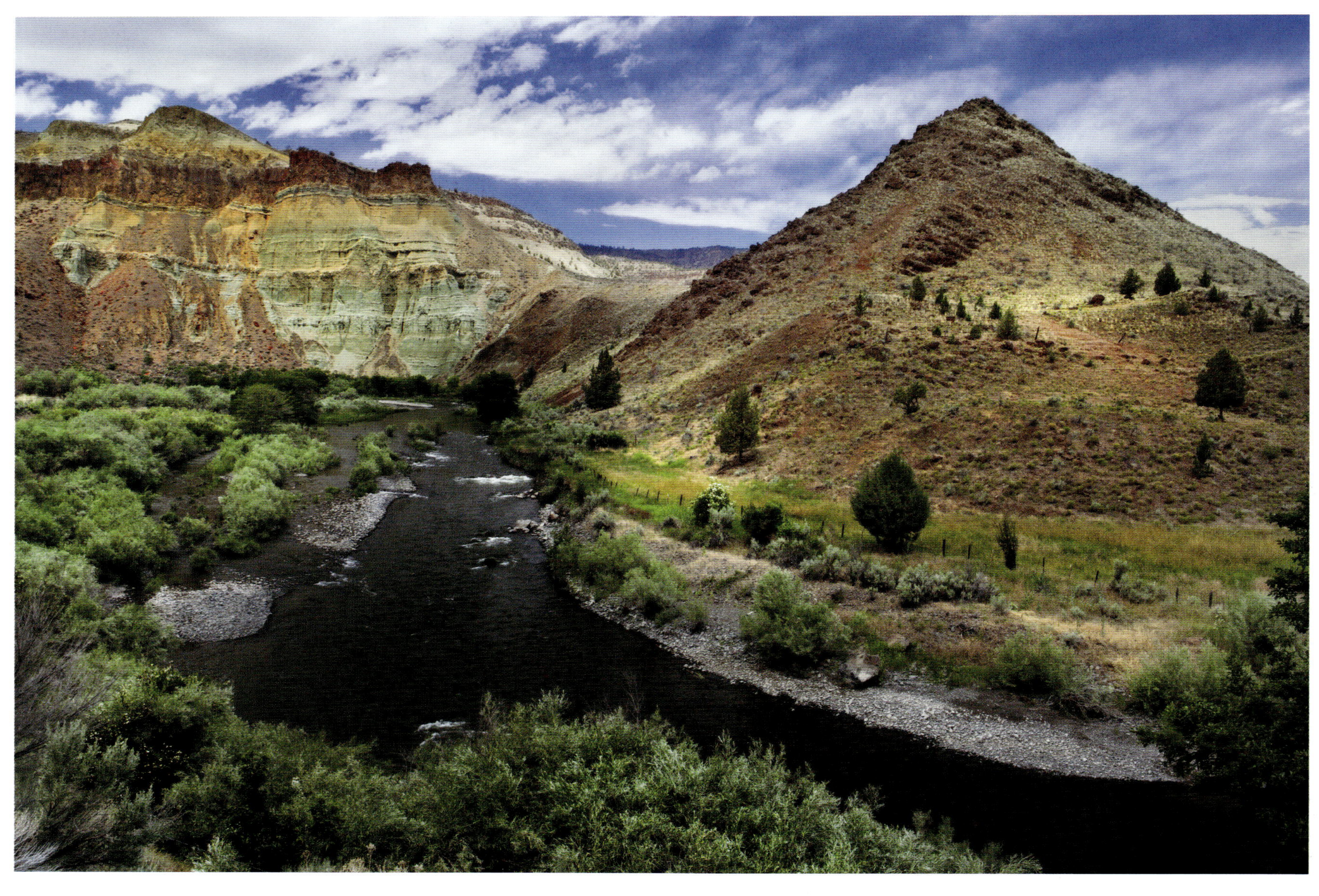

Cathedral Rock rises above the John Day
River in early summer.

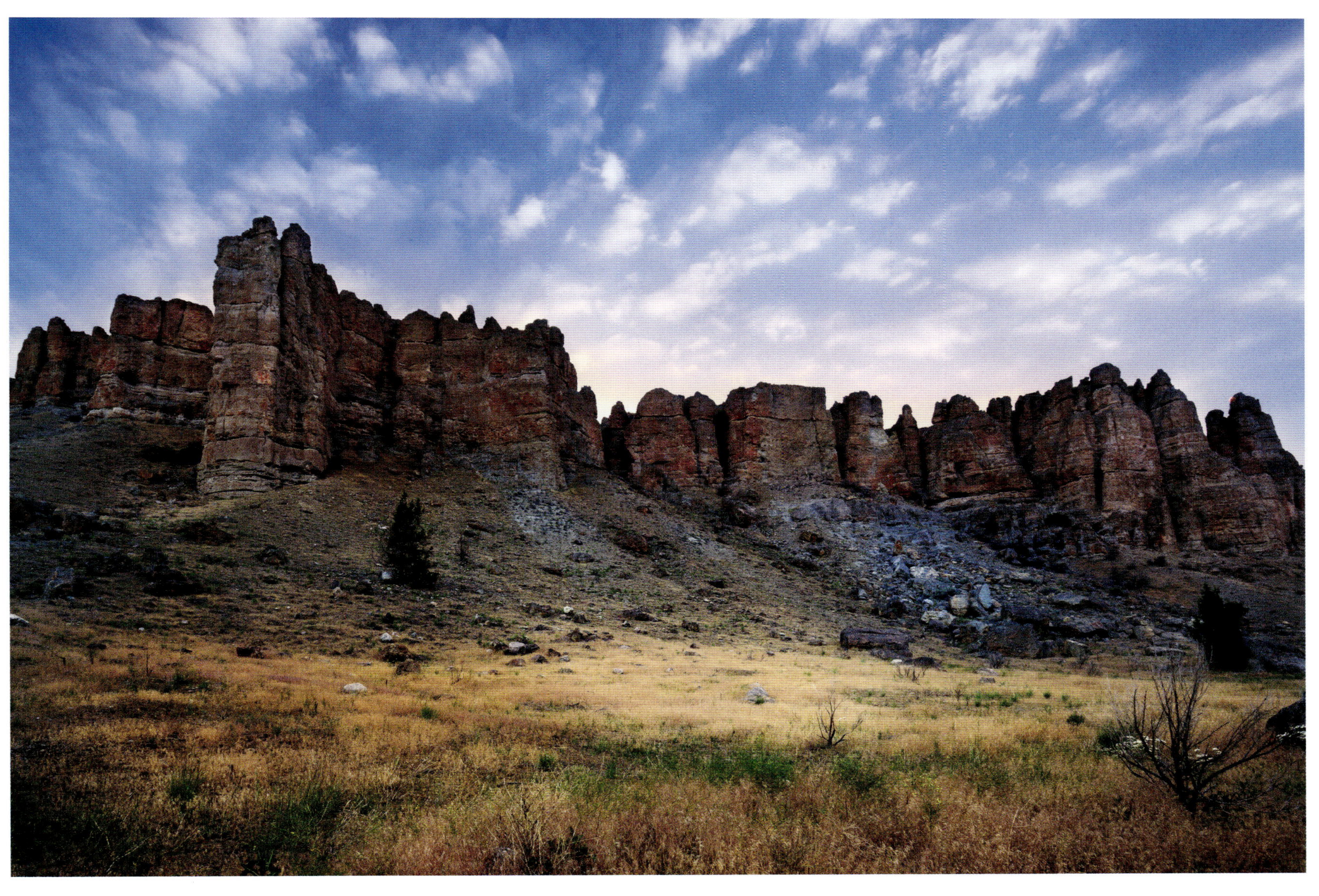

The Clarno Unit of John Day Fossil Beds National Monument, known for its Palisades of volcanic lahars that formed 54–40 million years ago. •

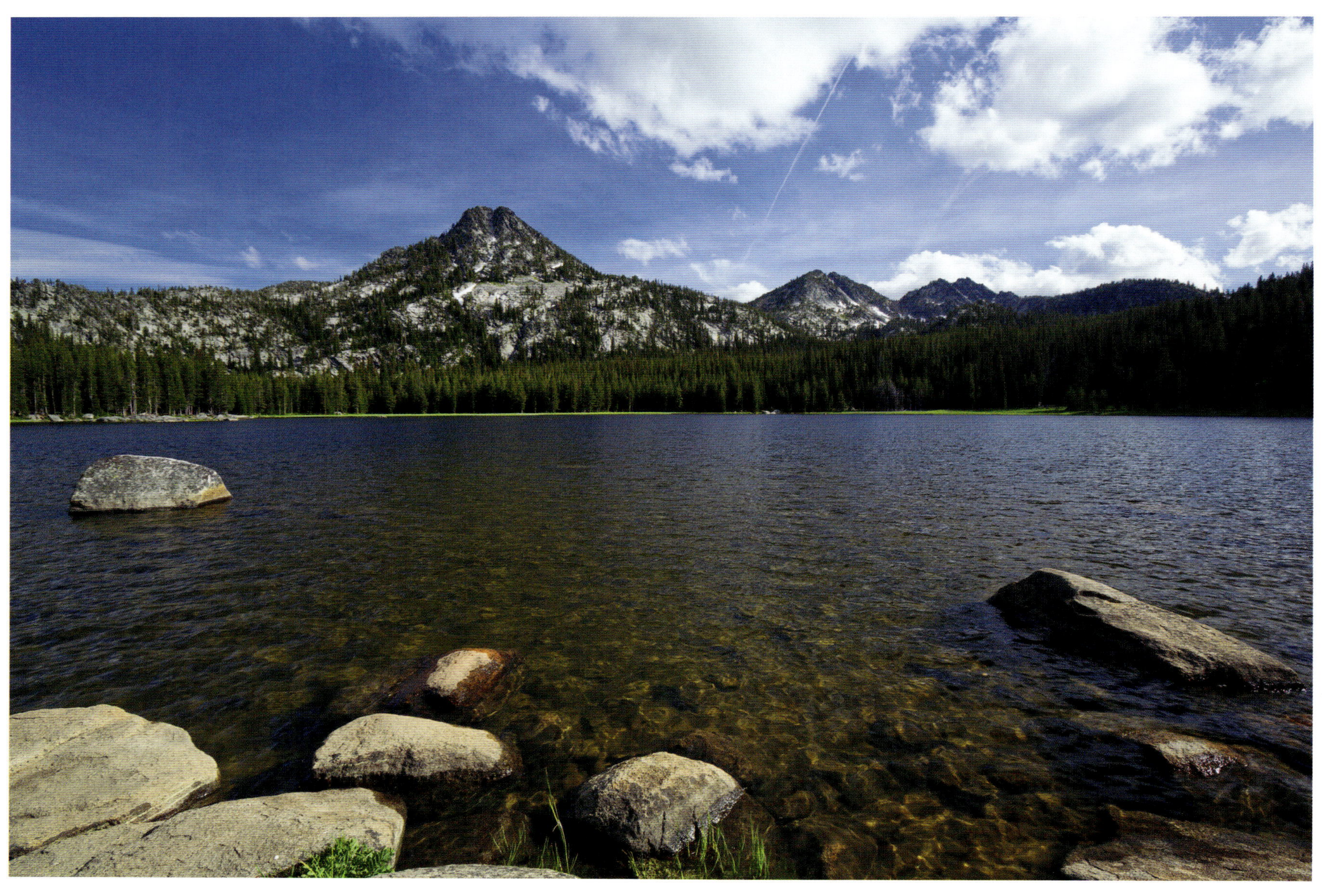

The peaks of the Elkhorn Mountains rise over the shores of Anthony Lake in the northeastern part of the state. •

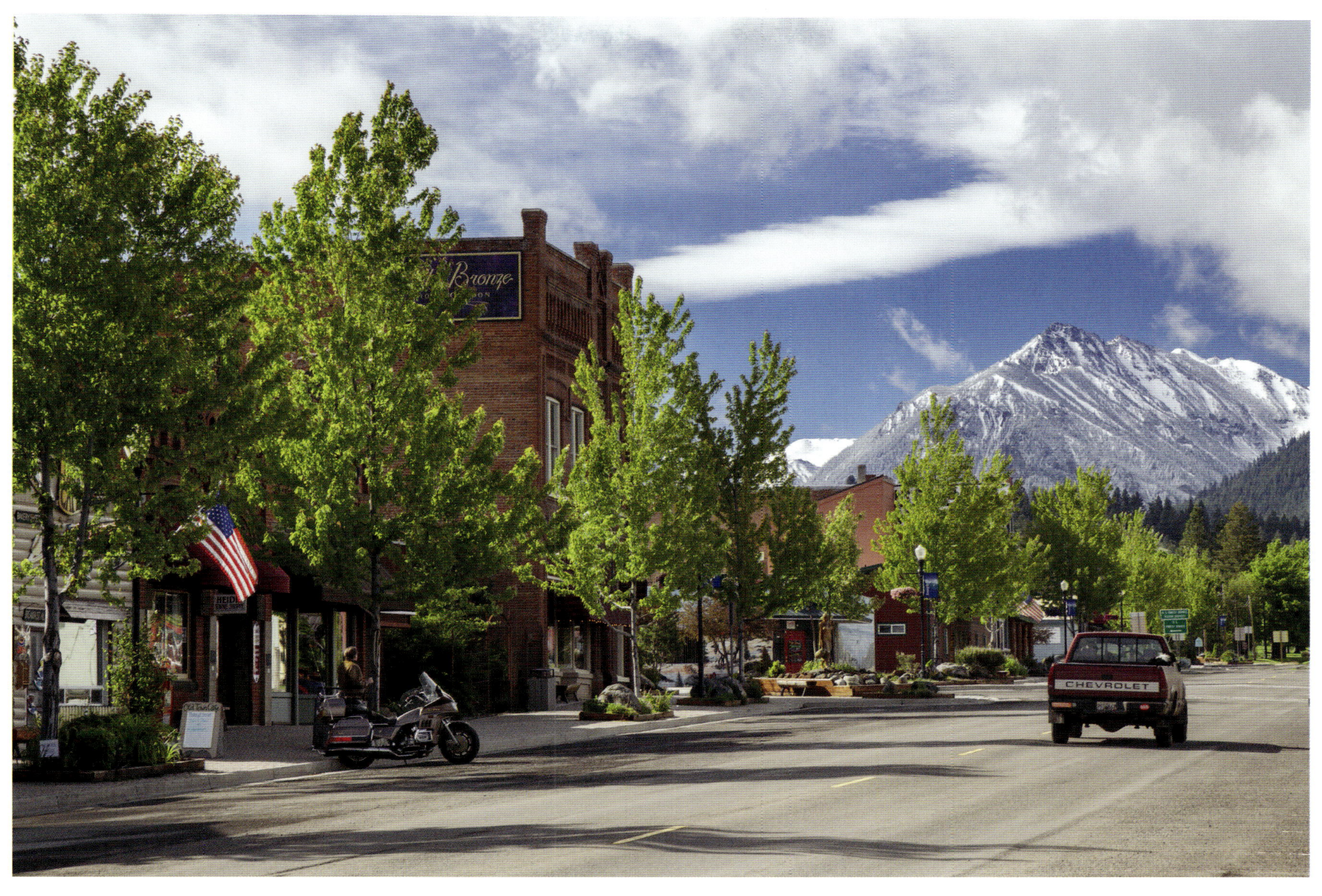

Main Street in the picturesque Old West
town of Joseph, which lies below the
Wallowa Mountains. •

Sunrise over the snow-capped peaks
during spring in the Wallowa Mountains
near Joseph. The Brennan Barn in the
valley below features an oversize white
cattle brand. •

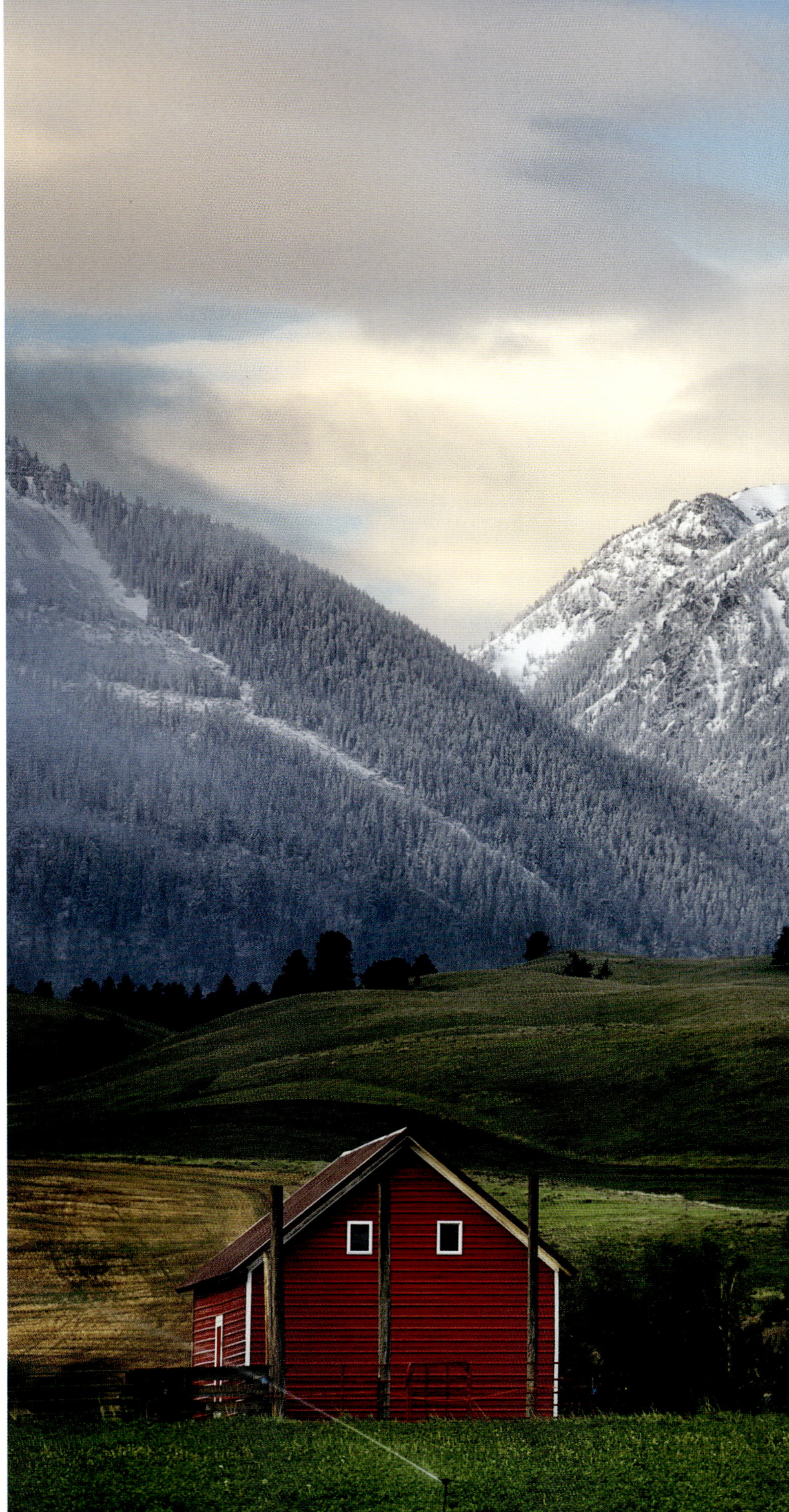

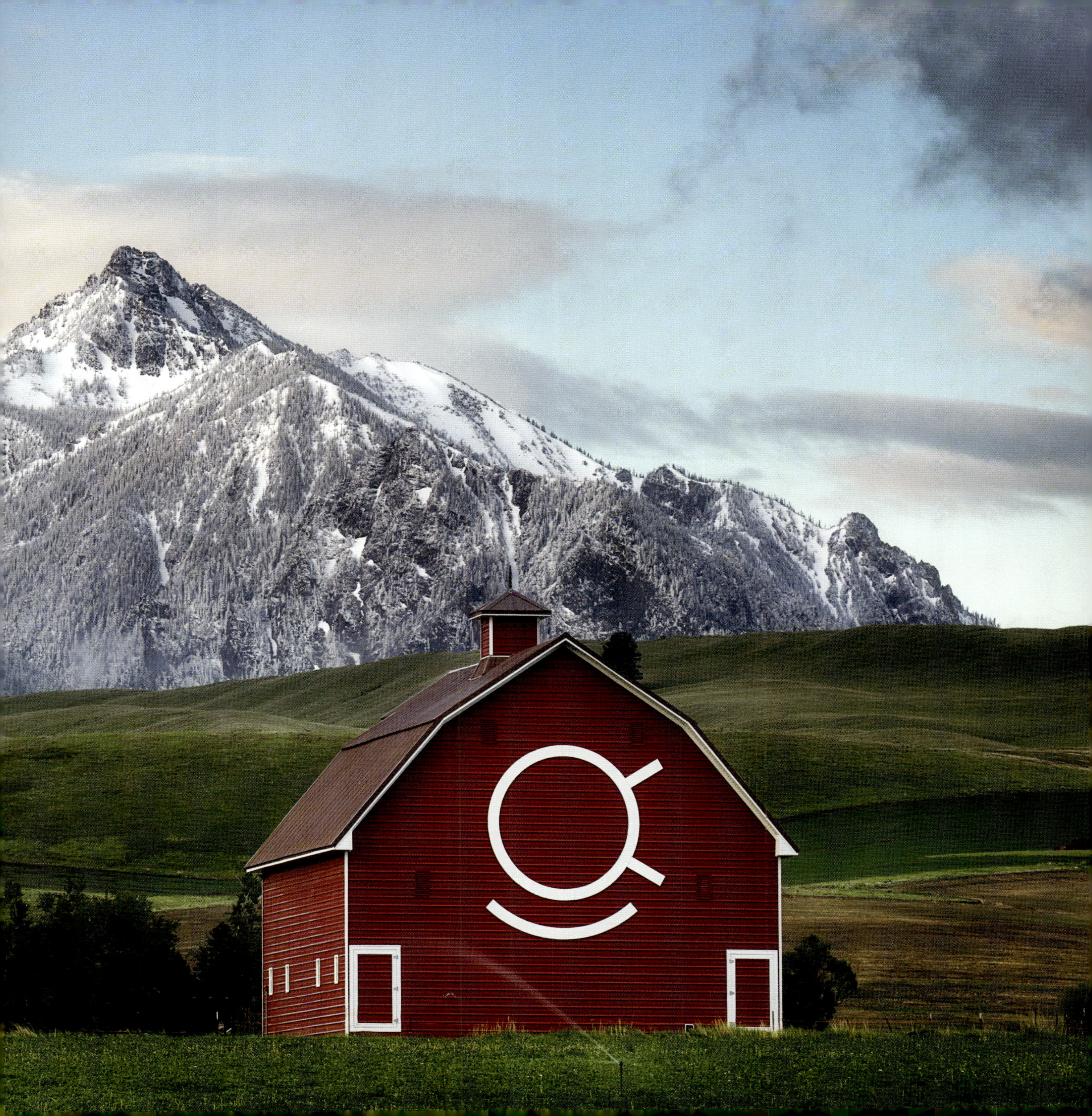

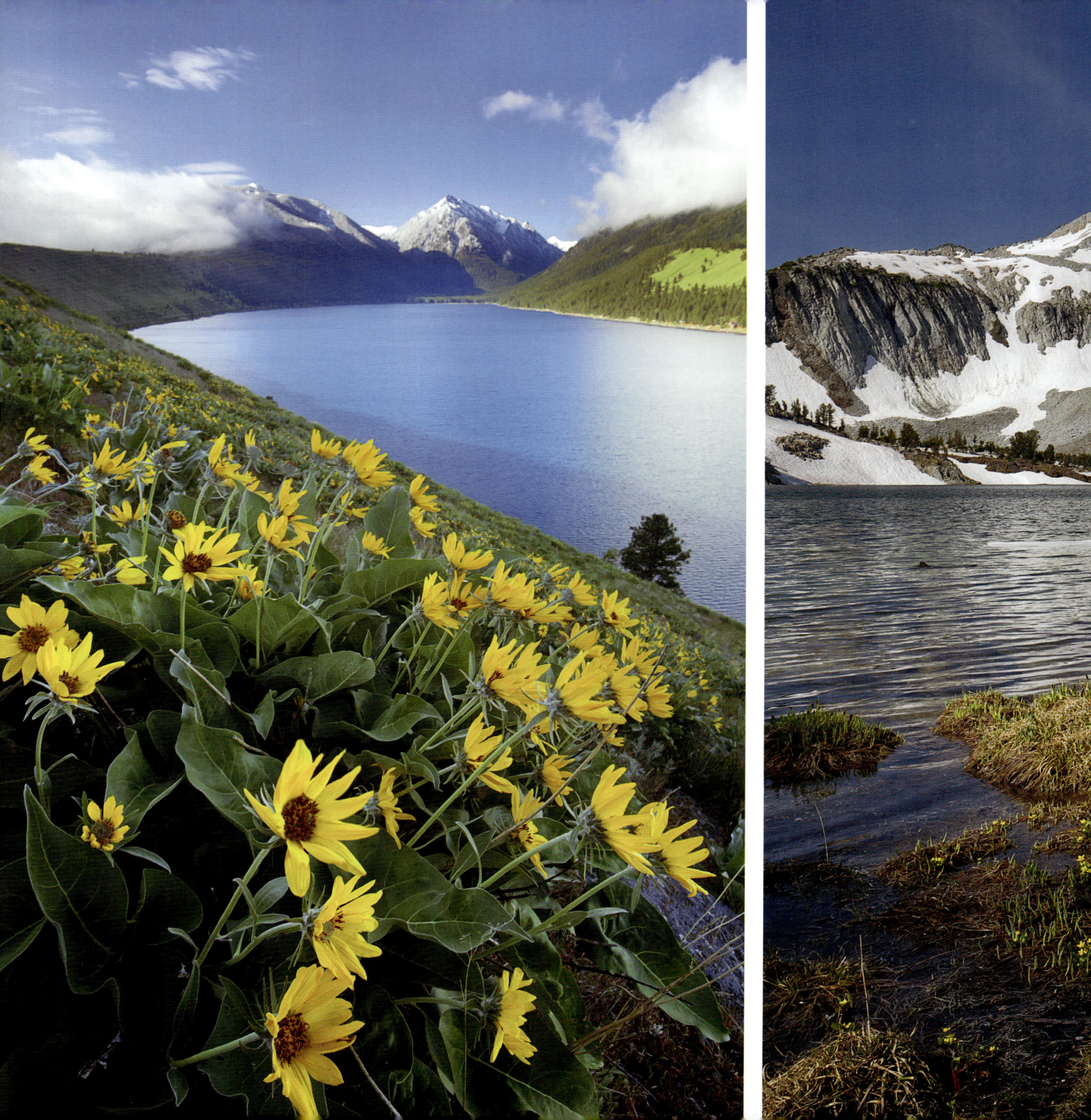

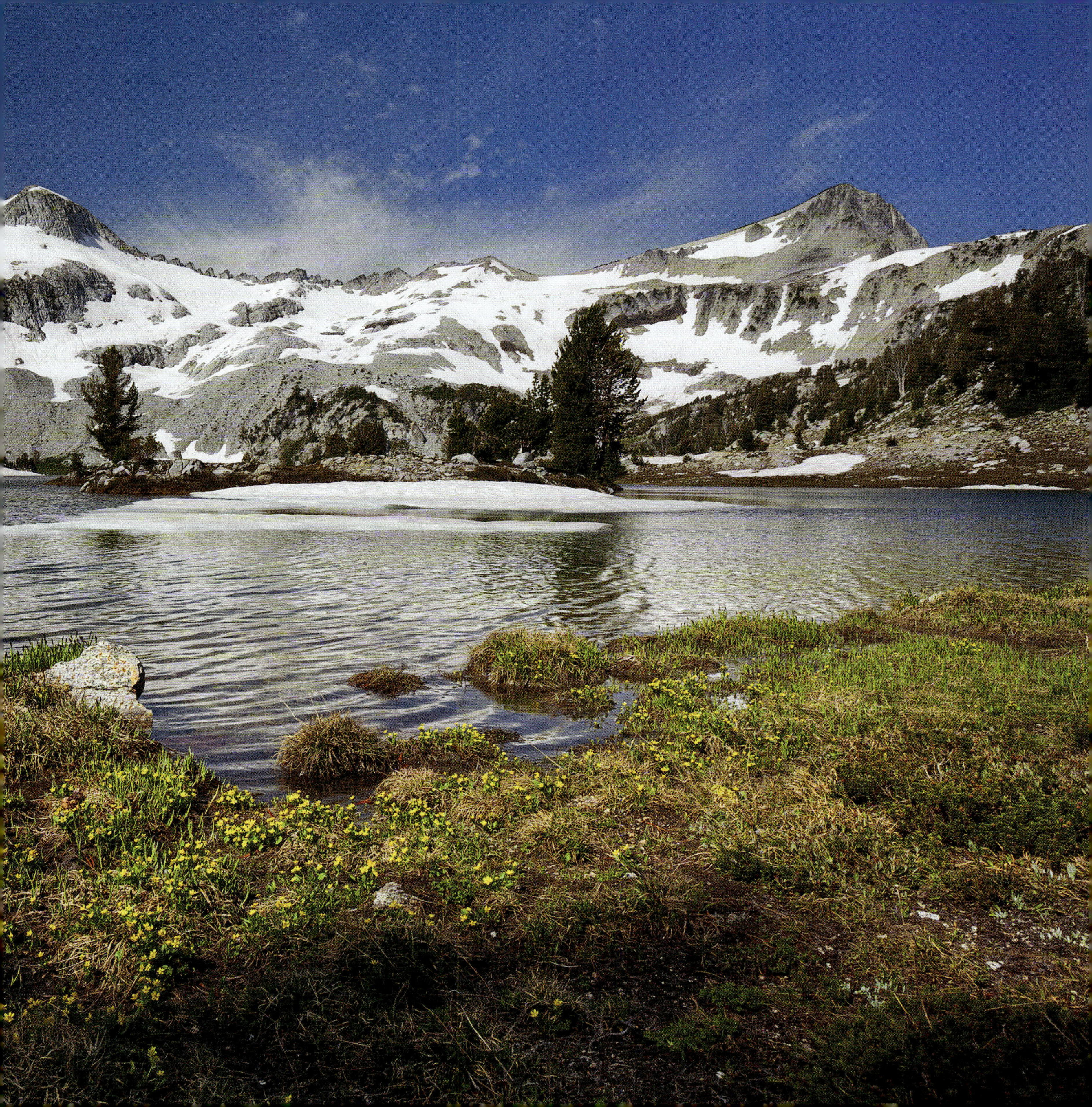

PREVIOUS PAGES, LEFT
Arrowleaf balsamroot (*Balsamorhiza sagittata*) covers the glacial moraine bordering Wallowa Lake and the Wallowa Mountains in summer. •

PREVIOUS PAGES, RIGHT
Glacier Lake lies high in the Eagle Cap Wilderness of the Wallowa Mountains. •

RIGHT   Snow melt flows into Mirror Lake; Eagle Cap catches the last rays of the summer day's sun. •

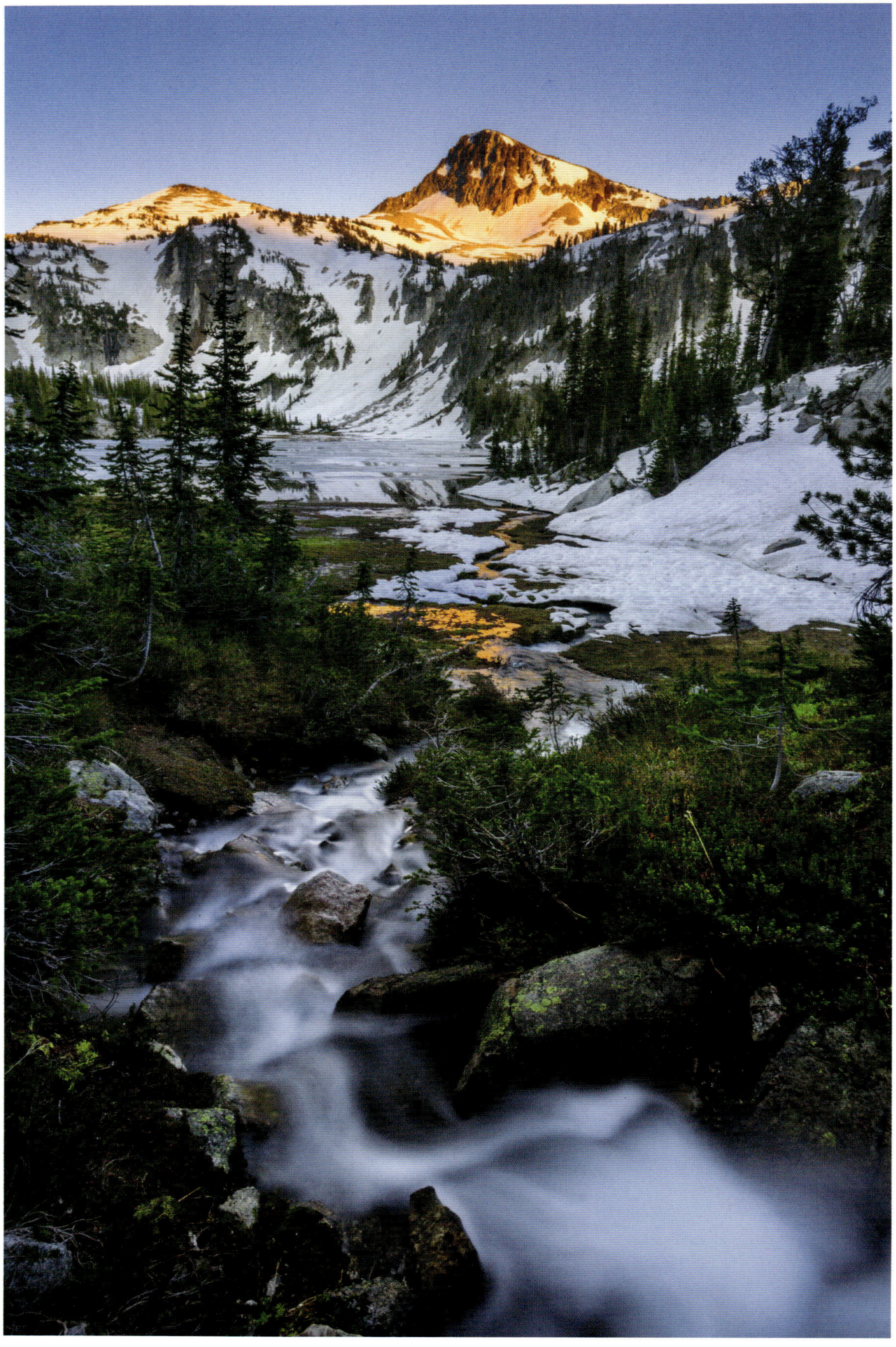

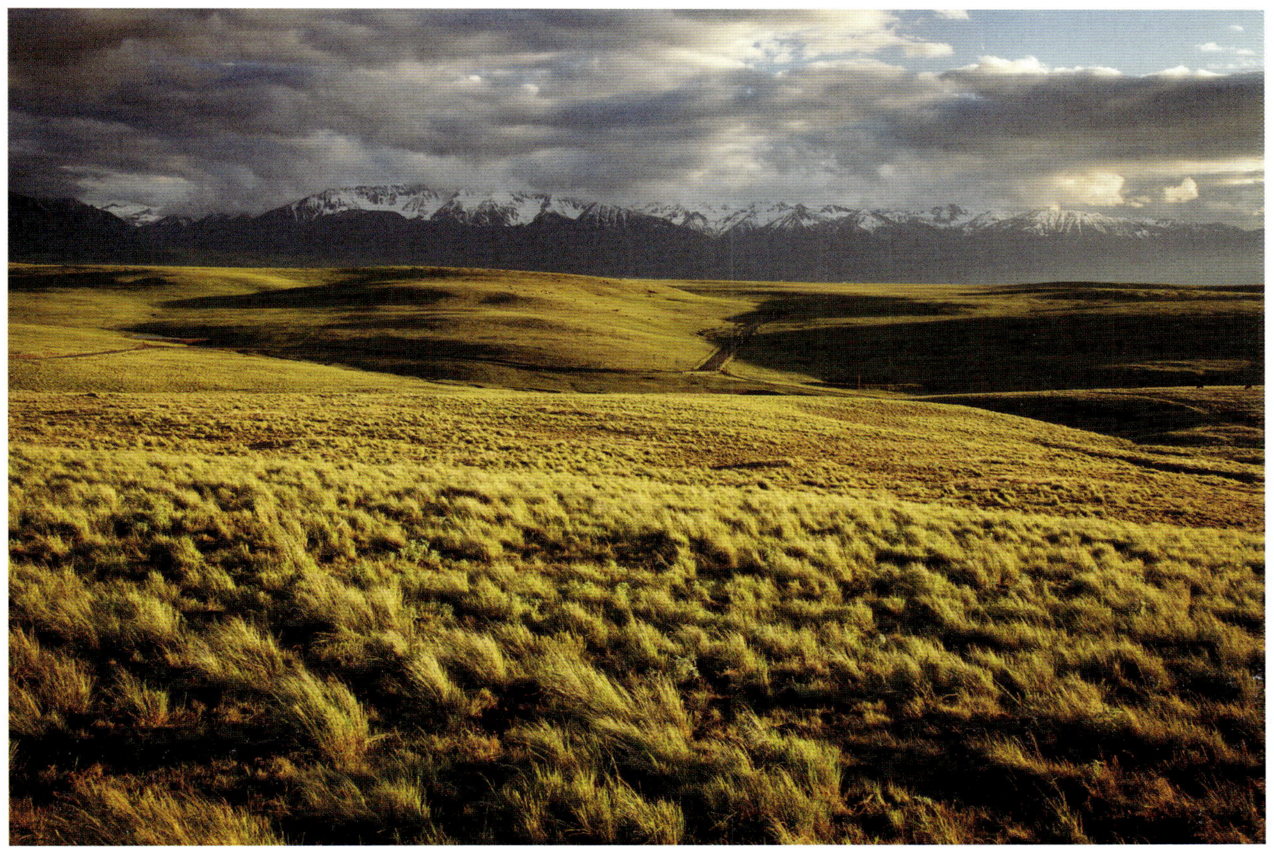

Late evening on the windswept Zumwalt Prairie in May, with the Wallowa Mountains in the distance. The prairie, which varies in elevation from 3500 to 5500 feet, is located on a basalt plateau west of Hells Canyon. •

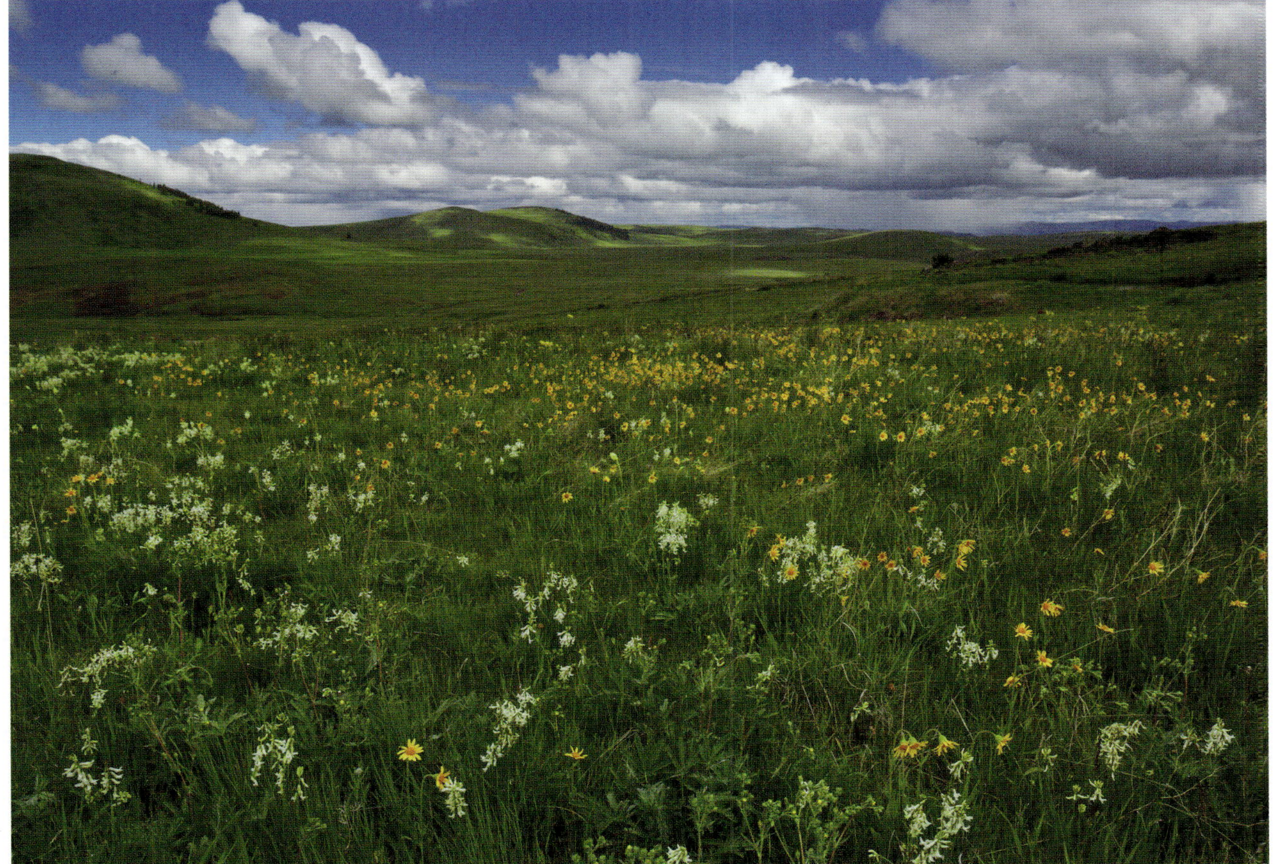

By early June, flowers, including twin arnica (*Arnica sororia*) and milkvetch (*Astragalus canadensis*), cover the Zumwalt Prairie. •

The Snake River is held back by the Hells Canyon Dam along the Oregon-Idaho border. Hells Canyon is North America's deepest river gorge at 7993 feet. •

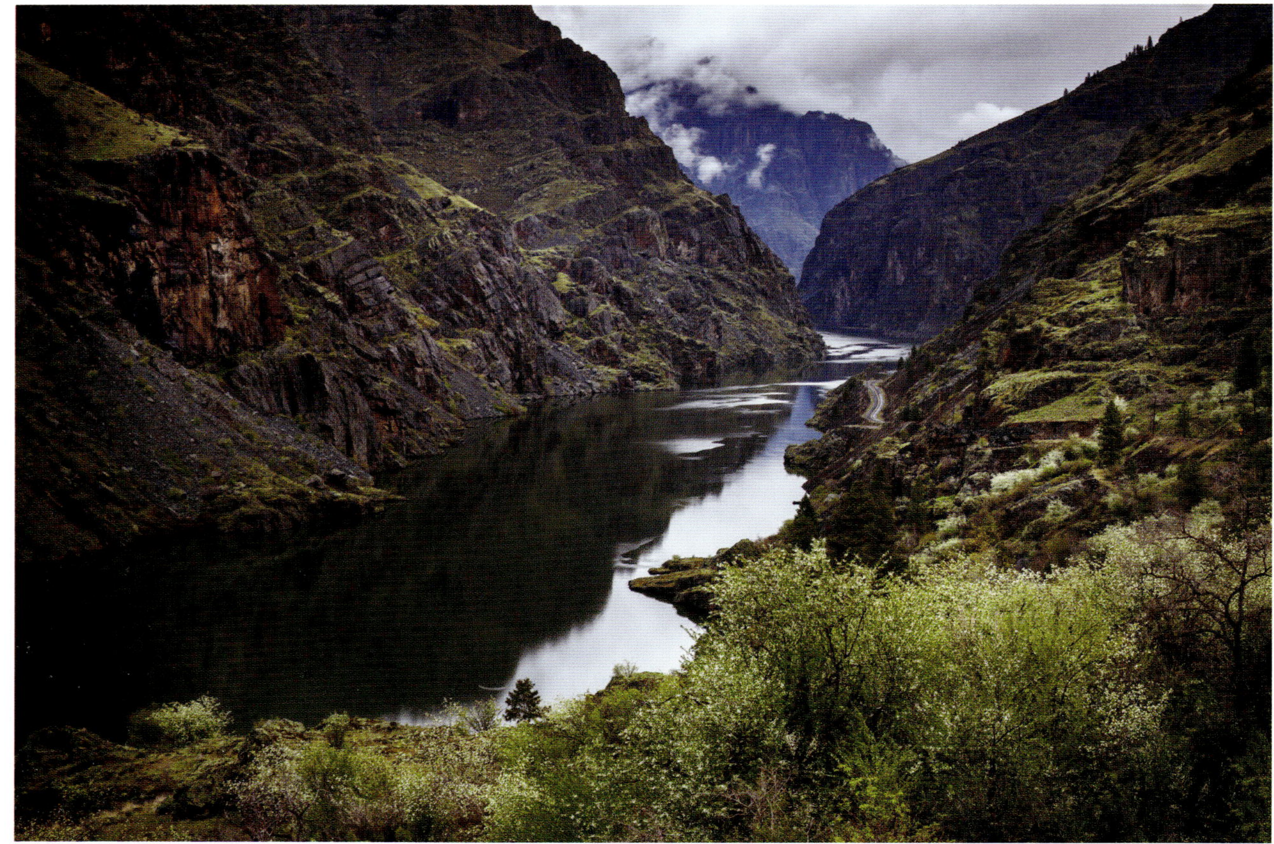

RIGHT An early summer view of the grasslands, peaks, and valleys of the Imnaha Canyon, near Hells Canyon in the northeastern corner of the state. •

OPPOSITE The Imnaha River is a designated National Wild and Scenic River; it follows a geologic fault from the Eagle Cap Wilderness to its confluence with the Snake River in Hells Canyon. •

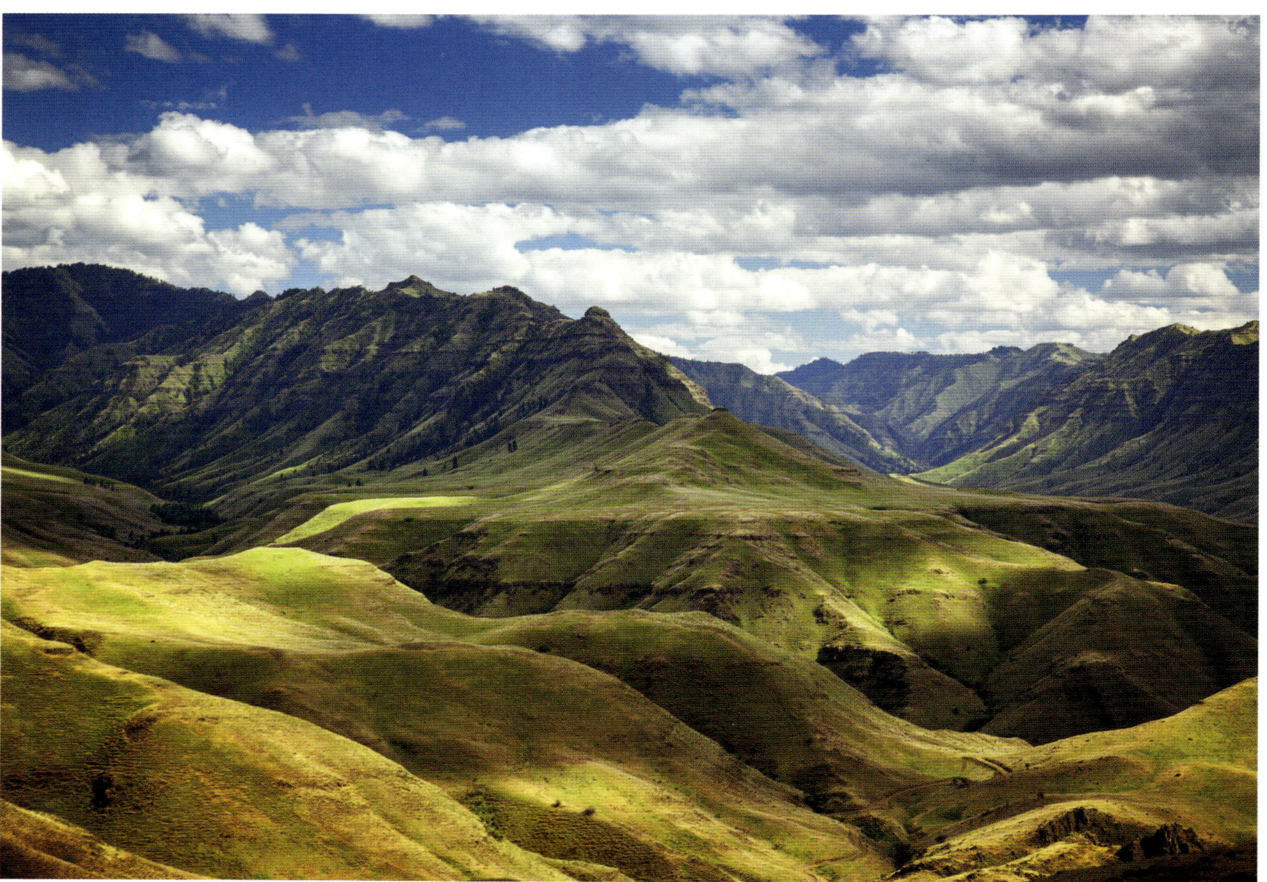

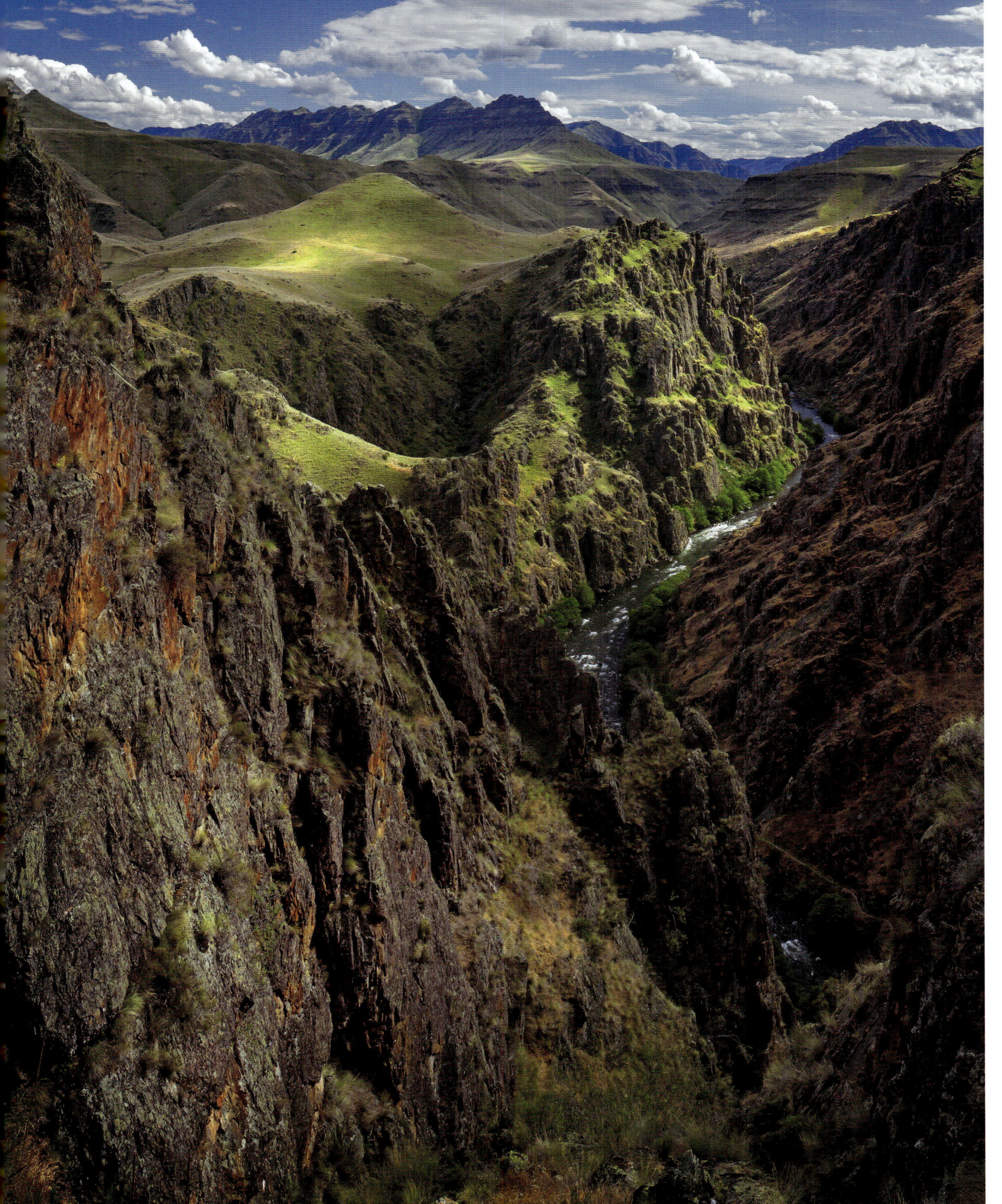

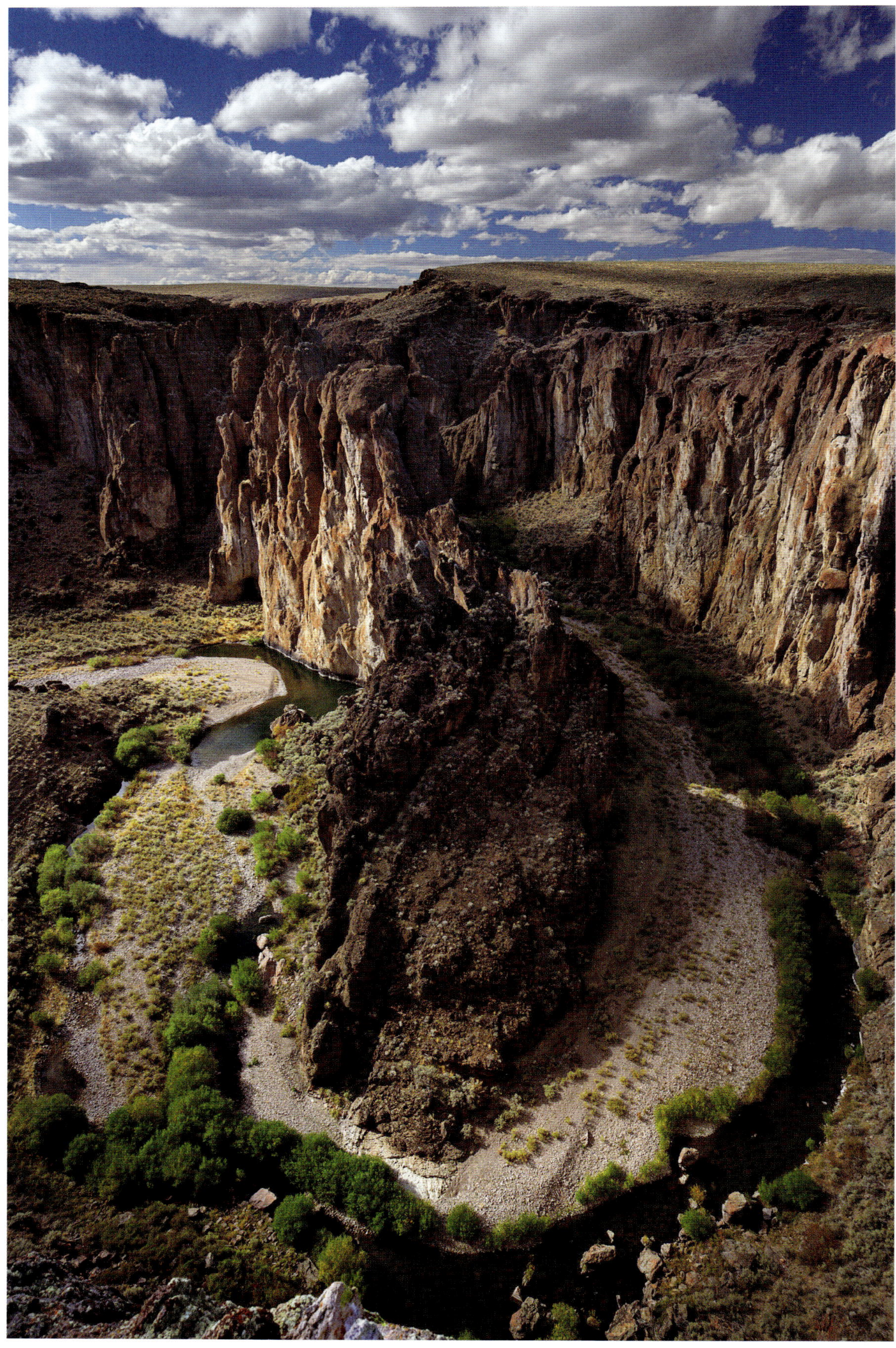

The Owyhee River, 120 miles of which are designated a National Wild and Scenic River, cuts a deep and winding path through the remote high desert plateau just north of the Great Basin in the southeastern part of the state. •

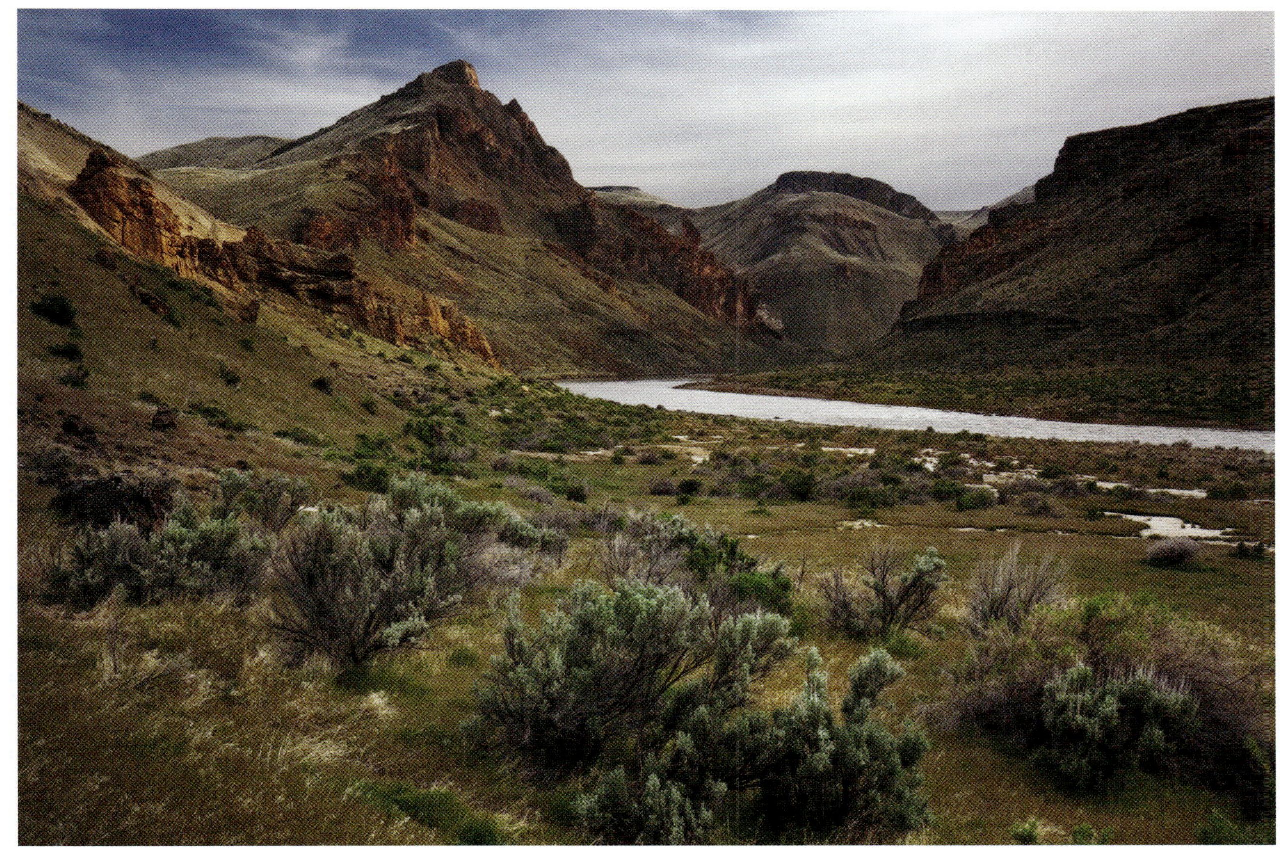

The Owyhee River flows from northern Nevada along the Oregon-Idaho border to the Snake River. Its high canyon rims are habitat for mountain lions, bobcats, mule deer, California bighorn sheep, and a large variety of raptors. •

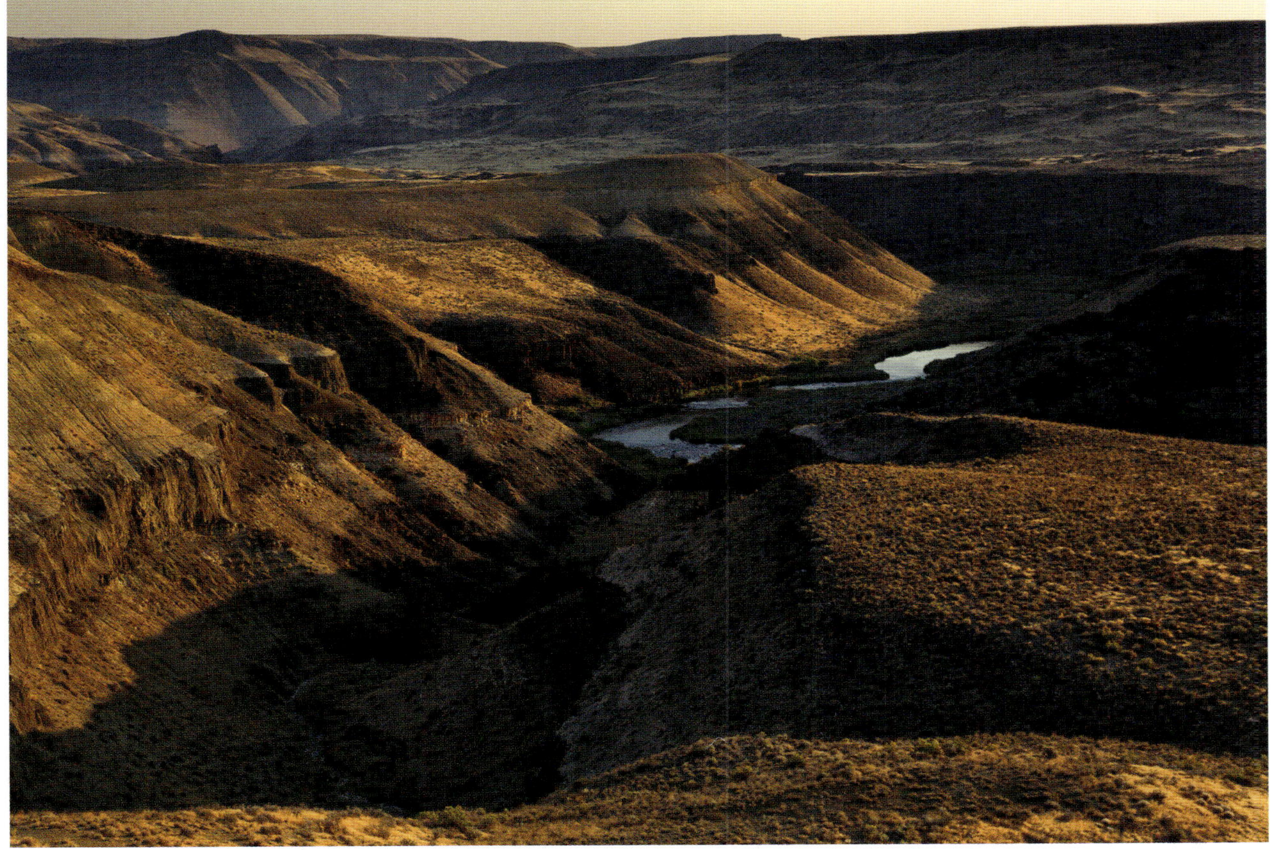

The Owyhee River winds through the canyons of eastern Oregon's high desert. •

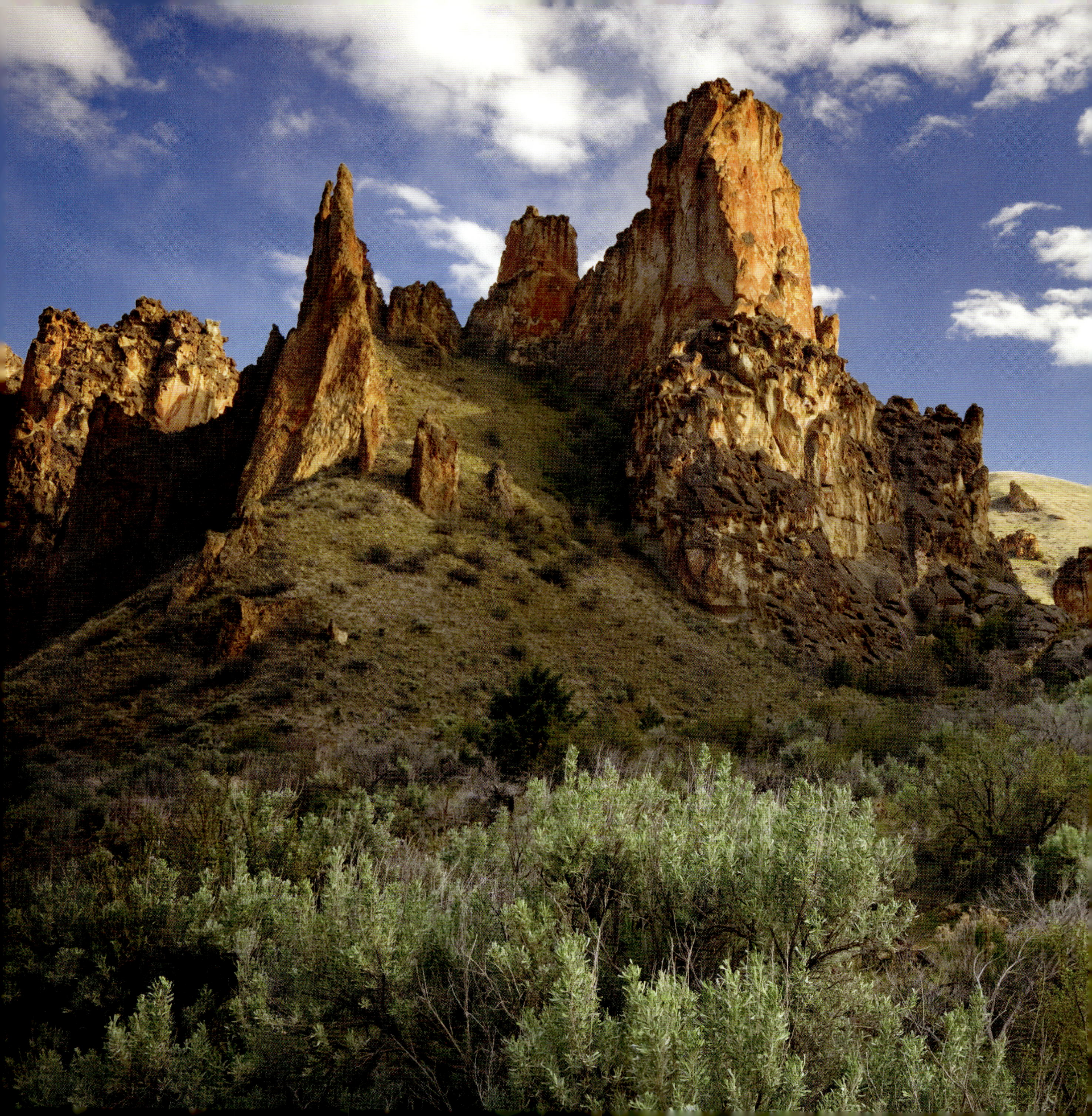

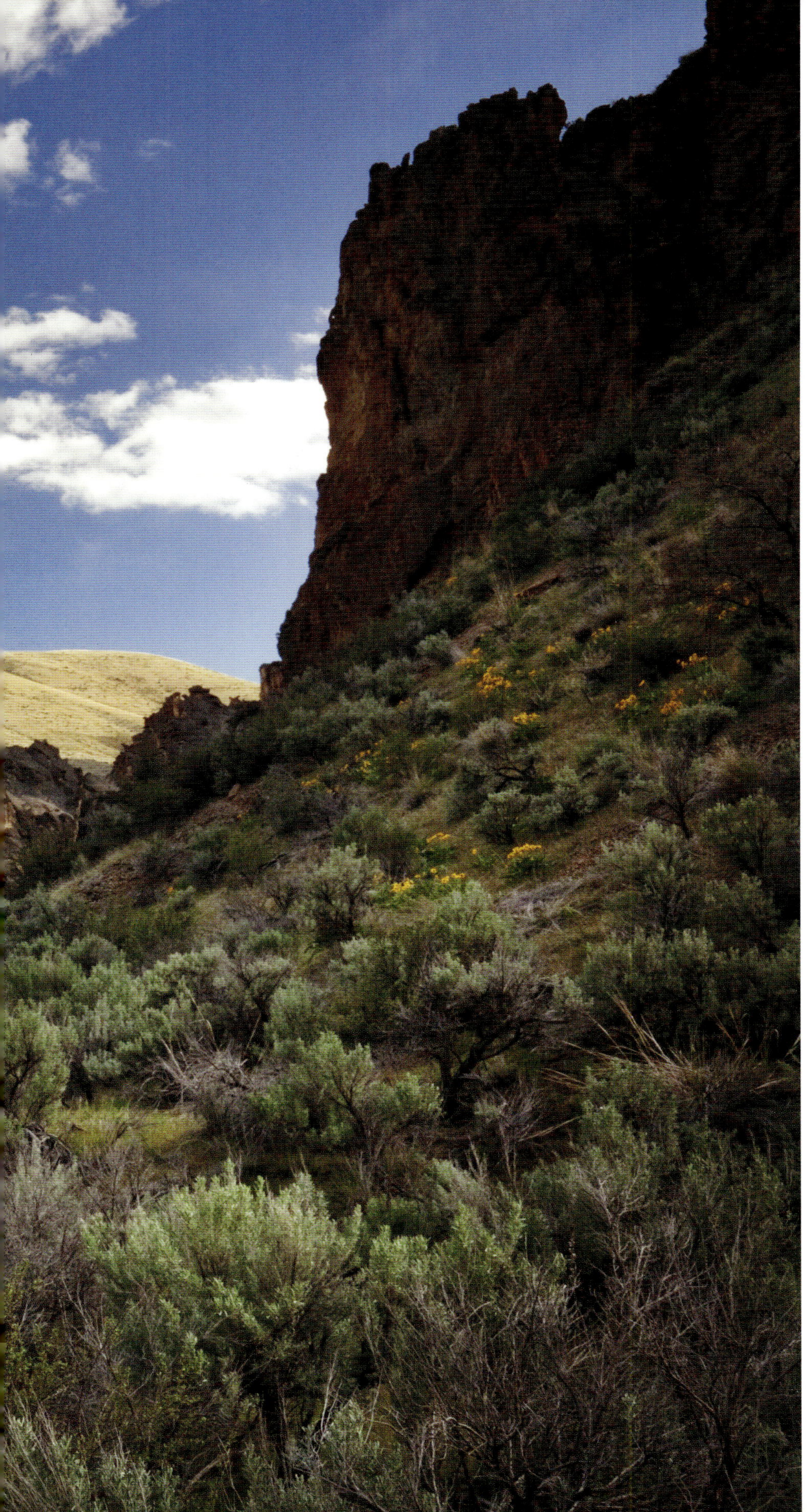

Leslie Gulch's most notable geological formations are towers of volcanic tuff; here they catch late-afternoon sun in spring. The gulch, located in the Owyhee Canyonlands, was named after a local rancher, Hiram E. Lesl e, who was struck by lightning here in 1882. •

Soft evening spring light in one of
the canyons along Succor Creek,
in the Owyhee Canyonlands. •

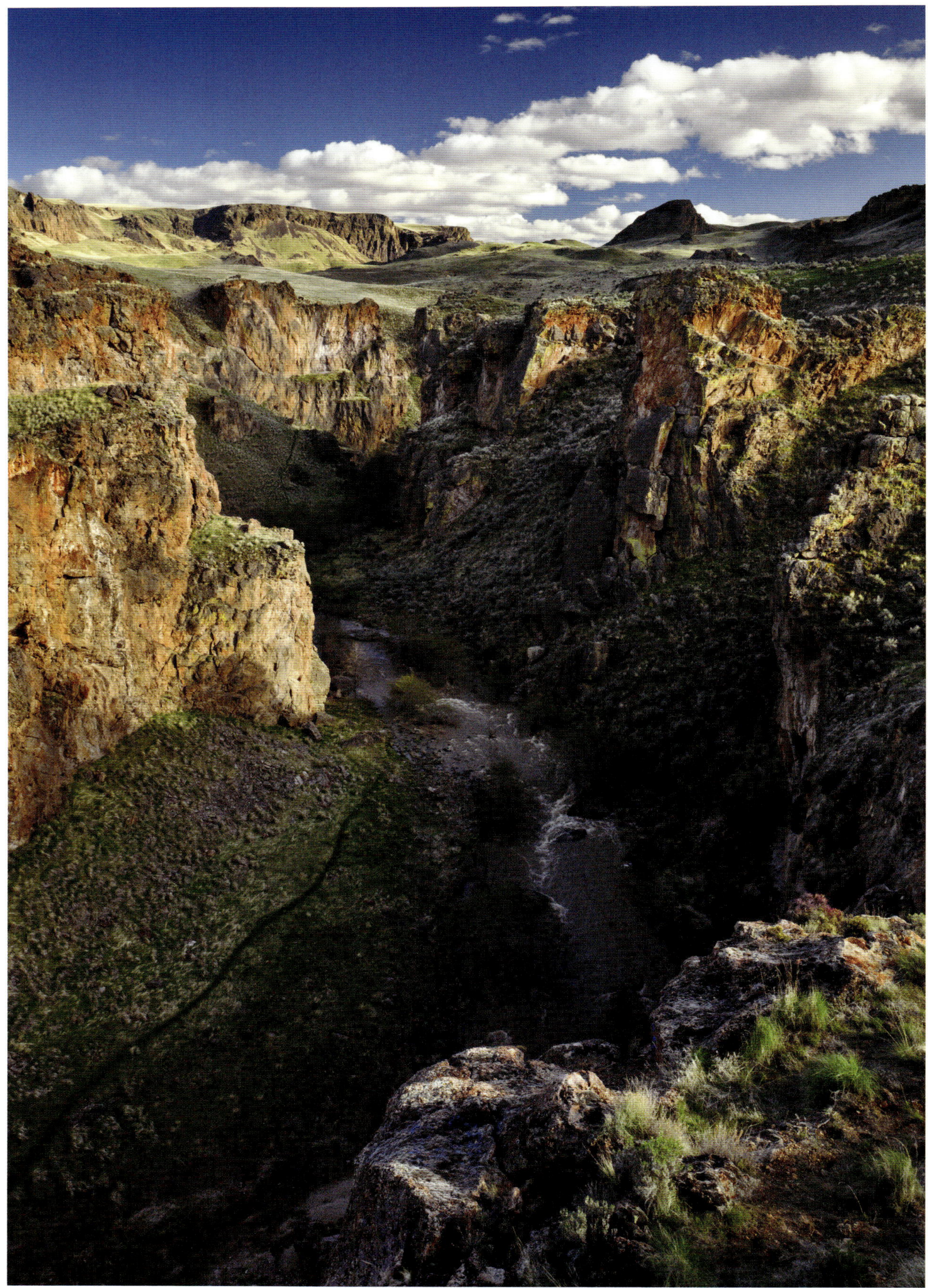

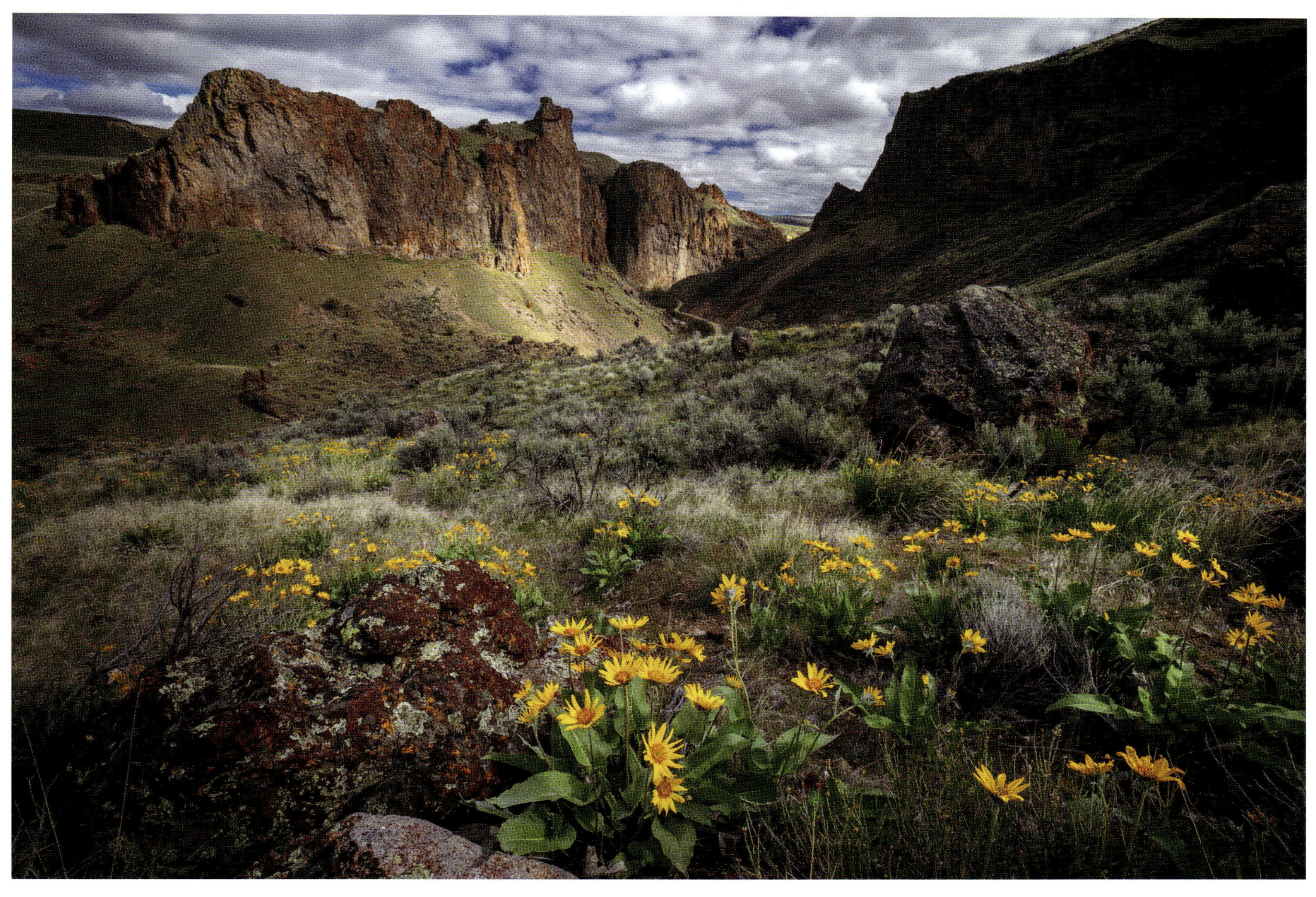

Balsamroot (*Balsamorhiza* sp.) and
dappled light in Succor Creek State
Natural Area. •

RIGHT The northernmost stand of redwoods in the United States lies just above the Chetco River in southern Oregon. •

OPPOSITE Rugged cliffs at Shore Acres State Park on the southern coast. •

OVERLEAF, LEFT TO RIGHT
Formations of eroded sandstone, tilted terraces, and bowling ball–shaped concretions make the coastline near Shore Acres State Park and Cape Arago a geologic wonderland. • Waves crash violently along the rocky shore at Cape Arago State Park on the southern coast. • Storm clouds move out and the sun makes an appearance behind the sea stacks of Bandon Beach. •

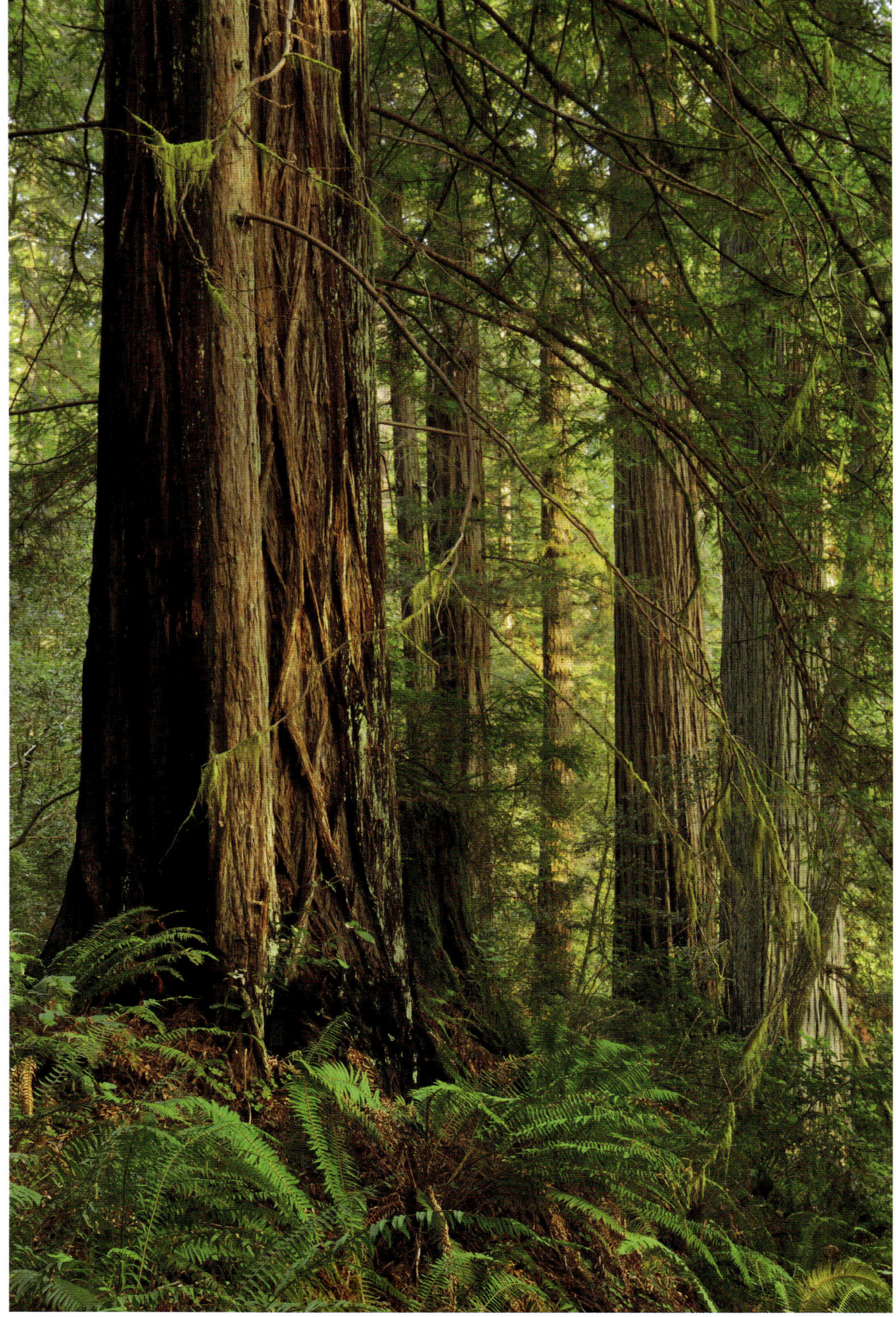

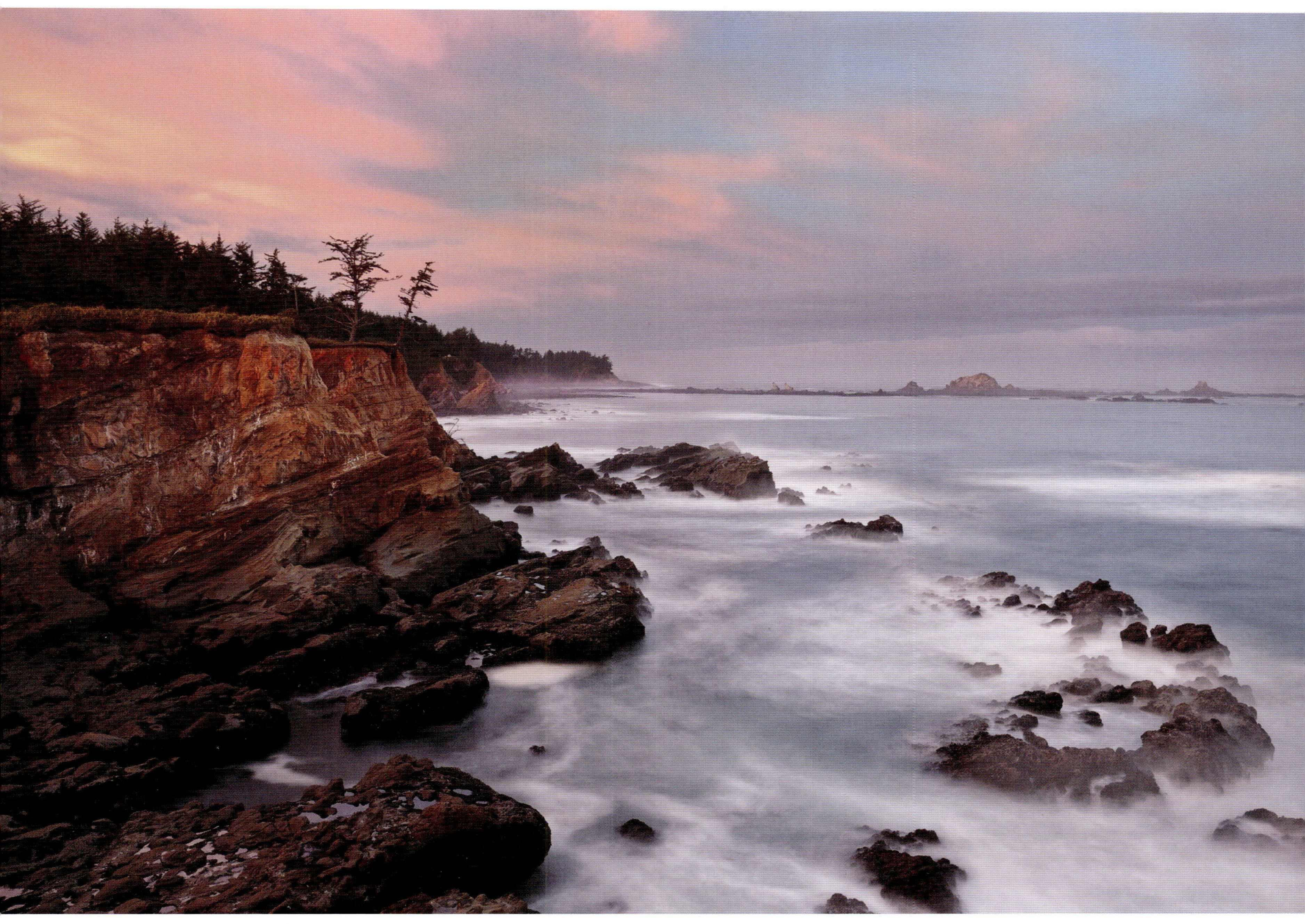

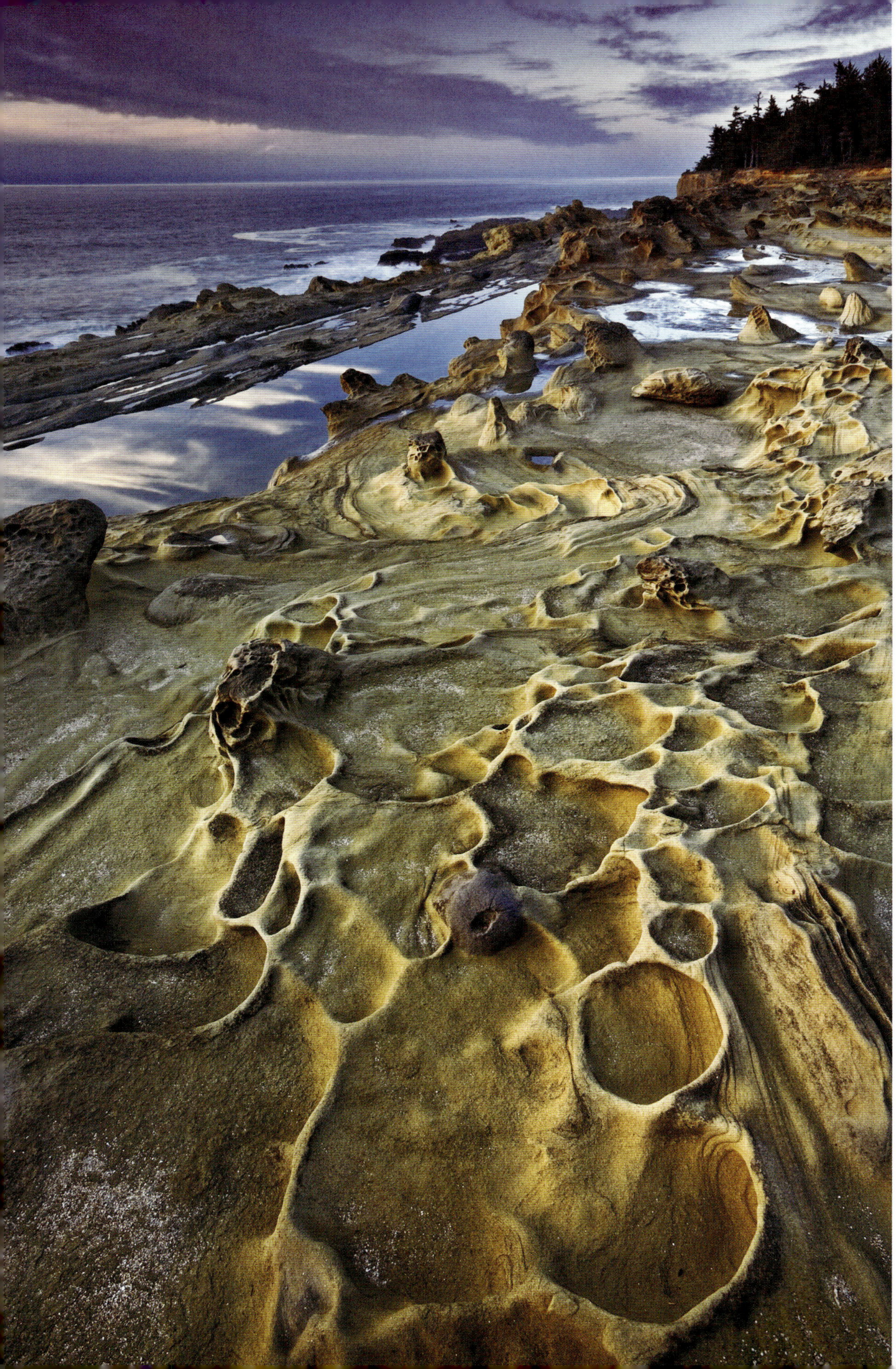

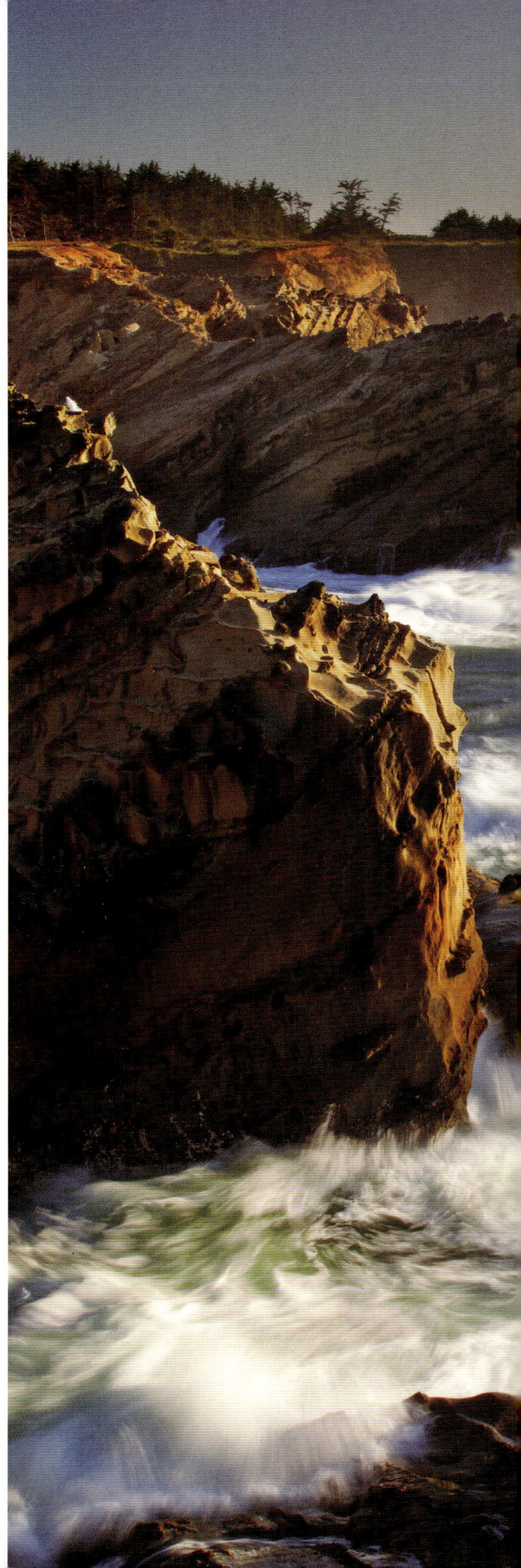

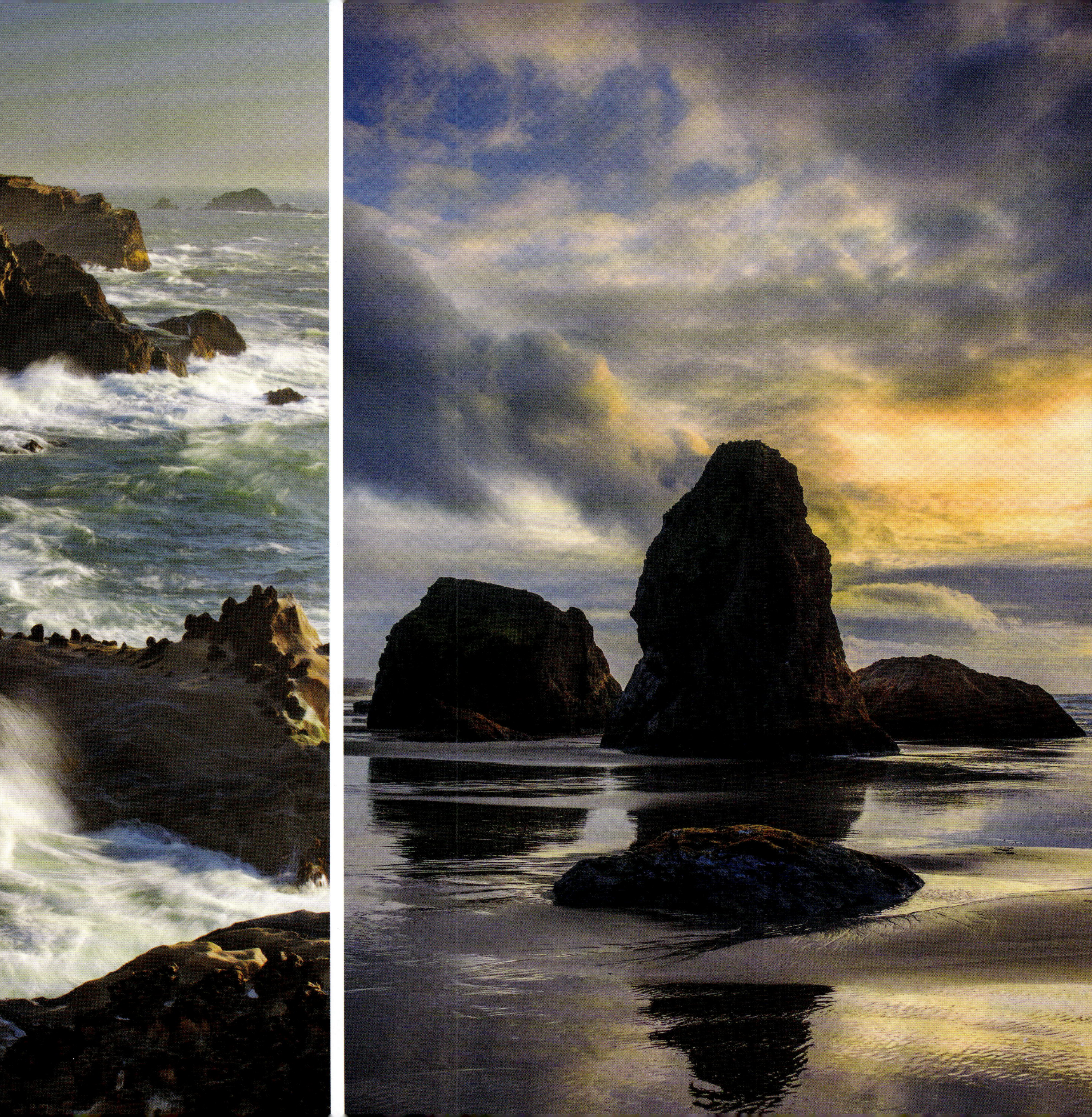

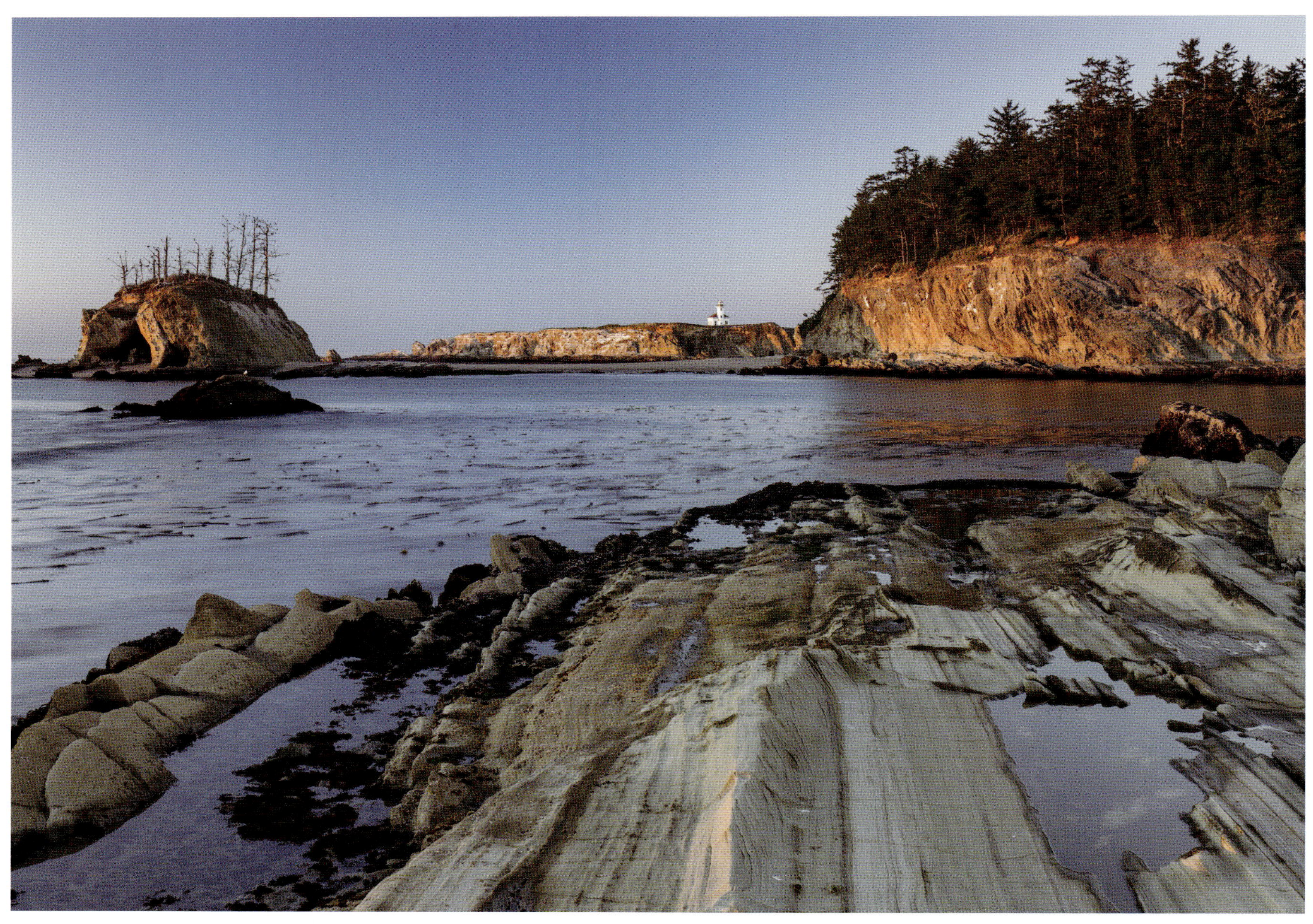

Evening light illuminates Cape Arago
Lighthouse and the cliffs at the entrance
to Sunset Bay. ●

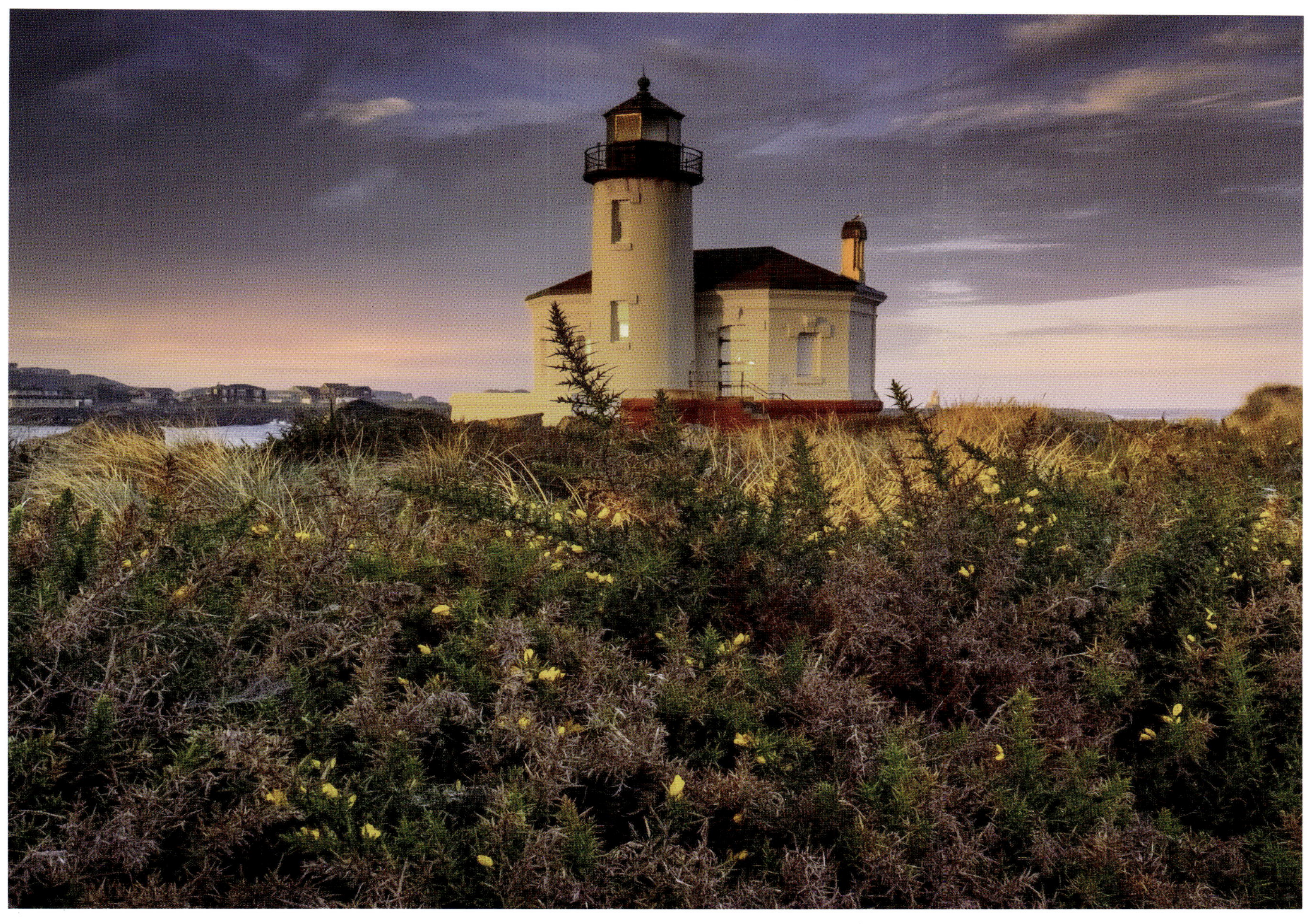

Warm colors highlight the Coquille River Lighthouse near the town of Bandon.

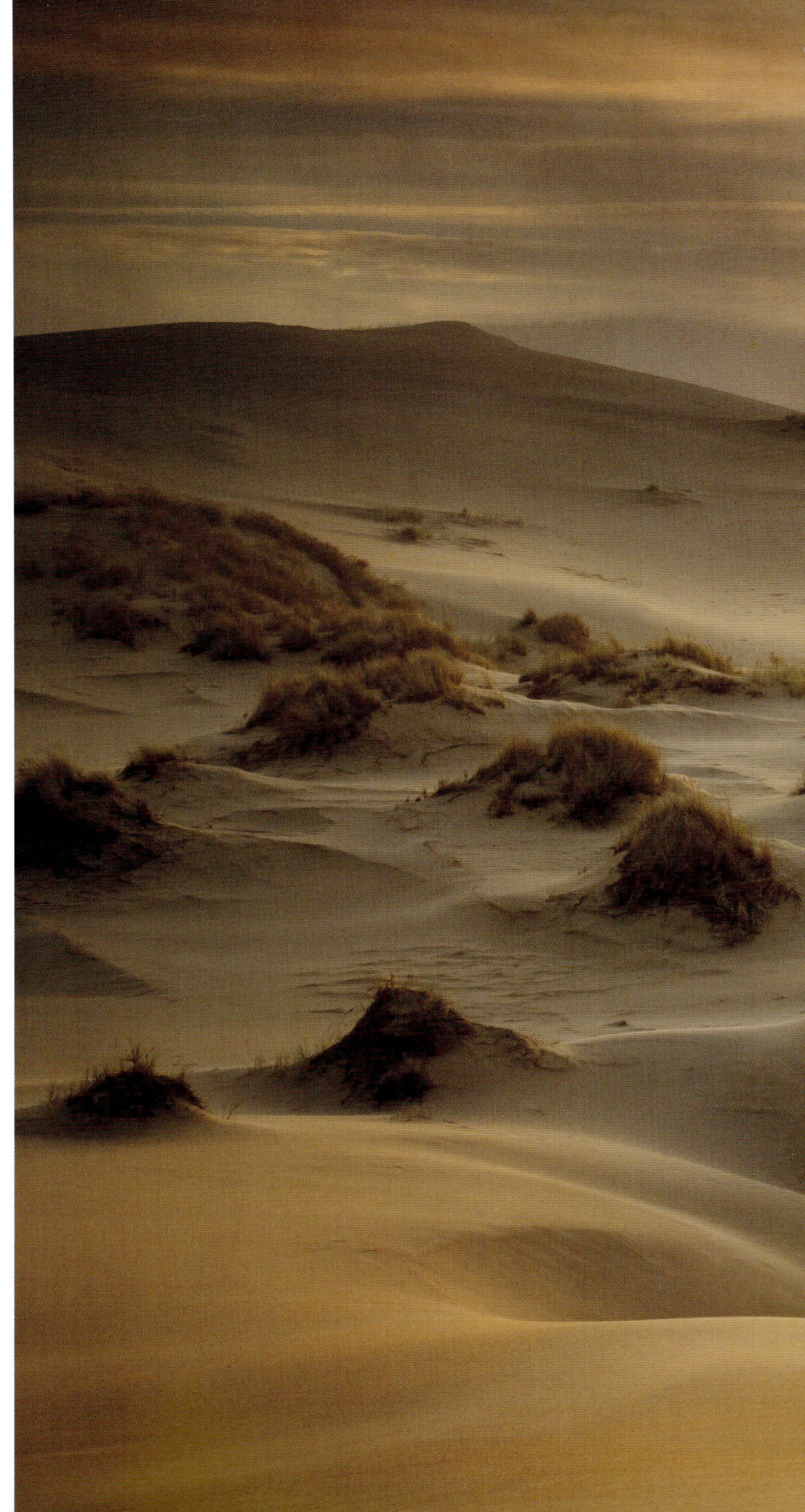

Sunrise through layers of atmosphere on the Dellenback Dunes. •

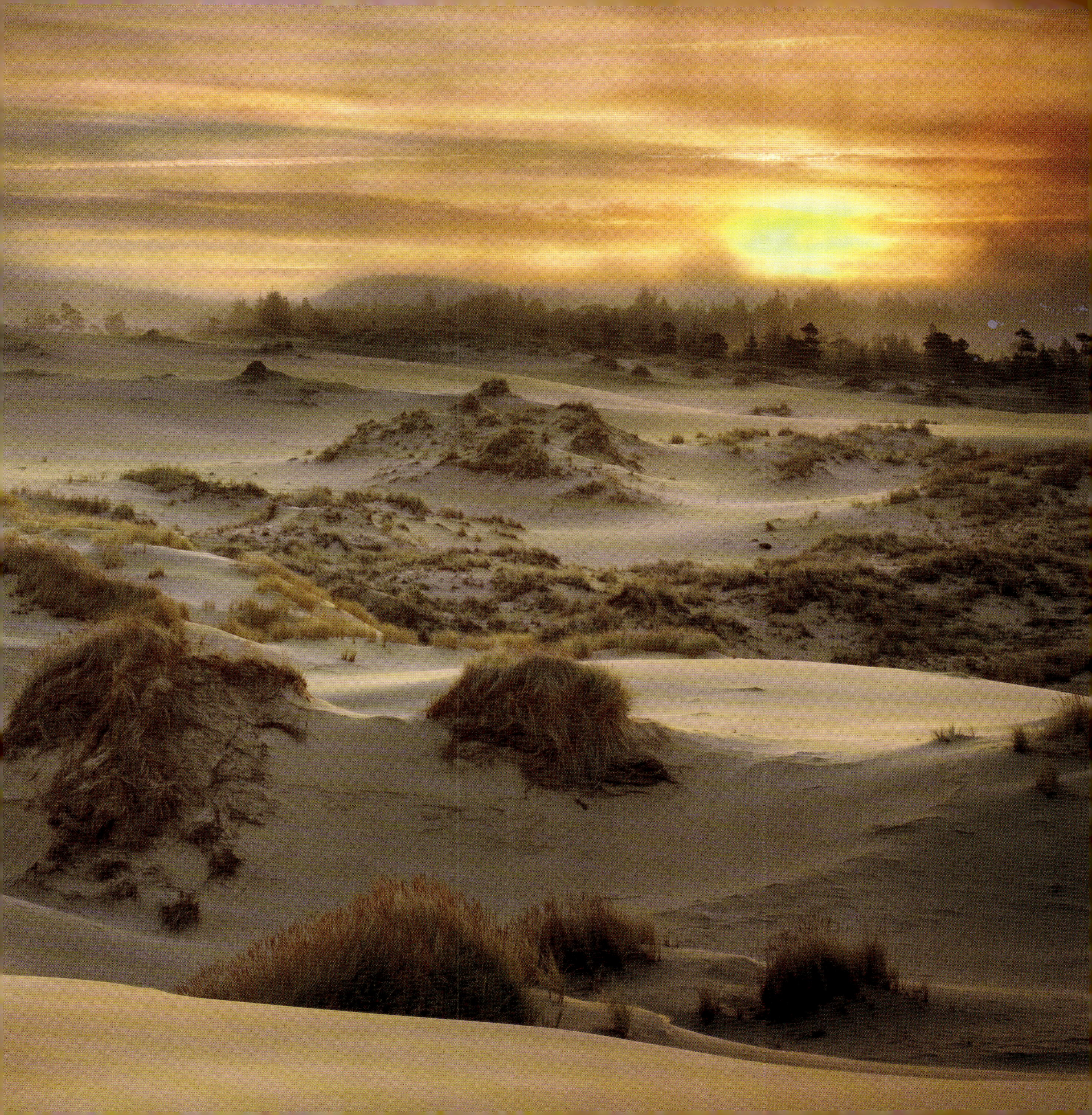

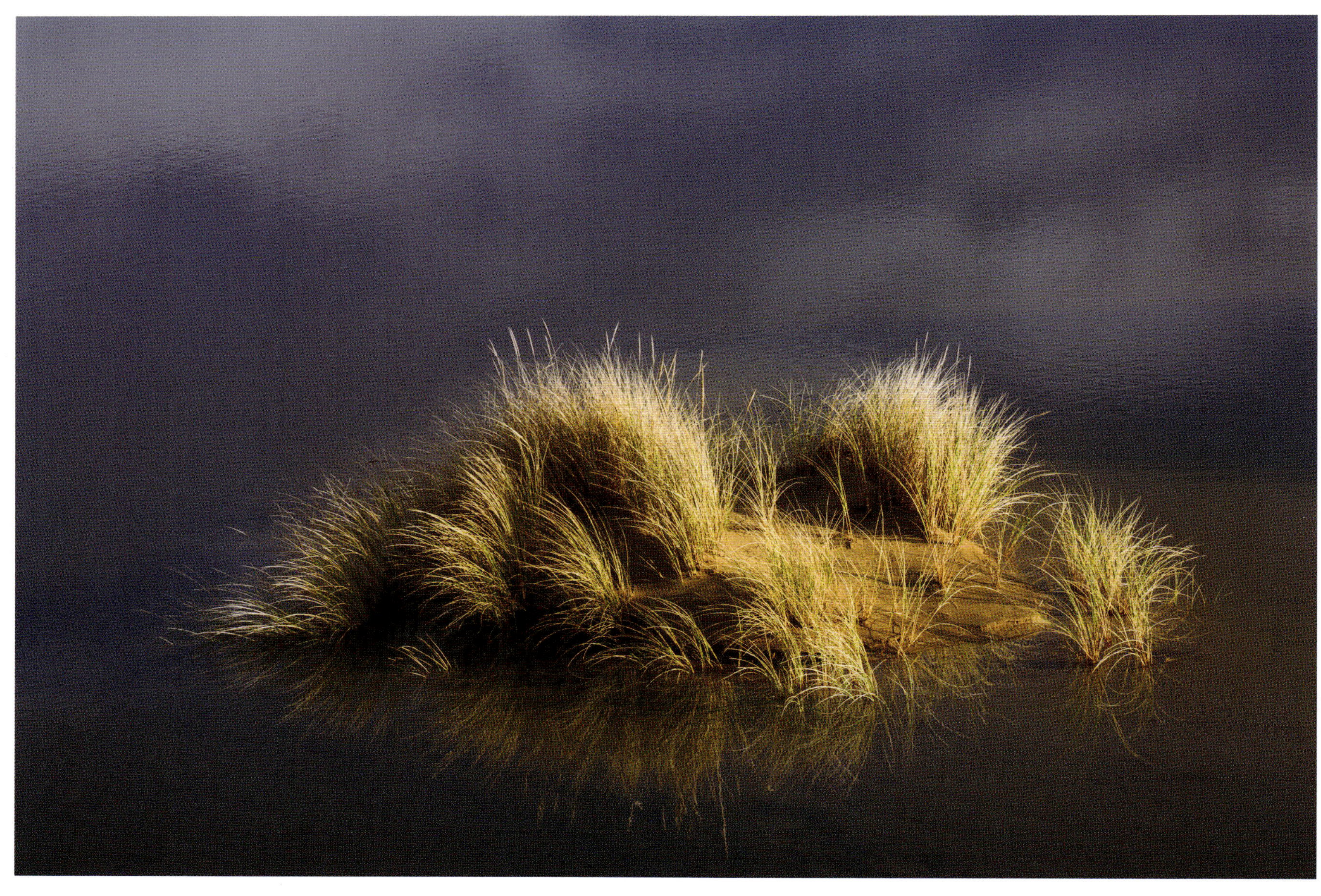

An island populated with bunch grass
sits in the middle of Dellenback Dunes
in spring. •

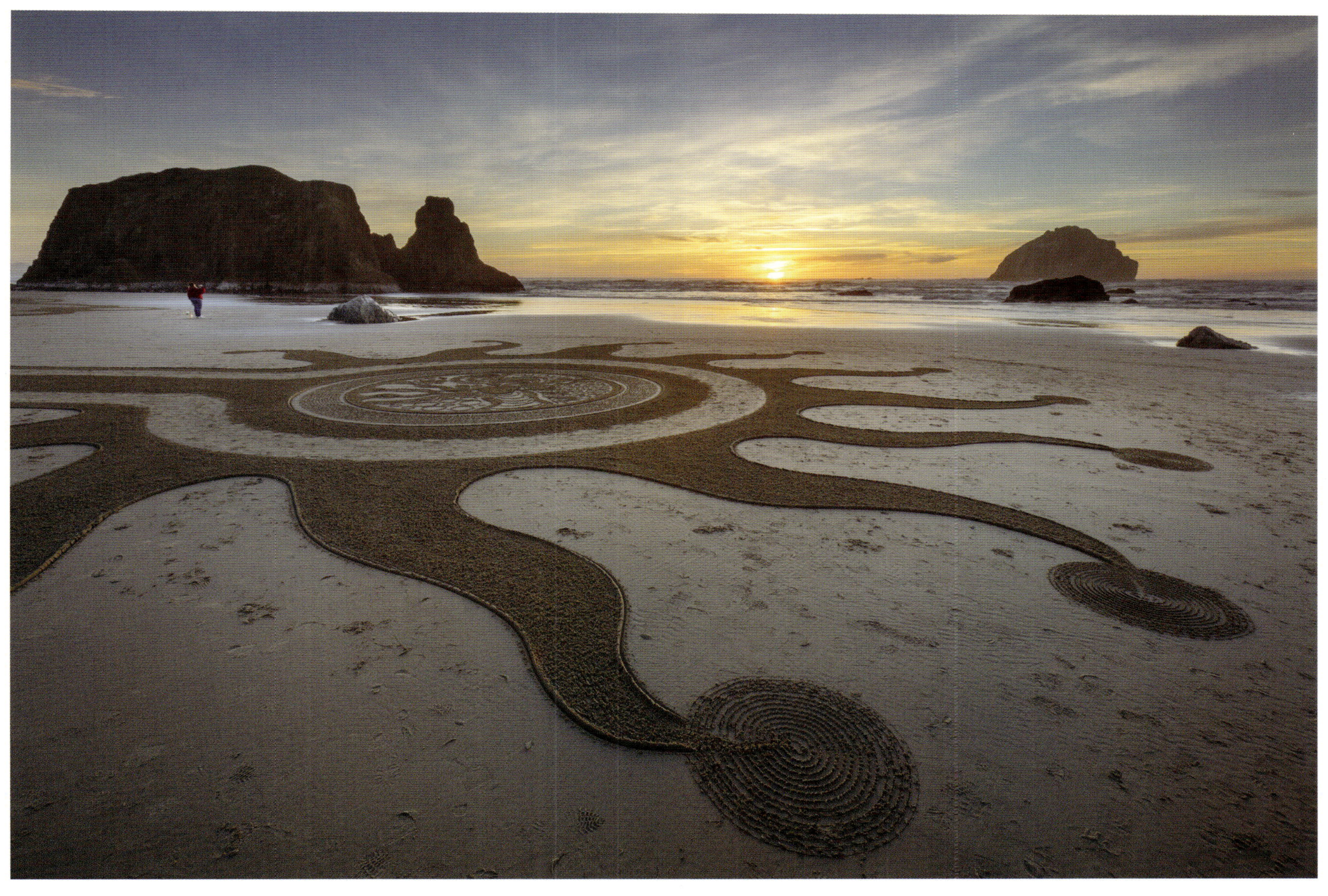

Sunset on a sand labyrinth created by
local artist Denny Dyke on Bandon Beach.
He creates his pieces during low tides for
the enjoyment of the public. ●

Low tide forms patterns in the sands of Bandon Beach during a winter sunset. •

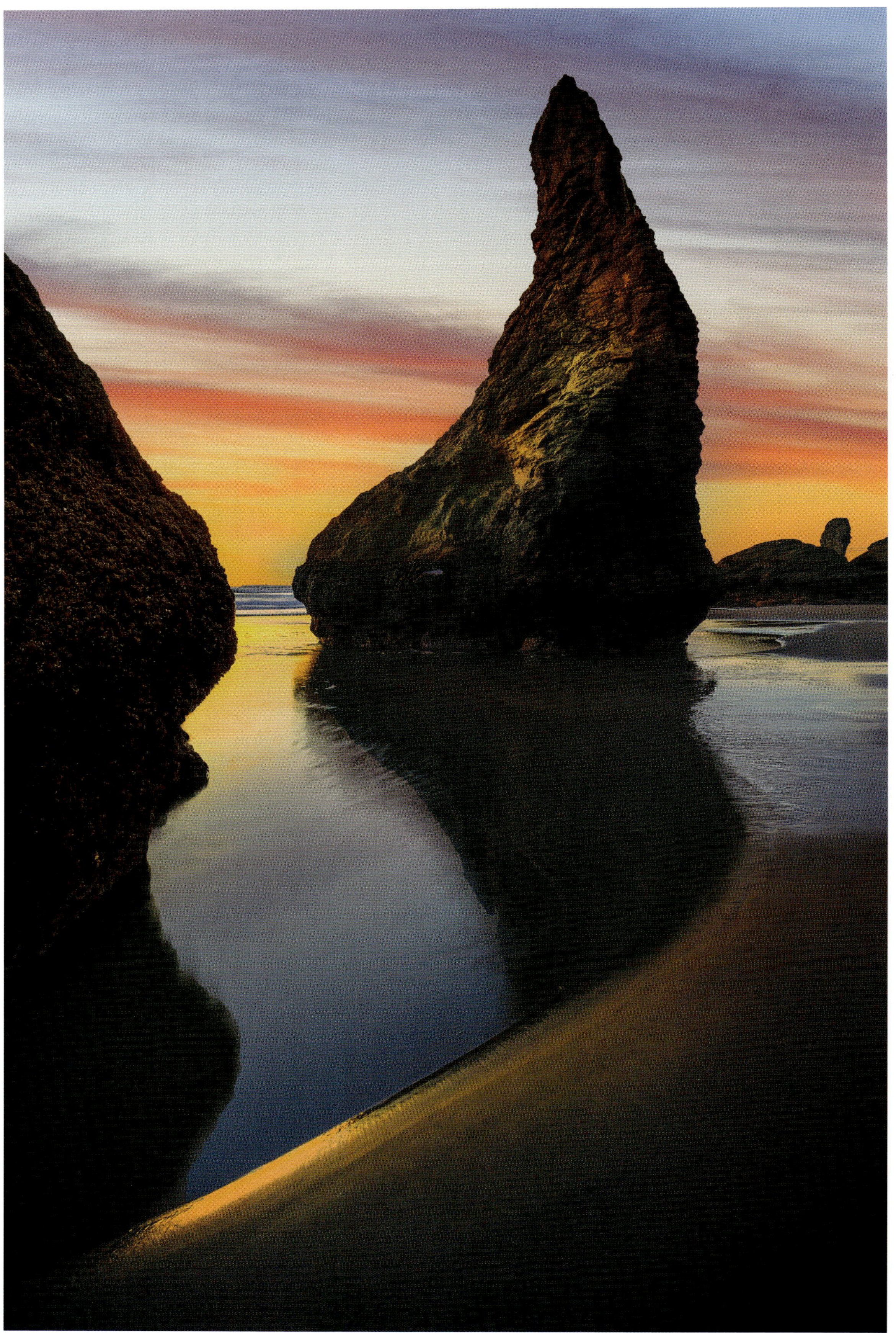

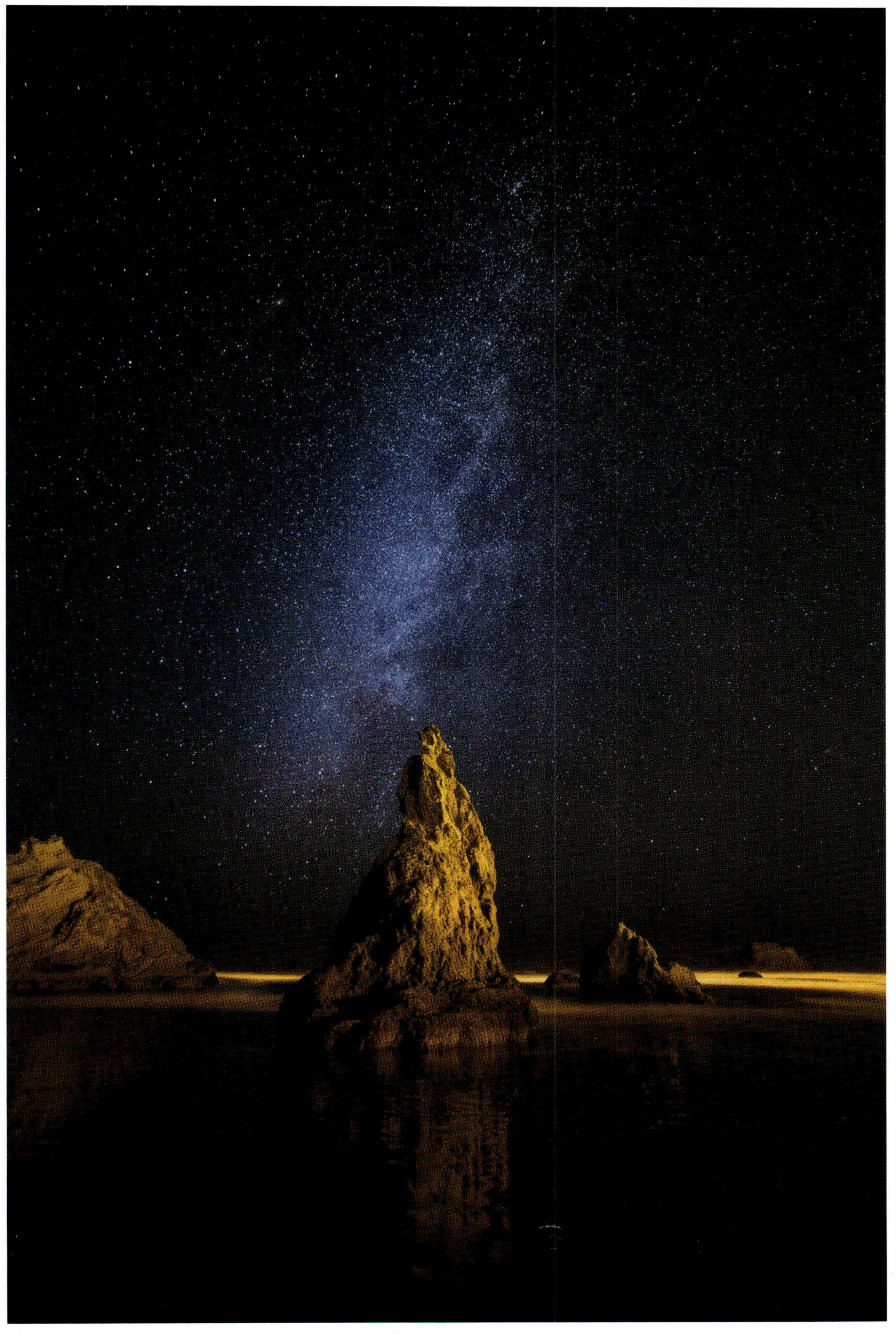

Just after sunset in January, the Milky Way sets over the sea stacks on Bandon Beach, which are in turn lit up by buildings on the bluff overlooking the beach. ●

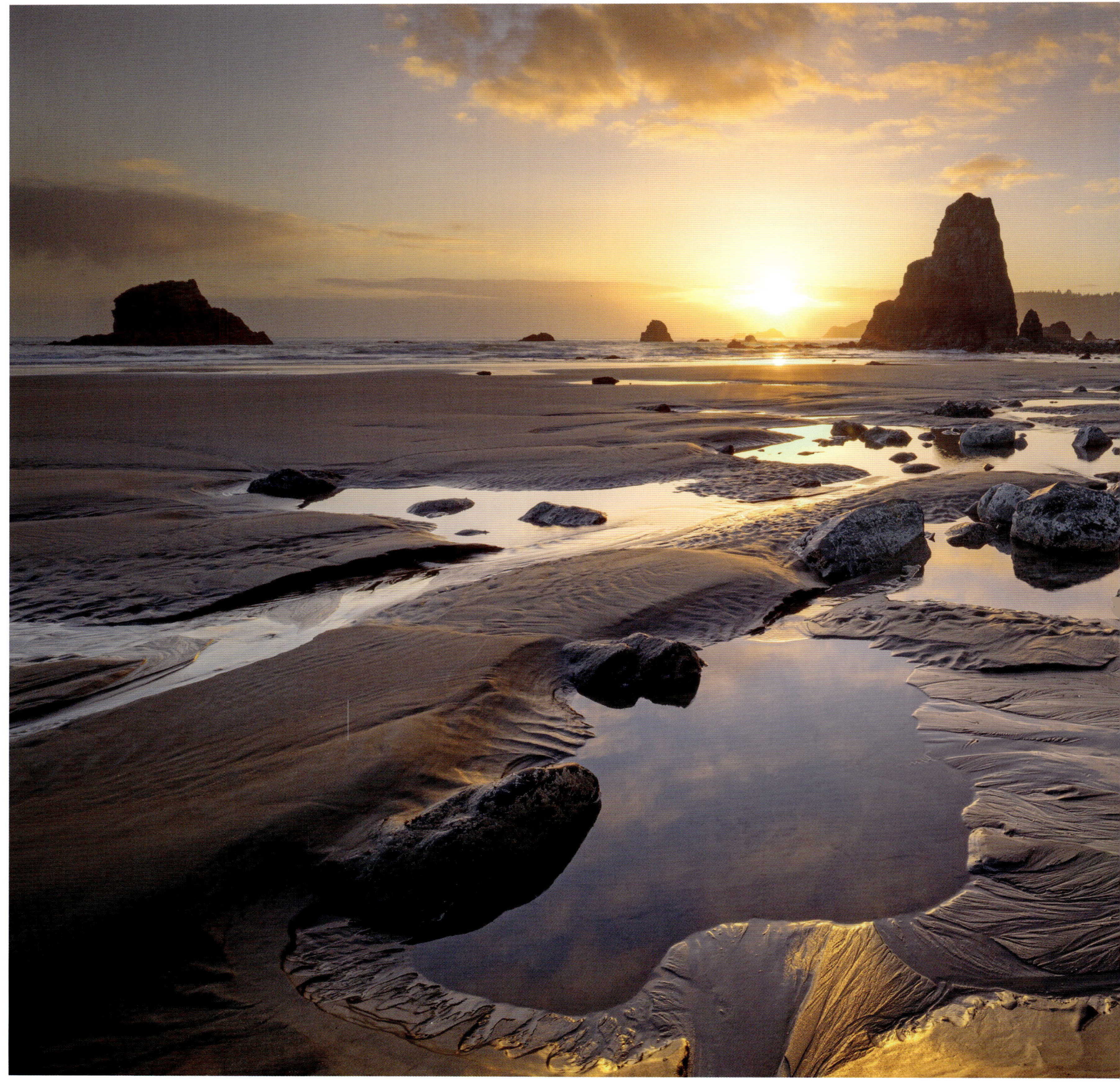

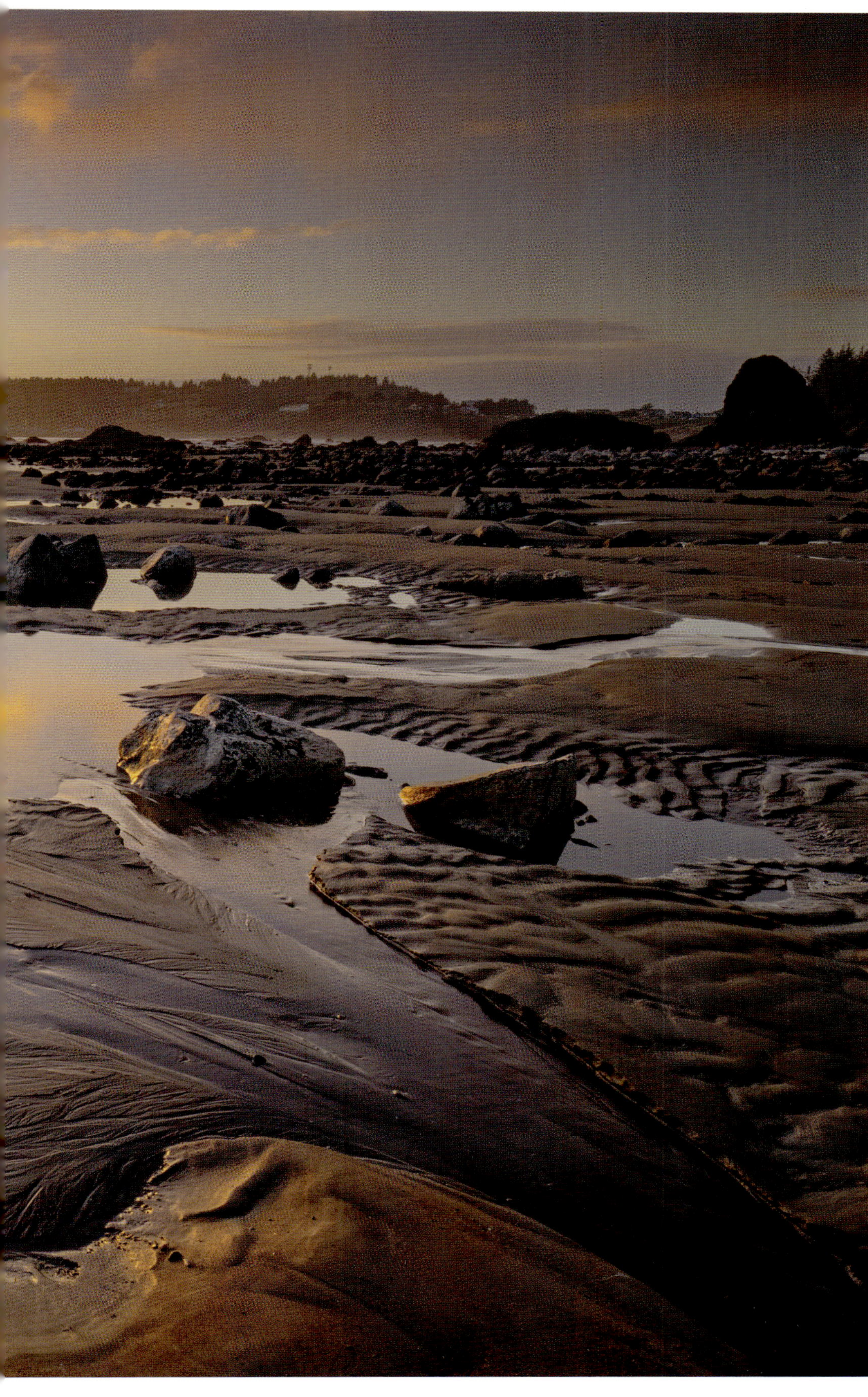

A rich bronze sunset reflects into the
tide pools of Battle Rock Beach near
Port Orford. ●

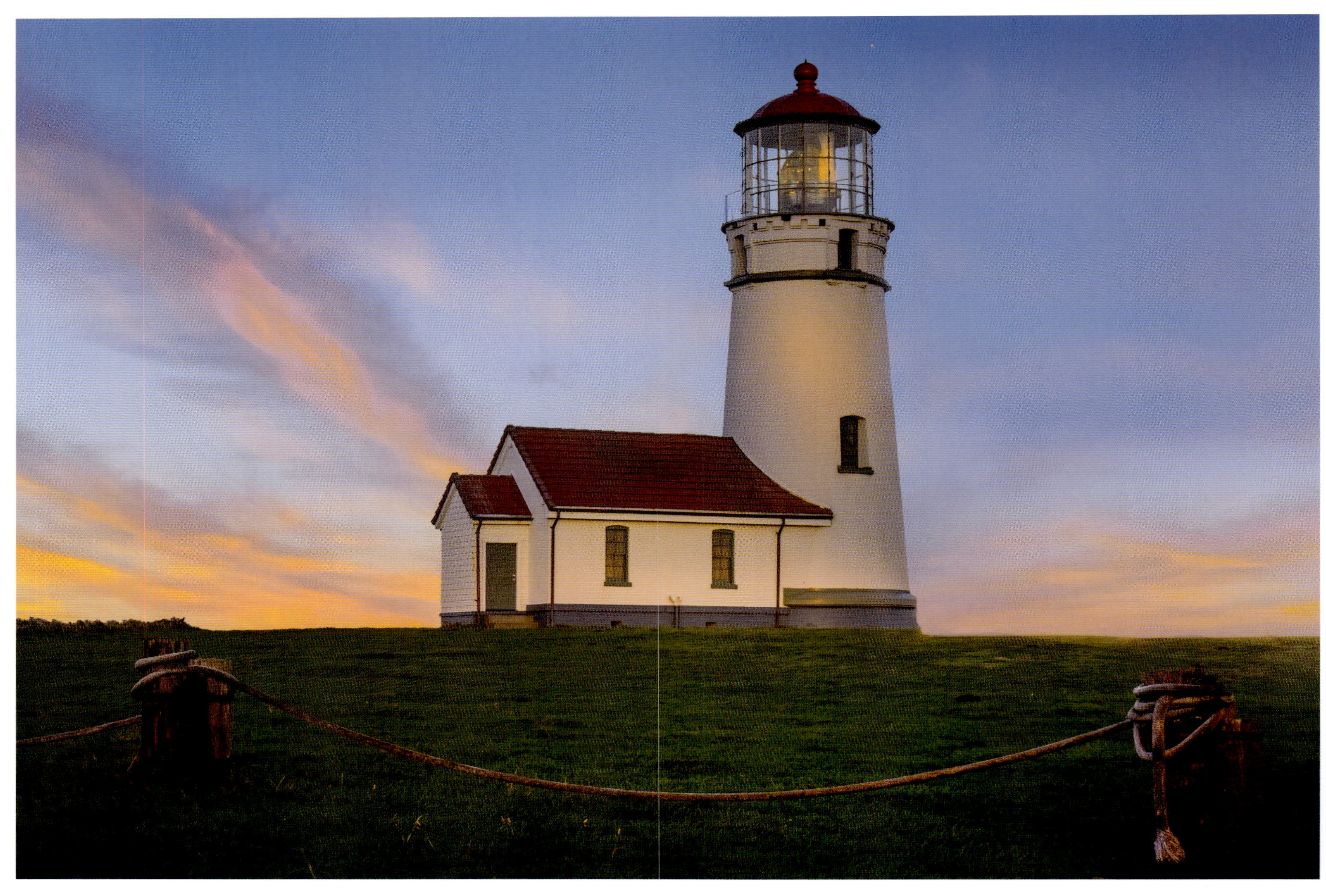

Clouds fan out at sunrise from
behind Cape Blanco Lighthouse
near Port Orford. •

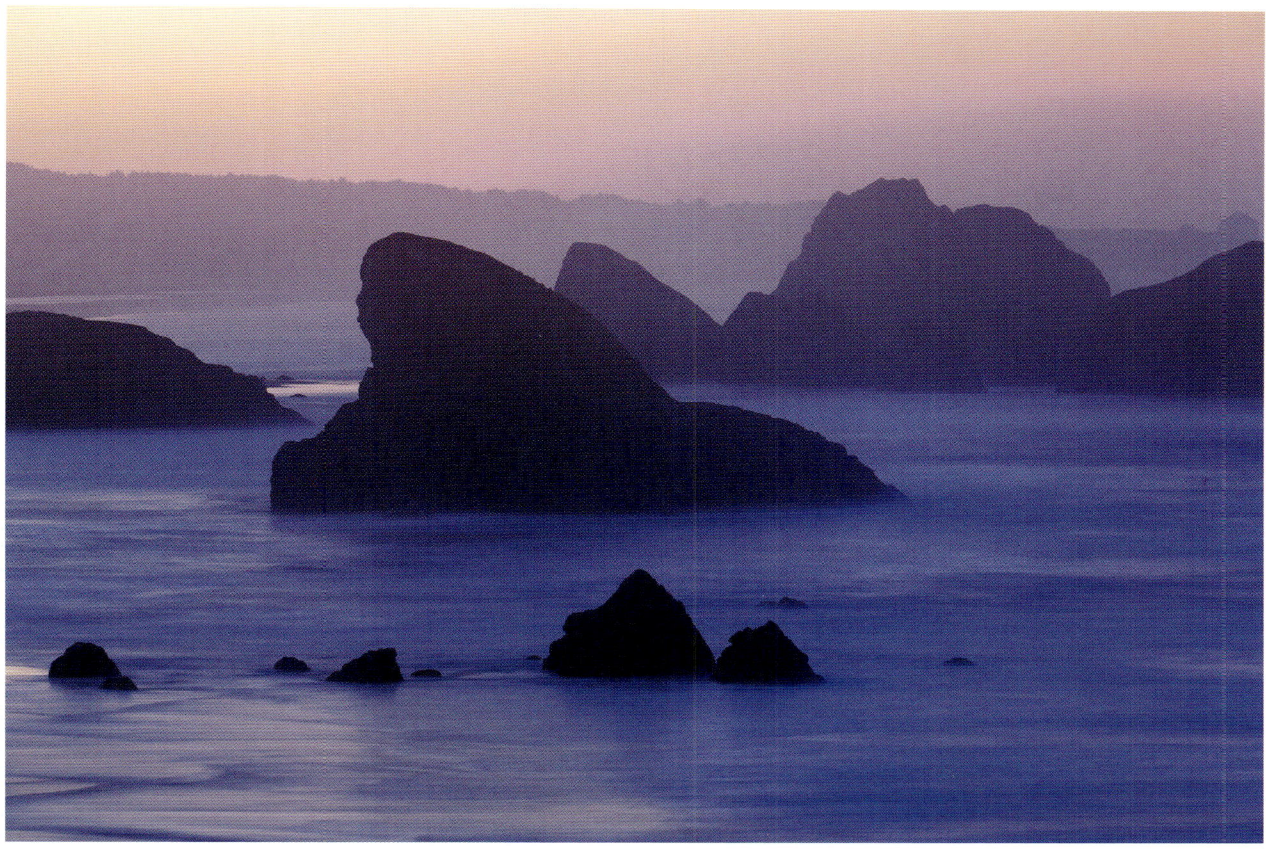

Morning mist turns rosy over the shark-fin sea stacks of Pistol River State Park. •

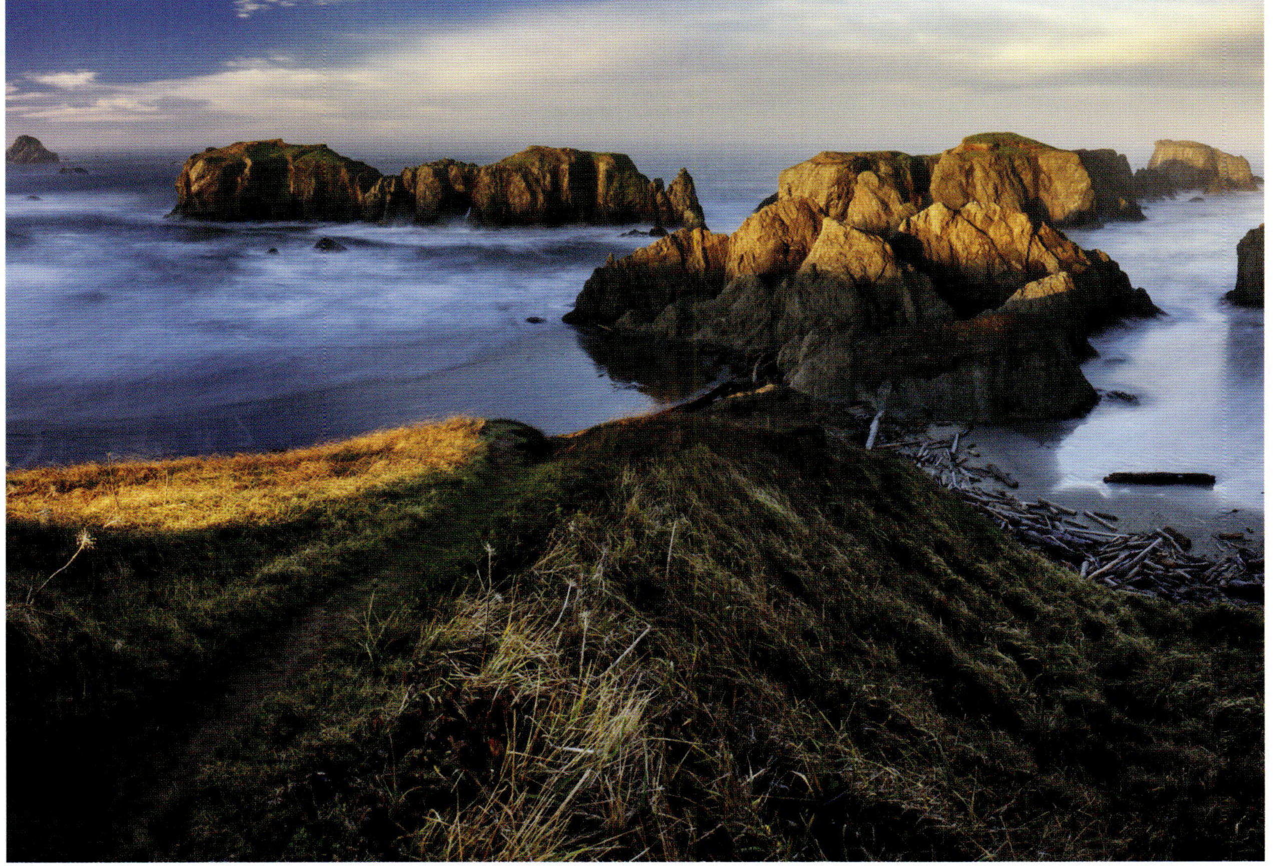

The first light of the rising sun brushes the tops of the rock formations at Coquille Point in Bandon. •

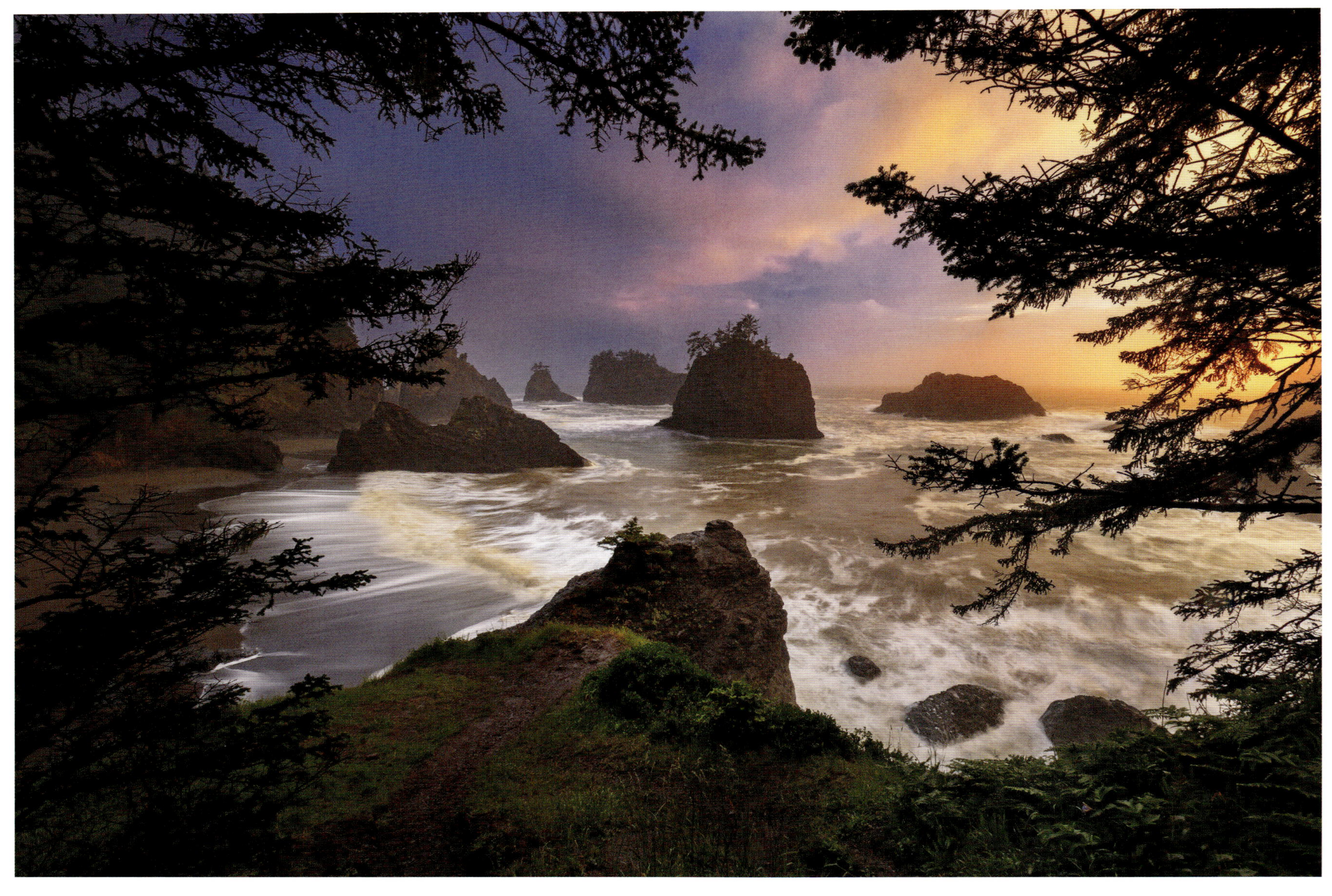

A spring storm breaks at sunset
over Secret Beach on the southern
coast, bathing the sea stacks and
waves in red light. •

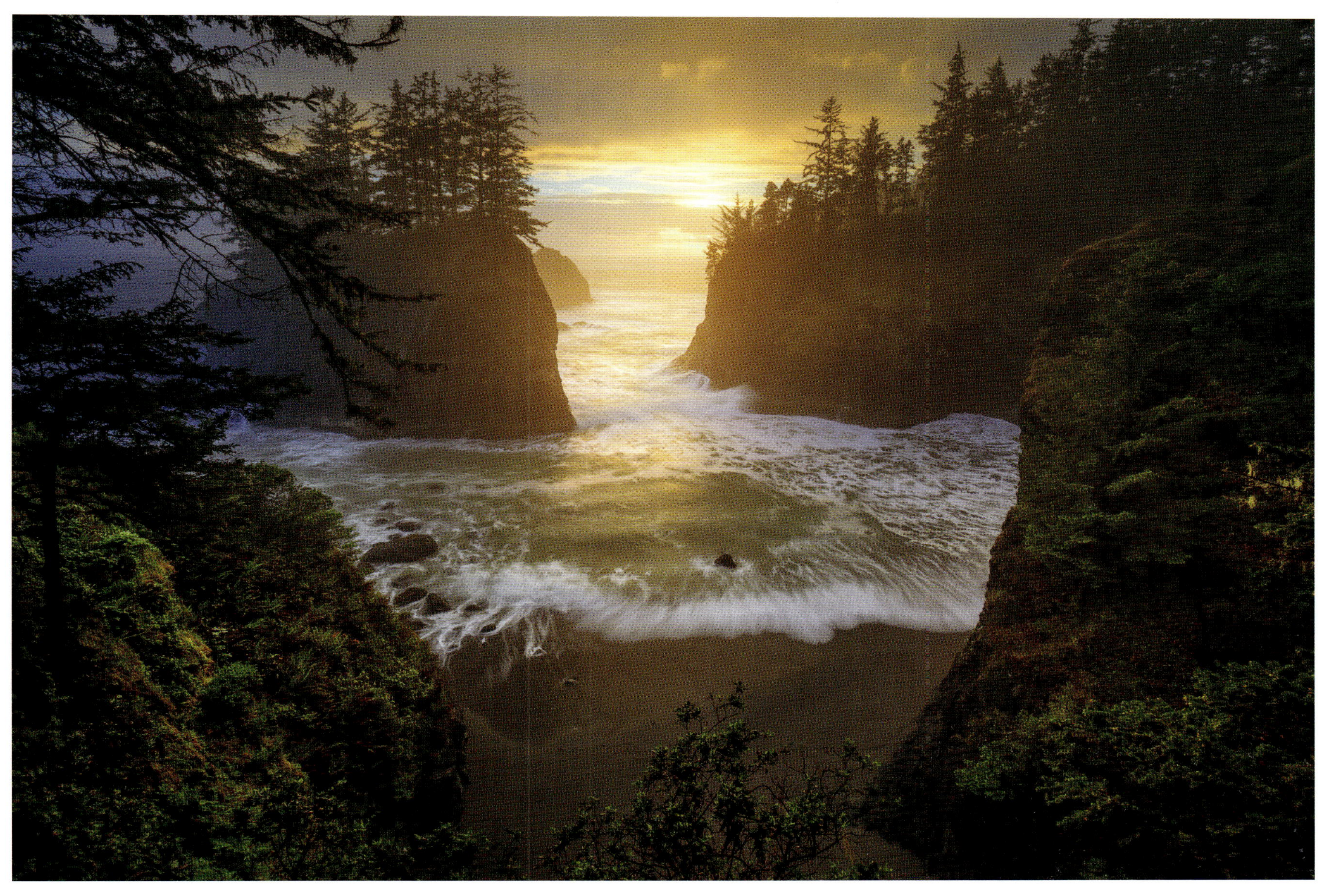

Moisture-laden marine air illuminated
by the setting sun at a small hidden cove
along the Samuel H. Boardman State
Scenic Corridor north of Brookings. •

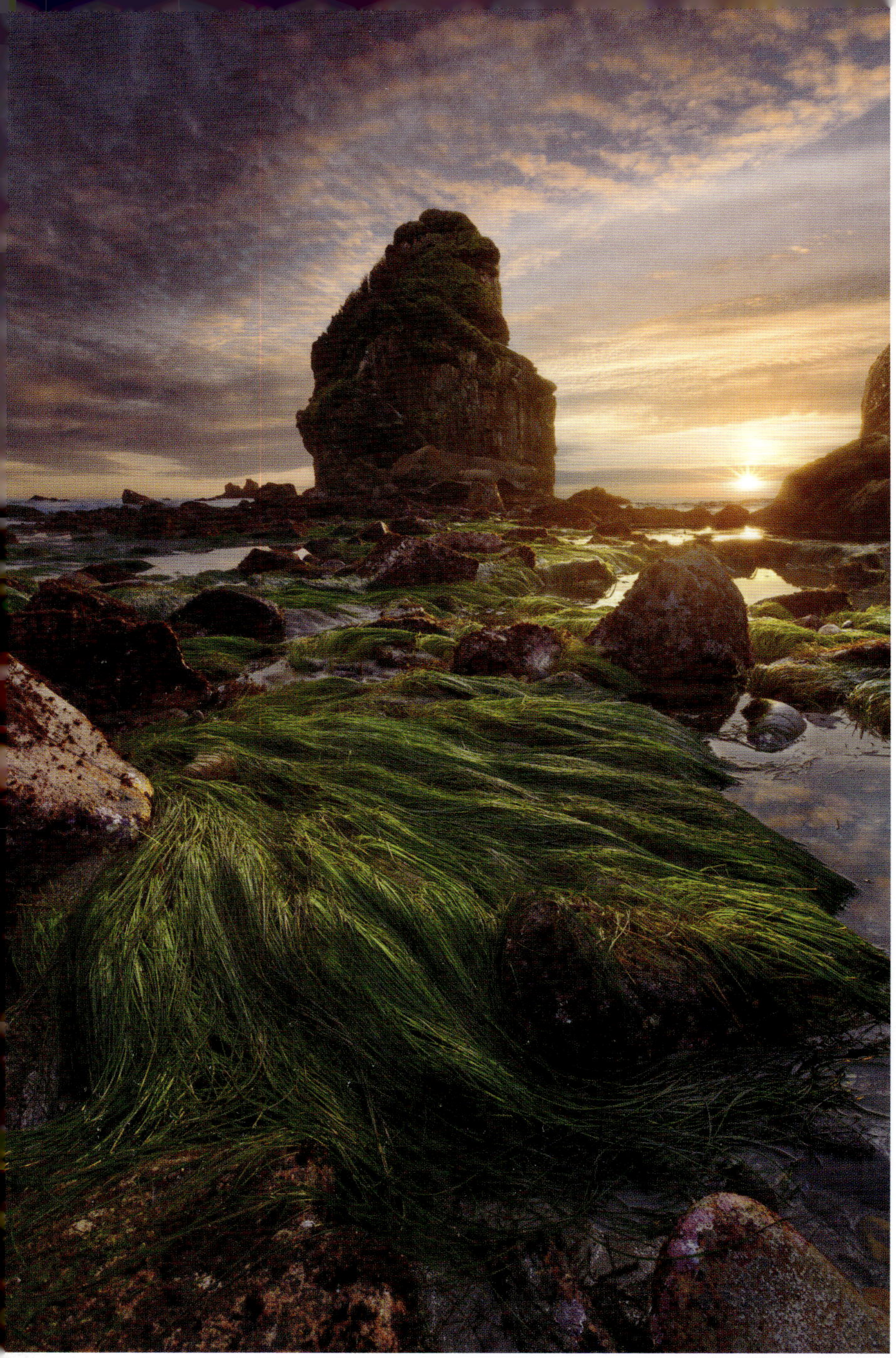

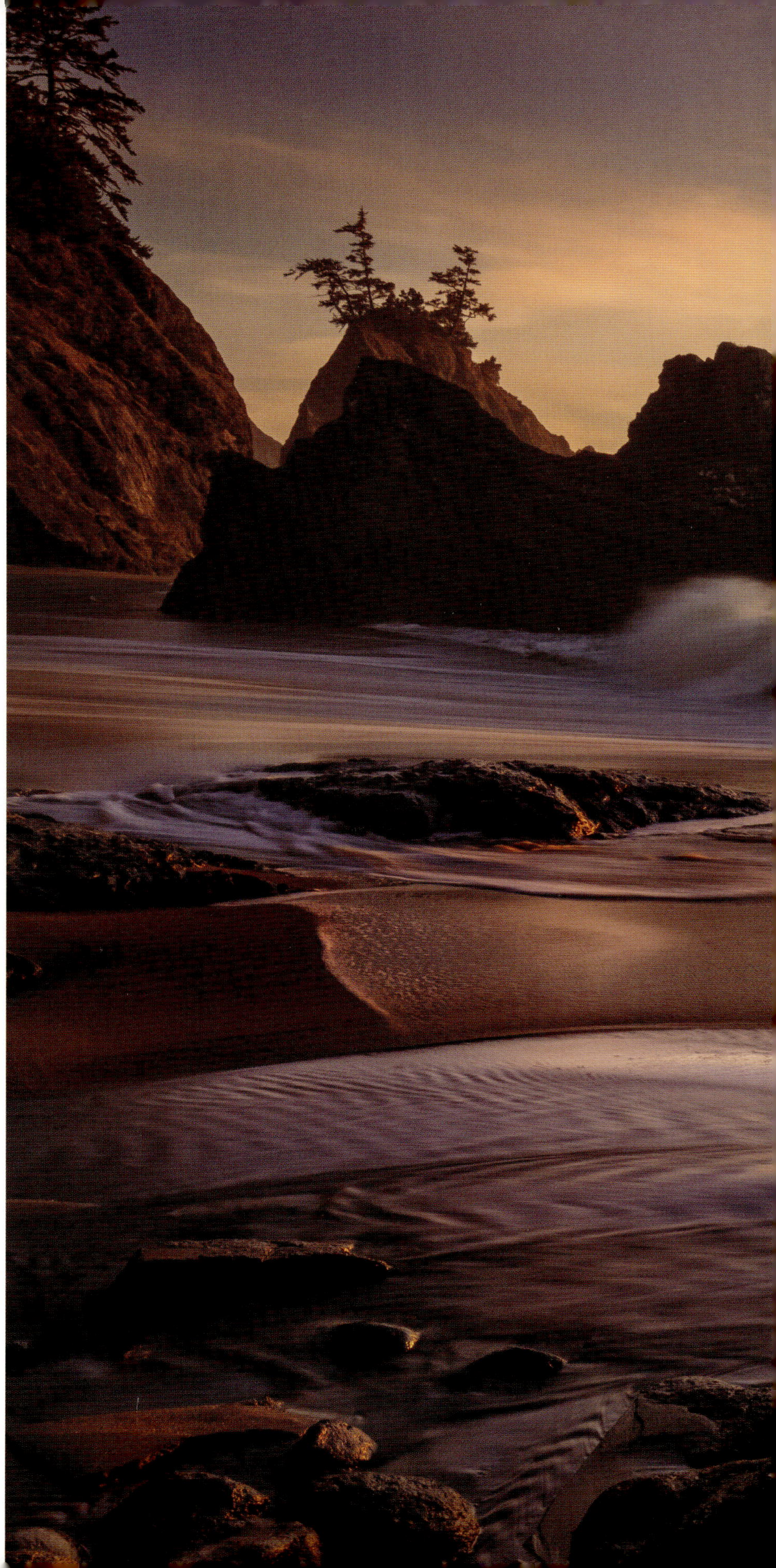

ABOVE A blanket of sea grass revealed
in tide pools at Harris Beach State Park. •

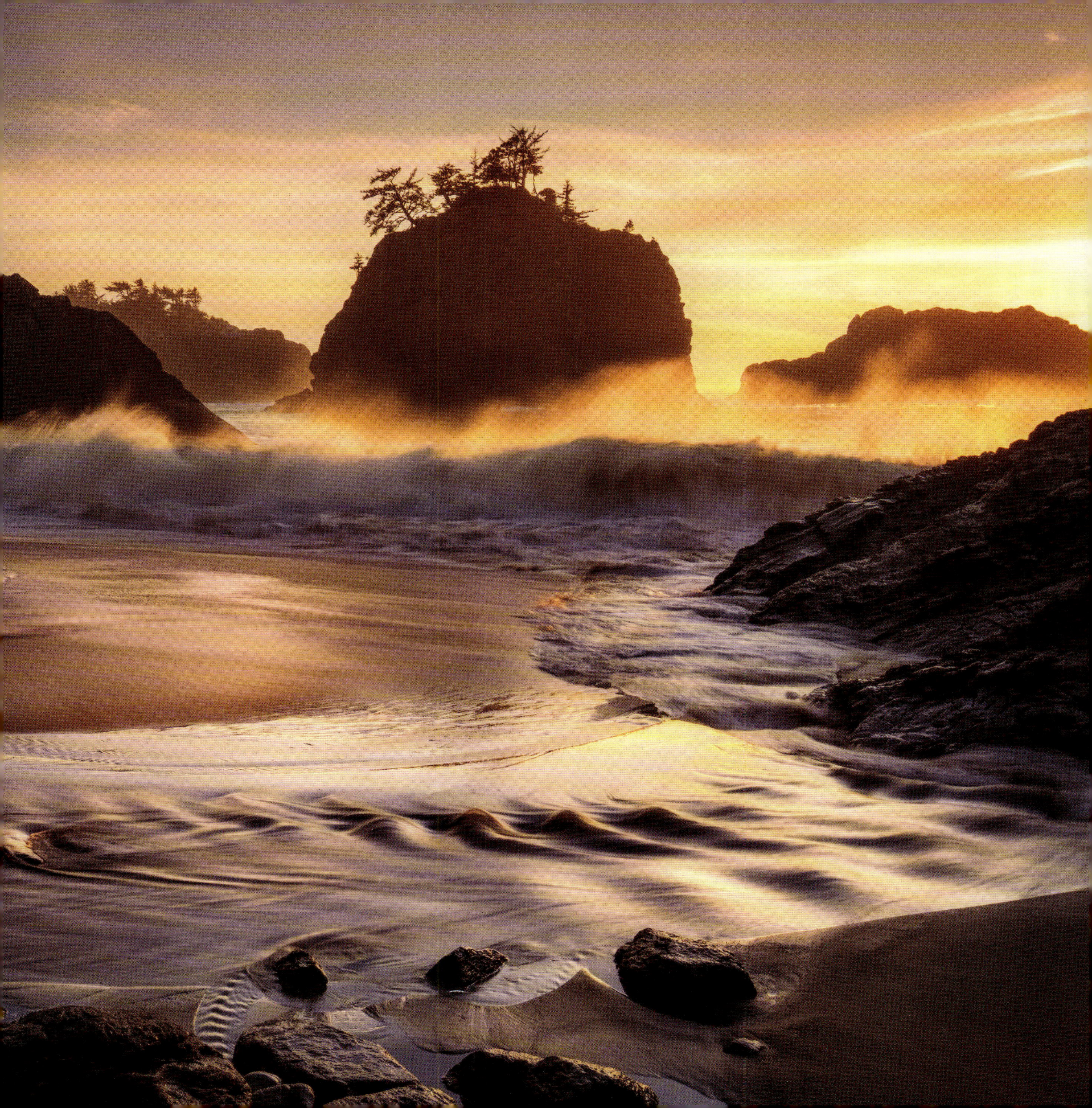

PREVIOUS PAGES High surf
during winter at Secret Beach on
the southern coast. •

RIGHT Looking south from the
Natural Bridges section of the Samuel
H. Boardman State Scenic Corridor. •

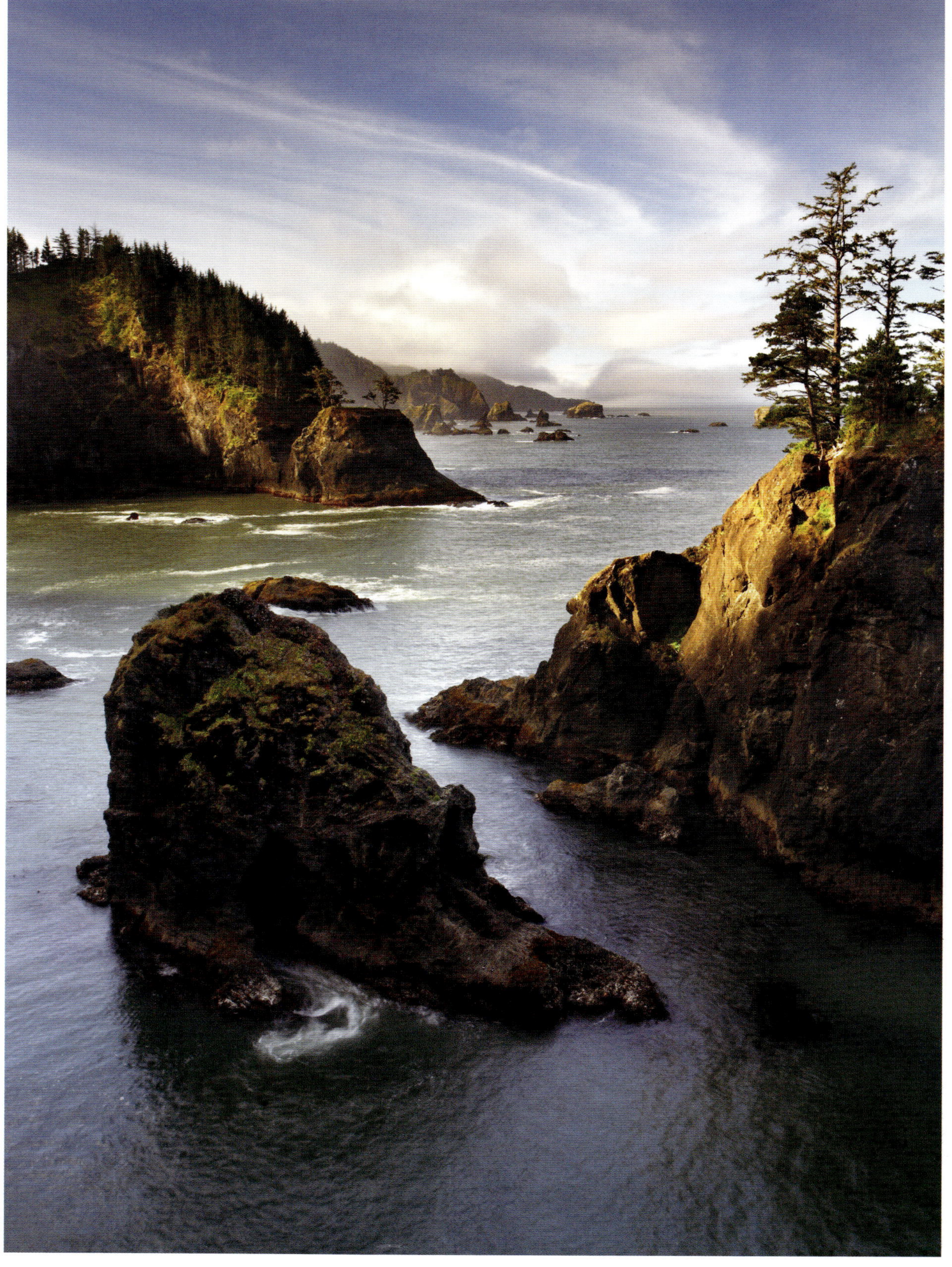

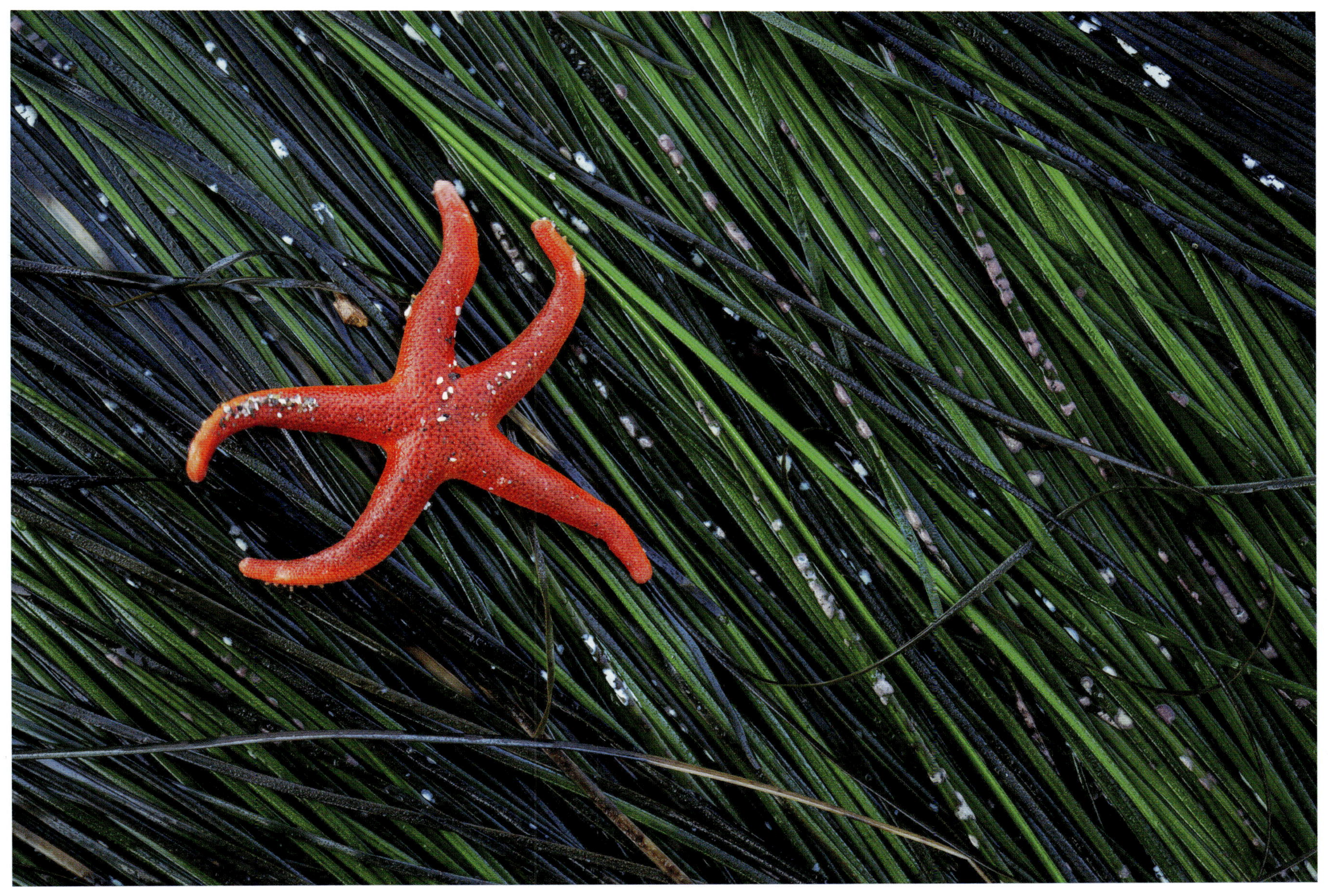

A blood star rests on eelgrass along the southern coastline. •

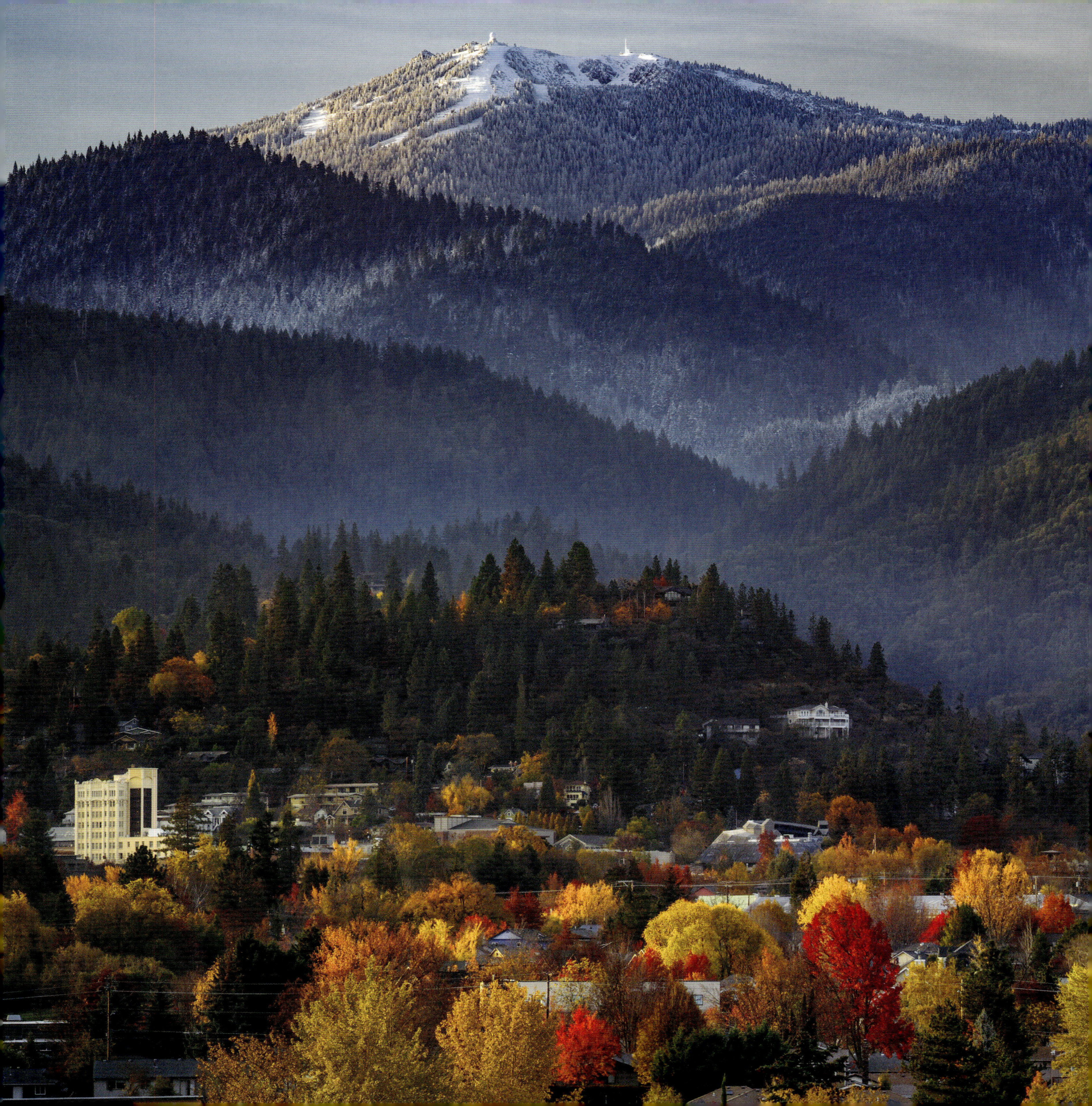

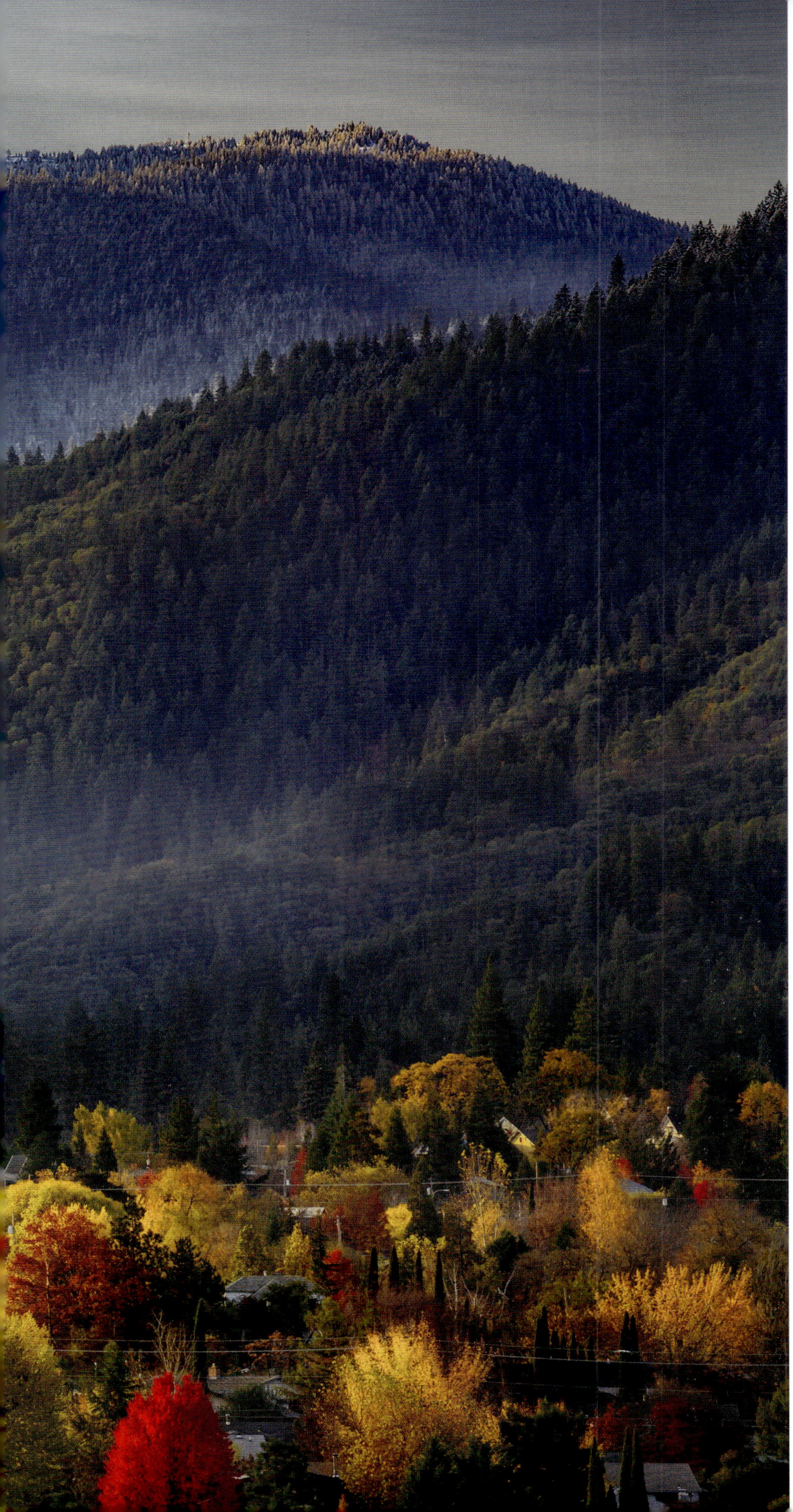

Fall and winter seem to overlap in the quaint town of Ashland, nestled in the foothills of the Sisk you Mountains and just below Mount Ashland. ●

The Allen Elizabethan Theater, one of
three theaters that hosts plays during
Ashland's renowned Oregon Shakespeare
Festival, surrounded by fall color in
Lithia Park. ●

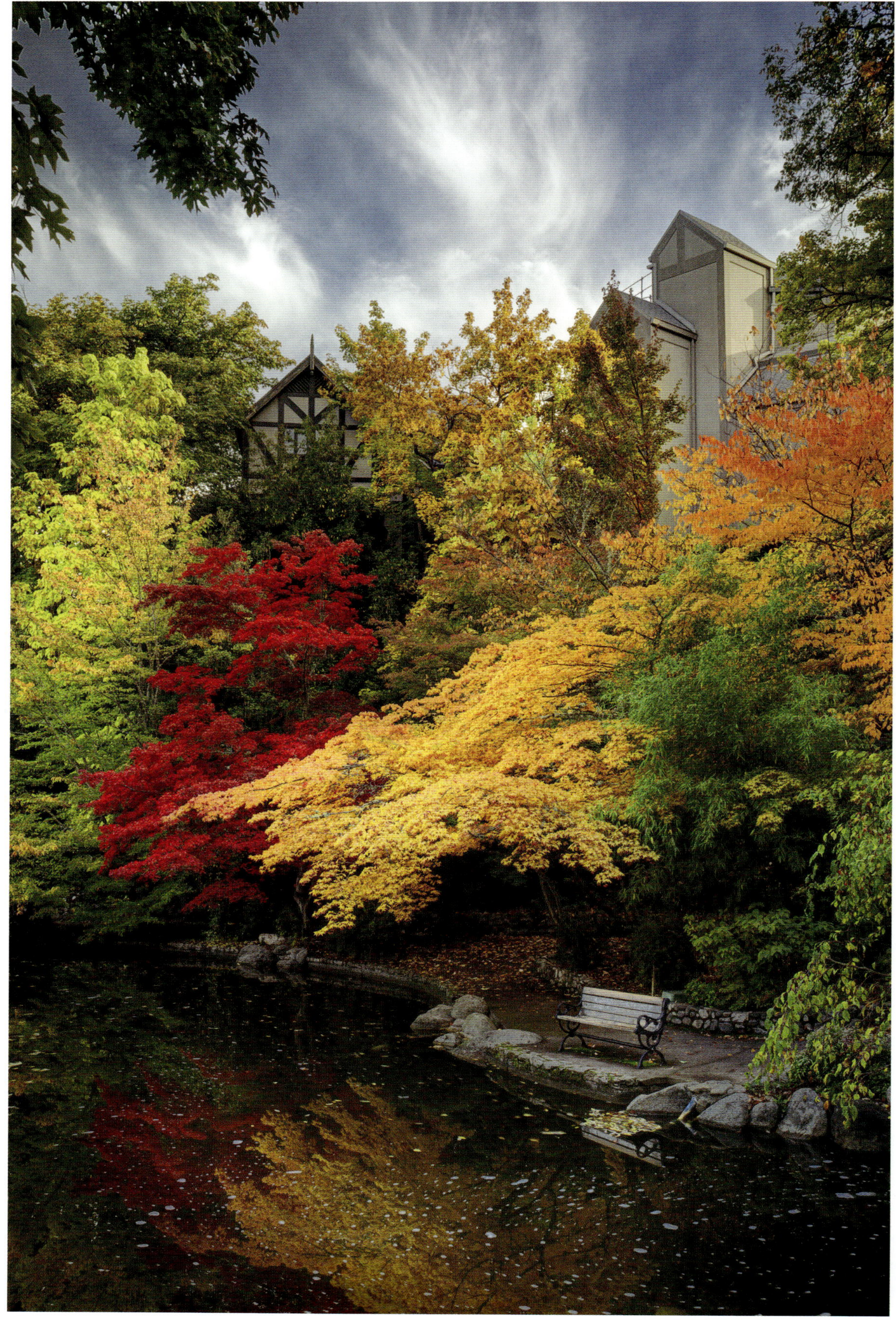

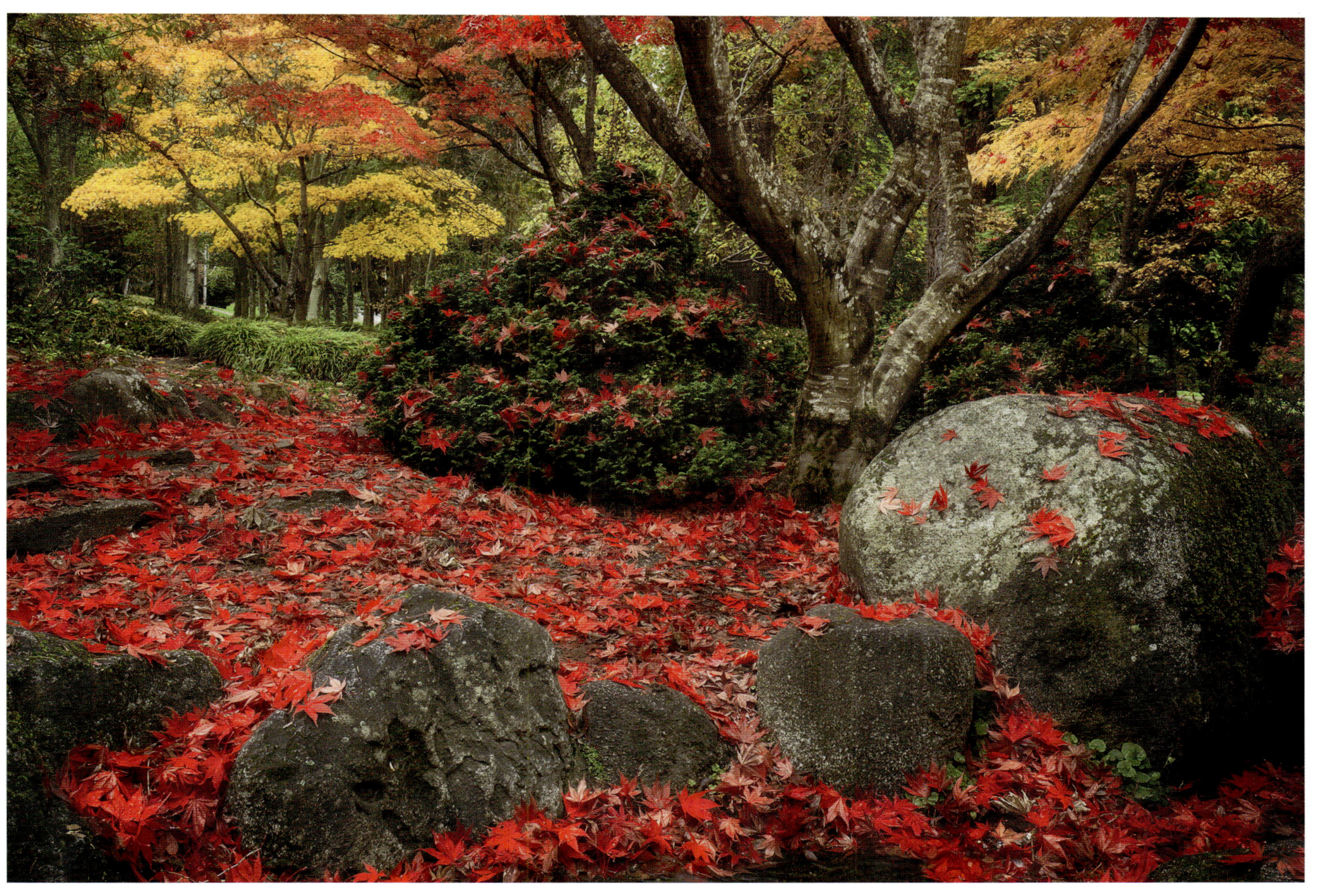

The Japanese Garden in Ashland's
Lithia Park, carpeted by maple leaves
in autumn. ●

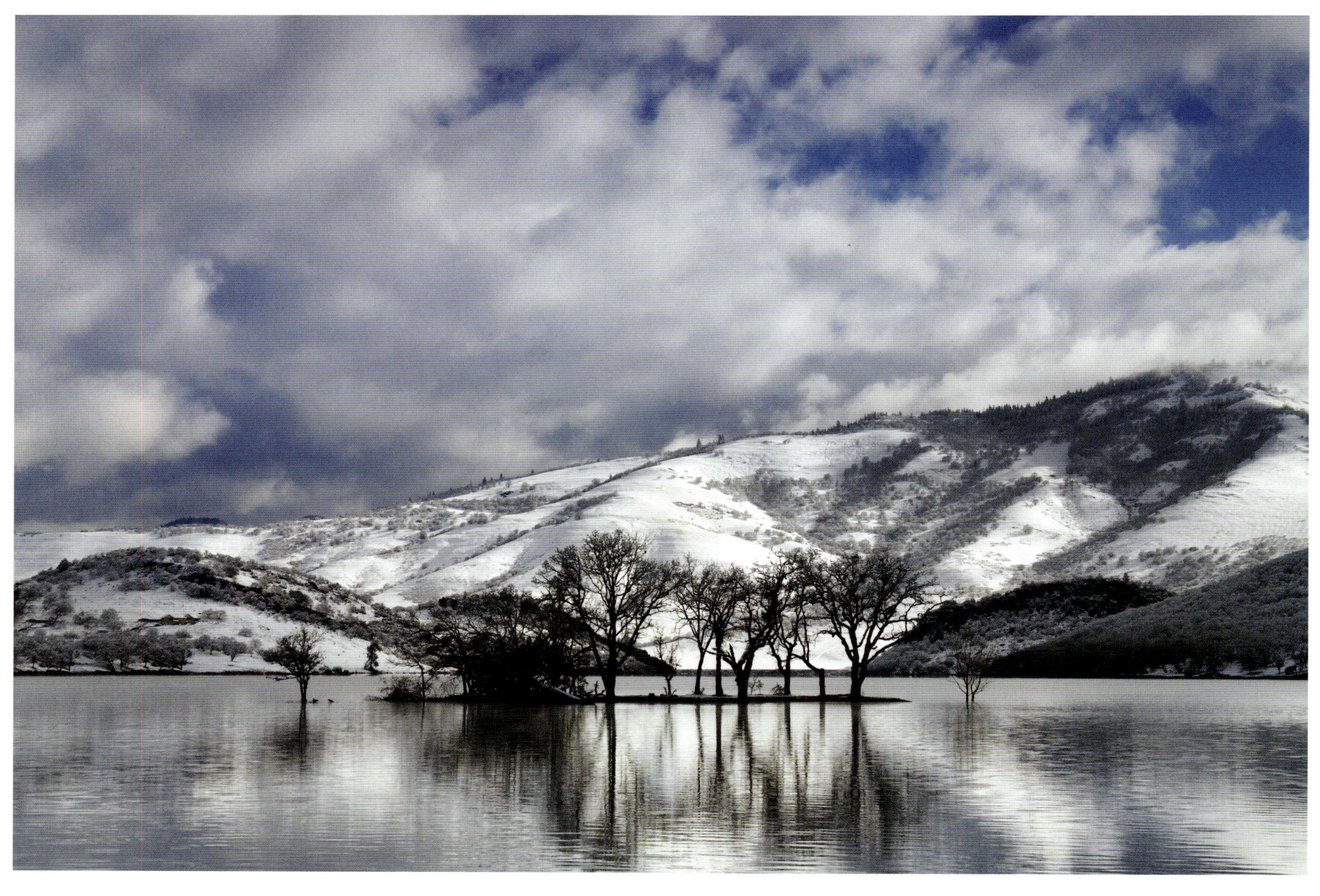

Emigrant Lake, nestled in the foothills
of the Cascade-Siskiyou National
Monument near Ashland. •

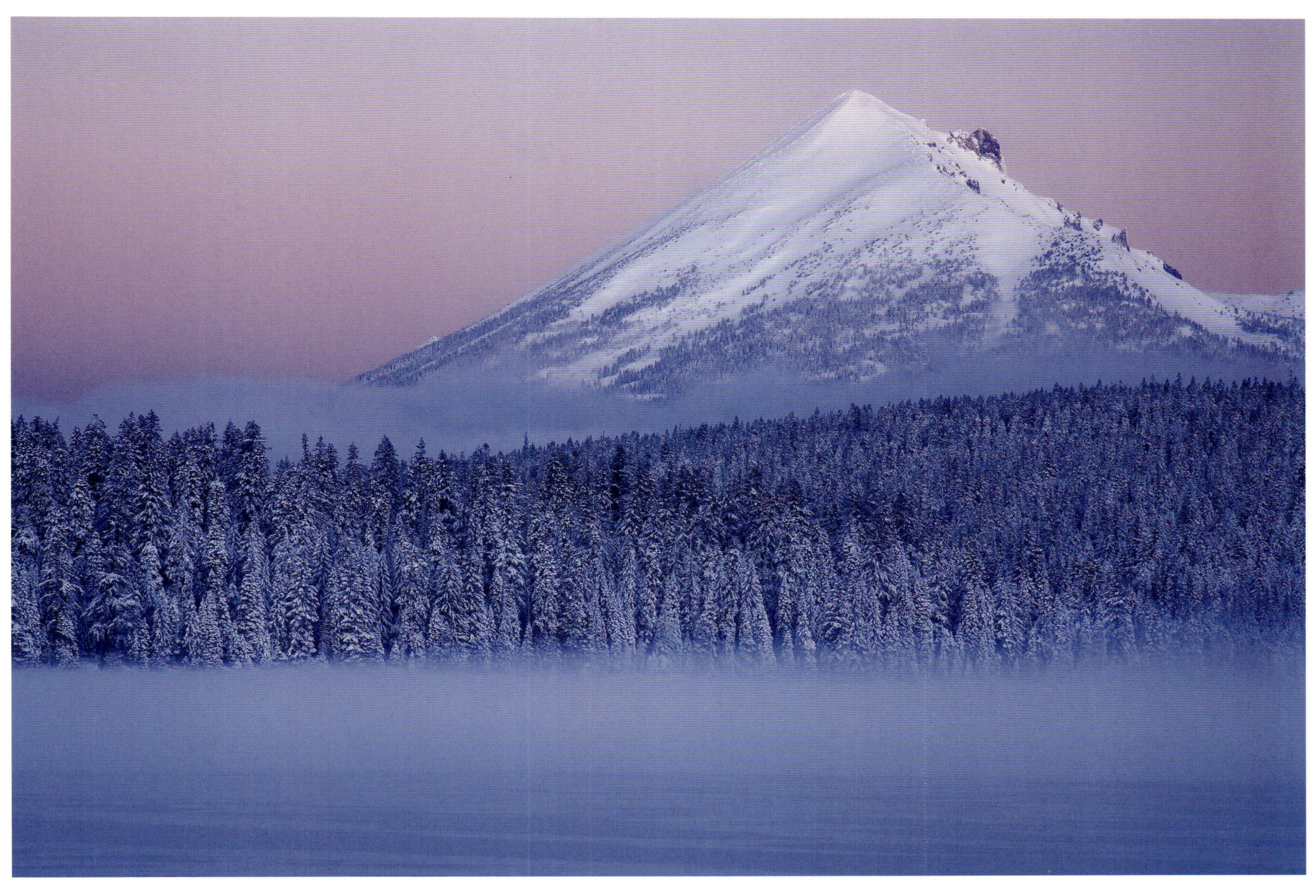

At 9493 feet, the volcanic Mount
McLoughlin rises in the predawn light
above a mist-covered Lake of the Woods
in the Cascade Range. •

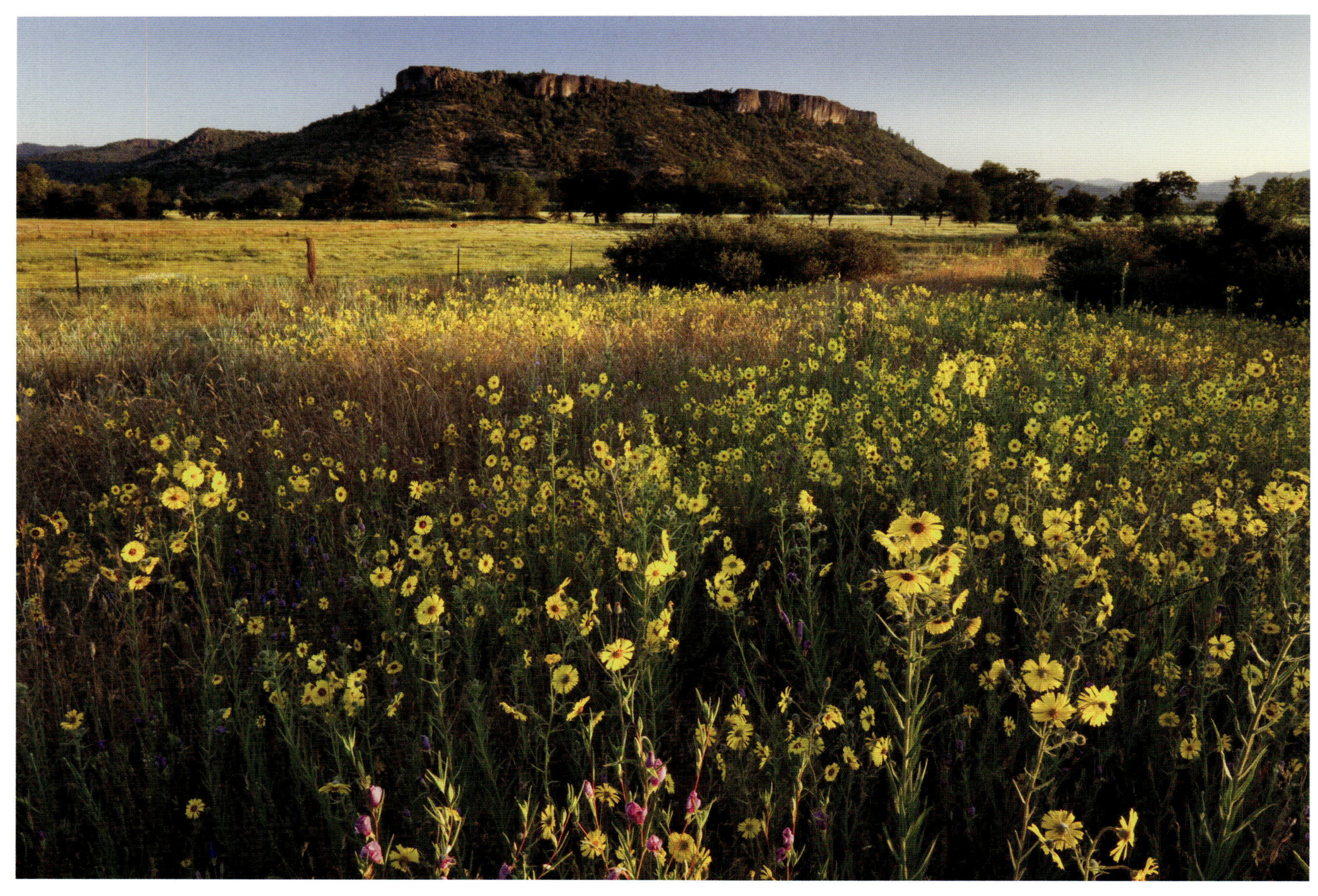

Lower Table Rock, one of two prominent
volcanic plateaus located just north of the
Rogue River, rises 800 feet above fields of
tarweed flowers (*Madia* sp.). •

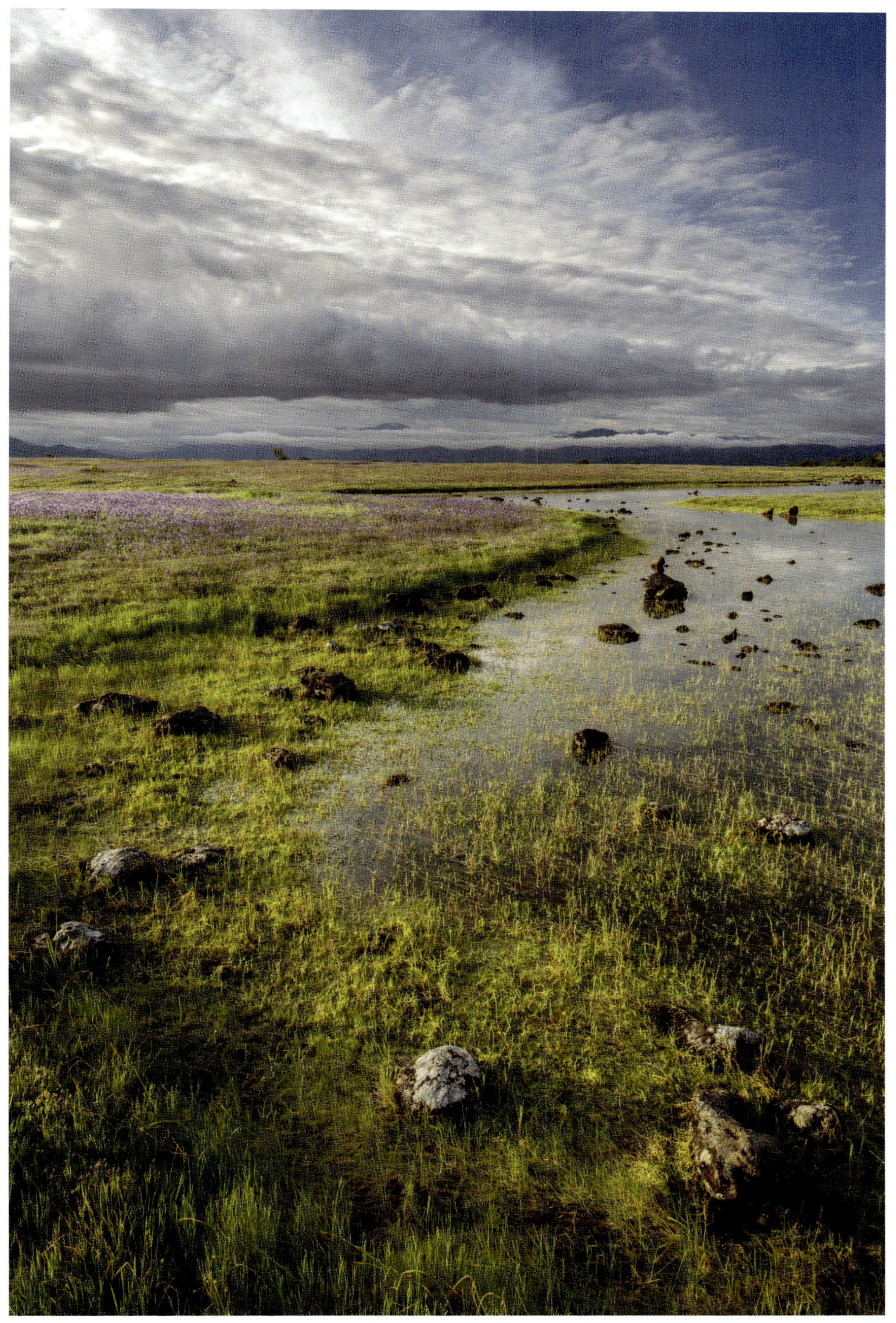

The tops of Upper and Lower Table Rocks are home to over 70 species of animals and 200 species of flowers. Vernal pools atop the rocks fill during winter and spring and are one of the few places a threatened species of freshwater fairy shrimp, *Branchinecta lynchi,* can live. ●

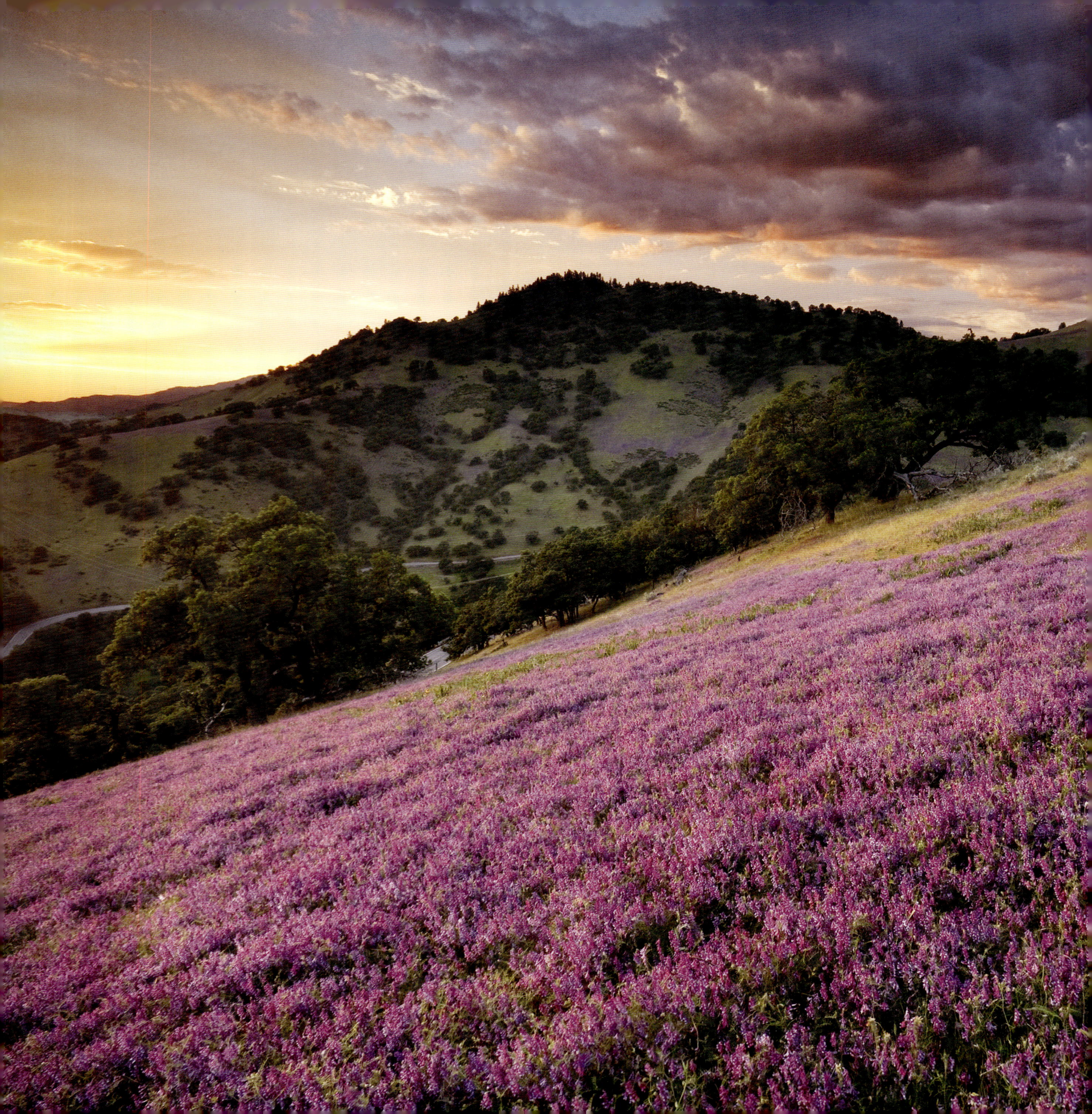

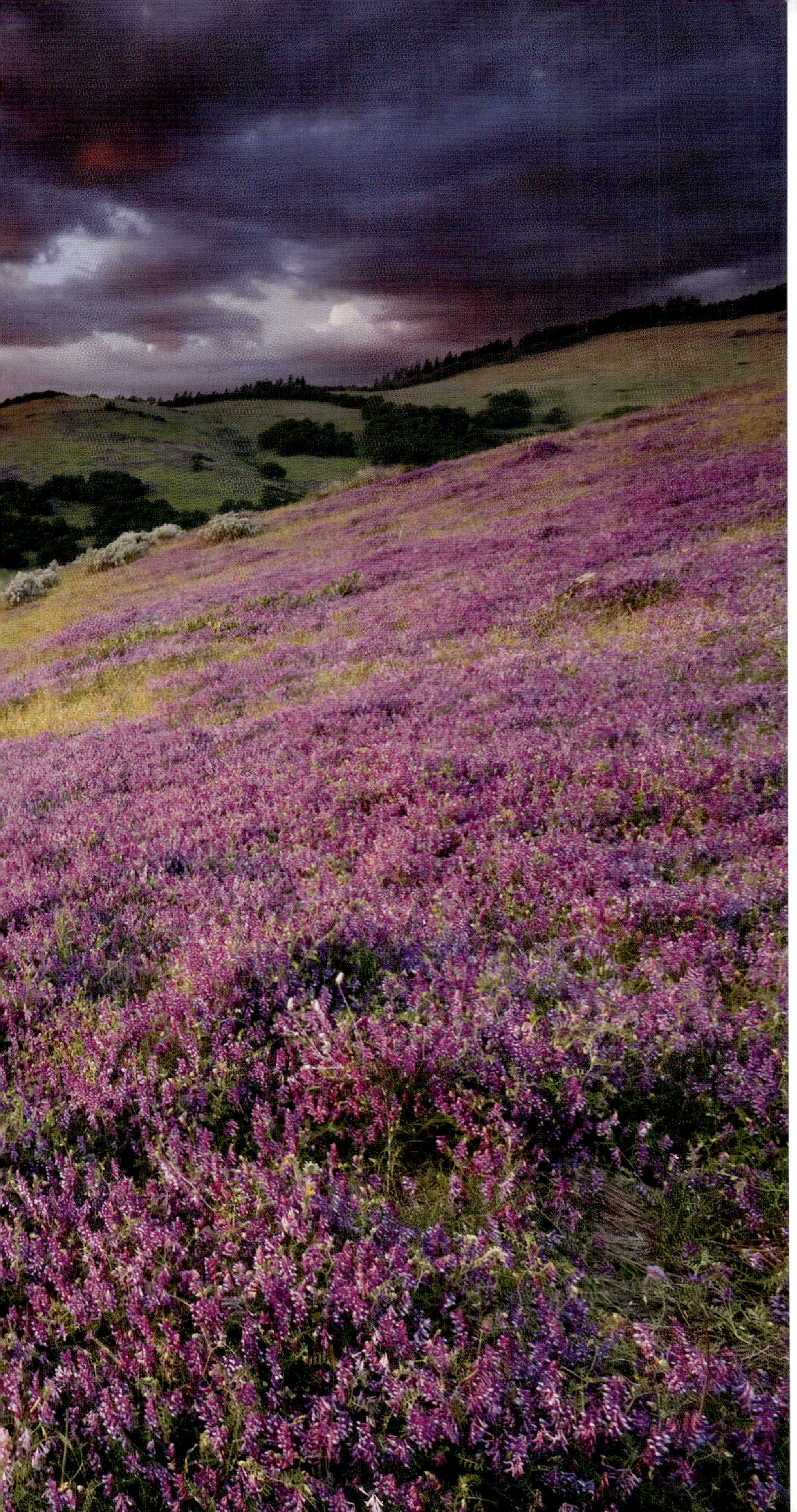

Colorful sunset light, dramatic clouds, and flowering vetch (*Vicia* sp.) in the hills along the Green Springs Highway in the southern Cascades. ●

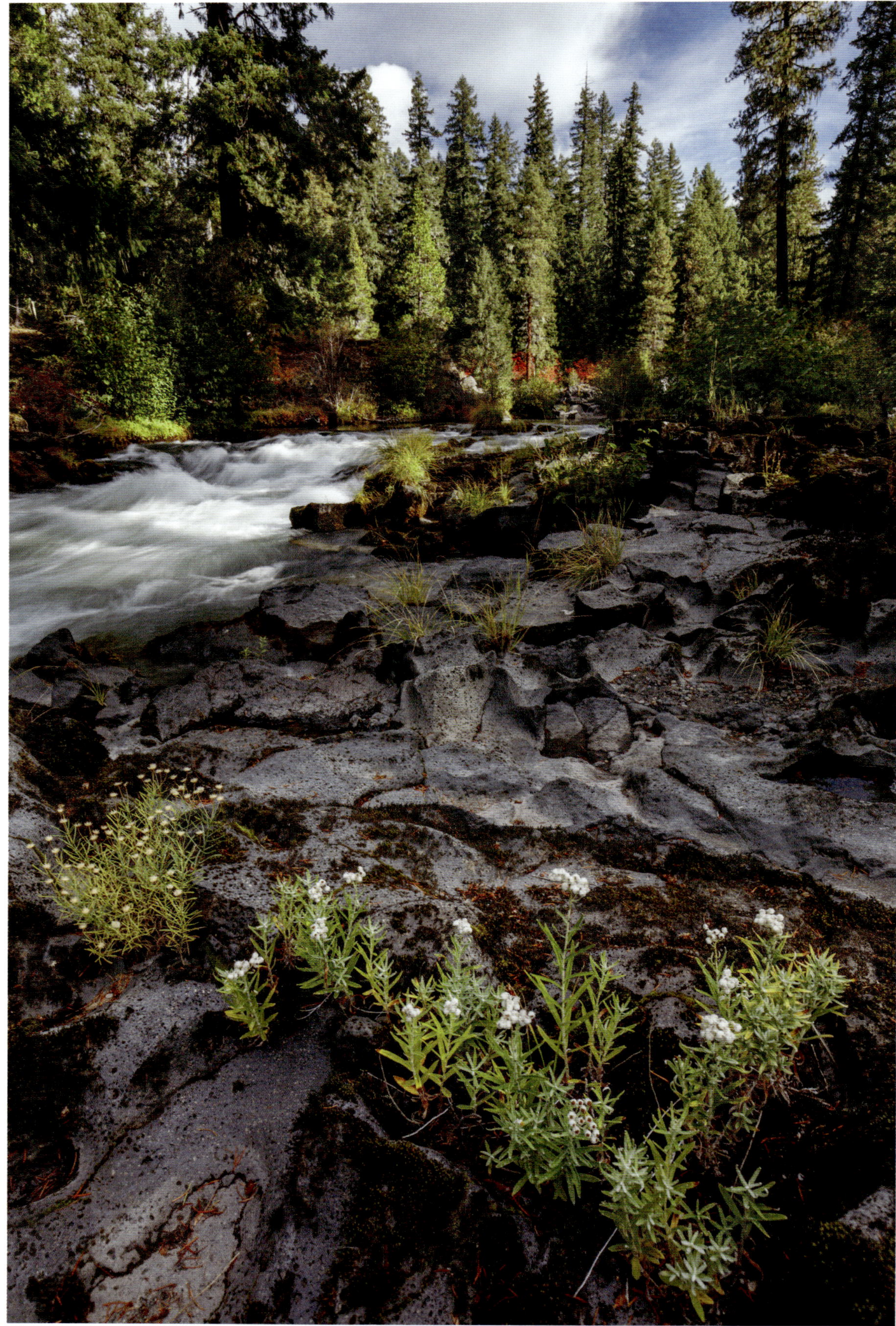

Fall color, wildflowers, and eroded
volcanic basalt along the Upper Rogue
River, which runs from its headwaters a
few miles upstream on the western
slopes of Crater Lake. ●

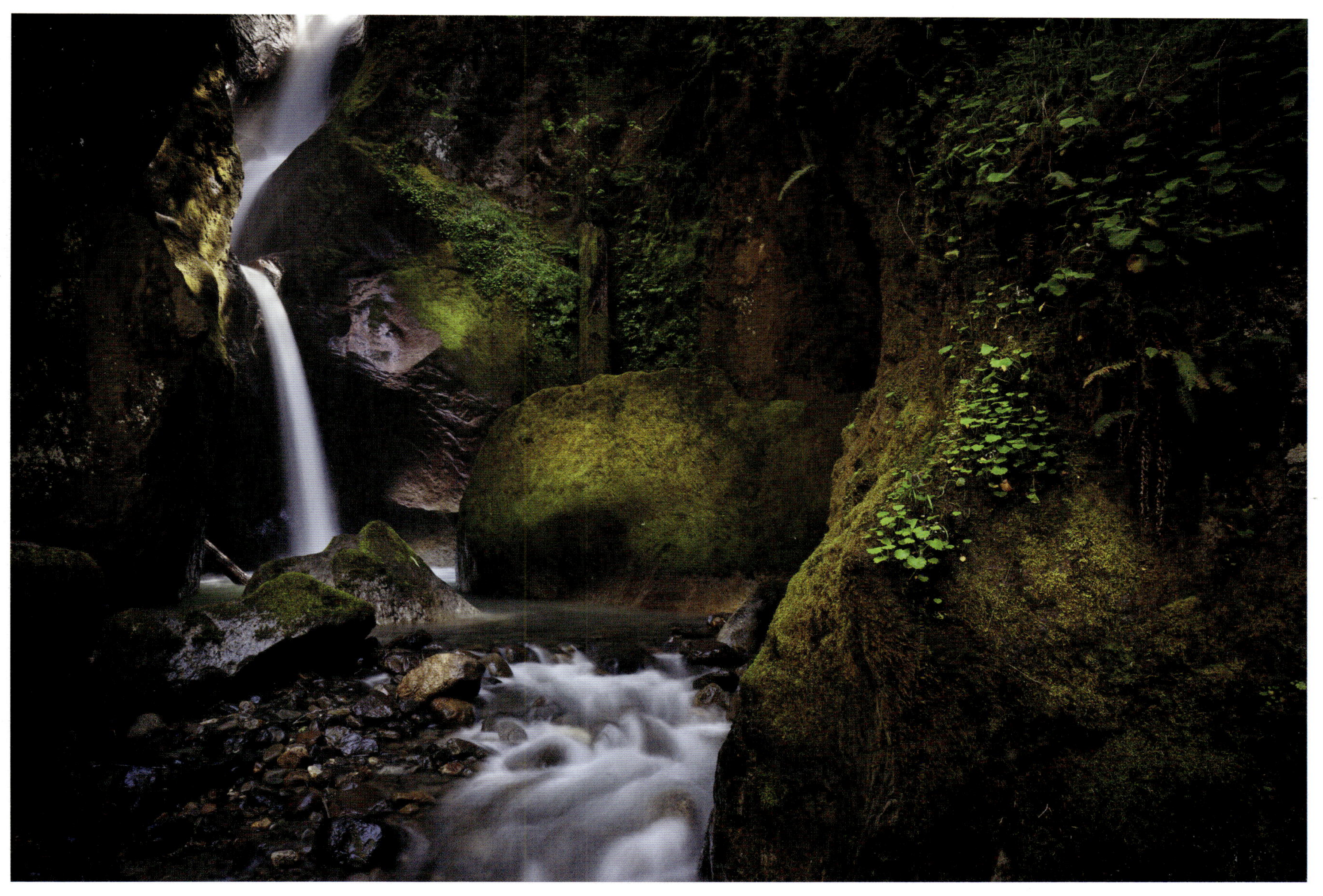

A small stream in the North Umpqua
River watershed on the west side of the
Cascade Range plummets 100 feet into
a dark, mossy canyon carved by erosion
over thousands of years. •

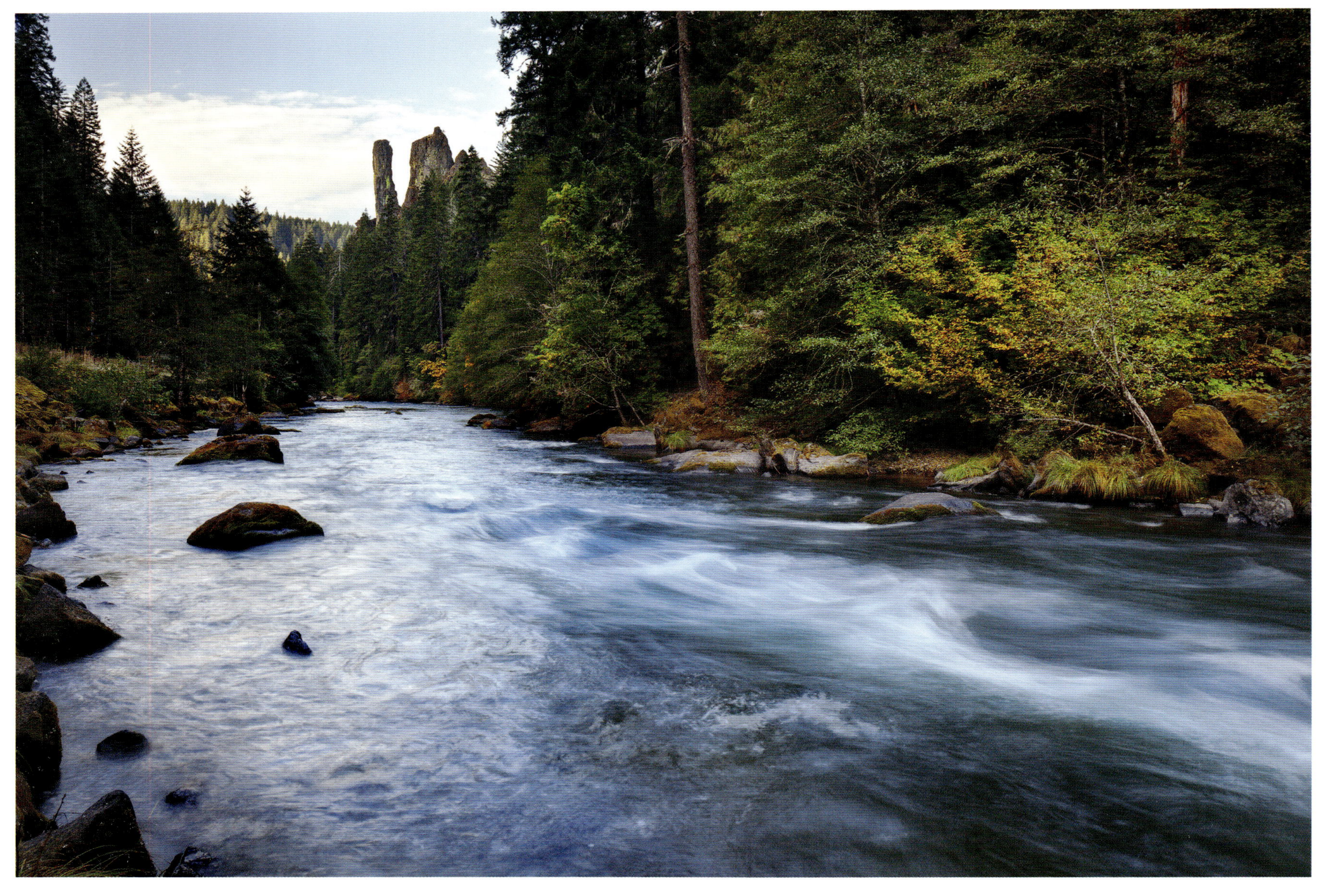

Two prominent rock spires called Old Man and Old Woman stand dominantly above the North Umpqua River east of the town of Glide. •

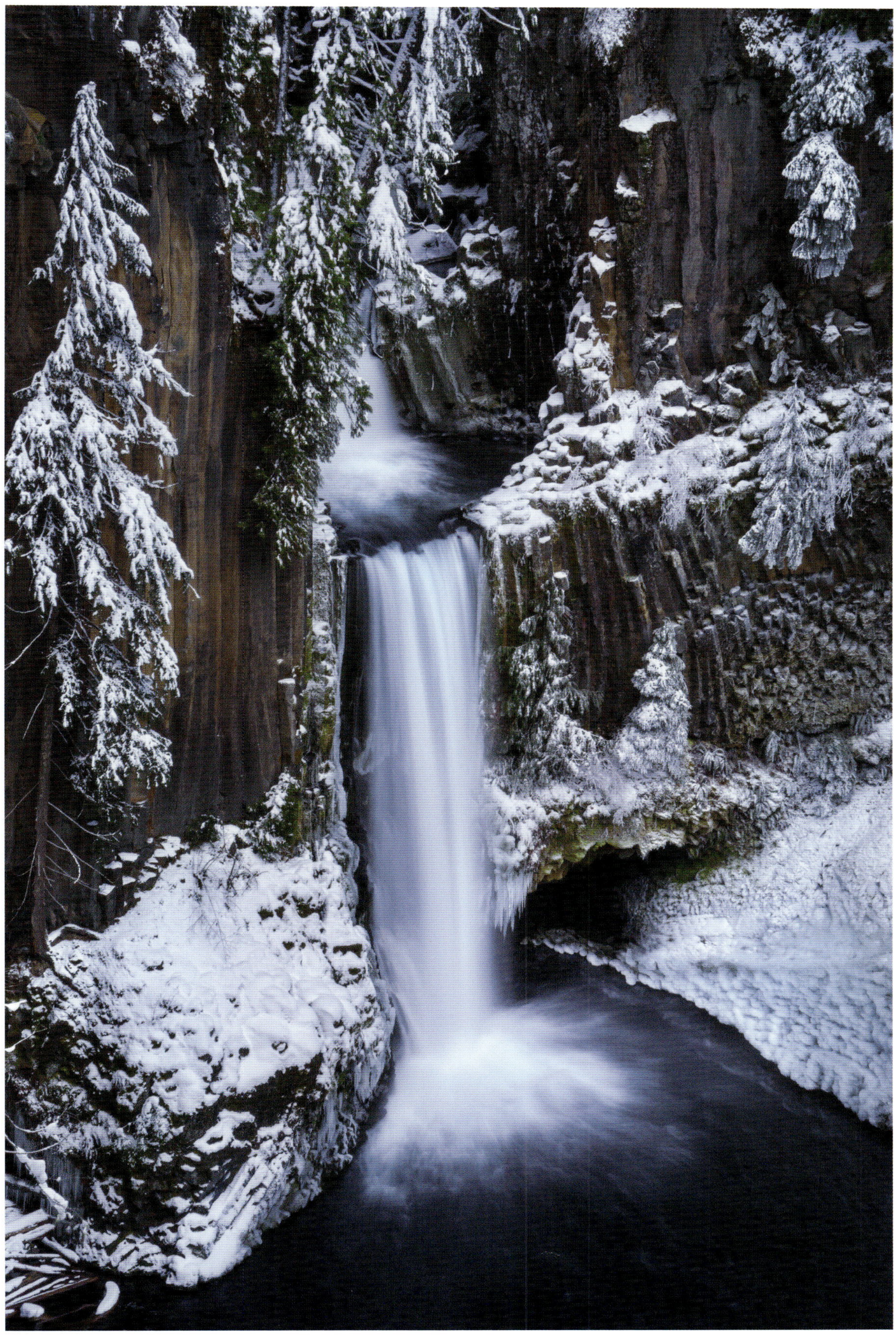

The icy waters of the North Umpqua River tumble over Toketee Falls after a fresh snowstorm. ●

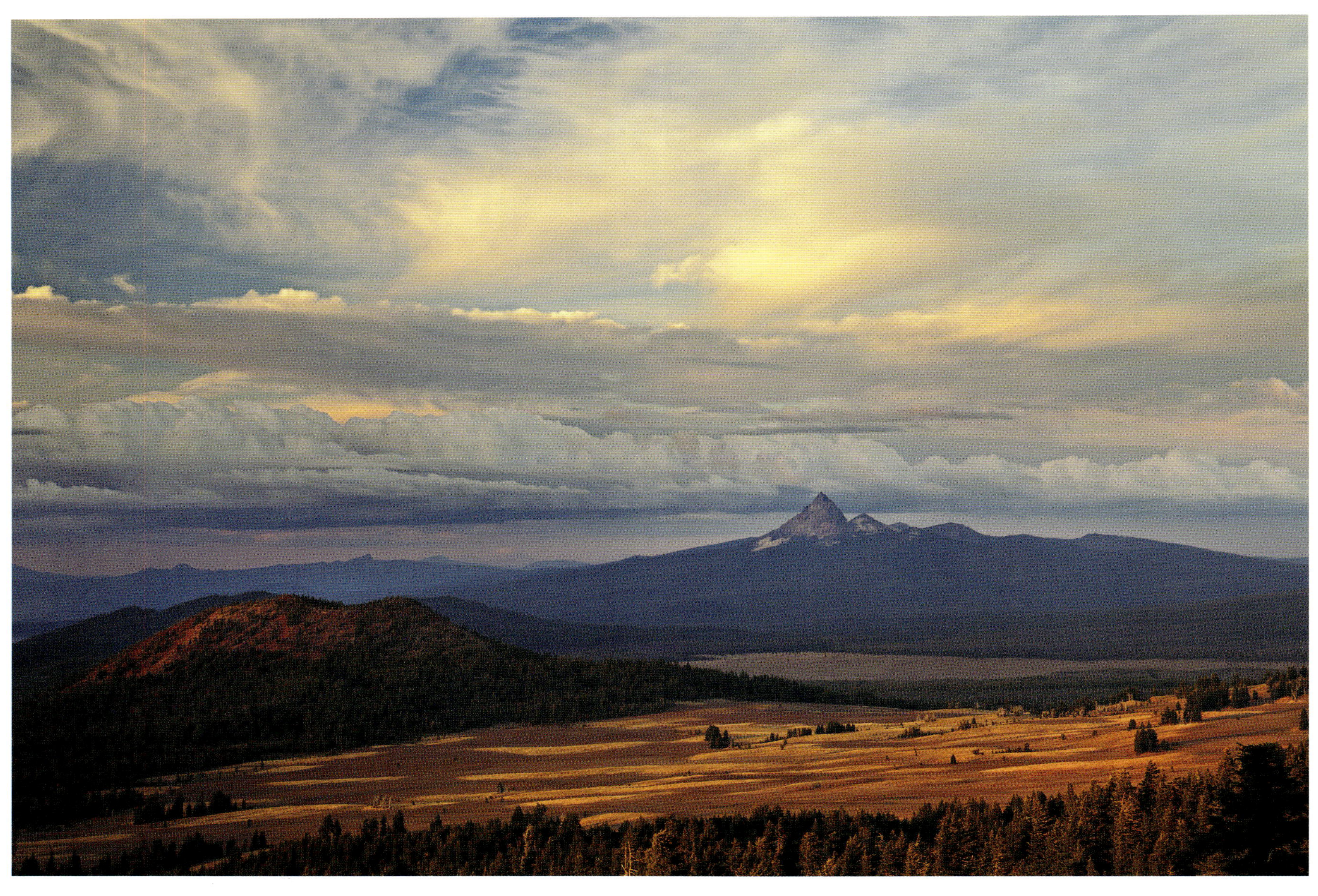

Summer thunderclouds over Mount
Thielsen and the Pumice Desert, viewed
from the north rim of Crater Lake. ●

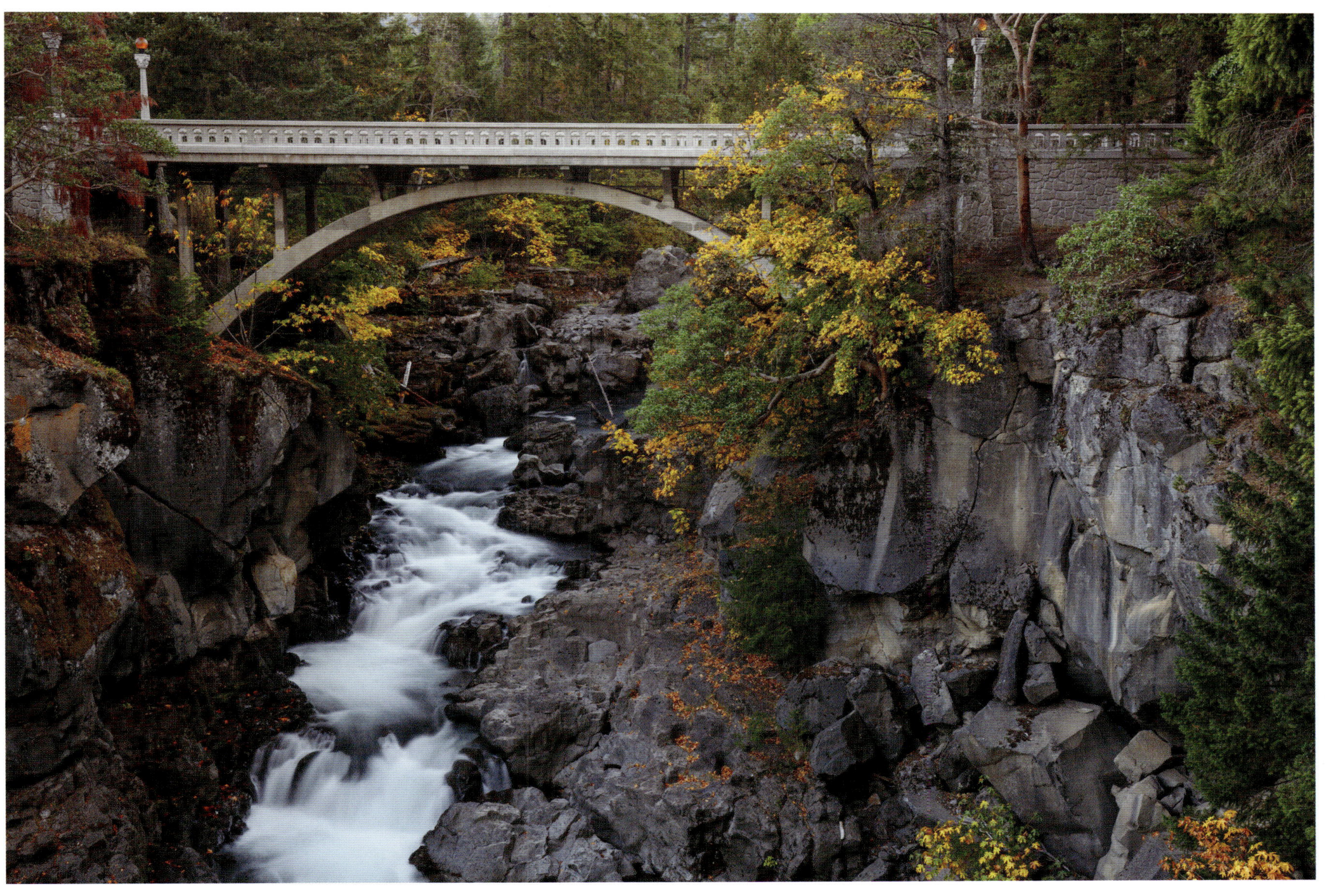

The Prospect Bridge, also known as the Mill Creek Drive Bridge, built circa 1930, spans the Avenue of the Boulders gorge on the North Fork of the Rogue River. •

OVERLEAF A hiker stands at the ecge of Crater Lake watching the sunrise on a cool morning in July. •

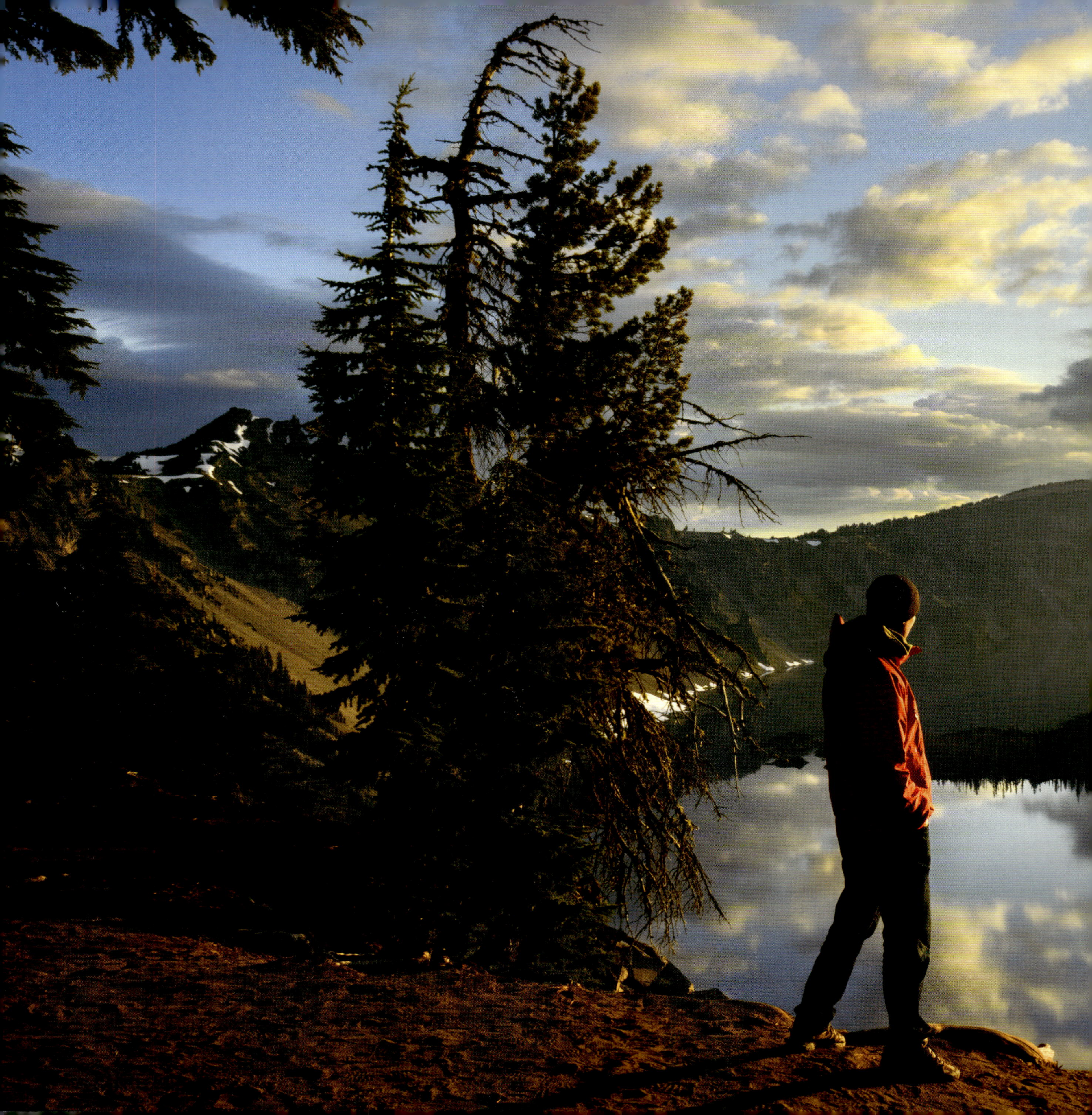

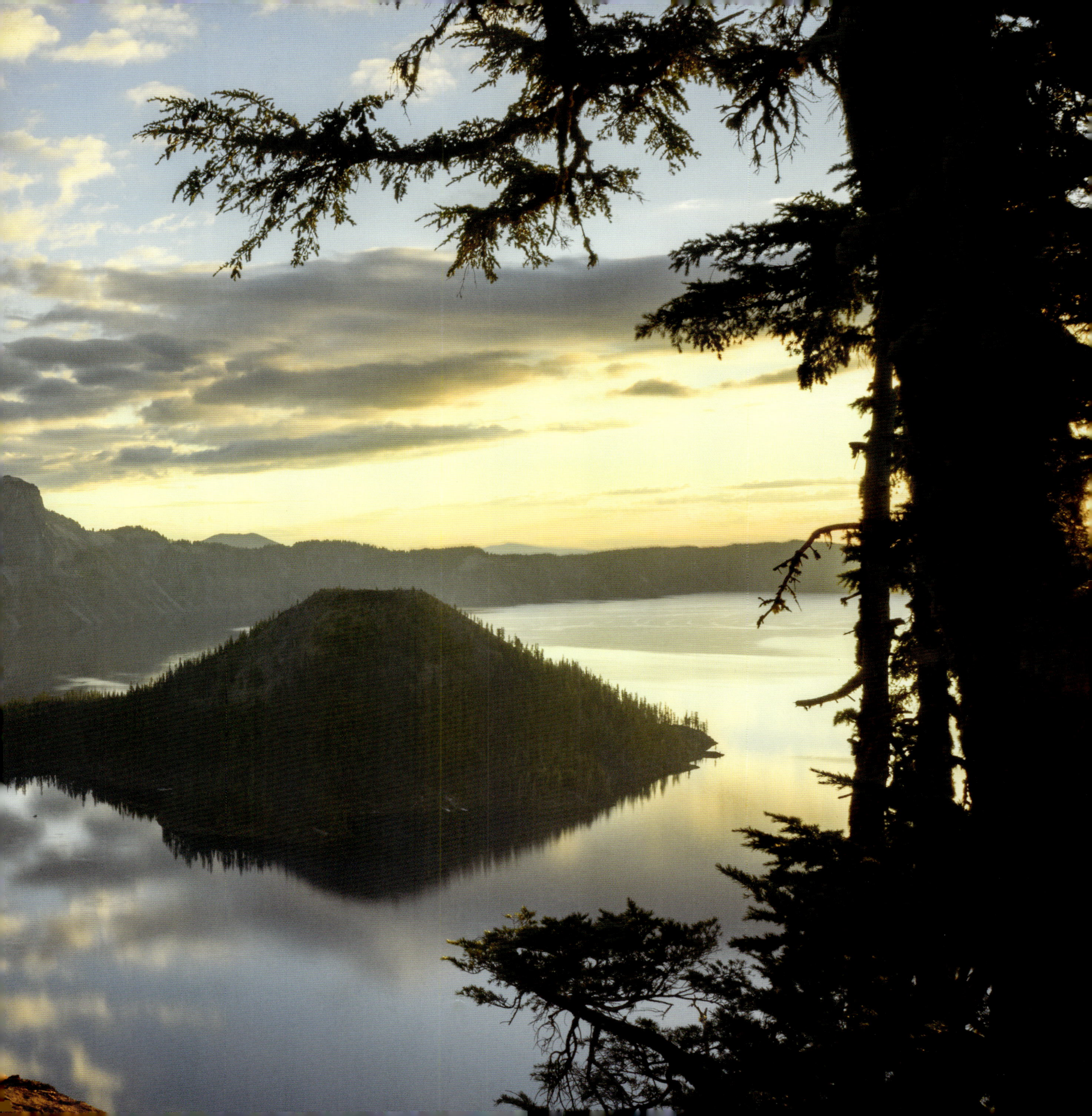

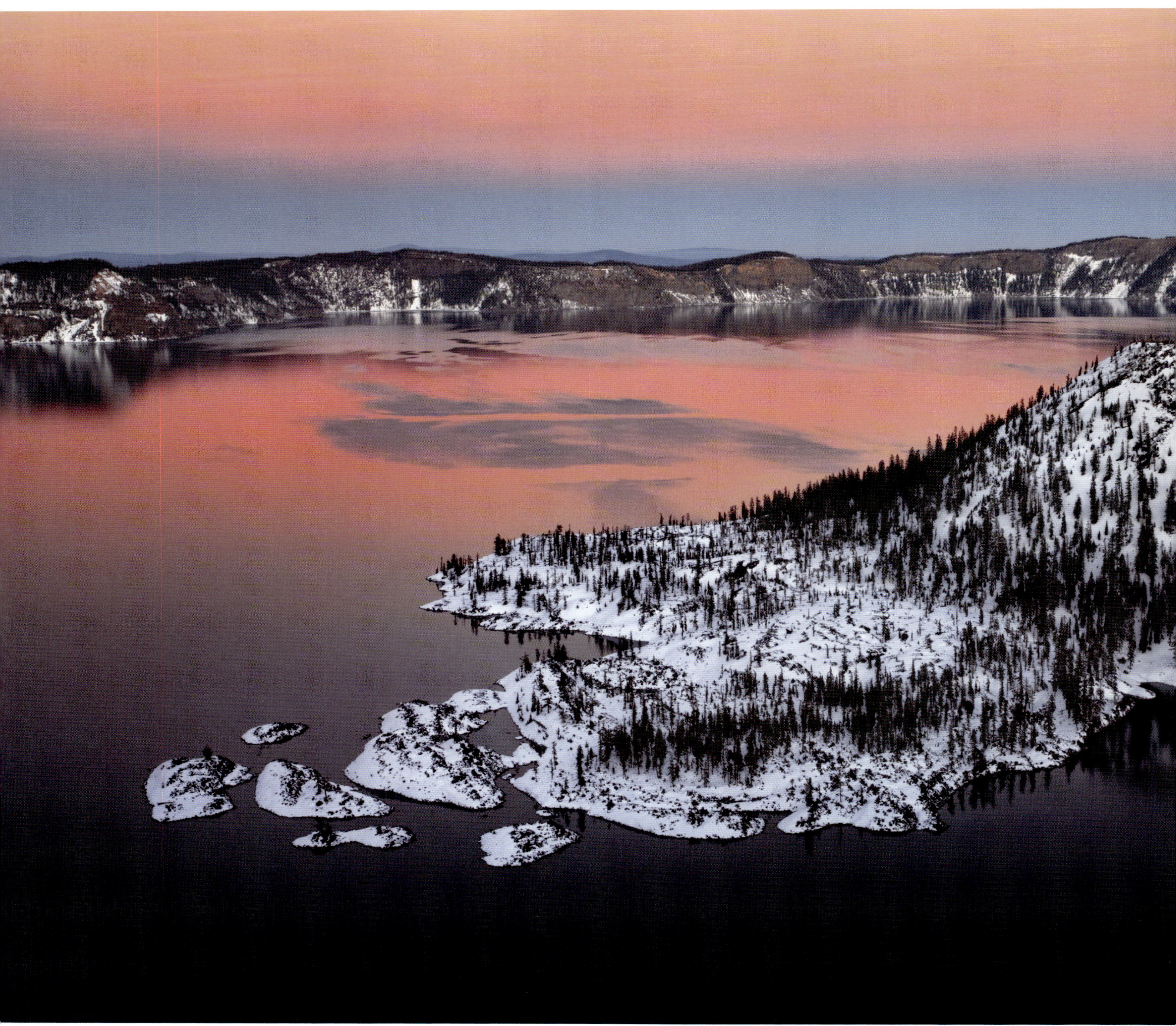

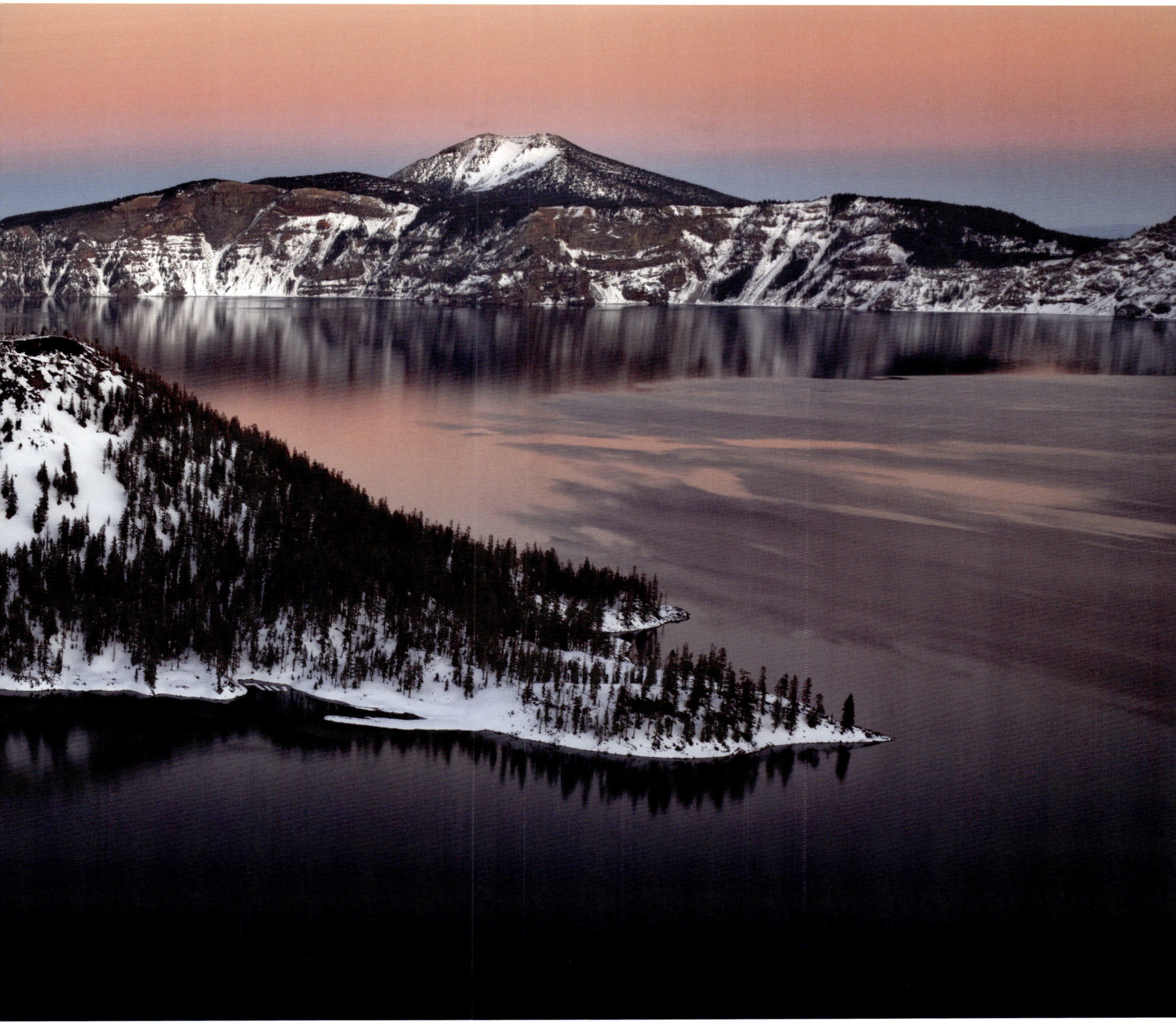

PREVIOUS PAGES Wizard Island seems to
float on the surface of Crater Lake during
a colorful winter sunset. ●

RIGHT Fog shrouds 100-foot-high
spires at Crater Lake National Park; the
pinnacles are fossil fumaroles from about
7700 years back in Mount Mazama's
history. ●

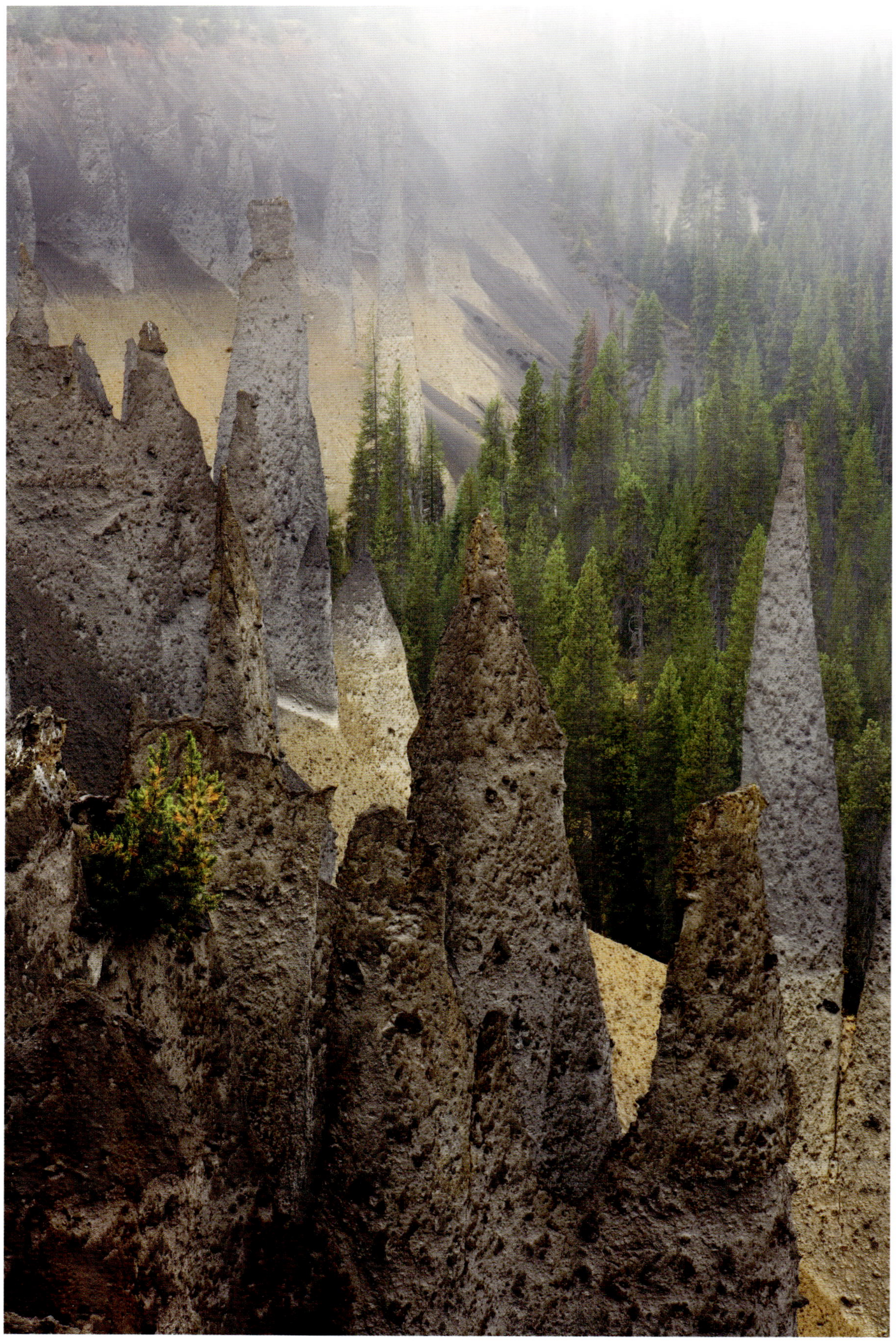

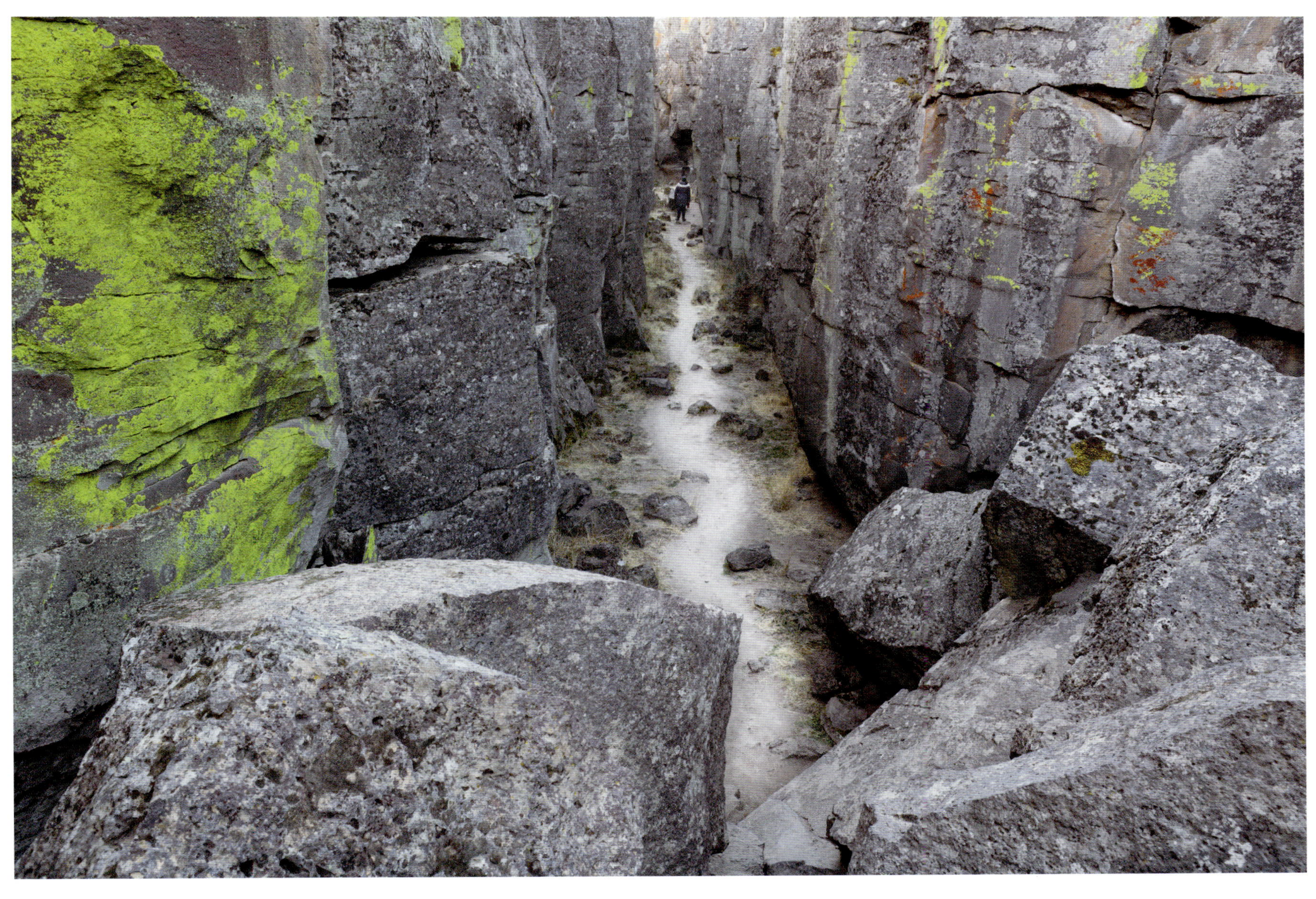

A hiker lends scale to Crack in the Ground, near Christmas Valley. This volcanic fissure is about 2 miles long with depths measuring nearly 30 feet. •

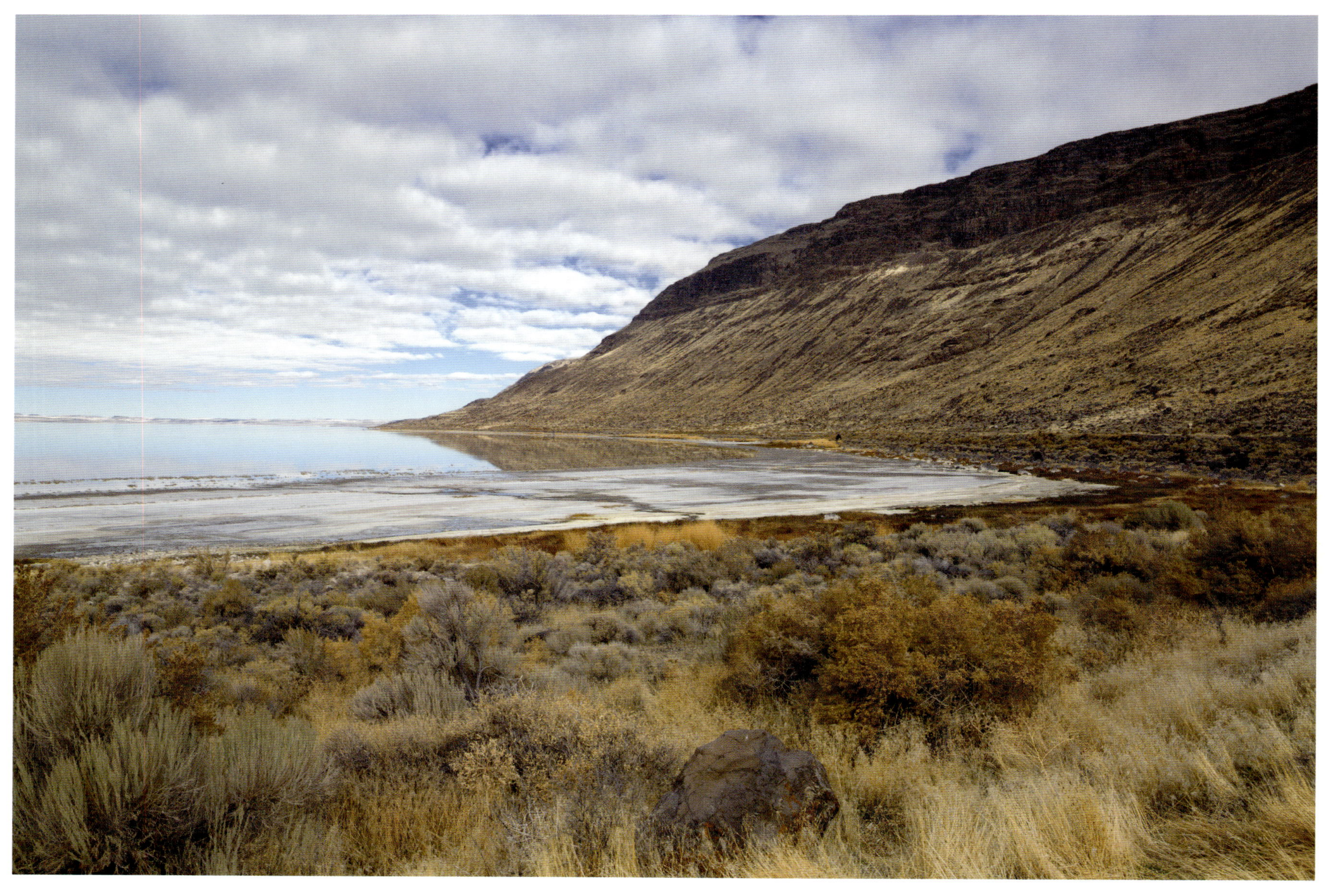

Lake Abert, Oregon's only saltwater
lake, during fall with Abert Rim in the
background. The lake has a dense
population of brine shrimp that supports
migratory birds. •

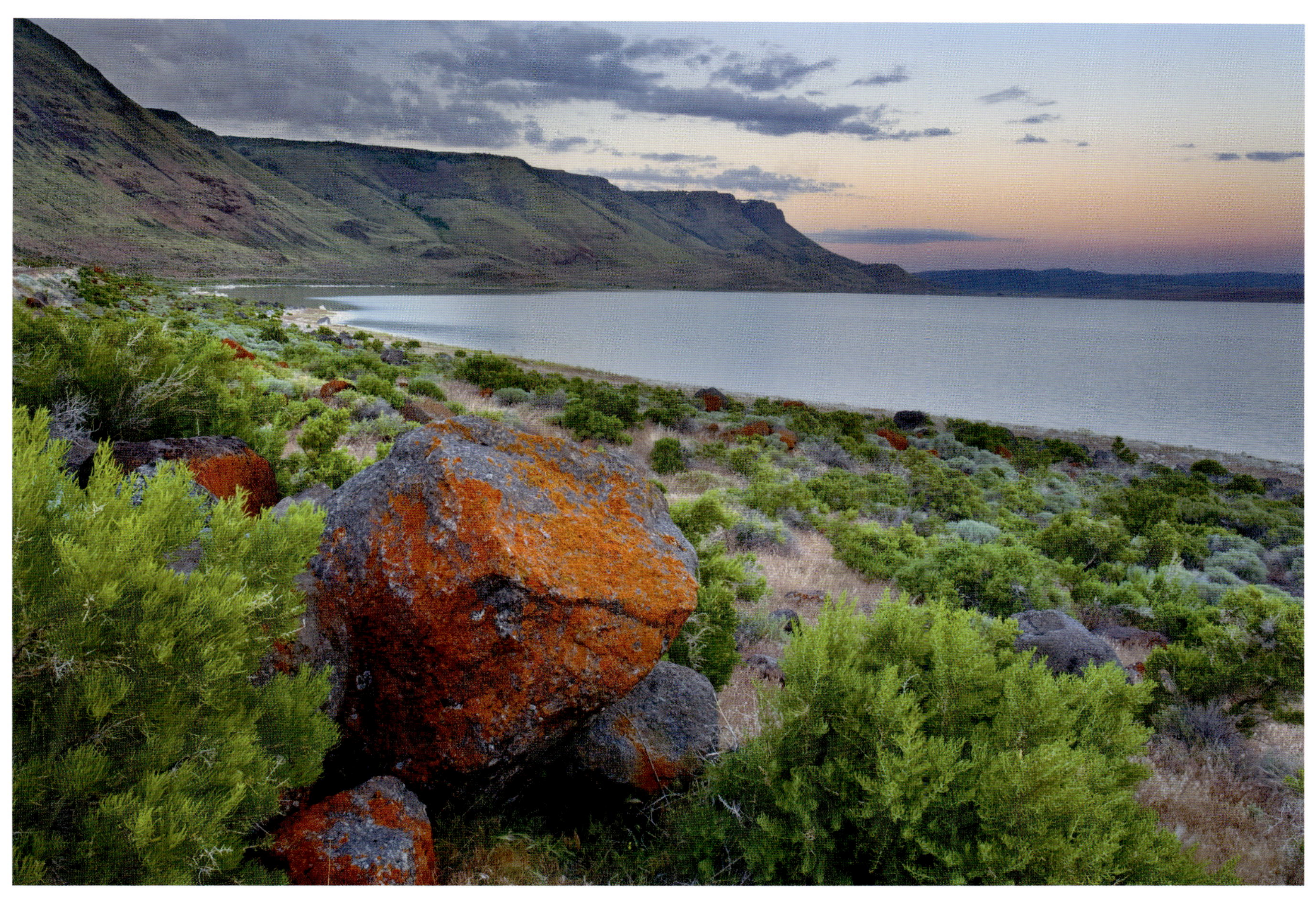

Lake Abert during a spring sunrise;
bordering Abert Rim is the longest
exposed fault scarp in North America. •

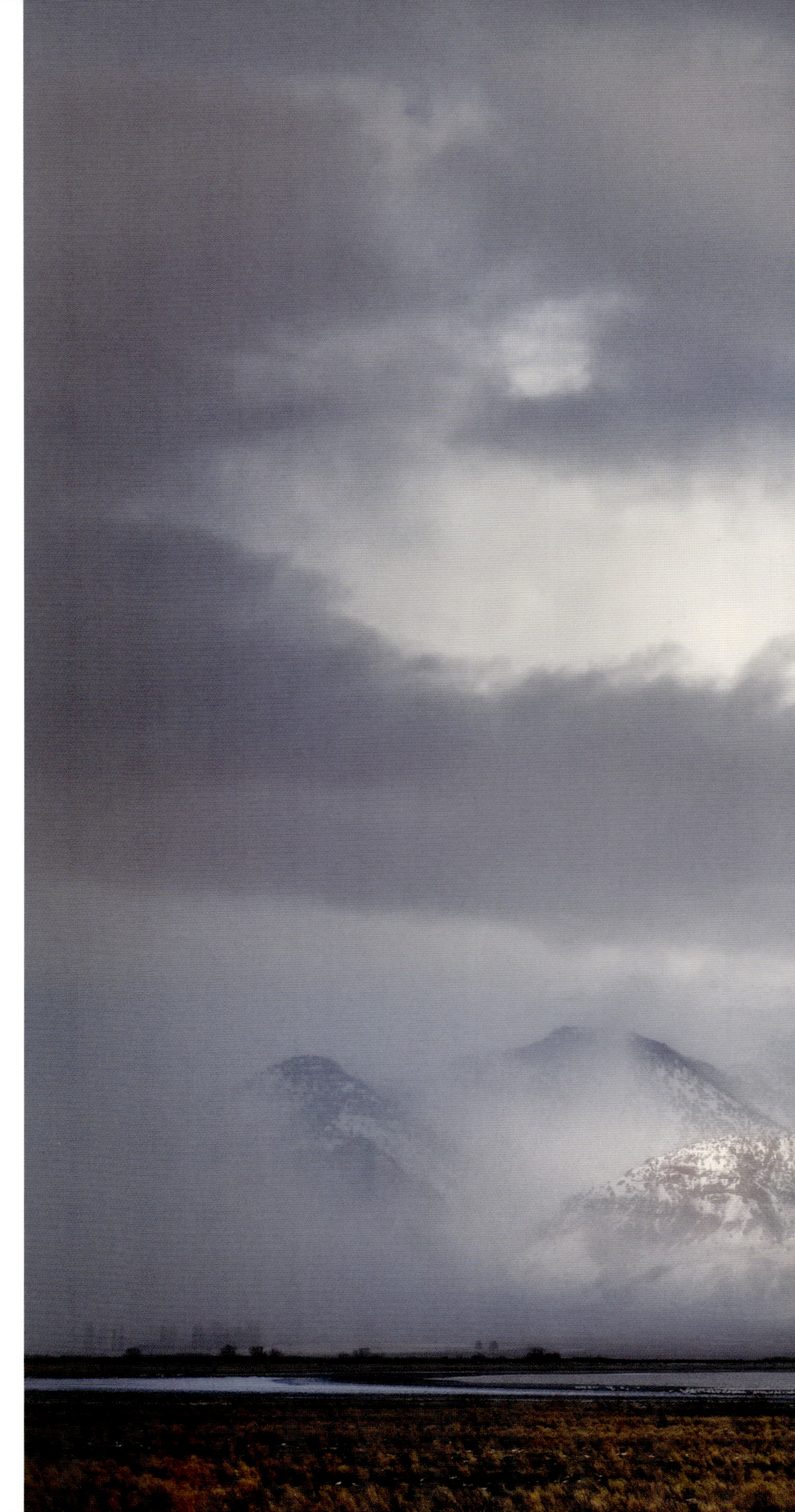

A winter storm clearing over Hart
Mountain and the Warner Valley
wetlands. •

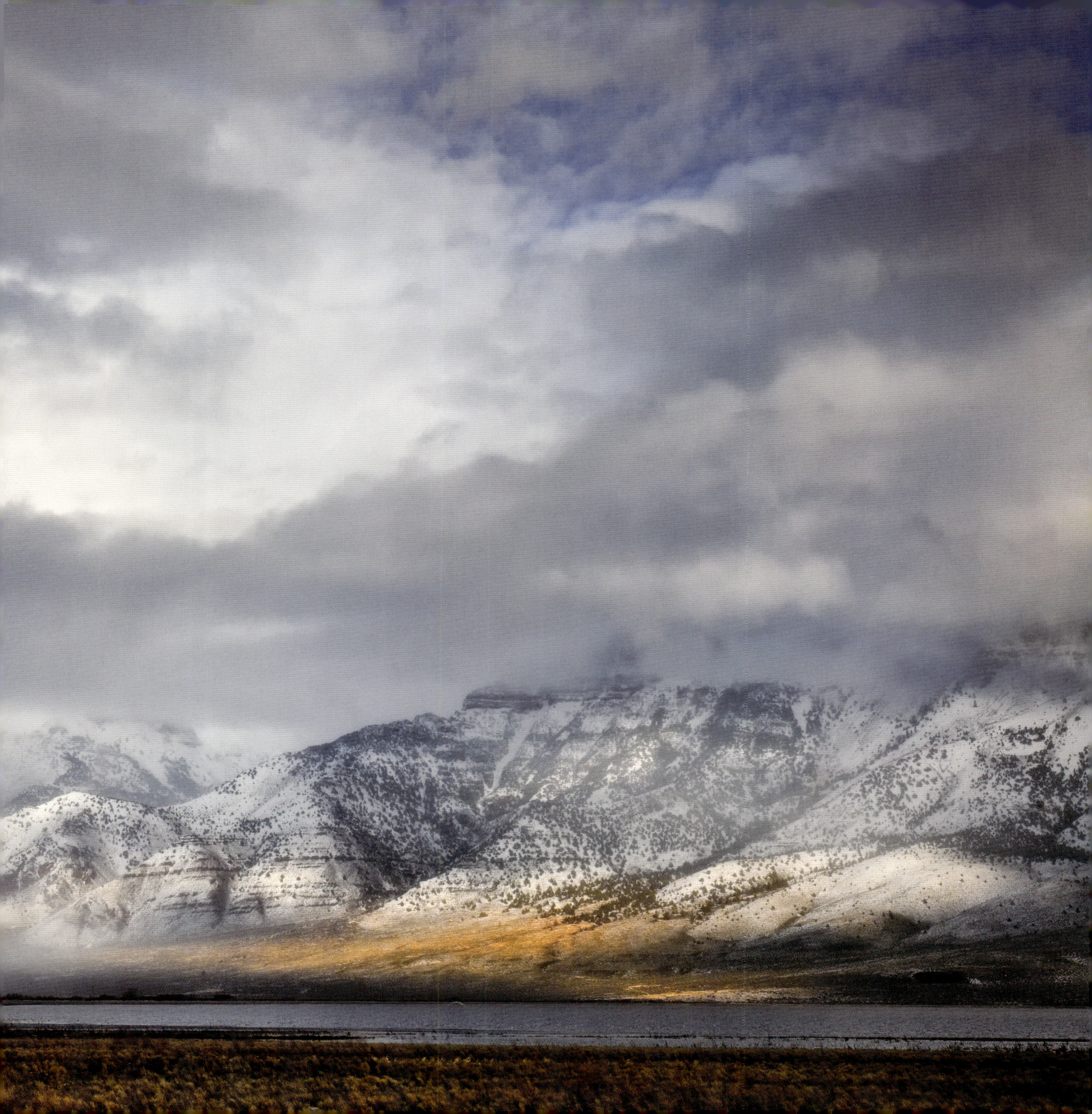

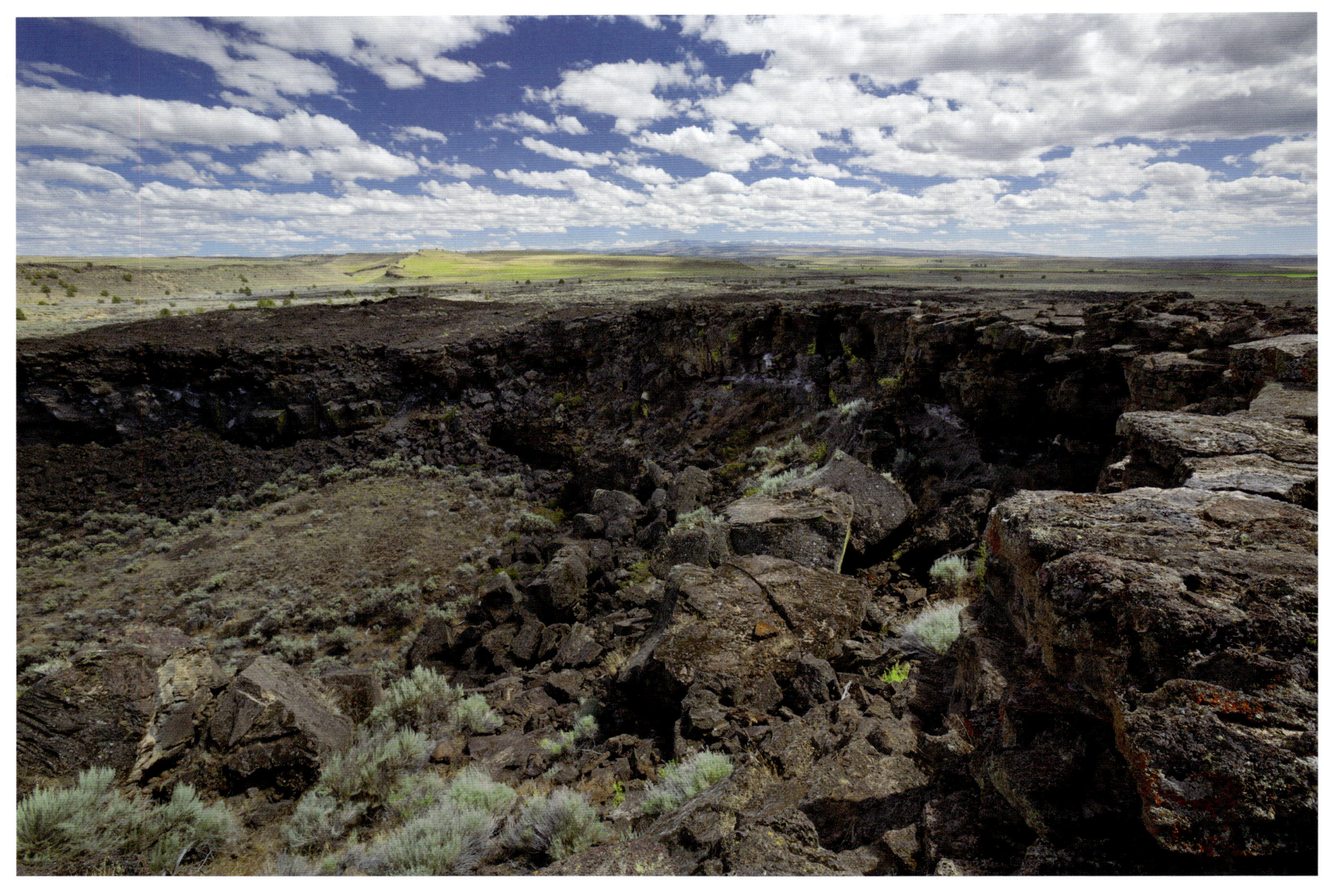

An ancient cinder cone in the Diamond
Craters Outstanding Natural Area, known
for its relatively compact collection of
diverse basaltic volcanic features. •

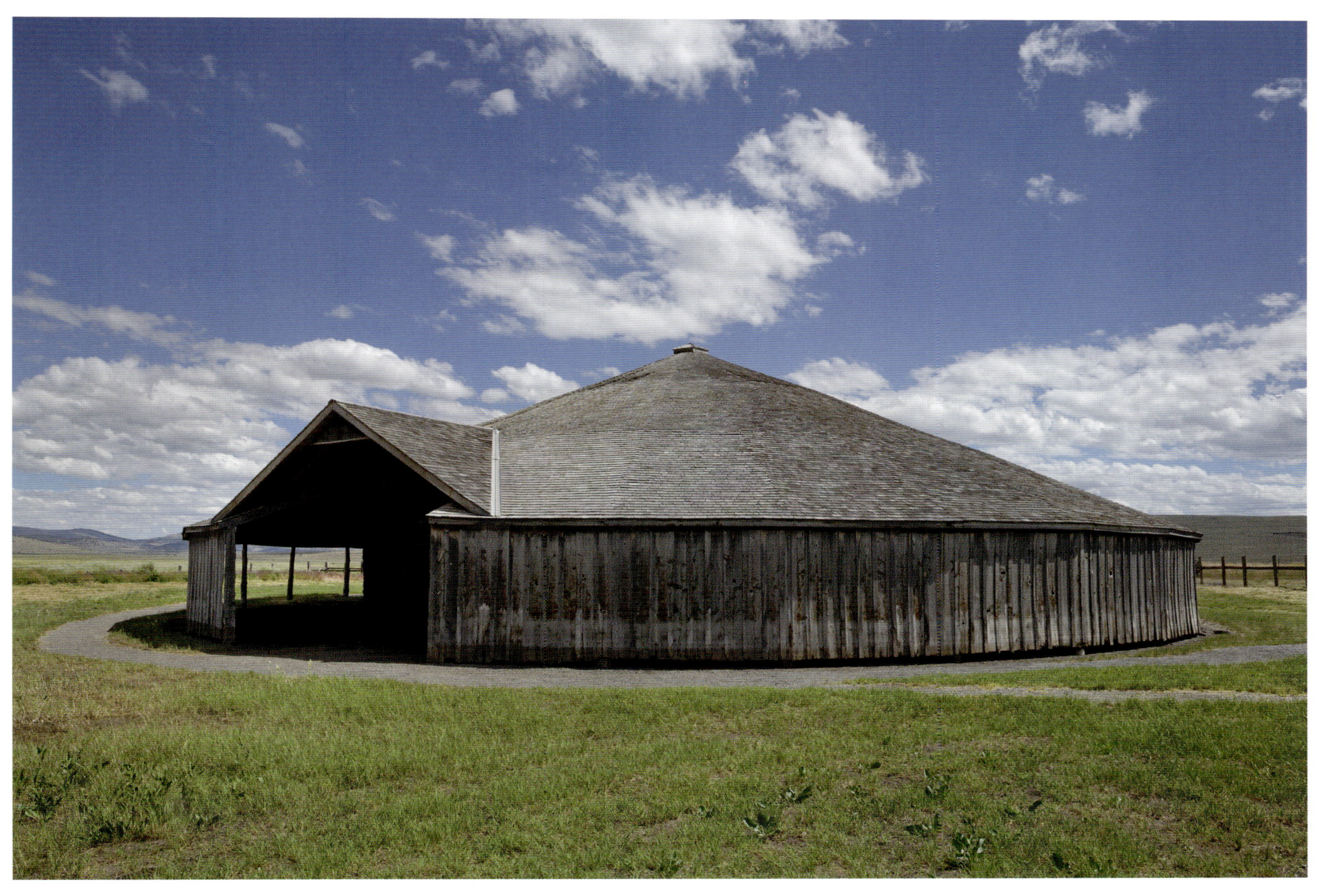

The renovated Peter French Round Barn, near Burns, still stands as the symbol of a bygone era in Oregon's early ranching days. •

First light falls on rabbitbrush in front of
the volcanic formation of Fort Rock in
central Oregon. •

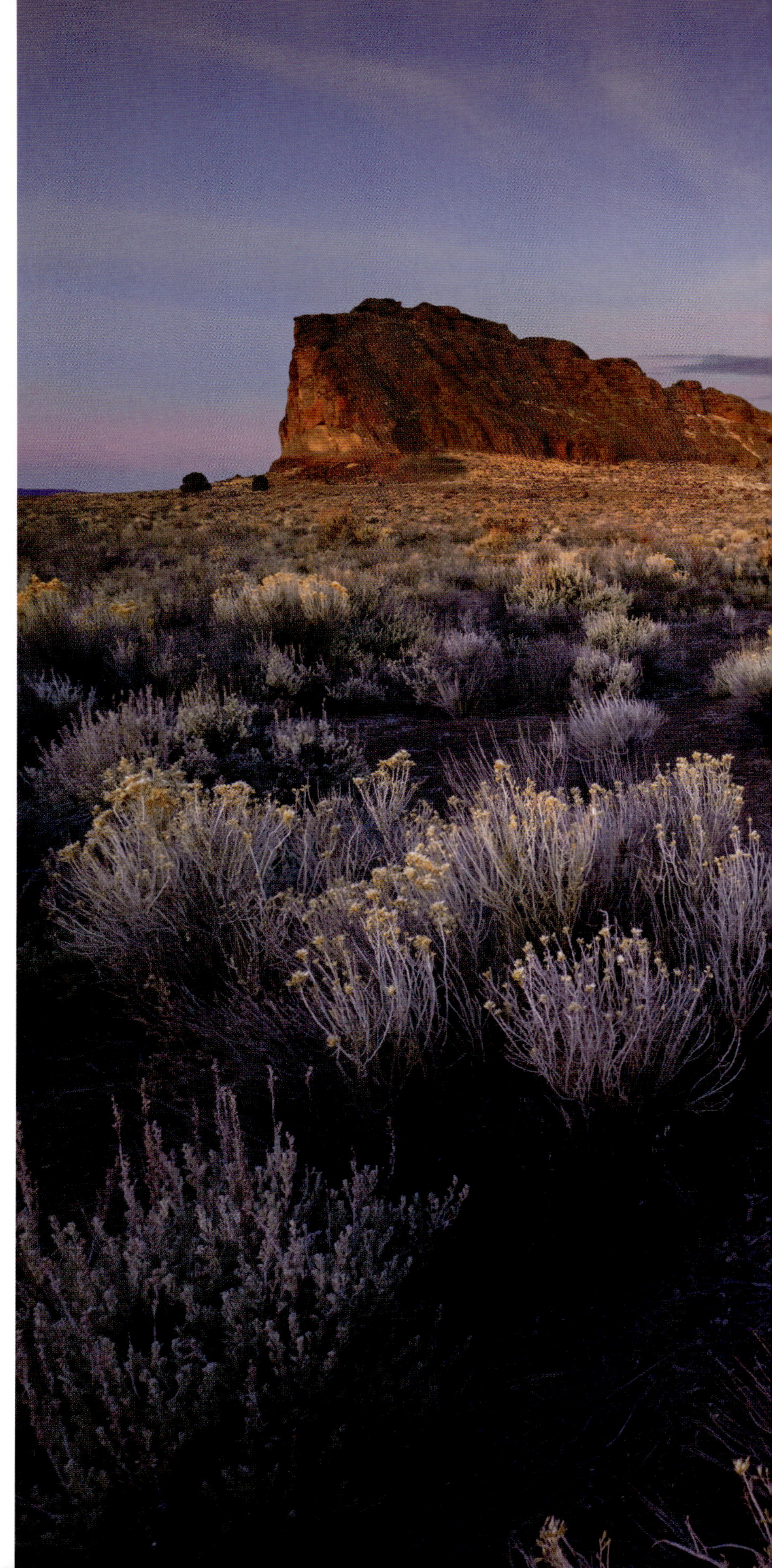

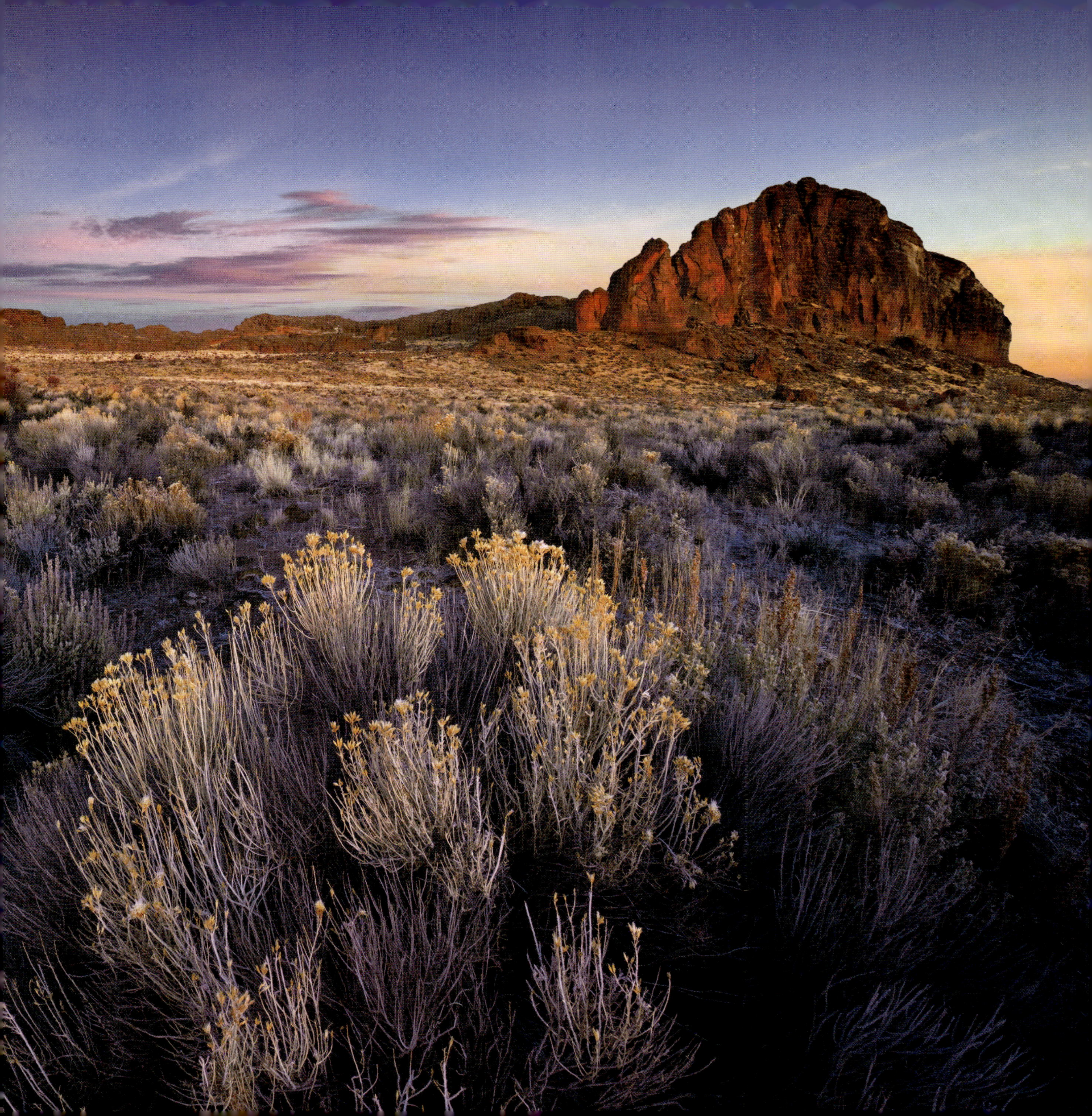

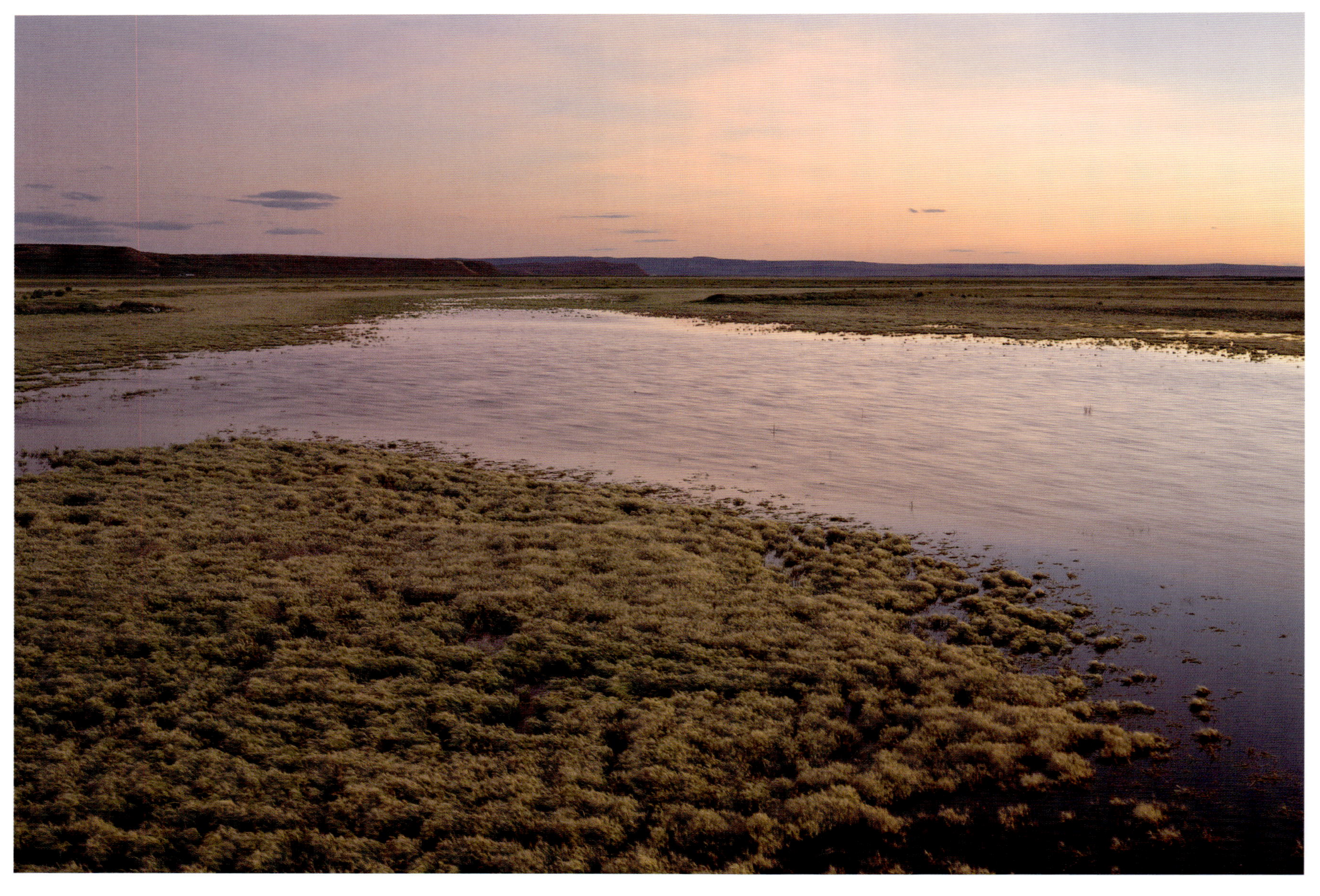

A colorful sunset lingers over the grasses
and ponds of the Malheur National
Wildlife Refuge. •

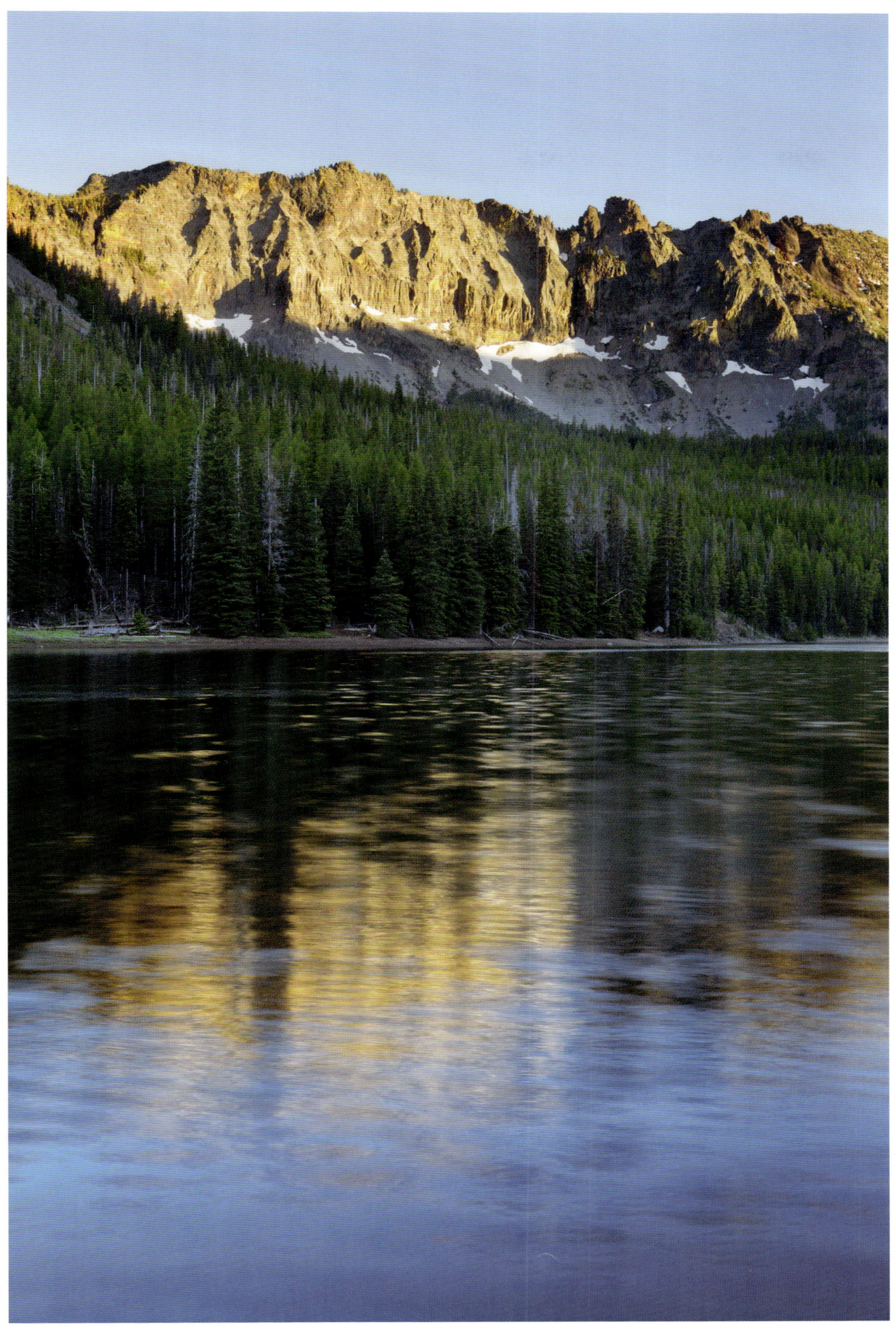

Rabbit Ears Mountain and Indian Spring Butte reflect into Strawberry Lake in the Strawberry Mountain Wilderness near John Day. •

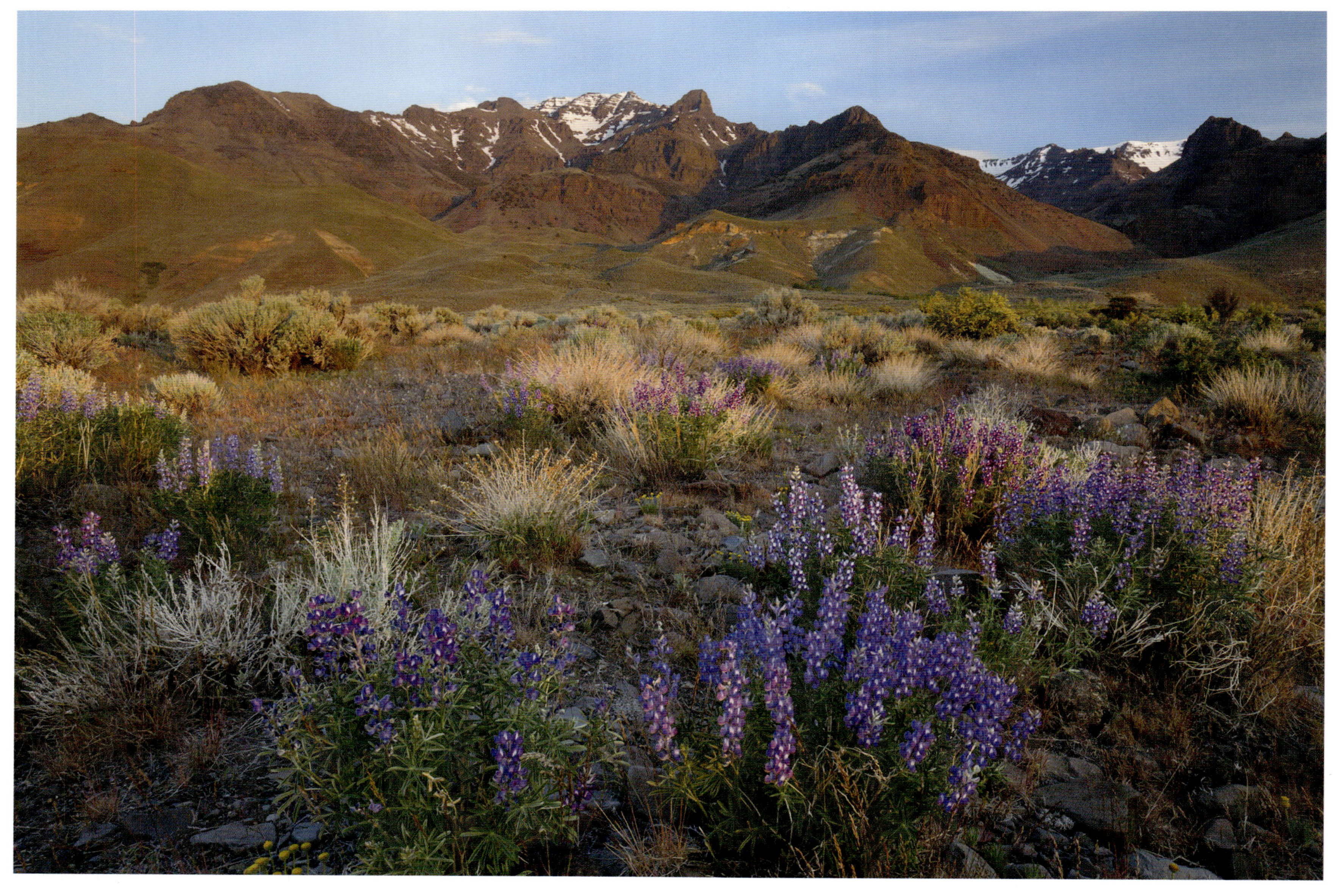

Lupine dots the landscape below a dramatic escarpment in the Steens Mountain Wilderness. •

OPPOSITE, TOP A variety of flowers bloom along the slopes of Steens Mountain in the early months of summer, including lupine (*Lupinus lepidus*), paintbrushes (*Castilleja* spp.), and arnica (*Arnica* sp.). •

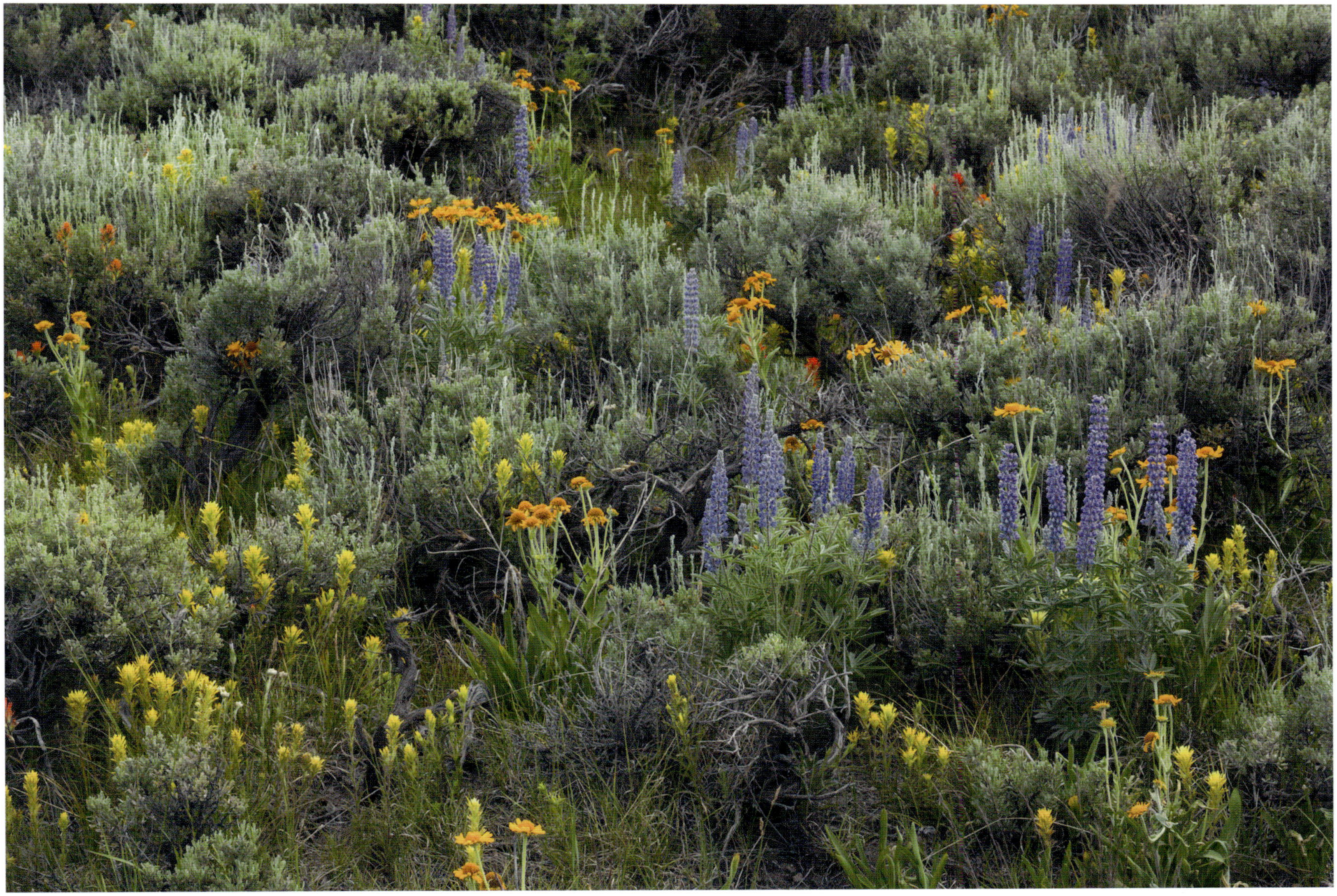

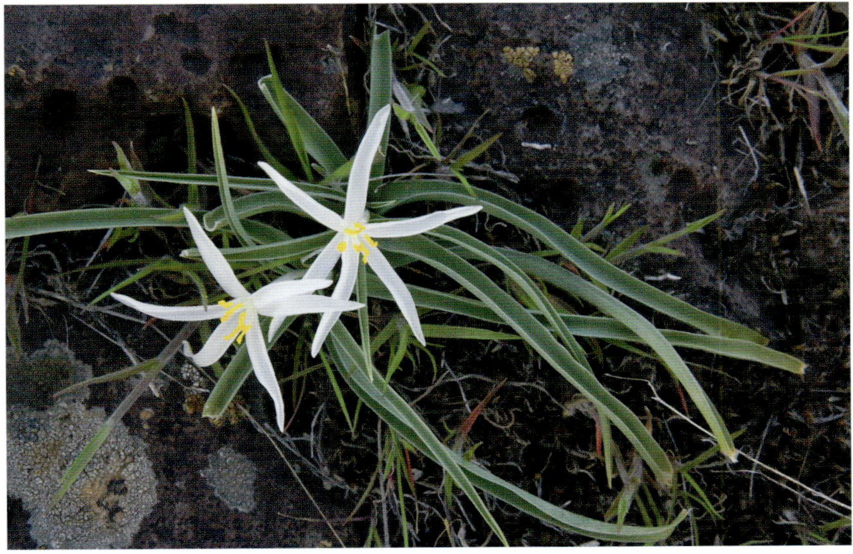

LEFT A sand lily (*Leucocrinum montanum*) breaks through the rocky soils of the high desert along the rim of the Owyhee Canyon. •

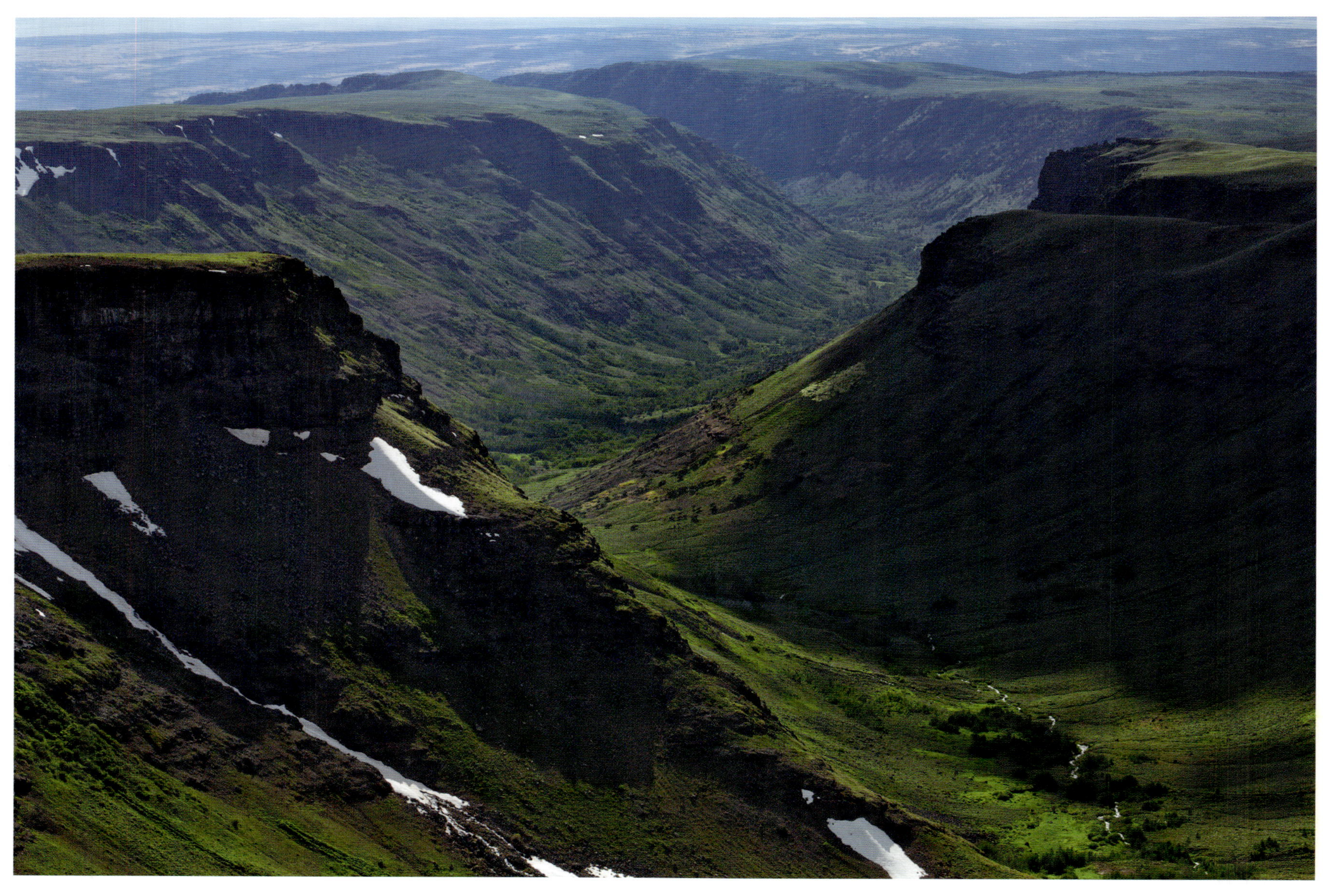

Kiger Gorge winds its way down from
Steens Mountain in early summer. •

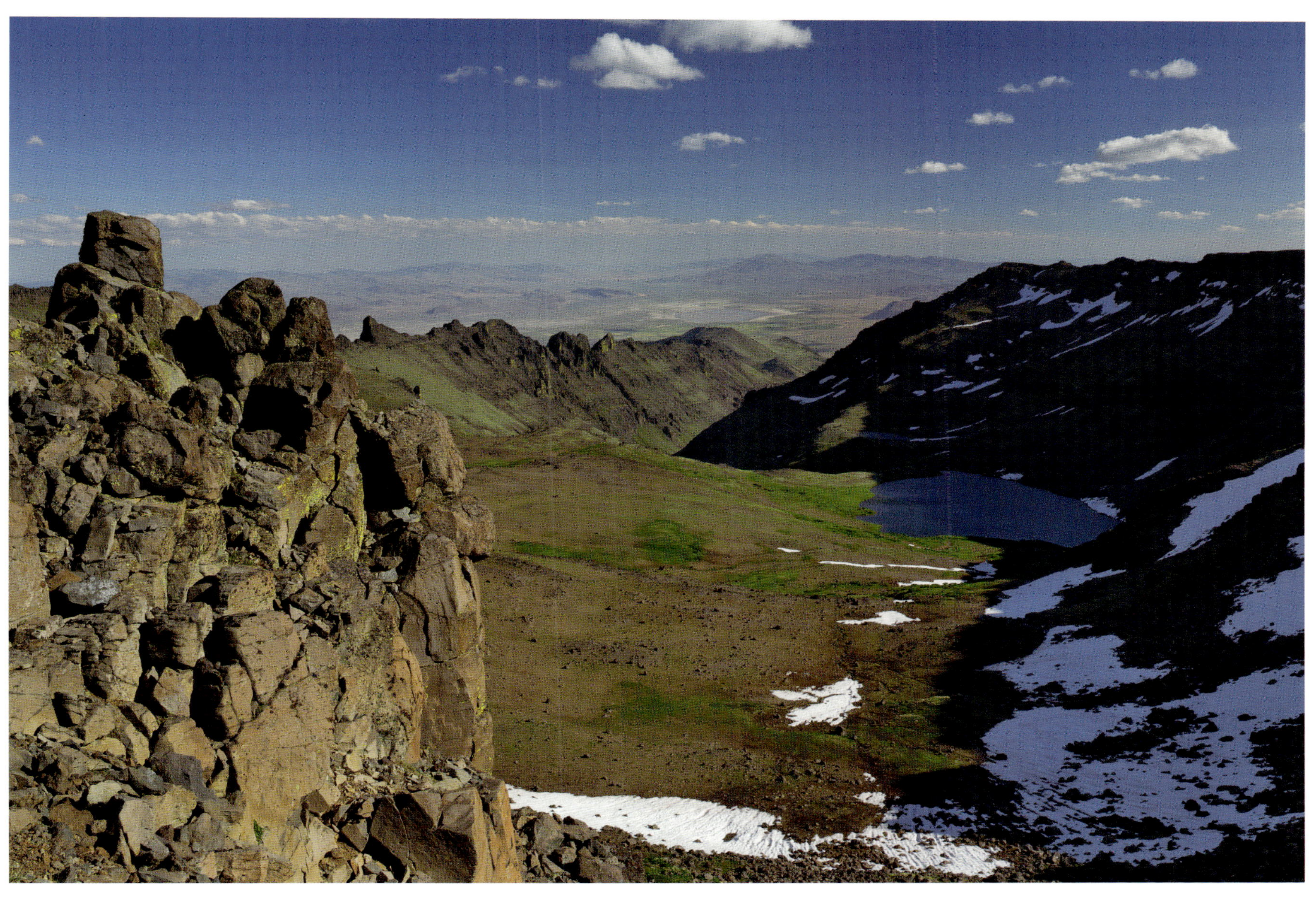

A summer view of Wildhorse Lake,
snug against the rugged Steens Mountain
Wilderness. •

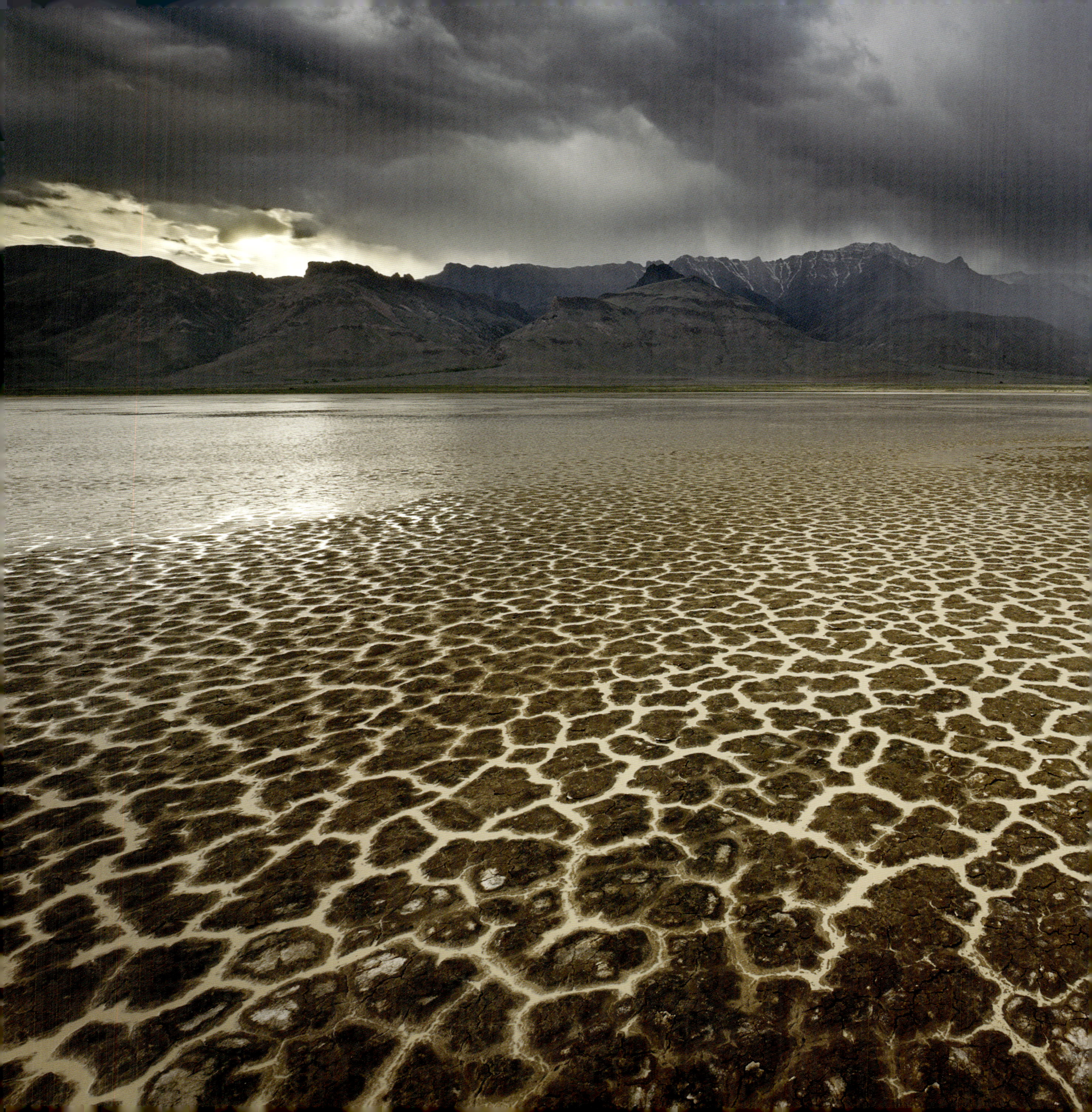

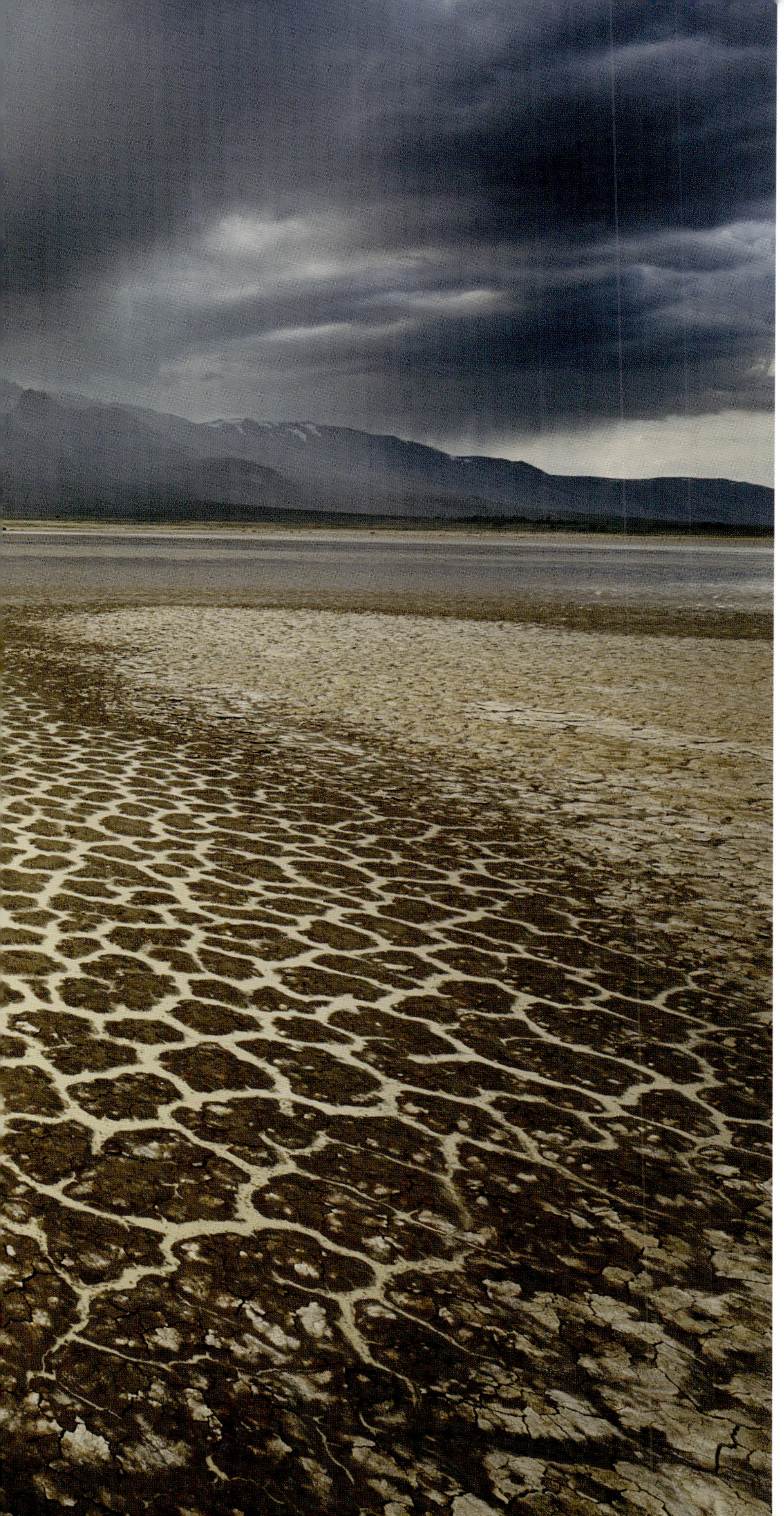

A late-afternoon thunderstorm builds over Steens Mountain and the tiled playa of the Alvord Desert. In the spring, rain and snowmelt can flood parts of the playa. •

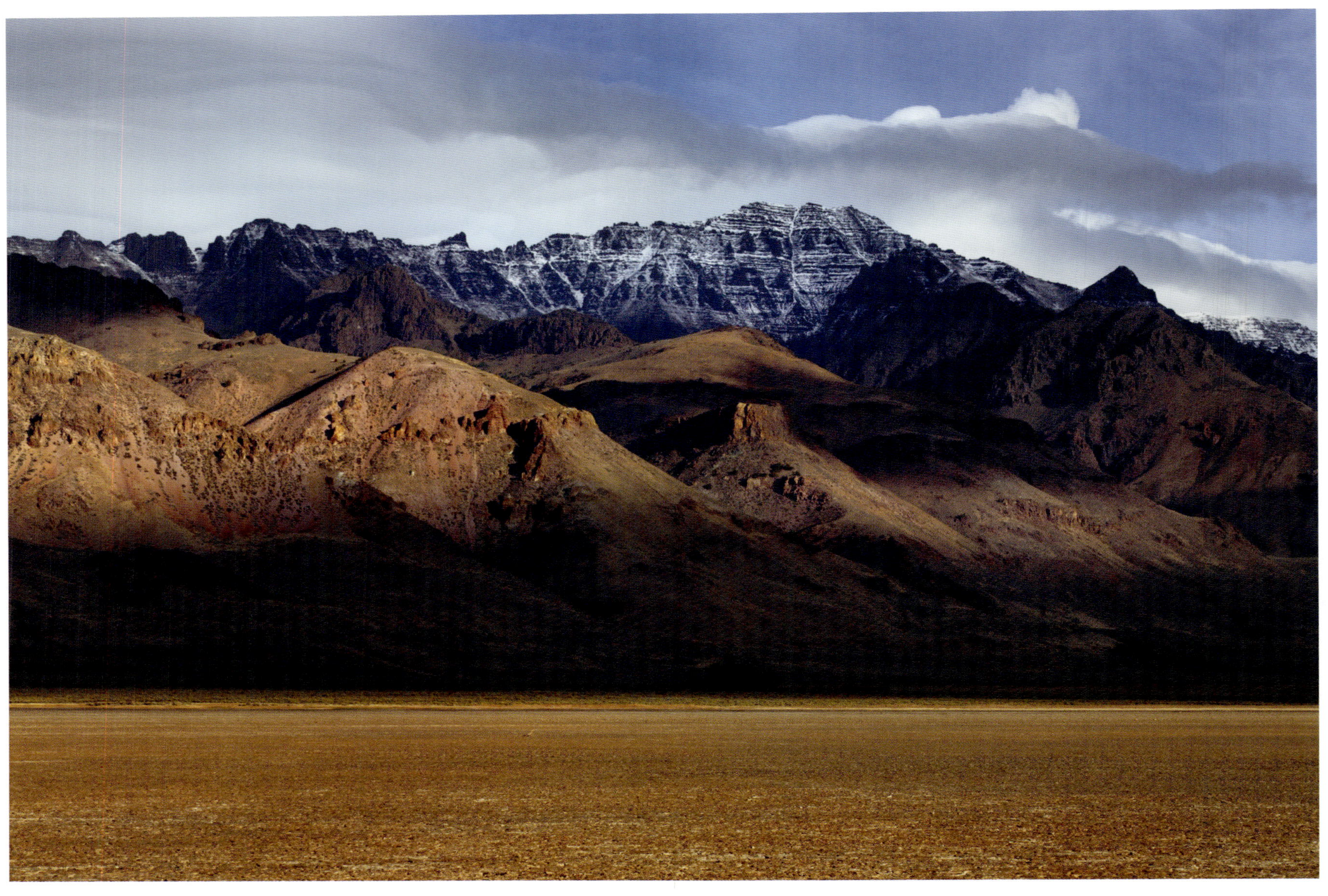

The Alvord Desert playa remains dry
and bathed in sunlight while fresh snow
dusts the Steens Mountain Wilderness
in fall.

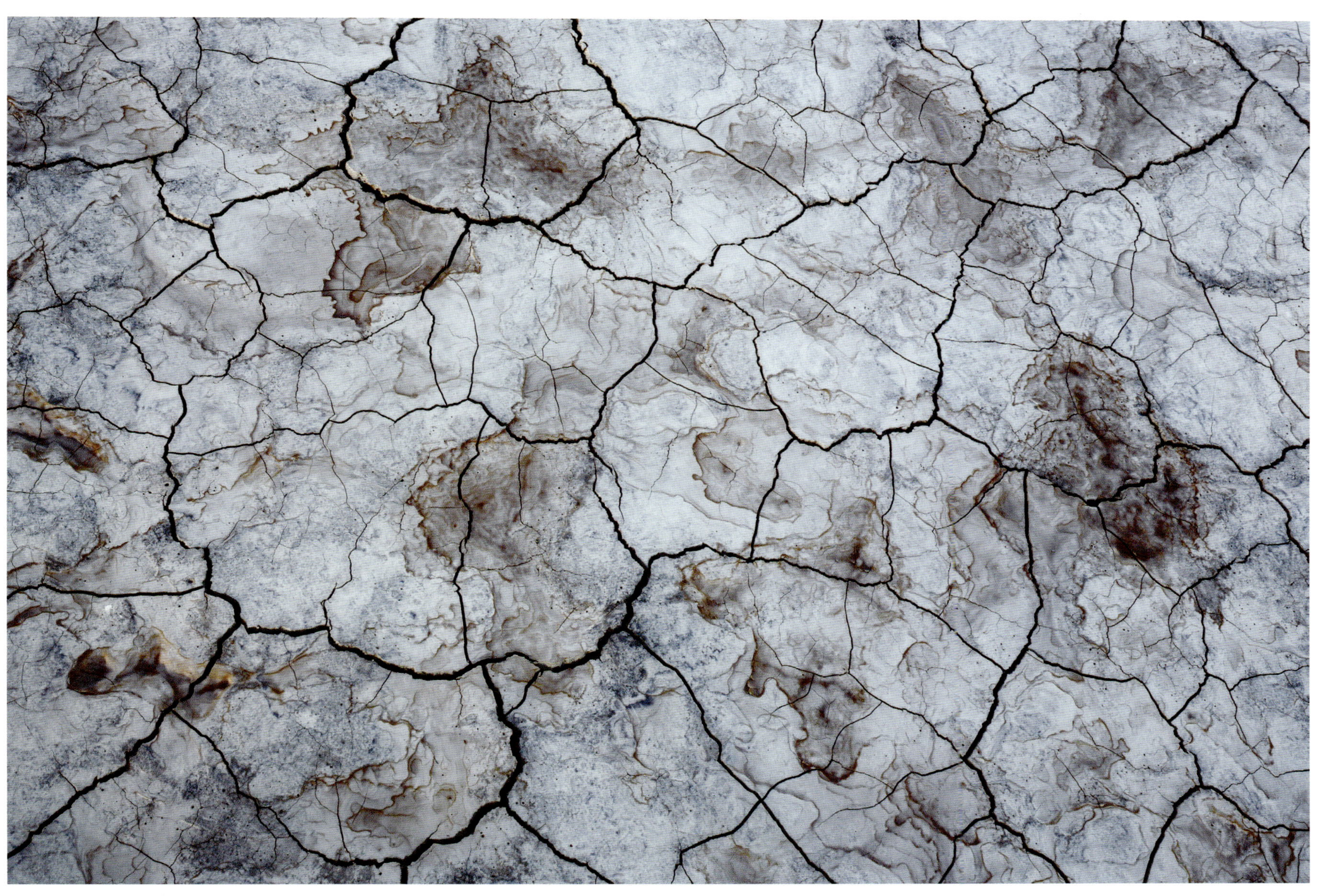

The mud of the Alvord Desert playa, which lies in the rain shadow of the Steens Mountain Wilderness, can crack from lack of moisture. •

Cumulus clouds building over Alvord Lake, a shallow and seasonal alkali lake in the Alvord Basin. At one time, Alvord Lake stretched 100 miles along the eastern side of Steens Mountain, but it now it spans just 4 miles. •

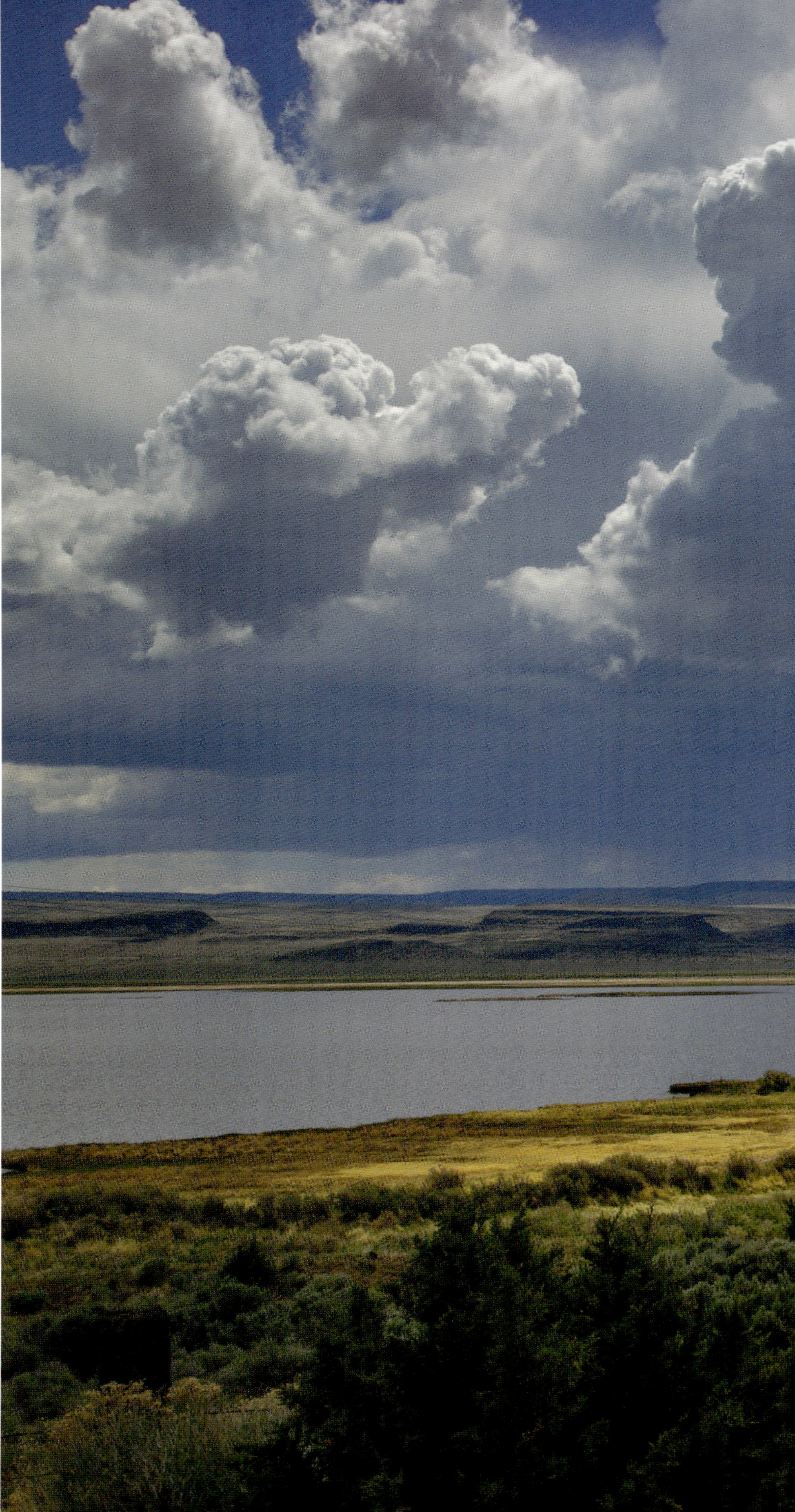

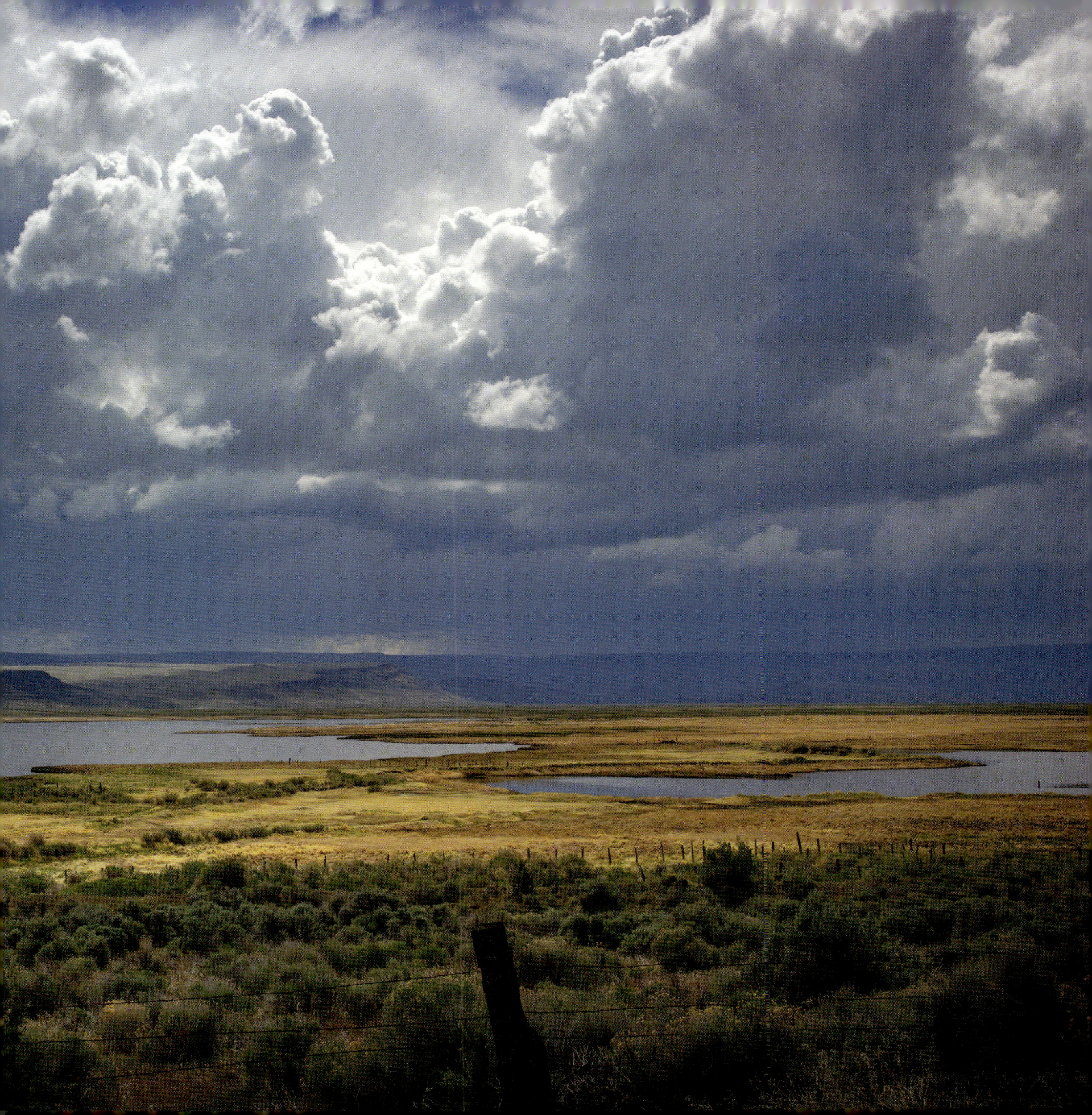

The Borax Lake Hot Springs are geothermal springs lying along a fault zone that runs north–south through the Alvord Valley east of Steens Mountain.

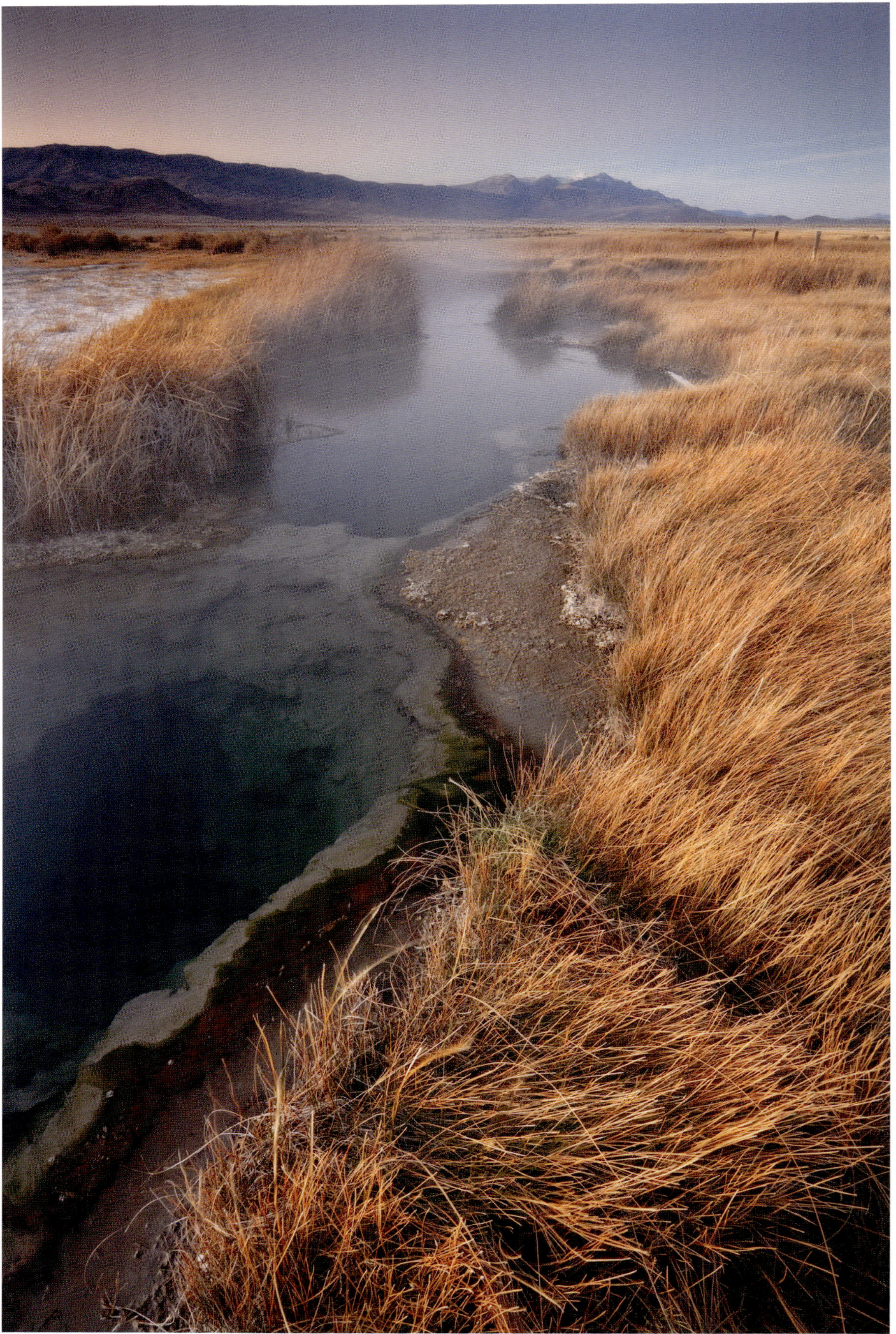

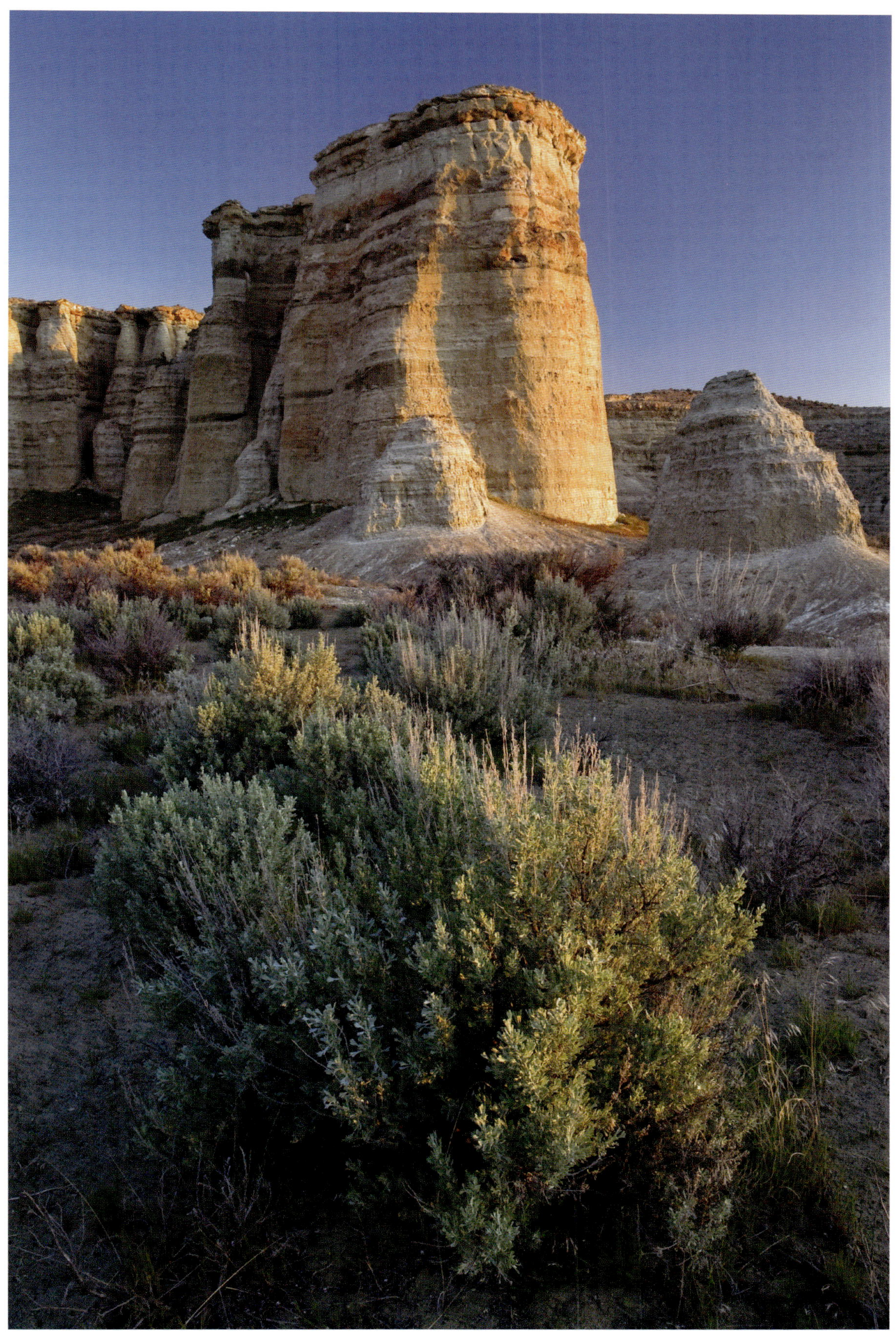

The white bluffs of the Pillars of Rome stand tall over the sagebrush of eastern Oregon.

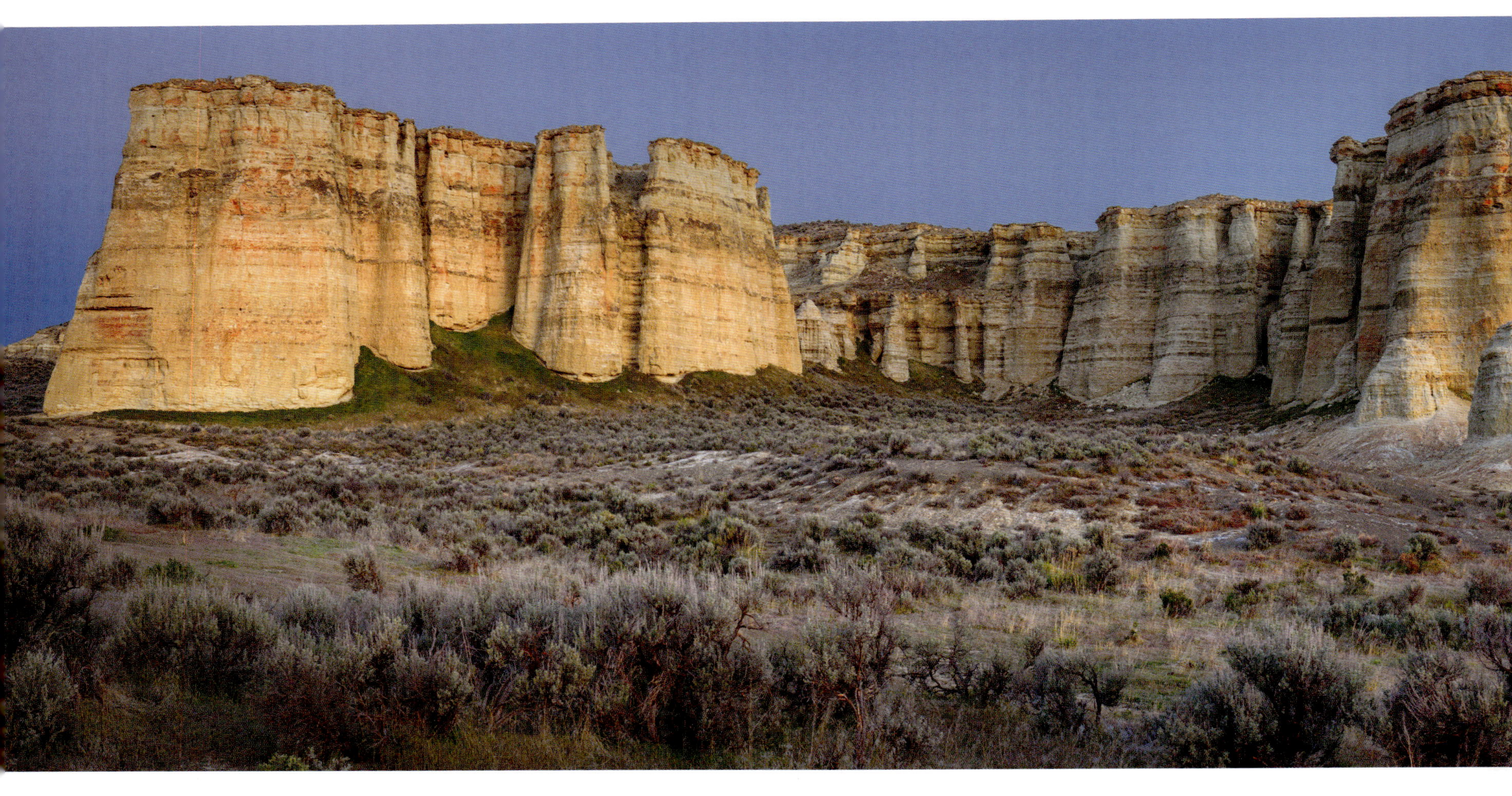

The 100-foot high Pillars of Rome
stretch for five miles along the Owyhee
River Valley and served as a landmark to
pioneers traveling the Oregon Trail. •

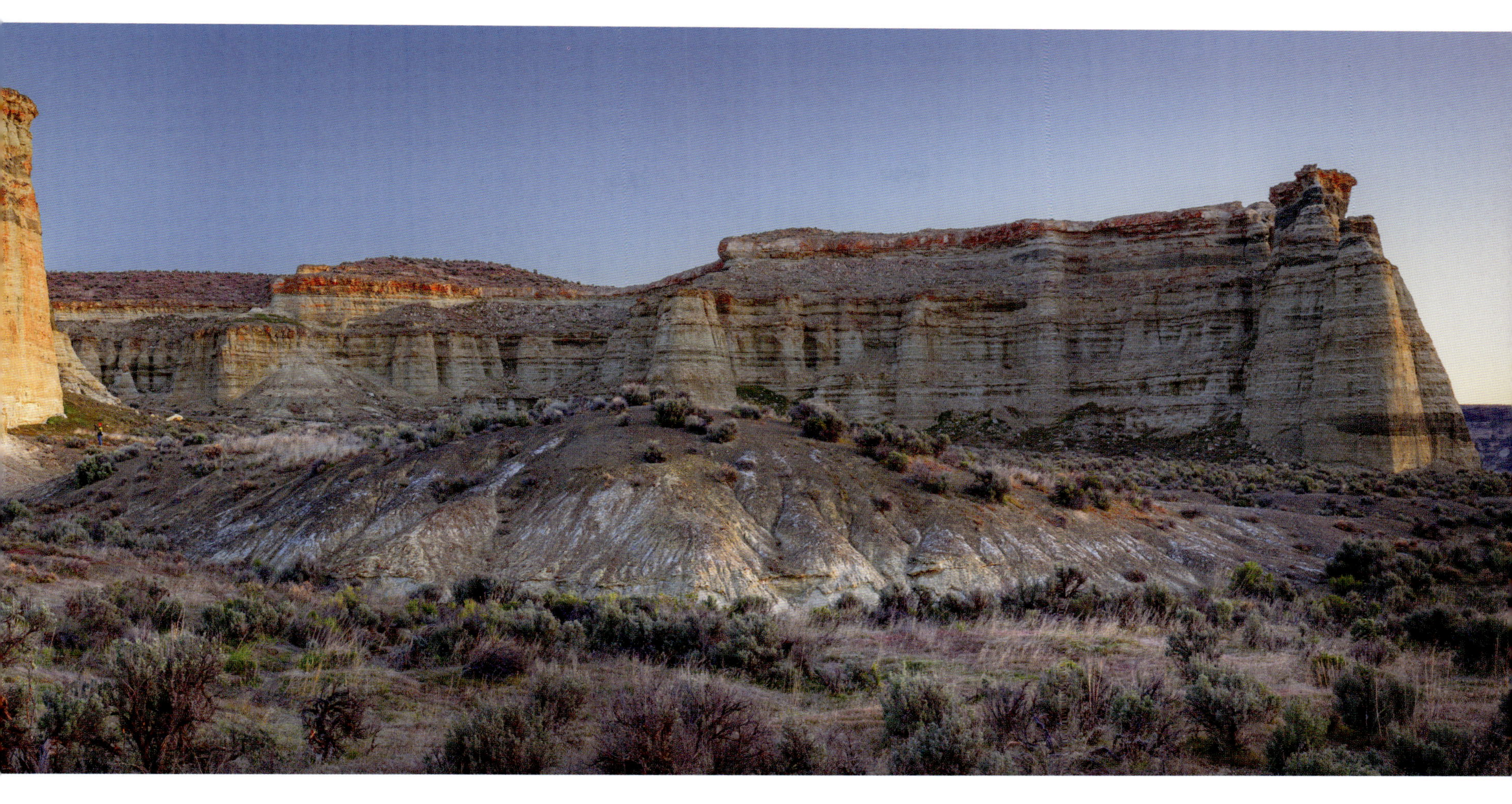

CREDITS

1
Page: 2
Zack Schnepf
Camera: Canon EOS 5D
Aperture: $f/16$
Focal Length: 29mm
Shutter Speed: 0.6 sec.
ISO: 100

2
Pages: 12–13
Kevin McNeal
Camera: Canon EOS 5D Mark II
Aperture: $f/16$
Focal Length: 17mm
Shutter Speed: 0.5 sec.
ISO: 100

3
Page: 14
Kevin McNeal
Camera: Canon EOS 5D Mark II
Aperture: $f/16$
Focal Length: 32mm
Shutter Speed: 25 sec.
ISO: 100

4
Pages: 14–15
Zack Schnepf
Camera: Canon EOS 10D
Aperture: $f/16$
Focal Length: 35mm
Shutter Speed: 1/15 sec.
ISO: 100

5
Pages: 16–17
David Cobb
Camera: Canon EOS 5D Mark III
Aperture: $f/22$
Focal Length: 45mm
Shutter Speed: 4 sec.
ISO: 200

6
Pages: 18–19
Adrian Klein
Camera: Canon EOS 5D Mark III
Aperture: $f/16$
Focal Length: 35mm
Shutter Speed: 0.5 sec.
ISO: 200

7
Page: 20
Adrian Klein
Camera: Canon EOS 5D
Aperture: $f/16$
Focal Length: 17mm
Shutter Speed: 3.2 sec.
ISO: 100

8
Page: 21
David Cobb
Camera: Canon EOS 5D Mark III
Aperture: $f/16$
Focal Length: 19mm
Shutter Speed: 2 sec.
ISO: 100

9
Pages: 22–23
Adrian Klein
Camera: Canon EOS 5D Mark II
Aperture: $f/16$
Focal Length: 29mm
Shutter Speed: 1/20 sec.
ISO: 200

10
Page: 24
Kevin McNeal
Camera: Nikon D800
Aperture: $f/9$
Focal Length: 48mm
Shutter Speed: 1.6 sec.
ISO: 200

11
Pages: 24–25
David Cobb
Camera: Canon EOS 5D Mark III
Aperture: $f/16$
Focal Length: 35mm
Shutter Speed: 1.6 sec.
ISO: 100

12
Page: 26
David Cobb
Camera: Canon EOS 5D
Aperture: $f/22$
Focal Length: 34mm
Shutter Speed: 1/4 sec.
ISO: 200

1	2	3	4
5	6	7	8
9	10	11	12

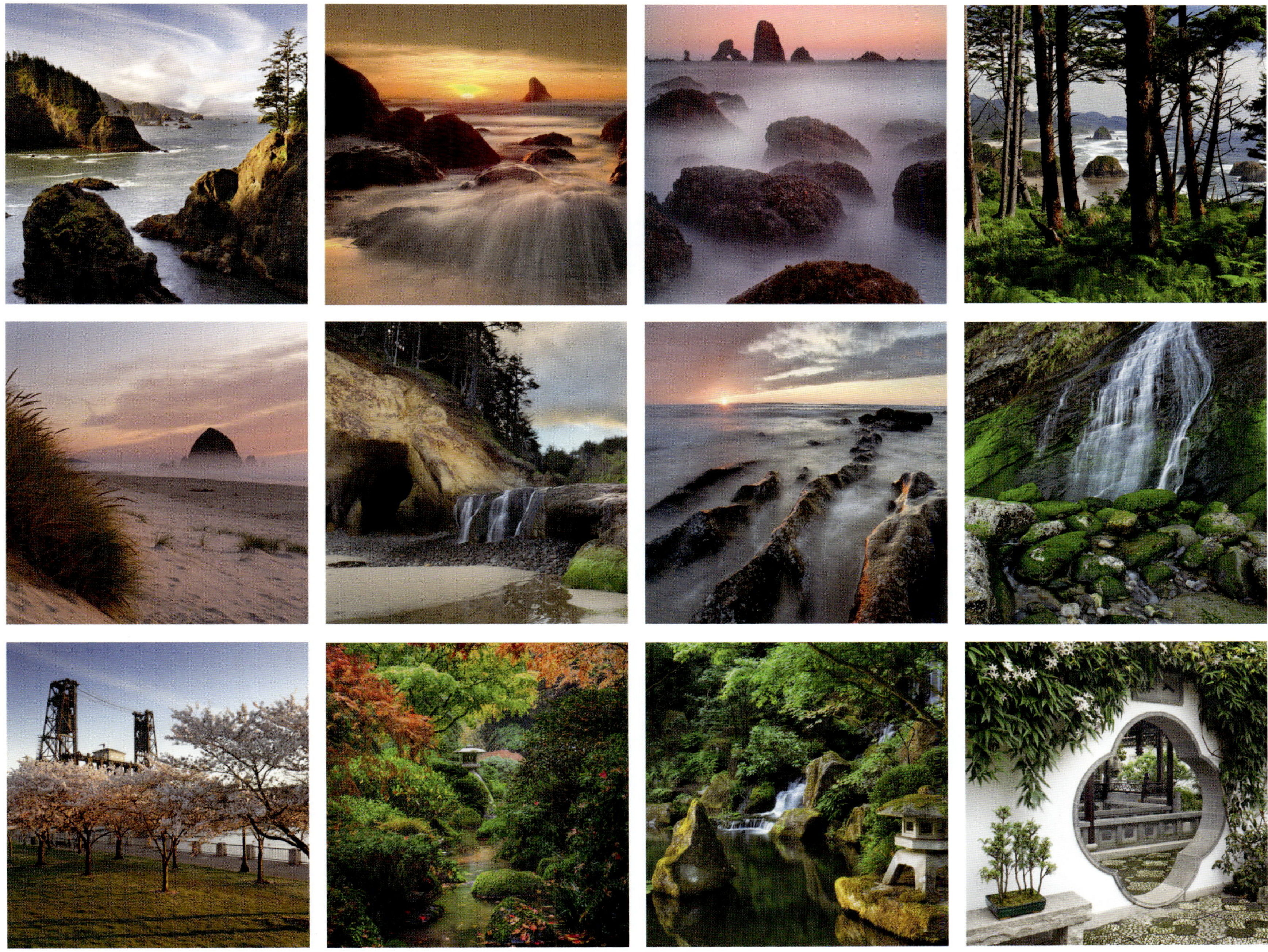

1

Page: 27
Adrian Klein
Camera: Canon EOS 5D
Aperture: *f*/16
Focal Length: 17mm
Shutter Speed: 83 sec.
ISO: 100

2

Pages: 28–29
Chip Phillips
Camera: Canon EOS 5D Mark II
Aperture: *f*/18
Focal Length: 70mm
Shutter Speed: 1/5 sec.
ISO: 100

3

Page: 30
Kevin McNeal
Camera: Canon EOS 5D Mark II
Aperture: *f*/16
Focal Length: 21mm
Shutter Speed: 1/5 sec.
ISO: 160

4

Page: 31
Adrian Klein
Camera: Canon EOS 5D Mark II
Aperture: *f*/14
Focal Length: 25mm
Shutter Speed: 0.8 sec.
ISO: 800

5

Page: 32
David Cobb
Camera: Canon EOS 5D Mark III
Aperture: *f*/16
Focal Length: 27mm
Shutter Speed: 0.4 sec.
ISO: 100

6

Pages: 32–33
Sean Bagshaw
Camera: Canon EOS 5D Mark II
Aperture: *f*/16
Focal Length: 24mm
Shutter Speed: 1/4 sec.
ISO: 800

7

Page: 33
Zack Schnepf
Camera: Canon EOS 5D
Aperture: *f*/22
Focal Length: 70mm
Shutter Speed: 25 sec.
ISO: 100

8

Pages: 34–35
Adrian Klein
Camera: Canon EOS 5D Mark II
Aperture: *f*/9
Focal Length: 19 mm
Shutter Speed: 1/8 sec.
ISO: 400

9

Page: 36
Zack Schnepf
Camera: Canon EOS 5D Mark II
Aperture: *f*/16
Focal Length: 40mm
Shutter Speed: 0.5 sec.
ISO: 250

10

Page: 37
Chip Phillips
Camera: Canon EOS 5D Mark II
Aperture: *f*/16
Focal Length: 84mm
Shutter Speed: 1/15 sec.
ISO: 100

11

Page: 38
Zack Schnepf
Camera: Canon EOS 5D Mark II
Aperture: *f*/20
Focal Length: 17mm
Shutter Speed: 2.5 sec.
ISO: 320

12

Pages: 38–39
David Cobb
Camera: Canon EOS 5D
Aperture: *f*/22
Focal Length: 16mm
Shutter Speed: 1.6 sec.
ISO: 100

13

Page: 39
Adrian Klein
Camera: Canon EOS 5D
Aperture: *f*/18
Focal Length: 73 mm
Shutter Speed: 1/4 sec.
ISO: 100

14

Page: 40
Adrian Klein
Camera: Canon EOS 5D Mark II
Aperture: *f*/16
Focal Length: 70mm
Shutter Speed: 1 sec.
ISO: 200

15

Page: 41
Chip Phillips
Camera: Canon EOS 5D
Aperture: *f*/14
Focal Length: 16mm
Shutter Speed: 13 sec.
ISO: 100

16

Page: 41
Adrian Klein
Camera: Canon EOS 5D
Aperture: *f*/16
Focal Length: 17mm
Shutter Speed: 0.6 sec.
ISO: 200

1	2	3	4
5	6	7	8
9	10	11	12
13	14	15	16

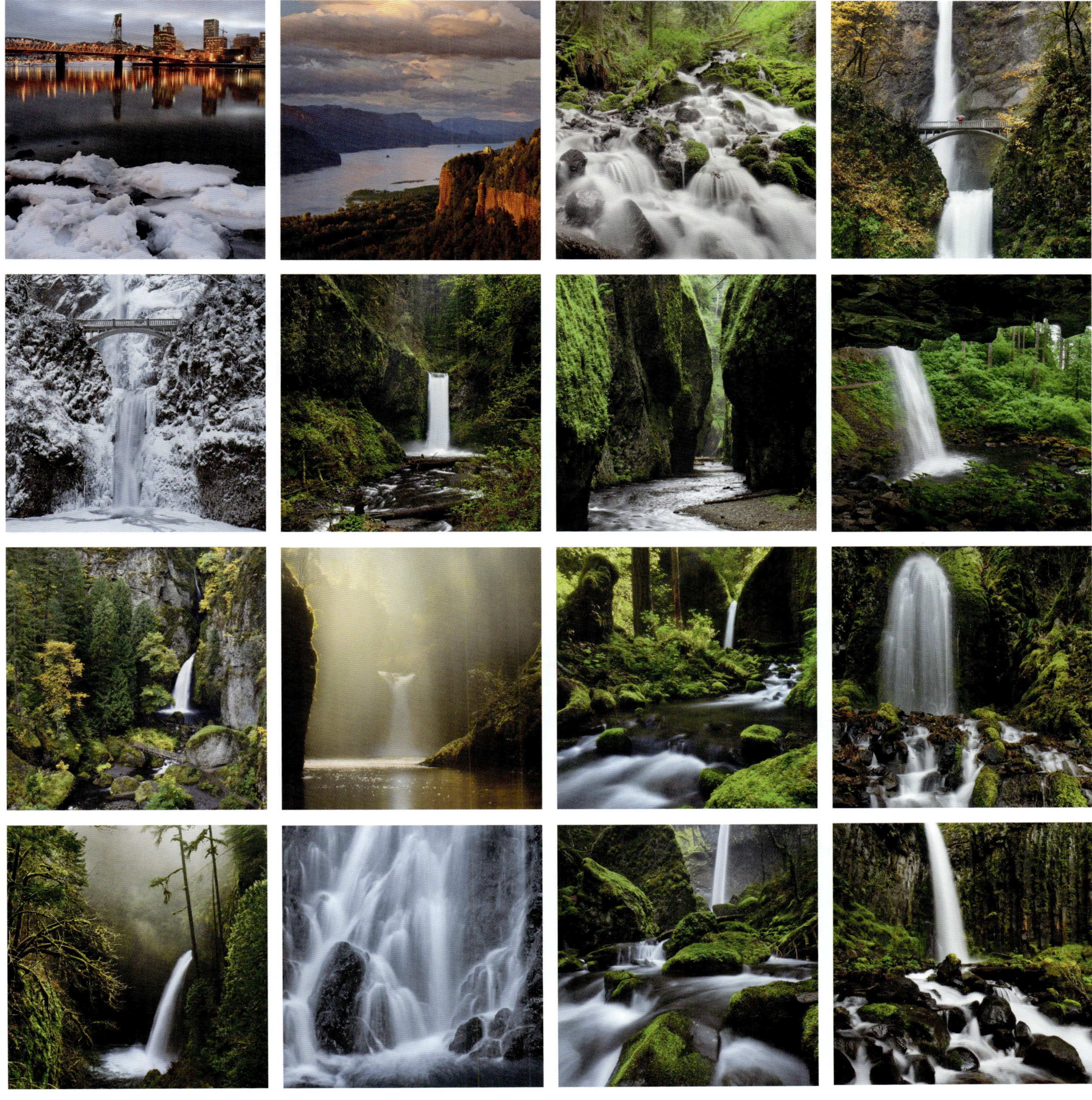

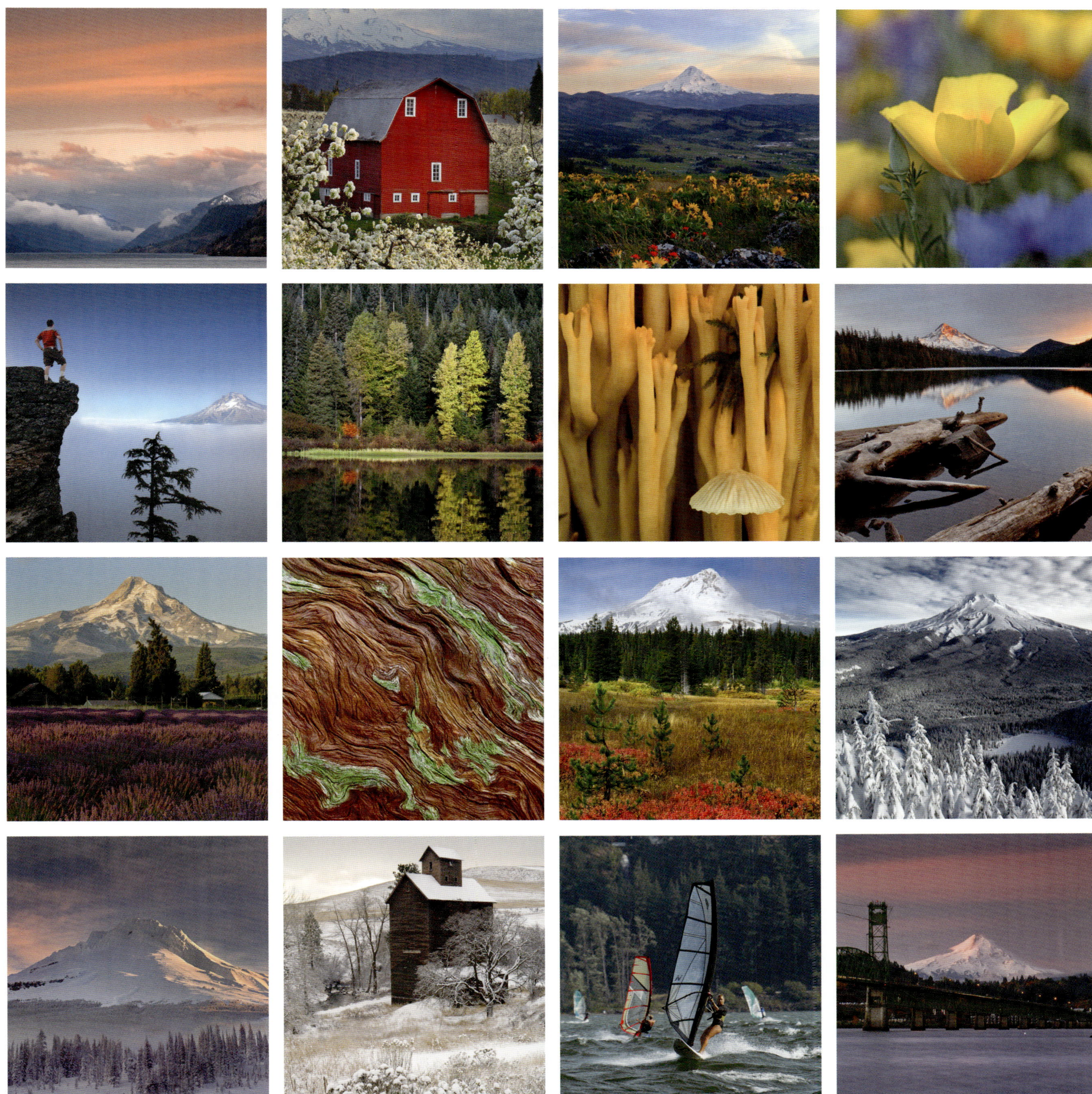

1

Page: 58
Adrian Klein
Camera: Canon EOS 5D Mark II
Aperture: f/16
Focal Length: 28mm
Shutter Speed: 1/50 sec.
ISO: 200

———

2

Pages: 58–59
David Cobb
Camera: Canon EOS 5D Mark III
Aperture: f/11
Focal Length: 23mm
Shutter Speed: 1/8 sec.
ISO: 100

———

3

Page: 60
David Cobb
Camera: Canon EOS 5D Mark III
Aperture: f/16
Focal Length: 27mm
Shutter Speed: 1.3 sec.
ISO: 125

———

4

Page: 61
David Cobb
Camera: Canon EOS 5D
Aperture: f/32
Focal Length: 180mm
Shutter Speed: 0.6 sec.
ISO: 100

———

5

Page: 62
David Cobb
Camera: Canon EOS 5D Mark III
Aperture: f/11
Focal Length: 59mm
Shutter Speed: 0.4 sec.
ISO: 200

———

6

Page: 63
Adrian Klein
Camera: Canon EOS 5D
Aperture: f/16
Focal Length: 28mm
Shutter Speed: 2.5 sec.
ISO: 100

———

7

Pages: 64–65
Adrian Klein
Camera: Canon EOS 5D Mark II
Aperture: f/16
Focal Length: 183mm
Shutter Speed: 1/10 sec.
ISO: 100

———

8

Page: 66
Kevin McNeal
Camera: Canon EOS 5D Mark II
Aperture: f/16
Focal Length: 17mm
Shutter Speed: 1.6 sec.
ISO: 500

———

9

Page: 67
David Cobb
Camera: Canon EOS 5D Mark III
Aperture: f/16
Focal Length: 98mm
Shutter Speed: 1/15 sec.
ISO: 200

———

10

Page: 68
David Cobb
Camera: Canon EOS 5D
Aperture: f/22
Focal Length: 200mm
Shutter Speed: 30 sec.
ISO: 100

———

11

Page: 69
Kevin McNeal
Camera: Canon EOS 5D Mark II
Aperture: f/16
Focal Length: 28mm
Shutter Speed: 1/100 sec.
ISO: 100

———

12

Pages: 70–71
Adrian Klein
Camera: Canon EOS 5D Mark II
Aperture: f/16
Focal Length: 46mm
Shutter Speed: 0.6 sec.
ISO: 100

———

13

Page: 71
Kevin McNeal
Camera: Nikon D800
Aperture: f/9
Focal Length: 122mm
Shutter Speed: 1/100 sec.
ISO: 800

———

14

Page: 72
Adrian Klein
Camera: Canon EOS 5D Mark II
Aperture: f/16
Focal Length: 43 mm
Shutter Speed: 0.3 sec.
ISO: 100

———

15

Page: 73
Kevin McNeal
Camera: Canon EOS 5D
Aperture: f/22
Focal Length: 17mm
Shutter Speed: 6 sec.
ISO: 100

———

16

Page: 74
David Cobb
Camera: Canon EOS 5D Mark III
Aperture: f/16
Focal Length: 30mm
Shutter Speed: 2.5 sec.
ISO: 100

———

PHOTO CREDITS

1	2	3	4
5	6	7	8
9	10	11	12
13	14	15	16

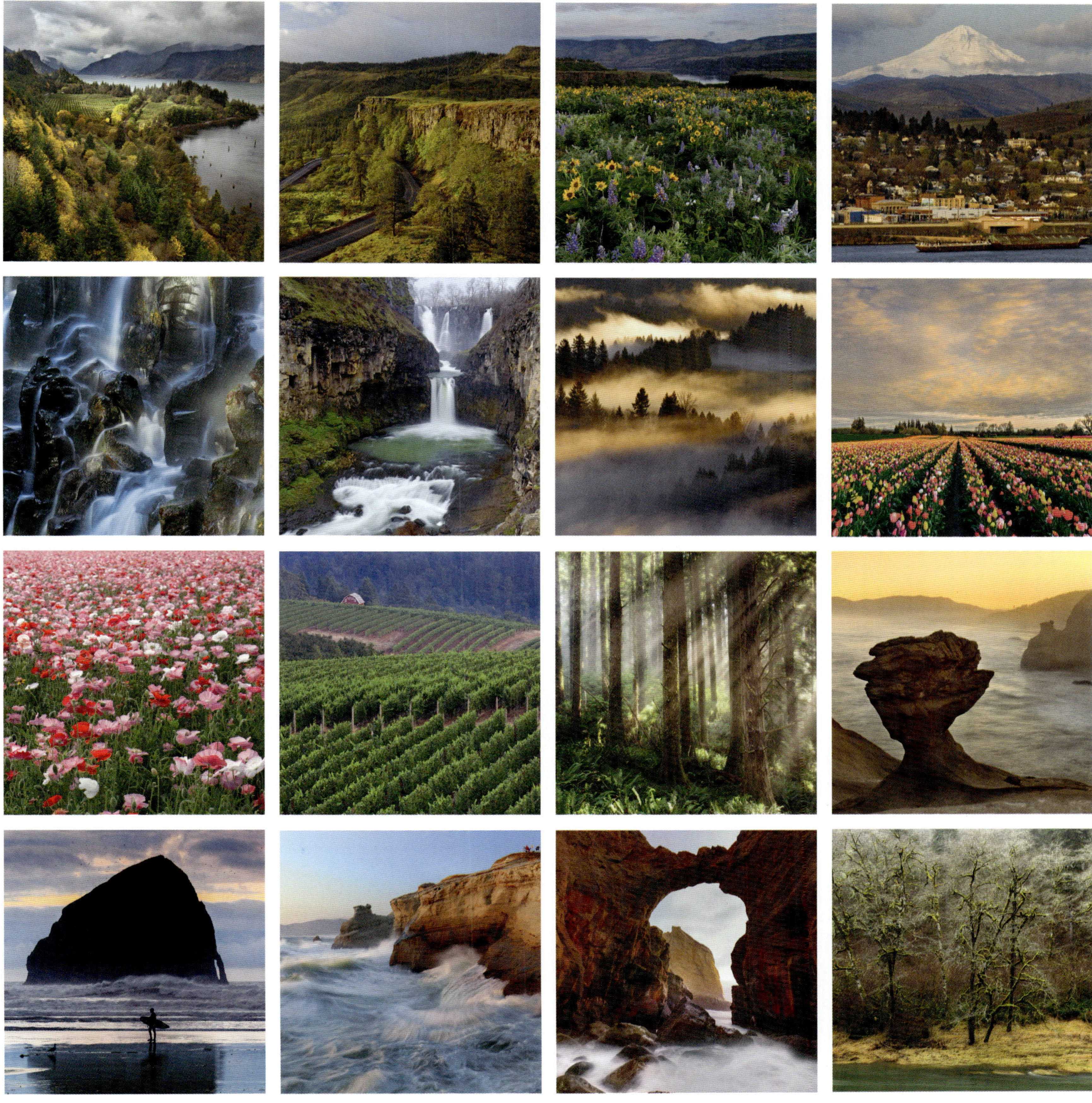

1
Page: 75
Adrian Klein
Camera: Canon EOS 5D
Aperture: $f/16$
Focal Length: 200mm
Shutter Speed: 1/50 sec.
ISO: 100
———

2
Page: 76
Kevin McNeal
Camera: Nikon D800
Aperture: $f/9$
Focal Length: 45mm
Shutter Speed: 45 sec.
ISO: 200
———

3
Pages: 76–77
Kevin McNeal
Camera: Canon EOS 5D Mark II
Aperture: $f/16$
Focal Length: 23mm
Shutter Speed: 1/4 sec.
ISO: 50
———

4
Page: 77
Kevin McNeal
Camera: Canon EOS 5D
Aperture: $f/11$
Focal Length: 17mm
Shutter Speed: 0.8 sec.
ISO: 50
———

5
Page: 78
Adrian Klein
Camera: Canon EOS 5D
Aperture: $f/16$
Focal Length: 23mm
Shutter Speed: 30 sec.
ISO: 160
———

6
Page: 79
Adrian Klein
Camera: Canon EOS 5D
Aperture: $f/16$
Focal Length: 24mm
Shutter Speed: 1/40 sec.
ISO: 200
———

7
Page: 80
Kevin McNeal
Camera: Canon EOS 5D Mark II
Aperture: $f/16$
Focal Length: 32mm
Shutter Speed: 1 sec.
ISO: 100
———

8
Page: 81
Kevin McNeal
Camera: Canon EOS 5D Mark II
Aperture: $f/16$
Focal Length: 94mm
Shutter Speed: 1 sec.
ISO: 200
———

9
Pages: 82–83
Kevin McNeal
Camera: Canon EOS 5D Mark II
Aperture: $f/22$
Focal Length: 29mm
Shutter Speed: 0.6 sec.
ISO: 50
———

10
Page: 84
Chip Phillips
Camera: Canon EOS 5D
Aperture: $f/25$
Focal Length: 163mm
Shutter Speed: 0.3 sec.
ISO: 100
———

11
Page: 85
David Cobb
Camera: Canon EOS 5D Mark III
Aperture: $f/16$
Focal Length: 43mm
Shutter Speed: 1 sec.
ISO: 100
———

12
Page: 86
David Cobb
Camera: Canon EOS 5D Mark III
Aperture: $f/11$
Focal Length: 35mm
Shutter Speed: 1/5 sec.
ISO: 160
———

13
Pages: 86–87
Kevin McNeal
Camera: : Canon EOS 5D Mark II
Aperture: $f/16$
Focal Length: 18mm
Shutter Speed: 0.5 sec.
ISO: 100
———

14
Page: 87
Sean Bagshaw
Camera: Canon EOS 5D Mark II
Aperture: $f/18$
Focal Length: 19mm
Shutter Speed: 1.3 sec.
ISO: 200
———

15
Page: 88
Adrian Klein
Camera: Canon EOS 5D Mark II
Aperture: $f/16$
Focal Length: 24mm
Shutter Speed: 0.5 sec.
ISO: 400
———

16
Page: 89
Sean Bagshaw
Camera: Canon EOS 5D Mark III
Aperture: $f/16$
Focal Length: 24mm
Shutter Speed: 4 sec.
Film Speed: ISO 100
———

1	2	3	4
5	6	7	8
9	10	11	12
13	14	15	16

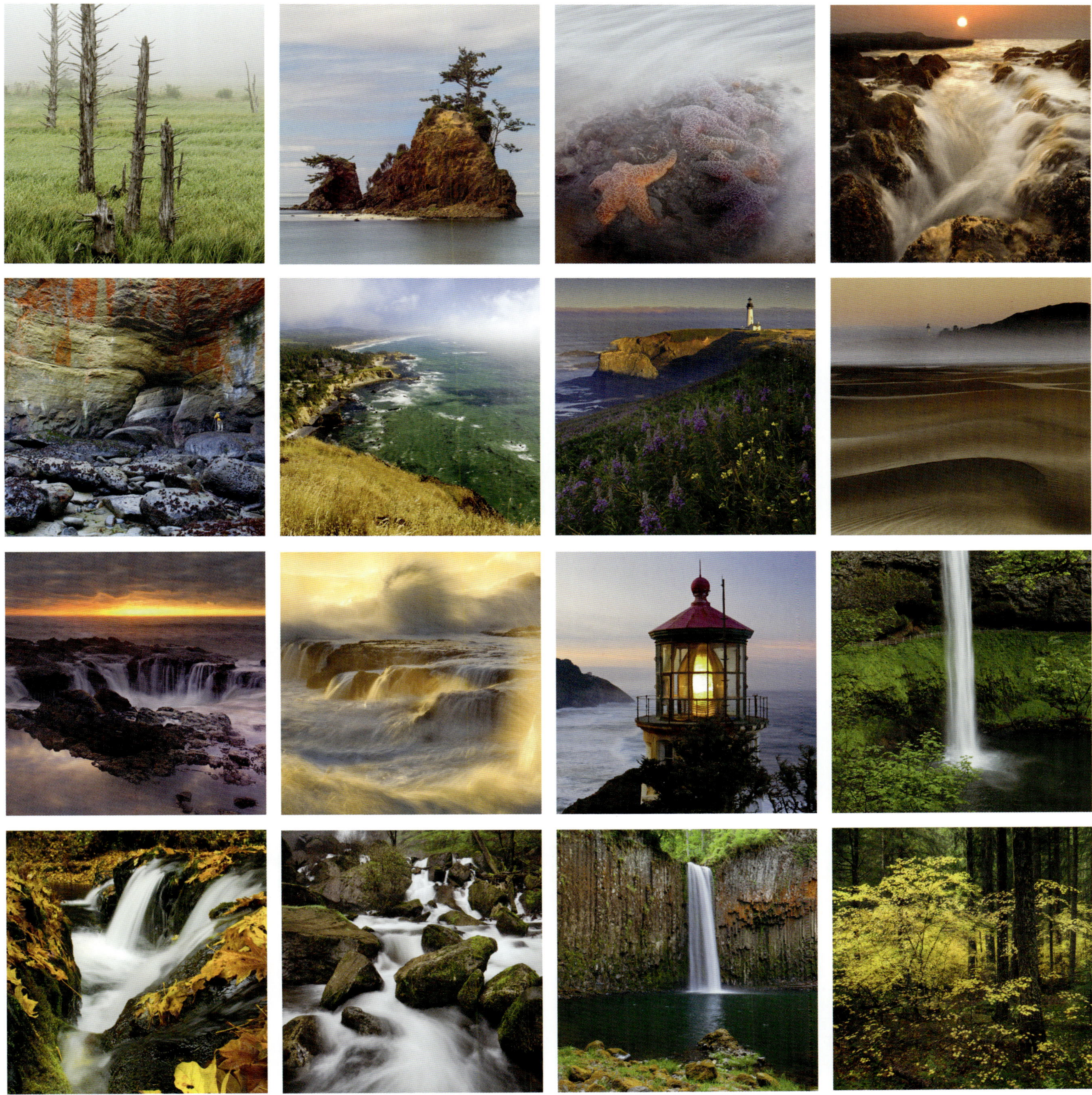

1
Page: 90
Adrian Klein
Camera: Canon EOS 5D Mark II
Aperture: ƒ/16
Focal Length: 29mm
Shutter Speed: 0.4 sec.
ISO: 200

2
Page: 91
Zack Schnepf
Camera: Sony A7r
Aperture: ƒ/18
Focal Length: 24mm
Shutter Speed: 0.2 sec.
ISO: 200

3
Page: 91
Adrian Klein
Camera: Canon EOS 5D
Aperture: ƒ/16
Focal Length: 17mm
Shutter Speed: 6 sec.
ISO: 200

4
Page: 92
Kevin McNeal
Camera: : Canon EOS 5D Mark II
Aperture: ƒ/16
Focal Length: 21mm
Shutter Speed: 1 sec.
ISO: 200

5
Pages: 92–93
Sean Bagshaw
Camera: Canon EOS 5D Mark IV
Aperture: ƒ/13
Focal Length: 27mm
Shutter Speed: 0.5 sec.
ISO: 100

6
Page: 94
David Cobb
Camera: Canon EOS 5D Mark III
Aperture: ƒ/22
Focal Length: 48mm
Shutter Speed: 1/13 sec.
ISO: 100

7
Page: 95
Sean Bagshaw
Camera: Canon EOS 5D
Aperture: ƒ/16
Focal Length: 16mm
Shutter Speed: 1/8 sec.
ISO: 100

8
Page: 96
Adrian Klein
Camera: Sony a6000
Aperture: ƒ/11
Focal Length: 33mm
Shutter Speed: 1/125 sec.
ISO: 200

9
Page: 97
Sean Bagshaw
Camera: Canon EOS 5D
Aperture: ƒ/18
Focal Length: 19mm
Shutter Speed: 10 sec.
ISO: 100

10
Page: 98
Zack Schnepf
Camera: Canon EOS 5D
Aperture: ƒ/6.3
Focal Length: 85mm
Shutter Speed: 1/40 sec.
ISO: 250

11
Page: 99
Sean Bagshaw
Camera: Canon EOS 5D Mark II
Aperture: ƒ/18
Focal Length: 28mm
Shutter Speed: 25 sec.
ISO: 160

12
Pages: 100–101
Kevin McNeal
Camera: Nikon D810
Aperture: ƒ/8
Focal Length: 28mm
Shutter Speed: 1/50 sec.
ISO: 400

13
Page: 102
Zack Schnepf
Camera: Sony A7r
Aperture: ƒ/16
Focal Length: 49mm
Shutter Speed: 1/5 sec.
ISO: 100

14
Page: 103
Adrian Klein
Camera: Canon EOS 5D
Aperture: ƒ/16
Focal Length: 19mm
Shutter Speed: 0.5 sec.
ISO: 100

15
Pages: 104–105
Zack Schnepf
Camera: Nikon D850
Aperture: ƒ/18
Focal Length: 24mm
Shutter Speed: 1/25 sec.
ISO: 100

16
Page: 106
Kevin McNeal
Camera: Nikon D810
Aperture: ƒ/22
Focal Length: 14mm
Shutter Speed: 0.6 sec.
ISO: 64

1	2	3	4
5	6	7	8
9	10	11	12
13	14	15	16

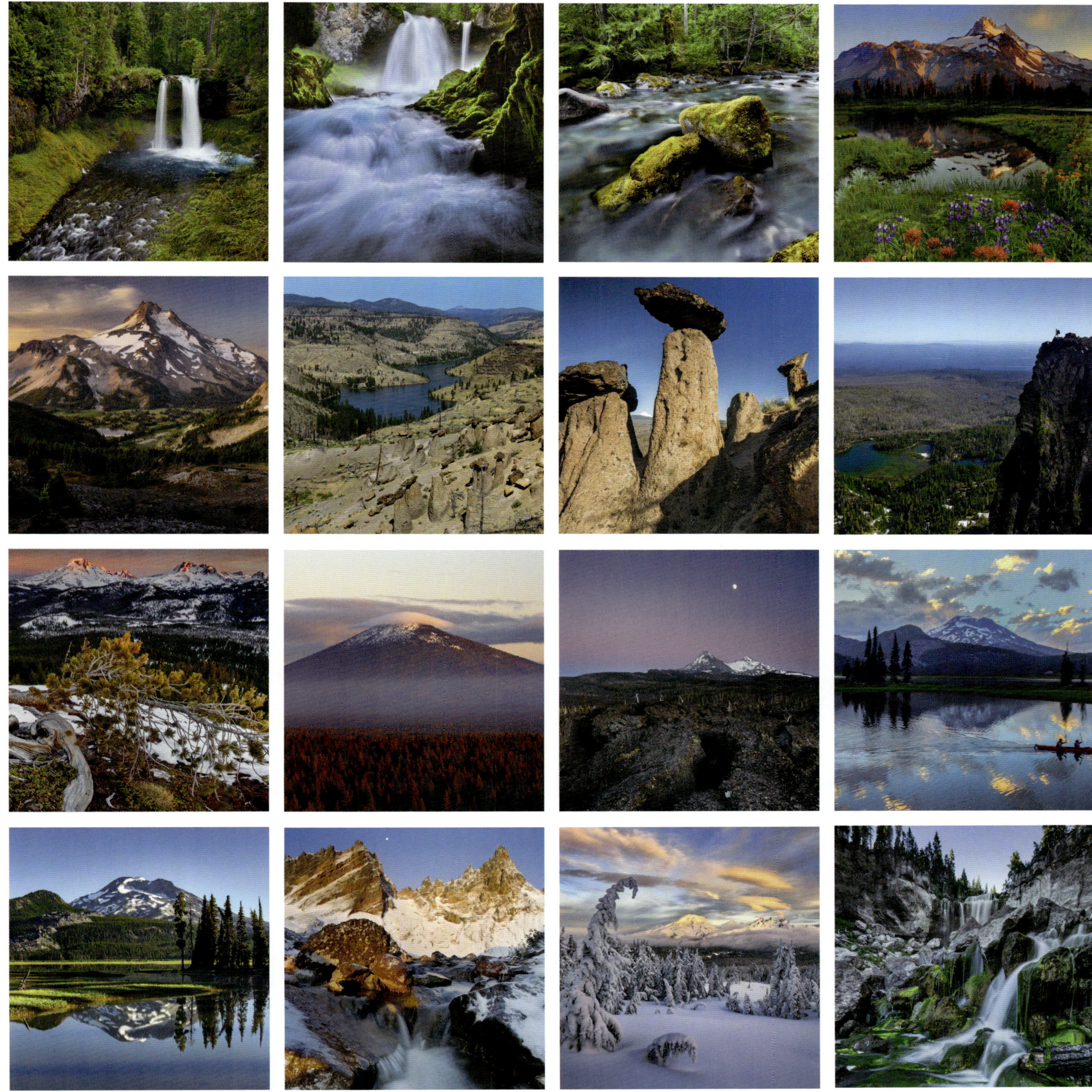

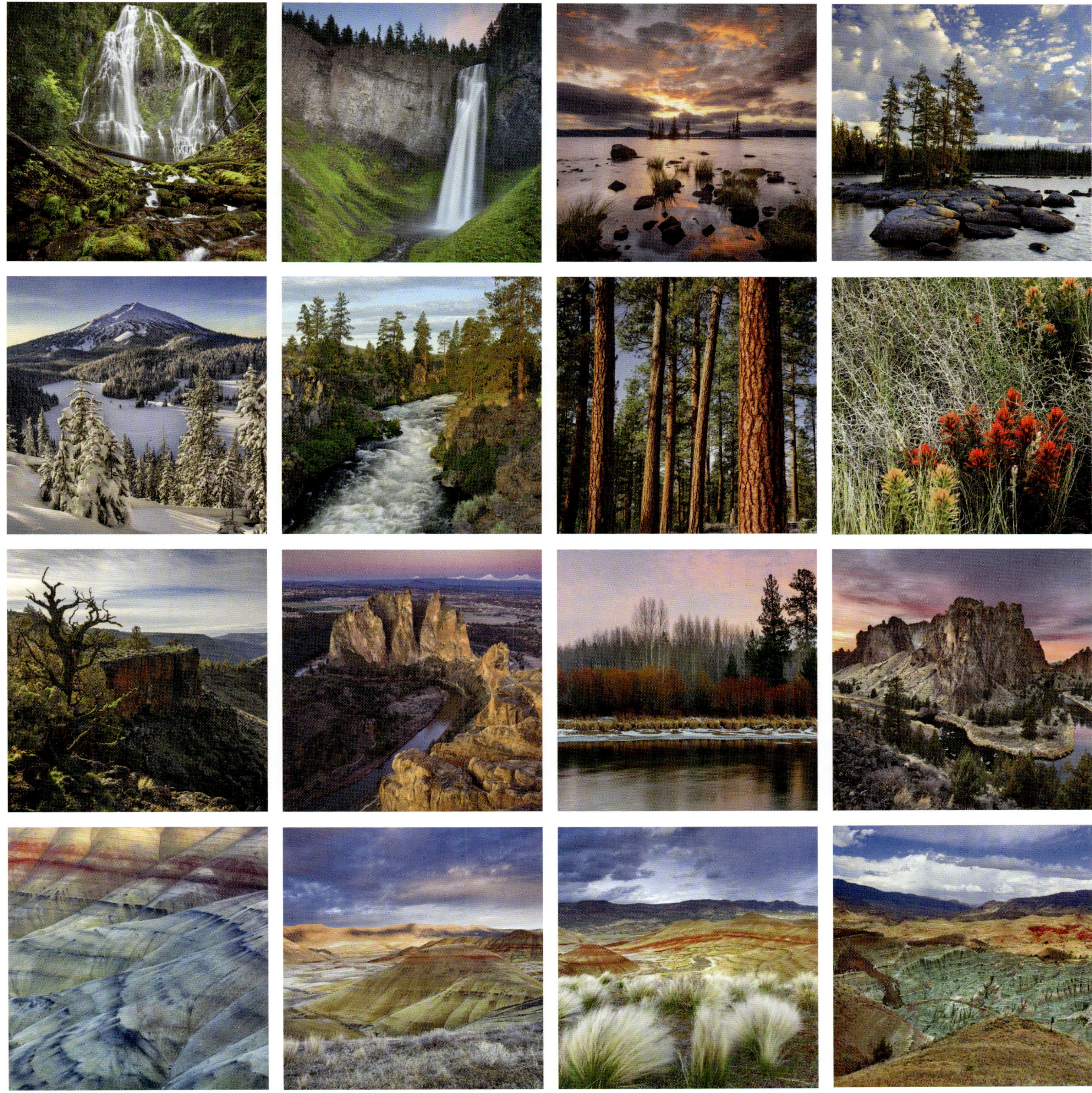

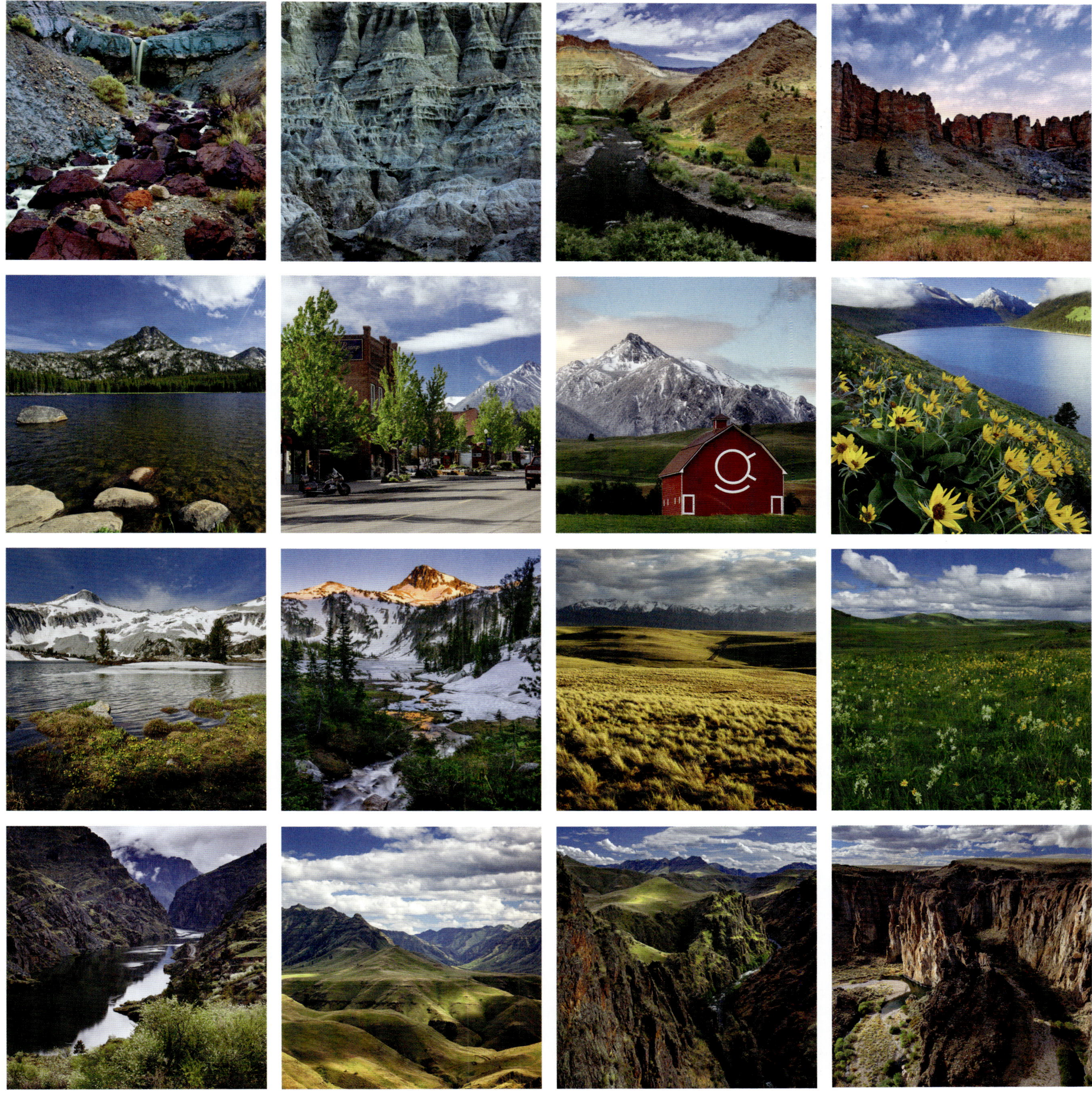

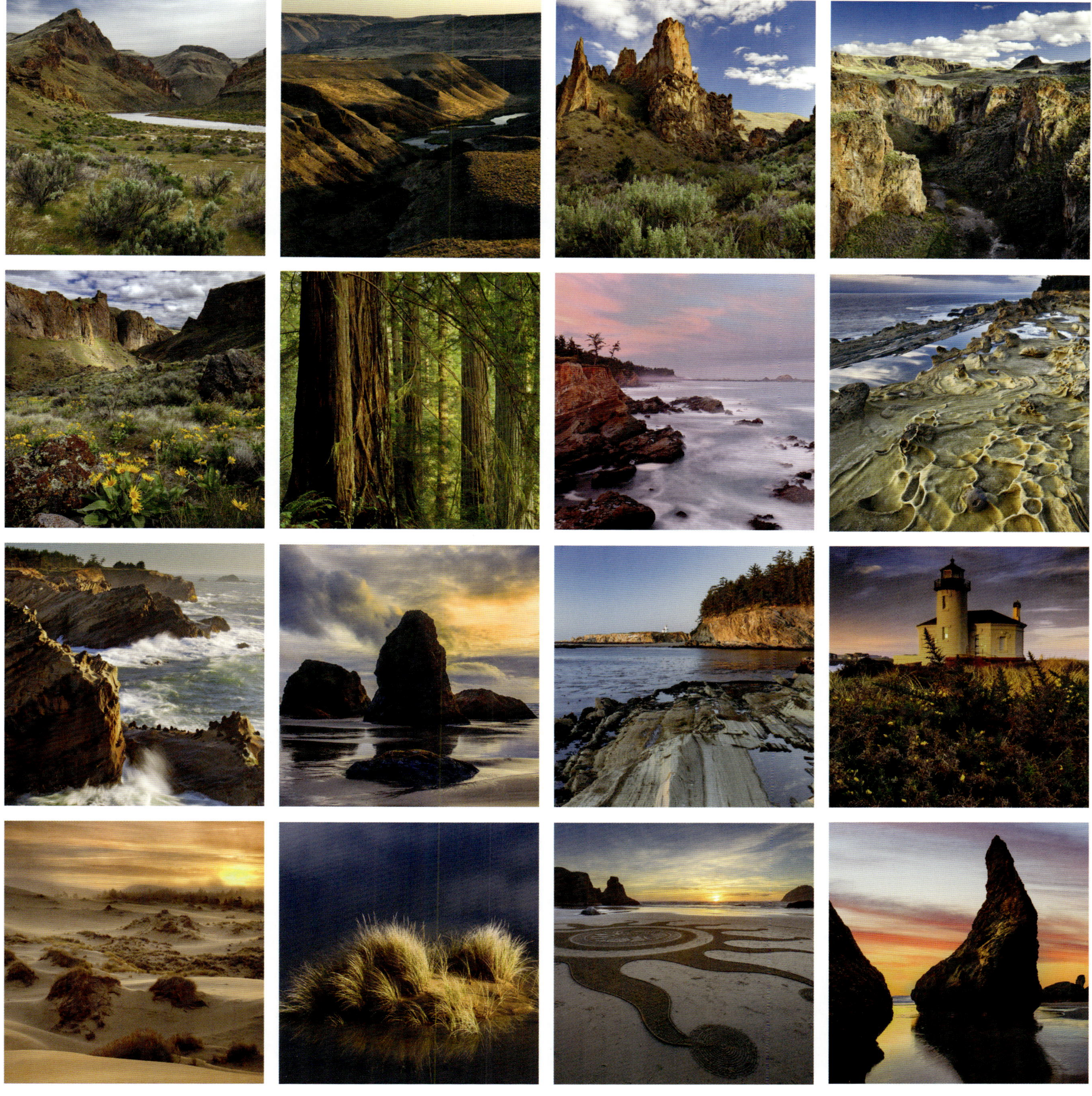

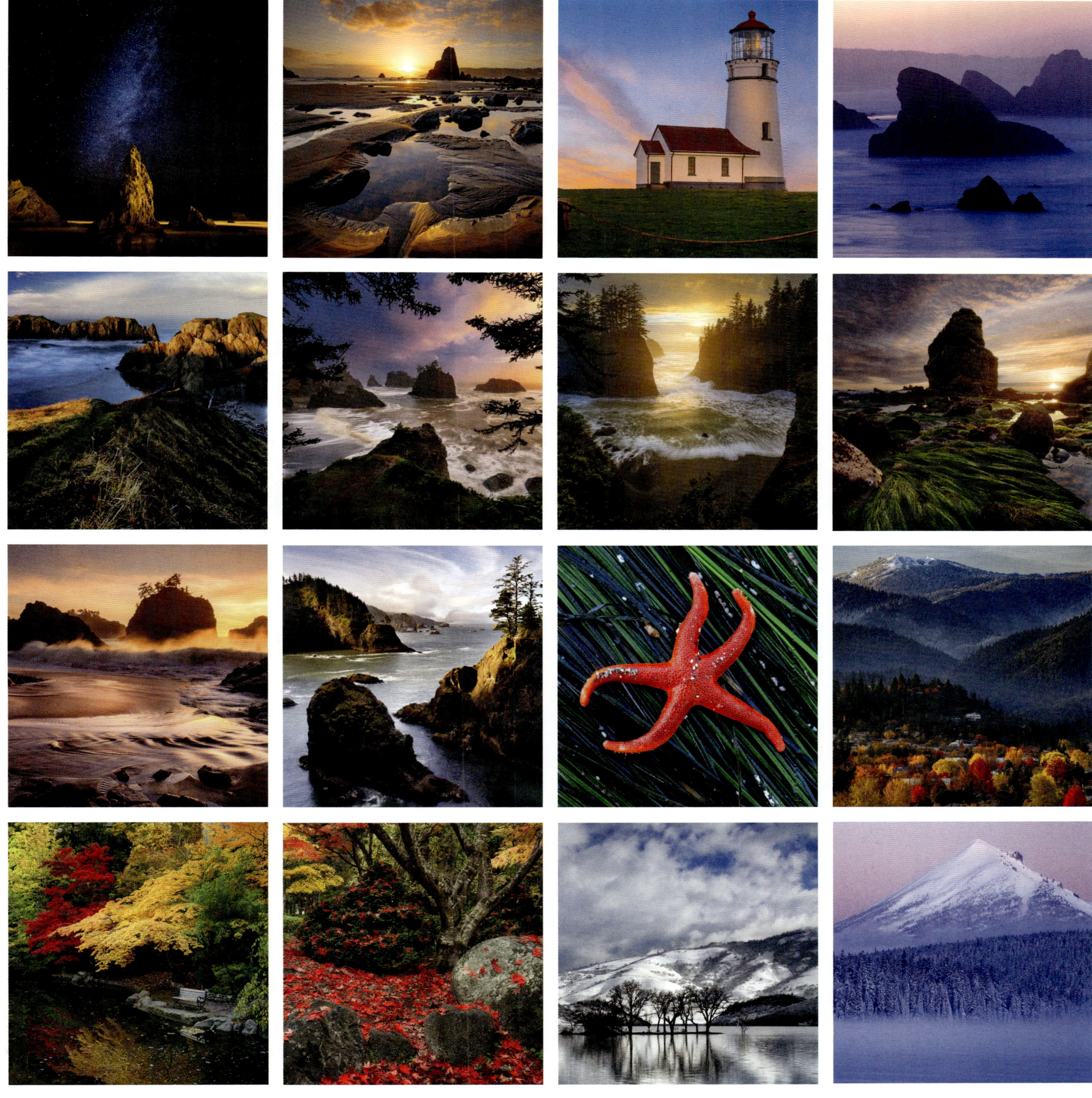

1

Page: 170
Sean Bagshaw
Camera: Canon EOS 5D Mark II
Aperture: $f/22$
Focal Length: 26mm
Shutter Speed: 1/4 sec.
ISO: 320

2

Page: 171
Sean Bagshaw
Camera: Canon EOS 5DS R
Aperture: $f/16$
Focal Length: 25mm
Shutter Speed: 1/13 sec.
ISO: 100

3

Pages: 172–173
Sean Bagshaw
Camera: Canon EOS 5D
Aperture: $f/16$
Focal Length: 16mm
Shutter Speed: 1 sec.
ISO: 100

4

Page: 174
Sean Bagshaw
Camera: Canon EOS 5DS R
Aperture: $f/14$
Focal Length: 22mm
Shutter Speed: 1/4 sec.
ISO: 100

5

Page: 175
Sean Bagshaw
Camera: Canon EOS 5D Mark IV
Aperture: $f/13$
Focal Length: 24mm
Shutter Speed: 0.8 sec.
ISO: 100

6

Page: 176
Sean Bagshaw
Camera: Canon EOS 5D Mark II
Aperture: $f/16$
Focal Length: 28mm
Shutter Speed: 0.6 seconds
ISO: 160

7

Page: 177
Zack Schnepf
Camera: Sony A7r
Aperture: $f/22$
Focal Length: 65mm
Shutter Speed: 1 sec.
ISO: 50

8

Page: 178
Sean Bagshaw
Camera: Canon EOS 5D Mark II
Aperture: $f/16$
Focal Length: 67mm
Shutter Speed: 0.3 sec.
ISO: 160

9

Page: 179
Sean Bagshaw
Camera: Canon EOS 5DS R
Aperture: $f/11$
Focal Length: 45mm
Shutter Speed: 4 sec.
ISO: 100

10

Pages: 180–181
Zack Schnepf
Camera: Nikon D850
Aperture: $f/22$
Focal Length: 24mm
Shutter Speed: 1/15 sec.
ISO: 200

11

Pages: 182–183
Zack Schnepf
Camera: Canon EOS 5D Mark II
Aperture: $f/16$
Focal Length: 39mm
Shutter Speed: 0.6 sec
ISO: 100

12

Page: 184
David Cobb
Camera: Canon EOS 5D
Aperture: $f/16$
Focal Length: 70mm
Shutter Speed: 2 sec.
ISO: 100

13

Page: 185
Adrian Klein
Camera: Canon EOS 5D Mark III
Aperture: $f/16$
Focal Length: 24mm
Shutter Speed: 0.6 sec.
ISO: 200

14

Page: 186
Adrian Klein
Camera: Canon EOS 5D Mark III
Aperture: $f/14$
Focal Length: 27mm
Shutter Speed: 1/100 sec.
ISO: 200

15

Page: 187
Adrian Klein
Camera: Canon EOS 5D
Aperture: $f/16$
Focal Length: 26mm
Shutter Speed: 4 sec.
ISO: 100

16

Pages: 188–189
Sean Bagshaw
Camera: Canon EOS 5D Mark II
Aperture: $f/13$
Focal Length: 55mm
Shutter Speed: 1/250 sec.
ISO: 320

PHOTO CREDITS

1	2	3	4
5	6	7	8
9	10	11	12
13	14	15	16

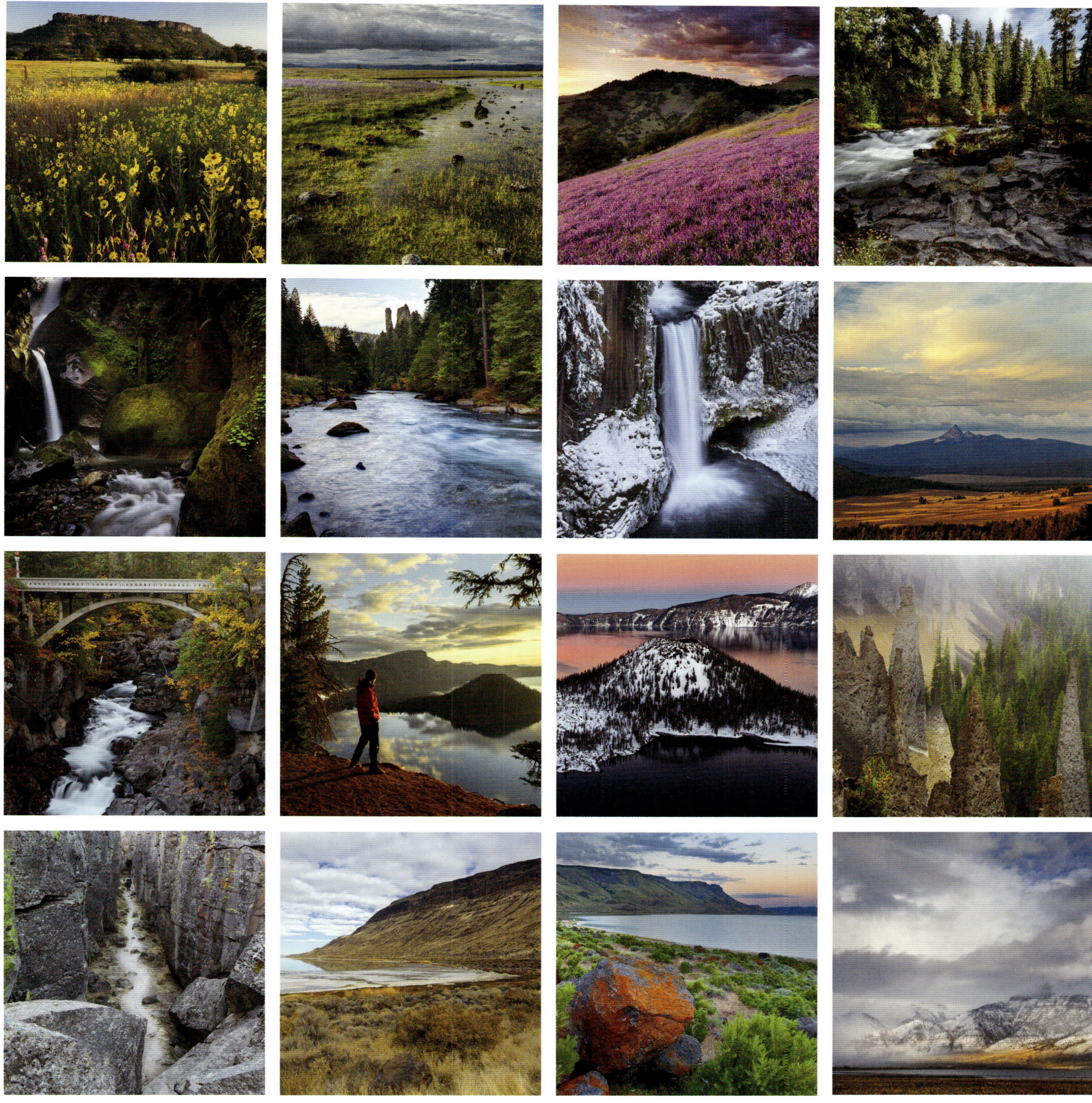

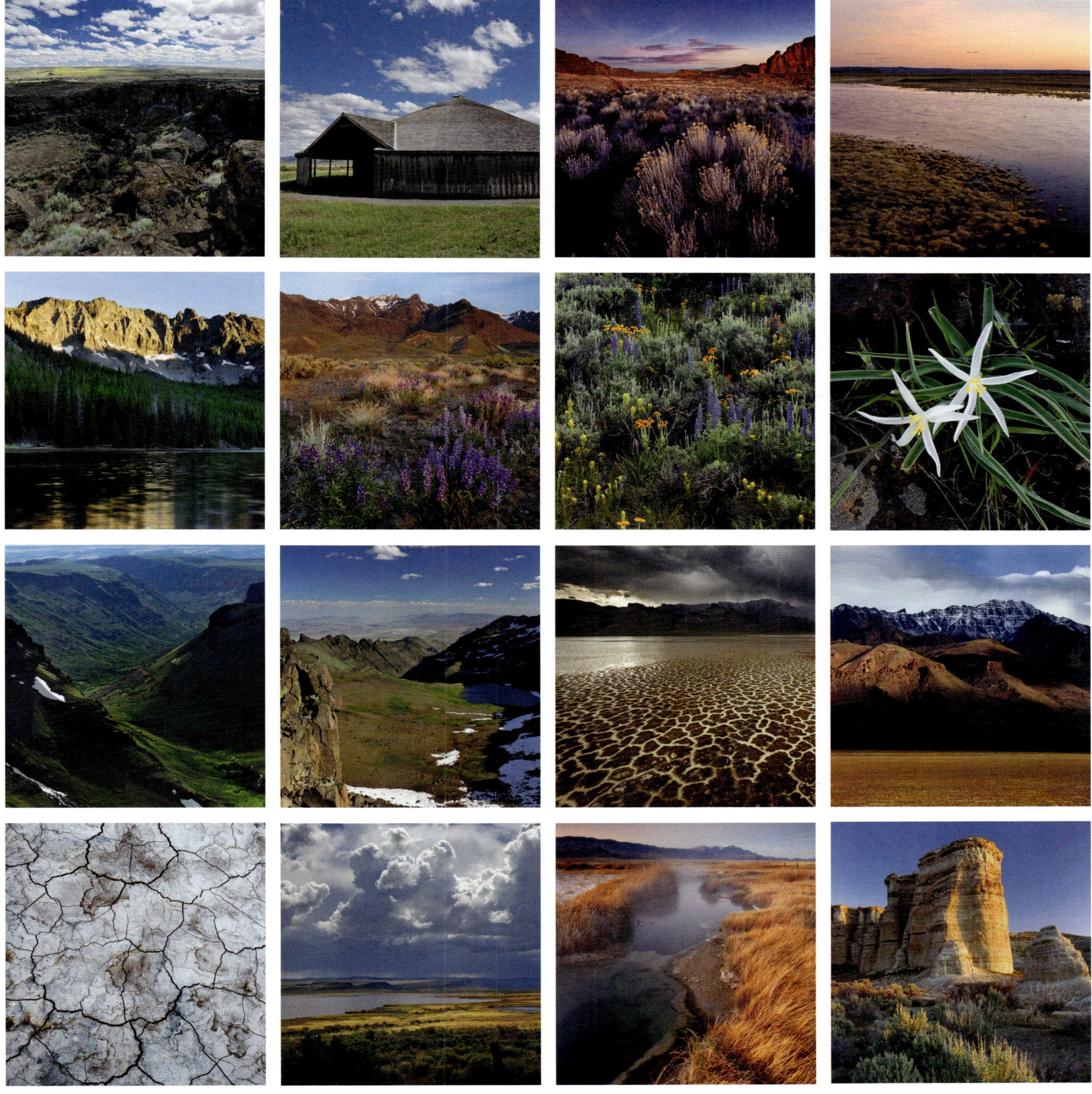

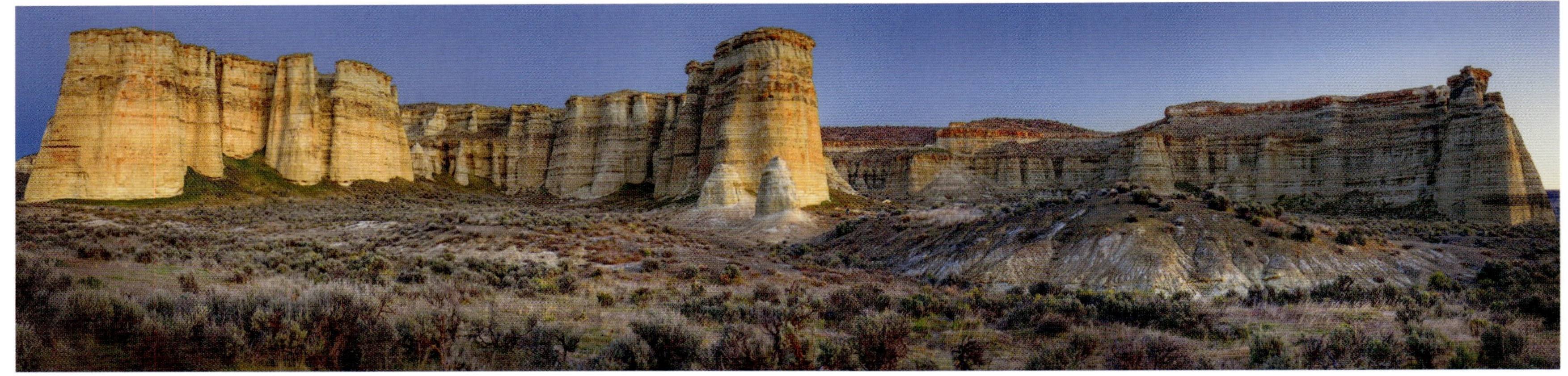

Pages: 208–209
Sean Bagshaw
Camera: Canon EOS 5D Mark II
Aperture: *f*/16
Focal Length: multiple frames at 47mm stitched into a panorama
Shutter Speed: 1 sec.
ISO: 320

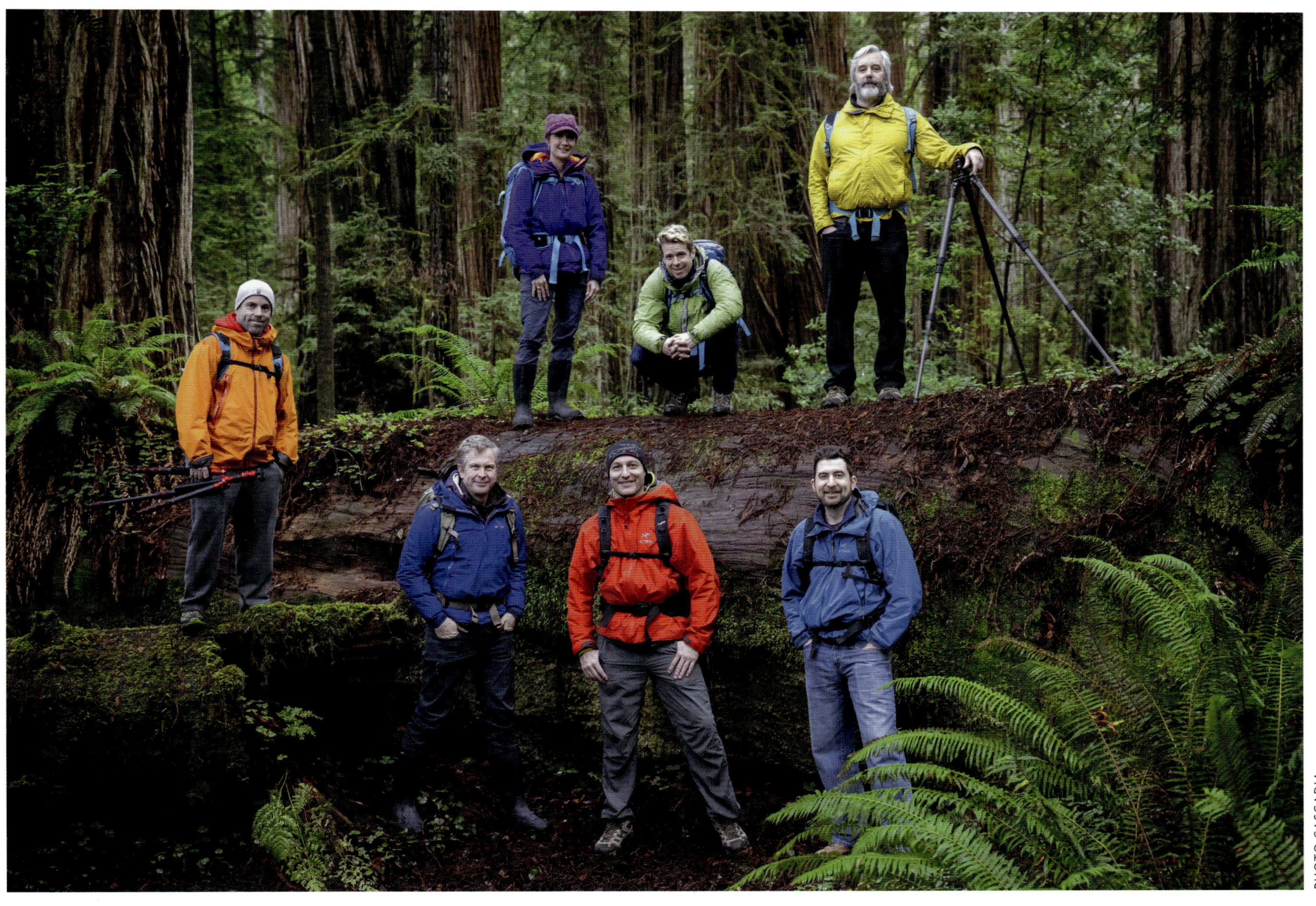

The seven photographers of the collective known as **Photo Cascadia**—Kevin McNeal, Sean Bagshaw, Erin Babnik, Zack Schnepf, Chip Phillips, Adrian Klein, and David Cobb—all live in the Pacific Northwest and have dedicated their careers to sharing its natural beauty while encouraging stewardship and conservation efforts. Active members of the photographic community, they regularly teach workshops and lead group photography tours throughout the region and beyond. Collectively they have mounted dozens of exhibitions and have received many industry and juried awards. Their images have been published in *Digital Photo Magazine, Digital Photographer, National Geographic, Nature's Best Photography, Northwest Magazine, OnLandscape, Outdoor Photographer, Outside, Popular Photography and Imaging,* and elsewhere. Erin Babnik is a Canon Explorer of Light.

See more of their work at **photocascadia.com**.

NICHOLAS D. KRISTOF is an op-ed columnist for the New York Times, and he was previously bureau chief in Hong Kong, Beijing, and Tokyo. He won his second Pulitzer in 2006 for his columns on Darfur.

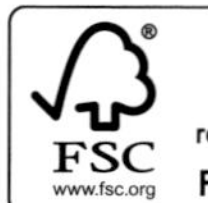

FSC
www.fsc.org
MIX
Paper from
responsible sources
FSC® C104723

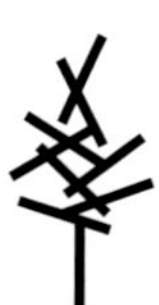